THE BANQUET YEARS

Alfred Jarry
Henri Rousseau
Erik Satie
Guillaume Apollinaire

Vintage Books
A DIVISION OF RANDOM HOUSE
New York

THE BANQUET YEARS

The Origins of the Avant Garde in France • 1885 to World War I

by *ROGER SHATTUCK*

R E V I S E D   E D I T I O N

. . . there remained awake only Socrates, Aristophanes, and Agathon, who were drinking out of a large goblet which they passed around, and Socrates was discoursing to them. Aristodemus did not hear the beginning of the discourse, and he was only half awake, but the chief thing which he remembered was Socrates insisting to the other two that the genius of comedy was the same as that of tragedy, and that the writer of tragedy ought to be a writer of comedy also.

—*Plato,* The Symposium or Banquet

PREFACE TO THE VINTAGE EDITION

This book was conceived one chilling March night eighteen years ago in Piana, Corsica. A year's work on Apollinaire translations had led me to a remarkable poet, and through him to an irresistibly attractive era. Yet the turn of the century in Paris seemed so teeming with energies all working at cross purposes that its shape forever escaped me. Then came the idea—a kind of gambler's hunch—that the trio Rousseau-Satie-Apollinaire represented several significant aspects of the period and could reveal them better than any single figure. The idea would not die. Two years later an appointment to the Society of Fellows at Harvard University allowed me to begin. Within a few weeks Jarry had forced his way into the group and established himself close to the center of things. He helped clarify my underlying subject: how the fluid state known as bohemia, a cultural underground smacking of failure and fraud, crystallized for a few decades into a self-conscious avant-garde that carried the arts into a period of astonishingly varied renewal and accomplishment. After the war, the generation of Dada and Surrealism could exploit a new layer of civilized discontent. But a mood and an era had expired.

The original conception presented me simultaneously with the comparative method of the book and its multiple subject. The title emerged unsummoned out of the reading at an early stage; I never looked for another. What I have written remains far from definitive both as cultural history and in its individual studies. But the method afforded a new purchase on all four figures and challenged me to attempt the synthesis to which Chapter 11 is devoted.

An enormous amount has been written on this era and these men since the first edition of this book in 1958. I have taken account of new biographical materials where they seemed important. Otherwise the text of the book is unaltered except for minor corrections.

I wish to thank Hortense Berman for her meticulous work on the proofs of this new edition.

Austin
October, 1967

ACKNOWLEDGMENTS

Research on this book was begun during a resident appointment to the Society of Fellows in Harvard University. An early draft served as the basis for a series of Lowell Institute Lectures delivered at the Boston Public Library in February, 1953. Sections have appeared in *La Revue Musicale, i.e. (The Cambridge Review), Arts,* and *Art News Annual.*

The materials of the book were assembled with the assistance of Marcel Adéma, Madame Jacqueline Apollinaire, Henri-Martin Barzun, Mrs. Robert Woods Bliss, Georges Braque, Madame Sonia Delaunay, Jean Denoël, Maximilien Gauthier, René Huyghe, William Lieberman, Madame Fernande Olivier, Amadée Ozenfant, Rollo Myers, Francis Poulenc, J. H. Sainmont, André Salmon, Georges Sirot, Alice B. Toklas, and Tristan Tzara; and of the Bibliothèque Jacques Doucet, the Collège de 'Pataphysique, the Conservatoire National de Musique, and the Dumbarton Oaks Library.

Many people have read chapters in manuscript, and their advice and encouragement have been invaluable: Harry Bober, Keith Botsford, LeRoy C. Breunig, Geoffrey Bush, Stanley Cavell, Herbert Dieckmann, Wallace Fowlie, Patrick Gowers, Harry Levin, Thomas McMahon, Robert Middleton, Lowry Nelson, Jr., Hubert Saal, Claudio Spiess, Wylie Sypher, and William Wise. My wife, Nora, has assisted me at every stage of composition.

To these individuals and these organizations I express my deepest gratitude.

ROGER SHATTUCK

Austin, 1958

CONTENTS

[THREE] THE CENTURY TURNED

PART ONE

TURN OF A CENTURY

The world has changed less since Jesus Christ than it has in the last thirty years. —Charles Péguy (1913)

THE GOOD OLD DAYS

The French call it *la belle époque*—the good old days. The thirty years of peace, prosperity, and internal dissension which lie across 1900 wear a bright, almost blatant color. We feel a greater nostalgia looking back that short distance than we do looking back twenty centuries to antiquity. And there is reason. Those years are the lively childhood of our era; already we see their gaiety and sadness transfigured.

For Paris they were the Banquet Years. The banquet had become the supreme rite. The cultural capital of the world, which set fashions in dress, the arts, and the pleasures of life, celebrated its vitality over a long table laden with food and wine. Part of the secret of the period lies no deeper than this surface aspect. Upper-class leisure—the result not of shorter working hours but of no working hours at all for property holders—produced a life of pompous display, frivolity, hypocrisy, cultivated taste, and relaxed morals. The only barrier to rampant adultery was the whalebone corset; many an errant wife, when she returned to face her waiting coachman, had to hide under her coat the bundle of undergarments which her lover had not been dexterous enough to lace back around her torso. Bourgeois meals reached such proportions that an intermission had to be introduced in the form of a sherbet course between the two fowl dishes. The untaxed rich lived in shameless luxury and systematically brutalized *le peuple* with venal journalism, inspiring promises of progress and expanding empire, and cheap absinthe.

Politics in *la belle époque* found a surprisingly stable balance between corruption, passionate conviction, and low comedy. The handsome and popular Prince of Wales neglected the attractions of London to spend his evenings entertaining in Maxim's restaurant, and he did not entirely change his ways upon becoming Edward VII. It was the era of gaslights and horse-drawn omnibuses, of the Moulin Rouge and the Folies Bergère, of *cordon-bleu* cooking and demonstrating feminists. The waiters in Paris cafés had the courage to strike for the right to grow beards; you were not a man or a republican without one at the turn of the century. Artists sensed that their generation promised both an end and a beginning. No other equally brief period of history has seen the rise and fall of so many schools of cliques and isms. Amid this turmoil, the fashionable *salon* declined after a last abortive flourishing. The café came into its own, political unrest encouraged innovation in the arts, and society squandered its last vestiges of aristocracy. The twentieth century could not wait fifteen years for a round number; it was born, yelling, in 1885.

It all started with a wake and funeral such as Paris had never staged even for royalty. In May, 1885, four months after an immense state banquet to celebrate his eighty-third birthday, Victor Hugo died. He left the following will: "I give fifty thousand francs to the poor. I desire to be carried to the cemetery in one of their hearses. I refuse the prayers of all churches. I ask for a prayer from all living souls. I believe in God." Four years earlier, during public celebrations of his eightieth year of vigor, the Avenue d'Eylau, where he lived, had been officially renamed in his honor. Now his remains lay in state for twenty-four hours on top of a mammoth urn which filled the Arc de Triomphe and was guarded in half-hour shifts by young children in Grecian vestments. As darkness approached, the festive crowd could no longer contain itself. "The night of May 31, 1885, night of vertiginous dreams, dissolute and pathetic, in which Paris was filled with the aromas of its love for a relic. Perhaps the great city was trying to recover its loss. . . . How many women gave themselves to lovers, to strangers, with a burning fury to become mothers of immortals!" What the novelist Barrès here describes (in a chapter of

Les déracinés entitled "The Public Virtue of a Corpse") happened publicly within a few yards of Hugo's apotheosis. The endless procession across Paris the next day included several brass bands, every political and literary figure of the day, speeches, numerous deaths in the press of the crowd, and final entombment in the Panthéon. The church had to be specially unconsecrated for the occasion. By this orgiastic ceremony France unburdened itself of a man, a literary movement, and a century.

Paris at the time was like no other place in the world. Even in retrospect her physical presence demands the feminine gender. The Seine, no mere frontier, as today, separating left and right banks, was a central artery carrying *bateaux-mouches* for suburban commuters, *bateaux-lavoirs* for the city's washer-women, heavy traffic of brightly painted and planted barges, and a fleet of light fishing skiffs. The Champs-Elysées was still a bridle path flanked by elegant *hôtels particuliers*. In the Bois de Boulogne, the rich and well born had their domain in which to parade in their carriages during the morning and in whose restaurants they dined and danced and made love at night. More cows and goats and chickens thrived on the open slopes of Montmartre among the windmills than artists lived in its steep village streets. Montparnasse lay quiet and far away across the river beyond the fashionable residences of the Faubourg Saint-Germain. Through the middle of Paris like an equator ran *les grands boulevards*, a busy and still fashionable quarter devoted to theaters, newspaper offices, and crowded cafés.

Most important of all, Paris had just had her face lifted. Baron Haussmann's ambitious plans for opening up the constricted city had been executed by 1880—except for his own unfinished Boulevard Haussmann, which came to a stop halfway through the eighth *arrondissement*. (It became the standard music-hall joke of the eighties.) The magnificent new Opéra, commanding its own avenue to the Louvre and the Théâtre-Français, the refurbished city hall, and wide tree-lined boulevards slicing through the most clogged quarters—these were more than architectural renovations. Paris now had the space to look at herself and see that she was no longer a village clustered about a few grandiose palaces, nor merely a city of bustling commerce and exchange. She had become a stage, a vast theater for

herself and all the world. For thirty years the frock coats
and monocles, the toppers and bowlers (*chapeaux hauts
de forme* and *chapeaux melon*) seemed to be designed to
fit this vast stage-set, along with the ladies' long dresses
and corsets and eclipsing hats. Street cleaners in blue
denim, gendarmes in trim capes, butchers in leather aprons,
coachmen in black cutaways, the army's crack chasseurs
in plumes, gold-braid, and polished boots—everyone wore
a costume and displayed himself to best advantage.

It is this theatrical aspect of life, the light-opera atmosphere, which gave *la belle époque* its particular flavor.
Since Offenbach's era, living had become increasingly a
special kind of performance presided over by fashion, innovation, and taste. History provides its own reasons for the
gaiety of the era: economic prosperity following rapid recovery from the defeat in 1871, the unexpected stability
of this third try at republican government, and innocence
of any world conflict of the kind that would put a stop to
it all. But such reasons do not explain why almost every
book of reminiscences about the period indulges an un-
ashamed nostalgia about a charmed way of life now lost.
One suspects the attitude of being pure sentimental illusion
until one perceives how truly different life was in Paris
in the nineties and in the early years of this century. More
than its debated public issues, the rarely challenged truisms of the age gave it its character. Without them the
city's boulevards and walled gardens, its *salons* and bou-
doirs might long since have been forgotten. These truisms
were simple and, in their own way, wise. Everyone loves
a crowd; everyone has a right to privacy. Equality is a
word reserved for public declarations and must not be
allowed to pervert justice and social distinctions. Politics
is a game played for fun or profit; business is a game best
mixed with pleasure. Love cannot last, but marriage must;
any vice can be forgiven except lack of feeling. The his-
trionic gifts of the French, concentrated in one city, en-
acted these themes with passion and conviction. Paris was
a stage where the excitement of performance gave every
deed the double significance of private gesture and public
action. Doctor and ragpicker alike performed their professional flourishes, and the *crime passionnel* was practiced
as a fine art.

In such an environment the theater, legitimate and illegitimate, operatic and naughty, was bound to thrive. The number of theaters in the city had been increasing since Molière, yet the actor came into his own as a public figure only toward the end of the nineteenth century, after the era of great literary-political heroes: Rousseau, Voltaire, Chateaubriand, Lamartine, Hugo. In the eighties, the roaring voice and sheer physical power of Mounet-Sully made him king in a world of mighty tragedians whose grandiloquence we no longer know. His furious integrity as an actor combined a cultist's intensity with the posturing of a buccaneer. For a few months, until she left him for further glory, Mounet-Sully found his queen in a young actress of illegitimate birth (with an illegitimate child of her own), violent disposition, slender figure, and haunting feline face. This woman, Sarah Bernhardt, lived for thirty-five years at the center of scandal and publicity; she was denounced by some for her love affairs and extravagances and lauded by others as the greatest genius of her time.

After eight years with the Comédie-Française she resigned in a quarrel with the director and made the first of eight triumphant tours in America. She dragged with her across the country, in addition to her score of pets, the famous gold-fixtured coffin which an admirer had given her at her request. After having been photographed in it to spite her director, she kept it at the foot of her bed wherever she went. In the United States dozens of pamphlets circulated in her path, with titles like *The Amours of Sarah*. The Bishop of Chicago thundered so eloquently from his pulpit against the corrupting influence of the French actress that her agent sent him a polite note: "Monseigneur: I make it a practice to spend $400 on publicity when I come to your city. But since you have done the job for me, I am sending you $200 for your needy." Every fortune Sarah amassed on her world-wide tours she proceeded to lose during the next season or two in Paris, even though she was idolized by all classes. One after the other, three major Paris theaters passed through her hands; each had to be sold to cover her mounting debts. When an injury to her leg first caused talk of amputation (which finally became necessary in 1915), P. T. Barnum approached her with an offer of $10,000 for the severed limb and the right to exhibit it. In 1896 a municipal *Journée Sarah Bernhardt* brought the whole of Paris to her

feet. It began with a banquet for six hundred at the Grand
Hôtel. The guests marveled at the undiminished youth of
the fifty-two-year-old beauty whose son was already over
thirty and managing her affairs. A procession of two hundred carriages followed hers to her own Théâtre de la
Renaissance. After her performance of the third act of
Phèdre, half a dozen poets, including François Coppée and
her new lover, Edmond Rostand (shortly to write two hits,
Cyrano de Bergerac and *L'Aiglon*), recited verses to her
on a stage banked with flowers. Four years later she attempted her most ambitious performance: *Hamlet, en tra-
vesti,* in Marcel Schwob's fastidious prose translation. For
twelve days running she rehearsed from noon until six in
the morning and finally staged a passionate, sometimes
sentimental version in which she whispered "To be or not
to be" almost *in secreto.* Colette described her in the performance as having "a face sculpted in white powder." Paris
loved it; London, despite her previous successes there, refused it in outrage; the festival at Stratford-on-Avon was
entranced. She went on acting for fifteen years, short one
leg at the end but never out of voice. Sarah Bernhardt's
was the most highly charged temperament of the era and
one of its greatest talents. Neither Caruso nor Nijinsky had
such a career of enduring public adulation, somersaulting
business adventures, and tumultuous private life. Only an
actress could replace the colossus of Victor Hugo, take
Paris for her private stage, and become what the French
have called ever since a *monstre sacré.*

But in reality it was the era of music hall and *café chan-
tant*—both of them popular adaptations of the light-opera
craze which Offenbach had brought to the Paris of the
Second Empire. Everyone was willing to pay to see even
brighter costumes and more sparkling antics than those
that filled the streets. La Goulue and, later, Mistinguett
(originally Miss Tinguette) were vivacious brassy enter-
tainers who worked themselves to the point of exhaustion.
Then out of this bubbling atmosphere emerged the appari-
tion of a thin nervous woman in a white dress and long
black gloves. No one could have predicted her success. In
a sensual grating voice she sang of heartbreak and cruelty
and unabashed crime. After hearing her, people never forgot the harsh diction and awkward eloquent gestures of
Yvette Guilbert. These were also the years when Colette

left her cultivated music-critic husband, Willy, for whom she had first set pen to paper. She danced in gold tights through the provinces and into the best *salons* of Paris before she reached fame as a novelist and one of the most penetrating chroniclers of the period. Three permanent circuses and a new Hippodrome fringed Montmartre along the boulevards. The clown, the horse, and the acrobat here earned their place in modern art; the Degas ballet dancer became the Toulouse-Lautrec cabaret entertainer, and then became the Picasso Harlequin. The team of clowns, Footit and Chocolat, developed the first comic-stooge act (known as *clown et auguste*). Grock and Antonet, the American Emmet Kelly, and the Fratellini brothers all achieved fame in Paris before the turn of the century.

Antoine, actor-producer and truant employee of the Paris gas company, brought a restrained naturalism and new dramatic talent (Strindberg and Ibsen) into his pioneering Théâtre Libre near the Place Pigalle. Actors learned to speak for, not at, the audience. He hung a bleeding side of beef in the set of a butcher's shop, and—it is hard to realize—for the first time in Paris, regularly turned the house lights out so that the attention of the audience would have to be directed to the stage. The theater reigned supreme. Yet it was all a show within a show. The frenzy on hundreds of stages all over Paris reflected the gala life around them. At the Opéra, unlike the concentration required at Antoine's Théâtre Libre, the performance never stopped the fashionable goings-on in the boxes. The city beheld itself endlessly and was never bored or displeased.

Of all the stages that made up the city, the most formalized and demanding was the *salon*. The aristocracy still cultivated the conversation of what were assumed to be great minds. The revolution had not destroyed the old aristocracy, but had set up beside it another: the Napoleonic. The most elevated member of the new nobility, Princesse Mathilde Bonaparte, Napoleon's niece, did not mince her words: "The French revolution? Why, without it I'd be selling oranges in the streets of Ajaccio." Her sympathy and loyalty had begun by attracting Théophile Gautier, Flaubert, and Renan to a dangerously liberal *salon* during the Second Empire. During the Third Republic she again began receiving in her house in the Rue de Berri (today the Belgian Embassy) and continued until after 1900, when she was over eighty. Dumas *fils*, Henri de Régnier, Maupassant, and Anatole France came to her simple early dinners, which Proust described affectionately in one of his best *Figaro* society articles.

In barely a generation, Princesse Mathilde had learned an aristocratic ease which gave her the proper "presence" for a *salon*. Her guests never felt like performing animals. Madame Aubernon, however, a somewhat vulgar aristocrat of the old school, passionately interested in literature and the theater, conducted her rival *salon* like a lion tamer. About a dozen guests attended her poorly cooked dinners in the Rue d'Astorg, and Madame Aubernon alone decided the subject for discussion. One guest at a time was permitted to orate, and his chances of a second invitation depended on the brilliance of his performance. The hostess silenced any disorderly interruption by ringing a little porcelain bell which stood at her right hand. One evening when Renan was discoursing at some length, she had several times to call to order the dramatist Labiche (author of *The Italian Straw Hat*). When she finally asked him to speak, he admitted with some reluctance that he had only wanted to ask for more peas. On another occasion Madame Aubernon asked D'Annunzio point-blank what he thought of love; his reply was not designed to bring him a second invitation: "Read my books, Madame, and let me eat my dinner." A lady, asked with similar abruptness to speak her piece on the subject of adultery, replied, "You must pardon me, Madame. For this evening I prepared incest."

As the *salon* declined for lack of ladies trained to conduct one and through disappearance of the basic attitude of *hommage* on which the institution rested, the need for a verbal arena increased. One of the principal changes of *la belle époque* was that the great performers moved from the *salon* into the café. Here anyone could enter, and each man paid for his drink. As far back as the mid-eighteenth century artists and writers in Paris had begun to rely increasingly on the stimulus and exchange of the café. (They were served by young boys, whence comes the word *garçon* for waiter.) The term *boulevardier* was now invented to describe men whose principal accomplishment consisted in appearing at the proper moment in the proper café. More than the *salon*, the café came to provide a free market-

place of ideas and helped France produce its steady succession of artistic schools. The Napolitain, the Weber, the
Vachette—the famous cafés of the period following 1885
—were sprinkled from the fashionable boulevards to the
Latin Quarter to the slopes of Montmartre. The Café
Guerbois and the Nouvelle Athènes in the sixties and seventies had nurtured the first artistic movement entirely
organized in cafés: impressionism. By the end of the nineteenth century the café represented a ritual which could
absorb the better part of the day. "In the old days," wrote
Jean Moréas, one of the great habitués and lion of the
Vachette, "I arrived around one in the afternoon . . .
stayed till seven, and then went to dine. About eight we
came back, and didn't finally leave until one in the morning." It was a life unto itself.

Salon and café demanded performances on a small and
intense scale from a group of highly trained actors. There
was an equally specialized class of Parisians who played,
however, to a larger audience. In the title of his famous
play, first produced in 1885, Dumas *fils* brilliantly named
this special world: *Le demi-monde*. The beautiful, cultured,
kept women had undisputed sway over styles in women's
dress. Fashion is the most unpredictable and competitive
theater of all, and they brought it to a peak of perfection.
Mesdemoiselles les cocottes (also more crudely known as
les horizontales) were on display mornings in the Bois in
their carriages, filled the tables at the Café de Paris and
the Pré Catelan in the evening, and entertained lavishly
at night in their own tastefully decorated *hôtels particuliers*.
One of the best known, Mademoiselle Jane Cambrai, practiced no deceit in exploiting her lover, a successful rag
dealer. He was in no way suitable company—or host—
at her brilliant parties, to which *Tout-Paris* swarmed at the
turn of the century. She saw to it that he remained happily
upstairs playing bridge with a few of his own friends, and
he showed no disgruntlement over the crowd below dancing and banqueting at his expense. These creatures of
pleasure and fashion and canniness lived truly in a "half-
world" from which they might fade into penury and loneliness, or out of which they might emerge dramatically by
marriage into nobility and respectability. A *cocotte* had
not arrived in her profession until she had inspired at least

one suicide, unsuccessful of course, and three or four duels, and had *déniaisé* (initiated) her lover's eldest son.

Fashion influenced every domain of life. Just after 1890 the velocipede had been introduced with little success. A few years later, the Prince de Sagan, the most prominent and dashing nobleman in Paris, pedaled through the Bois on a "little steel fairy," wearing a loud striped suit and specially designed straw boater. The city was delighted, and women's fashions changed immediately to allow them to ride astride. The bicycle, symbolizing everything democratic and modern (and supporting two weekly papers and a daily), led the way to an upsurge of sport which culminated in the revival of the Olympic games in 1894. After the bicycle, but without public participation, came the airplane. Blériot designed and stubbornly flew eight successive models before he finally drifted across the English Channel in 1909 in a ship that looked like a bicycle with fins. He was deliriously mobbed during the welcome-home parade in Paris.

One of the most fashionable annual social events in the nineties was the Bazar de la Charité. It was held in a rambling wood-and-canvas structure off the Champs-Elysées, and the ladies who organized it went to great lengths to include every kind of attraction. In 1897 they set aside a room for a showing of Louis and Auguste Lumière's recently perfected *cinématographe,* which had rendered obsolete Edison's unwieldly kinetoscope only a few months after the latter came into use. The film program at the Bazar attracted many children, and a turnstile was installed at the door to keep them orderly. An ether lamp provided light for projection, and one afternoon when the operator had difficulty keeping it lit, he inadvertently shot across the room a jet of flame which reached the canvas wall. The entire premises went up in flames in a few minutes, and adults and children found themselves blocked behind the turnstile. In the panic, scores of people died, including some of the most prominent aristocrats in France. The blame fell, naturally, upon the new invention rather than on the outmoded lamp, and promotion of films in France suffered a grave setback for several years.

The Bazar de la Charité disaster led to one of the strangest quarrels of the period. It involved the dandified Count Robert de Montesquiou, a scion of ancient French nobility, and the well-known symbolist poet, Henri de Régnier. In addition to a reputation for effeteness, wit, and the ability to mime at will, Montesquiou was to achieve literary notoriety as the model for Huysmans' unregenerate aesthete, Des Esseintes, in *A rebours*, and for Proust's cultured and corrupt Baron de Charlus. At Verlaine's funeral the count's silk-clad figure with curled mustache served as a pallbearer next to the poet Catulle Mendès. Montesquiou gives a partial account of the quarrel in his memoirs. It was rumored after the Bazar fire that some of the upper-crust youths, trapped with everyone else, had used their canes to clear a path out of the furnace and had simply abandoned their lady companions. During a visit to the Baroness de Rothschild's picture gallery a short time later, Henri de Régnier's two sisters-in-law encountered Montesquiou and made insinuations about a cane he was carrying. They compared it to those which had been used in the Bazar catastrophe, even though Montesquiou had not been present. According to the charges made by the Count, Régnier added some comments about how well the Count would look with a muff or a fan. Montesquiou challenged him to a duel, choosing pistols. Maurice Barrès was one of his seconds. But Régnier claimed to have said, on the contrary, "There are two things I wish I could use—a fan in summer and a muff in winter." The offender became the offended and chose swords. Régnier wounded his opponent. Both refused to be reconciliated.

Honor was still something out of a Corneille tragedy, and dueling perfectly suited the mood of the times. "On the field of honor" one could go beyond words to settle personal differences by serious dramatics. The papers carried announcements of each day's *affaires d'honneur*, with lengthy procès-verbaux drawn up by the seconds to establish how settlement had or had not been made. Engagements were fought until the first blood flowed, and afterward the combatants sometimes walked off the field arm in arm. Fatal encounters were rare. When an important duel was to be fought, numbers of spectators tried to follow the participants to the chosen spot on the outskirts of Paris. Journalists, who outdid one another in writing slanderous articles, constantly had their friends up at dawn to serve as seconds, and many doctors began their day by dressing a sword wound. Catulle Mendès almost lost his life defend-

ing Sarah Bernhardt's right to play the role of Hamlet.
Duels were fought on the slightest provocation, and no
effective attempt was made to outlaw the custom, so typically exhibitionistic, until after World War I.

The number of duels multiplied wildly during the two
contrasting political crises of the period. One was excellent
farce; the other serious melodrama. In 1886 a handsome
and apparently trustworthy officer, General Boulanger,
enjoyed a reputation for bravery, republicanism, and such
terse slogans as "The army doesn't take sides." In order
to introduce necessary reforms into the army, then regain-
ing full strength, Clemenceau maneuvered Boulanger's appointment as minister of war. The common people and
politicians alike believed that the full-bearded "man on
horseback" was destined to overcome the lethargy and
divisionism of the government. Parading everywhere on
his coal-black charger, his military figure appealed irresistibly to men and women alike. Because it supplied the
desired rhyme, his name was chanted across the country at
the end of the second stanza of a popular song, *En revenant
de la revue,* describing a Fourteenth of July parade:

> *Moi, j'faisais qu'admirer*
> *Not'brav'général Boulanger.*

When the hero was relieved of his ministry and sent back
to duty at Clermont-Ferrand, a cheering uncontrollable
mob surrounded the entire Gare de Lyon, and people lay
down on the tracks in front of the train to prevent his
departure. He escaped by jumping into a lone locomotive
on another track and riding off with the engineer. Two
secret affairs prevented him from exploiting the mob, as
he might easily have done. One was a consuming love
affair with Madame de Bonnemain, the divorced wife of
one of his subordinates at Clermont. The other involved
his political negotiations with the Royalists. After flirting
with all parties in succession, Radical, Republican, and
Bonapartist, he had begun to come to terms with the still-
powerful Royalists. They hoped to use him to bring back
the Orleanist pretender, the Comte de Paris, and to that
end they furnished him money and electioneering facilities.
Returning to Paris as a deputy, the general prepared to
seize power with the simple and simple-minded program:
"Dissolution and reform." The sixty-year-old Radical Flo-

quet mocked the fifty-year-old general in the Chamber of
Deputies by saying, "At your age, Napoleon was dead."
They chose sabers, and Paris held its breath. The old poli-
tician wounded the vigorous cavalry officer after some dazzling sword play on both sides, but even this shaming could
not hinder Boulanger's ascent. The plot, which had already
involved spies, disguises, secret conferences with powerful
emissaries, and midnight rendezvous with Madame de Bonnemain, thickened but never resolved. Enjoying the adulation of the populace and feted by the cream of the aristocracy (who took to wearing his insigne of a red carna-
tion), the general never conceived a plan of action and
opposed any use of force. The government cannily scared
Madame de Bonnemain out of the country and then let
word reach her eyes that a warrant was out for the general's
arrest. At the peak of his popular acclaim, listening to the
crowd outside shouting that he should march on the president's palace, and knowing that both the police and the
army would join him rather than arrest him if he did, General Boulanger lingered over his dinner at the Restaurant
Durand and pondered his mistress's plea that he follow her
to Belgium. As the minister of the interior said the next
morning, "The comedy is over." He was allowed to cross
the border unmolested. But it was not quite over. Madame
de Bonnemain died the following year, and the lover who
had abandoned the leadership of an entire nation to rejoin
her stabbed himself on her grave.

After this two-year national farce came the international
melodrama of the Dreyfus case. Almost by force it divided
public opinion into partisans of individual justice and defenders of vested authority; the poisons of anti-Semitism
and anti-clericalism flooded through the cleft. Zola's open
letter, *J'accuse*, in 1898 first brought the affair into the
open, helped by the publicity surrounding a duel between
the "two colonels": Picquart, the first officer to insist that
justice had miscarried, and Henry, who was arraigned
many months later for responsibility in forging key documents. (Henry finally slit his own throat in the Mont
Valérien military prison.) They met in an indoor cavalry
training ring, the worst possible spot because of tetanus
infection. Henry, fighting "with his tongue hanging entirely
out of his month," impressed the spectators (who had
climbed to the windows on ladders) as half insane. Two

minor wounds started him raving, and he had to be carried away.

The case followed its course of embattled trials, petitions
and public letters with scores, then hundreds, of signatures,
shooting of the defense attorneys, endless duels, and fist
fights in the street and in cafés. When Loubet, a new pro-
Dreyfus president, was elected, Baron Christiani smashed
in his top hat with a cane on the *pelouse* of the Auteuil
race track. In reply the incensed working classes demonstrated against the aristocracy at Longchamp race track
the day of the ultrafashionable Grand Prix. An anti-Semite,
Jules Guérin, who published the blatant *L'Anti-Juif*, barri-
caded himself for thirty-seven days against Lépine, the
Prefect of Police, until starvation brought him out. During
the Rennes retrial, the officers of the General Staff tried to
rattle their sabers loud enough to drown out the voice of
Dreyfus's lawyer. As soon as the important events took
place, they were restaged and filmed by the first great
movie producer, Méliès. It made a twelve-reel *grand film*
in scrupulous documentary style (*L'affaire Dreyfus*, 1899).

With only one exception, every aspect of the case
evolved into demonstration; there was no middle ground
between crusading and corruption. The exception was
Dreyfus himself, brought back from five years on Devil's
Island. Near collapse after a few minutes in public, his uniform visibly padded so as not to hang too pathetically on
his wasted frame, and talking in a rasping colorless voice,
he disappointed his most fervent partisans and settled for
a pardon. But even without a popular hero like Boulanger,
the melodrama had accomplished its work of dramatizing
the social and political issues of the times. Church, army,
government, nobility, newspapers, courts—every revered
institution revealed its profound taint. Waldeck-Rousseau,
the premier who formed a government in 1899 to meet the
crisis, conceived the most theatrical gesture of all. He welcomed the country's 22,000 mayors at a mammoth banquet
and assured the feasting company that he would be mod-
erate but firm in his legislation.

If not the profound effect, at least the bitter memories
of the Dreyfus case were dispelled by an immediate distraction: the International Exposition of 1900. The previous
exposition, in 1889, had feted the centenary of the revolu-

tion.* At this earlier event, scientific exhibits filled several buildings, including the colossal Hall of Industry, a monument of structural steel. Gaugin showed his paintings at the Café Volponi. A Cairo street scene was constructed with authentic imported Egyptians to live in it and perform the *danse du ventre*. The Javanese dancers became the rage of Paris, influenced music-hall routines for twenty years, and confirmed Debussy in his tendency toward Oriental harmonies. Thomas Edison, exalted by French scientists as "the sorcerer of Menlo Park," visited the grounds where his own pavilion was one of the largest. His latest invention, the incandescent bulb, augmented the miracle of the fair by lighting the silhouette of its principal buildings. Edison was so impressed by an allegorical statue called "The Fairy of Electricity" (a winged woman crouching on a dilapidated gas jet, surrounded by a Volta battery, telegraph key, and telephone, and brandishing an incandescent bulb—all in the best Carrara marble) that he bought it for his new West Orange laboratory.

After such a stunning success in 1889, Paris staged for the new century a still more fabulous and universal fair; it had been under construction for ten years. The nineteenth centenary of the birth of a certain well-known religious figure was not prominently featured. For more than a year after the April opening, the banks of the Seine for a mile on both sides of the Trocadero were transformed by exotic buildings—or at least exotic façades. Paris looked and acted like an overblown Venice.

Both expositions lay at the feet of the same gigantic monument. The Banquet Years received their symbol built to order in the heart of the city. The Eiffel Tower, raised at the cost of fifteen million uninflated francs in 1889, aroused protest from a committee of prominent citizens from Gounod to Dumas *fils*. Their outraged letter condemned the "Tower of Babel" which would "disfigure and dishonor" the city—but to no avail. When work was completed, tables were set up on the lower level, and three hundred workmen still in overalls feasted and drank cham-

* After the first, in 1867, the second Universal Exposition, in 1878, had proclaimed the recovery of France from the defeat of 1871 and the overwhelming subscription of forty-two billion francs to a requested three billion government loan. Among the French there is no surer expression of confidence.

pagne. Later an official banquet with full official pomp opened the tower to the public. This great anomaly of modern engineering expressed all the aspirations of a period which set out to surpass its heritage. And it remained: styleless, functionless, unhistoried, and soon as familiar as an *urinoir*. Tourists visited it, artists painted it, newlyweds with innocent faces were photographed beside it, suicides and inventors of devices for human flight jumped off it. In the end it became a symbol of Paris as famous as the Seine itself. The Eiffel Tower in its truculent stance is the first monument of modernism. For half a century it remained the tallest man-made structure in the world.*

The expositions turned every resident and visitor in the city into an actor in the extravaganza of human progress and vanity. There was no resisting such pageantry. The closet performances of *salon* and café, the social drama of Dreyfus, were only part of the show. For the Banquet Years, all Paris was a stage.

In its prolonged romp through the eighties and nineties and into the *avant-guerre*, Paris scarcely knew what it was excited about. Was it a liberation? A revolution? A victory? A last fling? A first debauch? Amid the externals of funerals and fashions the city knew only that it was having a good time and making a superb spectacle of itself. Sensing this prevailing mood, artists, more than any other group, saw their opportunity. Exactly in the years following Hugo's funeral in 1885, all the arts changed direction as if they had been awaiting a signal. Along a discernible line of demarcation they freed themselves from the propulsion of the nineteenth century and responded to the first insistent tugs of the twentieth.

In painting, impressionism fell into public domain after its last group show in 1886. While Gauguin and Van Gogh, working together in Arles, were finding two different paths leading away from the literal vision of impressionism, Signac, Redon, and Seurat founded the "Société des Artistes Indépendants." Membership was open to all; its annual

* Another prominent structure associated closely with Paris was also rising at this time on the heights of Montmartre. The white wonder of the Sacré-Cœur basilica, a symbol of penance for the Commune massacres, took forty years to build; the Eiffel Tower, two.

salon had no jury. The Société marks one of the crucial dates in the formation of modern Western art, for, more than those of the impressionist group, its growing exhibitions gave space to every new tendency in painting. The first show came in 1884, a reasonable public success, but rocked by internal upheavals.* Reorganized the same year, the group tried to hold another show in December "for the benefit of cholera victims." This event was totally snowed out. Thus the second exhibition of the Société des Artistes Indépendants in August and September, 1886, was the real beginning. Two hundred paintings were hung in the Rue des Tuileries in a huge barracks of a building originally erected to house postal and telegraph offices. Two of the canvases have become landmarks in modern painting: Seurat's *Un dimanche d'été à la Grande Jatte* and Rousseau's *Un soir de carnaval.*[7]

Only two years before Hugo's death, music had lost its own last genius-artist of romanticism. Although Wagner's popularity swelled until 1900 at least, his death in 1883 finally made possible the liberation of French music from German domination. The best works of Chabrier and Fauré followed almost immediately, as if these composers needed no other inducement to find themselves. Debussy and Ravel were only a few years behind. In literature, the very different writings of Verlaine and Huysmans, Laforgue and Rimbaud, and, above all, Mallarmé, converged in an era of endeavor that earned its name in 1886. Symbolism meant everything from intense verbal lyricism to spiritual defiance. In all the arts, 1885 is the point from which we must reckon the meaning of the word "modern."

The forces that thus began to give a new impetus to the arts hover just below the exuberant surface of *la belle époque*. These less-known aspects of its life still partake of the theatrical posturing without which no action seemed

---

* Apparently the treasury was mercilessly raided by idle members wanting fishing rods; the Seine flowed temptingly nearby. Nonangler members demanded to see the accounts, and the cashier had to defend himself by producing a revolver. "Members of the Organizing Committee had fist fights in the exhibition rooms during the day and waylaid one another at night on street corners, and then went to denounce each other at local police stations." (R. Rey in *Histoire de l'art contemporain*, ed. Huyghe.)

possible or meaningful. They distinguish themselves from superficial events by both their destructiveness and their sense of purpose. One must probe behind the quirks of Madame Aubernon's *salon* and General Boulanger's romantic failure in politics in order to find what supported that gaudy façade. Only a few people had an inkling of what was happening. Beneath the careening of the Banquet Years, something pulled hard and long to establish the direction the new century would travel.

The most turbulent force of all is almost forgotten. Anarchism had been seething for many years in the south, principally in the industrial city of Lyon. Its way was prepared by the surge of antimilitarism after the war of 1871 and by the fresh memory of the Commune. Traveling inexorably northward, the libertarian movement finally shook Paris in a series of bomb explosions and controversial trials.

> Anarchists come from the most varied backgrounds. But a specific mentality links them—the spirit of revolt and its derivatives, the spirit of examination and criticism, of opposition and innovation, which leads to scorn and hate of every commitment and hierarchy in society, and ends up in the exaggeration of individualism. Decadent literature furnished the party with a strong contingent; in recent years there has been, especially among young writers, an upsurge of anarchism. (Maurice Boisson, *Les attentats anarchistes.*)

First Ravachol, with five murders behind him, blew up the homes of several magistrates in 1892. He was caught in a restaurant, brought to trial, and let off with penal servitude for life. Then another jury, intimidated by public outcry, reversed the decision and sent him to the guillotine. The end of the same year Vaillant, of illegitimate birth and hysterical disposition, tossed a weak bomb full of nails into the Chamber of Deputies from the visitor's gallery. None of the deputies was killed, and Vaillant, pleading in his defense that the bomb was intended only as a "warning," quoted Darwin, Spencer, Ibsen, and Octave Mirbeau in support of his doctrine. After his execution he was widely acclaimed as a martyr. At a literary banquet the evening of Vaillant's bombing, the polemical critic Laurent Tailhade was interviewed about the violence in the Chamber. "What do a few human lives matter," he replied, *"si le geste est beau?"* Two years later he lost an eye when a bomb exploded in the restaurant where he was eating, and the next morning's paper chastised him with his own Nietzschean sentiments. Yet his sympathies were shared by many.

A few weeks after Vaillant's death, a young intellectual of good family named Emile Henry exploded a bomb in the Café Terminus in the Gare Saint-Lazare. He had to be saved by the police from being lynched on the spot. The trial brought out the full challenge of anarchist convictions. Judge (in red robe): "Your hands are stained with blood." Henry: "Like the robes you wear, Your Honor." His coolness on the stand allowed him to discuss the precise chemical composition of his bomb and regret that it had not taken the lives of more victims. He died bravely under the knife crying, *"Vive l'anarchie,"* and it was discovered that he had spent his last days in prison reading *Don Quixote.*

In the summer of 1894 began the mass trial of thirty ill-assorted men accused of anarchist leanings and treasonable acts. Among them was the prominent literary figure Félix Fénéon, an early champion of the impressionists. The prosecution could not produce significant evidence, and Fénéon in his response to cross-examination was concise to the point of parody.* The climax of the trial came when the government attorney unwisely opened in the courtroom a package which had been sent to him containing, not explosives, but *de la matière fécale*. He asked for a recess to wash his hands. Fénéon's voice rose over the assembly: "Never since Pontius Pilate has a magistrate washed his hands with such ostentation." The trial led to no convictions.

During the years preceding 1894 the anarchists had gained wide amateur support. Several literary reviews and daily papers defended the "brave gestures." There were strange chapters in the history of the movement, like the story of the prefect of police in Paris who anonymously founded and subsidized an anarchist magazine in order

---

* One exchange went thus: Magistrate: *On vous a vu causer avec un anarchiste derrière un bec de gaz.* Fénéon: *Pouvez-vous me dire, Mon Président, ce que c'est que le derrière d'un bec de gaz?*

to have a reliable source of information. During a raid on the Bal des Quat'-z-Arts for immodest attire, the police killed an innocent bystander. The students, fired with an-archist ideas, resisted this invasion of their rights. For sev-eral days the full Paris police force kept the Latin Quarter in a state of siege while the issue almost came to a vote of confidence in the Chamber of Deputies.

By 1894 most sympathizers realized that the defiance of the anarchists exceeded defensible bounds, and the out-rages died out quickly. But their effects remained. Anarch-ism served not only to unsettle the political smugness of the Third Republic, but also to challenge any formulated aesthetic. The dynamism of prewar artistic activity ran a close parallel to anarchism; postwar Dada and surrealism look like its artistic parodies. By acting on their ideas, the anarchist "martyrs" inspired artists to demonstrate as boldly.

And so they had been doing since the eighties in the new setting of the literary cabaret. The organized yet authentic Bohemia of the Chat Noir, the most famous of the cabarets, was a *salon* stood on its head. Its origins go back to a group of young Latin Quarter poets, *chansonniers*, and painters, calling themselves the Hydropathes, who had begun meeting regularly in the seventies to recite, sing, and issue a magazine. Among them were the sardonic poet Charles Cros, close friend of Rimbaud and Verlaine and legitimate inventor of a pre-Edison phonograph, and Al-phonse Allais, chief *fumiste* (perpetrator of tall tales and hoaxes) and short-story writer, with the mixed talents of Poe and Mark Twain. In 1881 an unsuccessful painter named Rodolphe Salis had the idea of opening a cabaret with its own weekly paper and literary evenings. Serving both as chief performers and dependable clientele, the entire Hydropathe group let itself be lured across the Seine to Salis' Chat Noir on the slopes of Montmartre. Within a few months the establishment was turning away cus-tomers attracted by wild stories and farcical publicity. The Chat Noir claimed to have been founded under Julius Caesar and displayed on its cobwebbed walls "cups used by Charlemagne, Villon and Rabelais." The surly waiters wore the formal garb of the Académie française, and Salis insulted each customer as he entered. No one had tried such a "democratic" enterprise before, and the snobs loved it. A few years later Aristide Bruant opened his famous Le

Mirliton, where he served as rudest of hosts and perambulating singer, probably the best of the era. A dozen more such establishments flourished until the turn of the century.

By 1885, in an operation twice delayed by the elaborate maneuvers of Hugo's funeral, the rowdy crowd of the Chat Noir burst out of its old quarters and paraded in costume through the streets with a mounted escort to occupy an entire building in the Rue Victor-Massé. The inaugural banquet and festivities included among the guests (for once the account in the Chat Noir paper told the truth) Léo Delibes, Maupassant, Jules Lemaître, Huysmans, Villiers de l'Isle-Adam, Waldeck-Rousseau and eleven other deputies, two Paris mayors, and three respected septuagenarians: Renan, Bouguereau, the academic painter, and Théodore de Banville, the Parnassian poet. The weekly paper thrived, publishing poems by Verlaine and Mallarmé, humorous *chroniques* by everyone, and cartoons by Forain, Steinlen, Caran d'Ache, and Willette. The *chansonnier*-dramatist Maurice Donnay had the dizziest success of all: ten plays and twenty years after his debut at the Chat Noir, he was elected to the Académie française—the real one—and was not out of place. The most original undertaking on the three-story premises was the Théâtre d'Ombres, which developed the crude technique of shadow plays into a convincing art form ten years before the advent of films. This menagerie of writers turned performers of their own work kept Paris entranced for a decade; their brand of sentimental humor both mocked and exploited the era.

The atmosphere of permanent explosion in artistic activity is evidence not only of anarchistic tendencies but also of the fierceness of its experiments. New reviews appeared, principally *La Vogue* (founded in 1886; in a brief life of nine months it reached the staggering circulation of 15,000 and published major texts by Mallarmé, Verlaine, Rimbaud, Villiers de l'Isle-Adam, and Laforgue), the long-lived *Mercure de France* (1890), with its monthly banquets and weekly editorial receptions, and the Natanson brothers' *Revue Blanche* (1891). The Salon des Indépendants outgrew one building after another with more and more work from young painters, while ethnological museums were being filled with astounding art from Africa, the Pacific, and Egypt. The new Schola Cantorum brought back old church modes, and composers began to collect the ancient songs of France. Modernism coincided in significant fashion with primitivism. Gauguin's "flight" to Tahiti in 1891 may not have produced his best work but it reveals the integrity of his desire for another vision. Anarchism itself can be seen as a form of political primitivism trying to return to an earlier stage of social evolution. What one can overlook most easily in all this demonstration is its stubborn purpose to change the aspect of both life and art. There was a connection and a difference between the irrepressible frivolity of the upper classes and the resolute gaiety of young artists.

Deep down at its center of gravity, however, the century turned slowly despite all this ferment. It changed its pace for no man. Artists who strained forward into the future found that their fresh trail was rarely being followed in a prosperous and complacent France. In response they did what was only natural: they banded together for support. They constituted what we have come to call the avant-garde,* a "tradition" of heterodoxy and opposition which defied civilized values in the name of individual consciousness. They developed a systematic technique of scandal in order to keep their ideas before the public. It amounted to an artistic underground, which began to break through to the surface in the latter part of the Banquet Years.

The avant-garde was not radically new, for it grew out of the nonconformist tendencies of the romantic movement. The lucid frenzy of Gérard de Nerval and the sentimental Bohemia of Murger crystallized into a determined group of artists who maintained a belligerent attitude toward the world and a genuine sympathy for each other. The Chat Noir was no ivory tower; it was, in fact, closer to the gutter, with Villon as its patron saint. Arbitrarily one can establish the origin of the avant-garde in 1863, when Napoleon III consented to a Salon des Refusés. Artists rejected by the official exhibit were able to protest loud enough to gain recognition as a group and a separate showing. Unfortunately, both Emperor and Empress were offended by

---

* First used in journalistic writing in the expression "*les artistes de l'avant-garde*," the term gradually outgrew the military metaphor and achieved independent existence during the last decade of the nineteenth century. Unquestionably the polemics of the Dreyfus case, with its military associations and political crusading, promoted the new usage.

Manet's *Le déjeuner sur l'herbe;* the exhibit was not repeated. By 1885 there was a crying need for fresh outlets
of expression, a need met in part by the new literary reviews, the Salon des Indépendants, and influential private
gatherings of artists such as Mallarmé's *mardis* (1884) and
Edmond de Goncourt's *grenier* (1885). Even more important, café and cabaret provided the artist with social independence and produced their own variety of conversational
wit and brilliance. The cultured public, no longer dom-
inated by the *salon,* gradually came to realize that there
existed a small group of people thinking and living and
creating beyond the pale of ordinary behavior. Today the
persevering remnants of the avant-garde are generally
scoffed at, often exploited, and occasionally glorified beyond all measure. Modernism wrote into its scripture a
major text, which demands, at least in retrospect, our gratitude: the avant-garde we have with us always.

Like everyone else, they had their own banquets. These
untrammeled gatherings tended to gain momentum toward
wild farce or orgy. The Lapin Agile (also known as the
Lapin à Gill or Là peint A. Gill), the Montmartre cabaret
that succeeded the Chat Noir around the turn of the century, housed many celebrations, which always included
Frédé, the bushy-bearded proprietor, and his unhouse-
broken donkey, Lolo. A group of young artists, inspired by
the author Dorgelès, there concocted the celebrated hoax
of a canvas brushed entirely by Lolo's twitching tail. The
resulting work, distinctly "impressionist" in style, was hung
at the Salon des Indépendants with the title "And the Sun
Went Down over the Adriatic." Dorgelès signed it "Joachim
Raphael Boronali," and the painting was praised by a respectable number of critics on their marathon tour of the
show.

The rival reviews the *Mercure de France* and the *Revue
Blanche* joined forces in 1895 to organize a dinner for the
Belgian poet Emile Verhaeren. It soon became apparent
that Verhaeren would not be able to attend, but no one was
dismayed; once under way, such a banquet had a life of its
own. An upper room in the Vachette Café on the Left Bank
held the guests, who, before entering, had to make their
way through a street demonstration against Oscar Wilde's
prison sentence and sign a petition of protest. It was carnival time, and women were speedily found for all males

who had come alone. Drinking ran heavy, and after
speeches of tribute to the absent guest of honor, a letter
from the ailing Verlaine was read by a handsome painter.
His embroidered silk vest and rich voice so attracted the
ladies' admiration that he soon found himself engaged in
a scuffle with several jealous males. Thereupon the whole
company moved off to le bal Bullier, a disreputable Latin
Quarter dance hall for students and street-walkers, and
spent the rest of the night with the cancan girls. It was,
obviously, always carnival time for many of the guests.

The larger the banquet, the better occasion it provided
to demonstrate one's exuberance. At a three-hundred-plate
affair in the Palais d'Orléans to celebrate the erection of a
monument to Verlaine after his death, the dignified critic
Charles Morice was chosen to give the major speech. The
younger generation rapidly decided he was too conservative
to do justice to the former Prince of Poets, and, after some
preliminary whistling and heckling from the back, china
and glassware began to fly. The bombardment succeeded
in breaking up the banquet, and the ladies present had
difficulty escaping the brawl that followed.

By 1900, then, old-world gaiety had taken on an aspect of methodical demonstration. Montmartre and the
Latin Quarter do not merely provide a colorful background for these years. Their cabarets and cafés represented a new aesthetic. The banquet called for gaiety and
scorn of convention, and also for an assimilation of popular art forms and a full aliveness to the present moment.
This was the setting for a great rejuvenation of the arts.
The Chat Noir and the Lapin Agile fostered a group of
artists who ventured far into the realm of pure buffoonery
without abandoning their loyalty to artistic creation. A similar pursuit of newness for its own sake was taking place
in England with the *Yellow Book* and the *Savoy*. But Au-
brey Beardsley and Oscar Wilde and Max Beerbohm found
no surroundings in London to equal a Paris café.

The frenetic gaiety of the *bistro* had its reverse side.
Some of the most high-spirited artists lived in poverty and
at times frightful physical hardship. The way they bore
their lots demonstrates the dedication of their lives. The
long antic of the Banquet Years was not a matter of mere
frivolity, for in many cases the demonstrations arose out of
basic earnestness. Referring to what underlay the extrava-

gance of his Chat Noir days, the Catholic revolutionary Léon Bloy wrote: "I brought with me, along with my religious preconceptions, a raging hunger for the Absolute, and an overpowering need for the trigonometric spirit in criticism, and even in the simple version of external reality." Bohemian surroundings could produce both a "Pilgrim of the Absolute" like Bloy, and a familiar macabre humorist like Alphonse Allais.

It has been said of men like Degas and Lautrec that they lived in the decade before it became necessary for the artist to be a part of the absurdity he described. The statement applies to most impressionists and symbolists. Mallarmé may have envisioned a "shipwrecked" universe, but his outward life moved on an even keel. The Banquet Years brought on stage a set of artists whose waggishness was not intended to serve as an interlude of comic relief. Their lives matched their art in a fashion that does not even now seem natural. Their "act," an intensification of the exuberant play-acting of *la belle époque*, generated the energy necessary to change the direction of things. There had been something of this deliberate creation of a way of life in the "frenetic" romanticism of Pétrus Borel, in Théophile Gauthier's and Baudelaire's pose of the dandy, and in Rimbaud's short-lived *dérèglement*. Now figures as heterogeneous as Max Jacob and Picasso and Modigliani worked in concert as if the world around them were the gala start of a voyage of discovery. They made fools of themselves and broached the limits of art. It is doubtful that they could have done so by clinging to their sanity. Their enthusiasm survived the catastrophe of World War I, but only in that severely modified form that we know as the twenties.

The climax of it all—for a climax was still to come after so long a period of stimulation—shook the world far beyond the limits of Paris. The year was 1913. Vorticism, the English version of cubism and simultanism, broke out in London; D. H. Lawrence published *Sons and Lovers*, and, after eight years of fruitless attempts to place it, Joyce sent the manuscript of *Dubliners* to the man who would publish it the following year. The Armory Show scandal aroused New York. Italian futurism tried to annex painting by issuing a new manifesto. In Paris, everything was happening at once. Picasso and Braque had carried cubism, then five years old, into its second stage of growth, which influenced even the reluctant Matisse; Apollinaire, looking on, contributed the forthright declarations of *Les peintres cubistes*. He was also sitting for a portrait by Chirico and working with Delaunay toward simultanism-orphism. Jacques Copeau founded the Vieux Colombier theater and launched Dullin and Jouvet on their careers in productions of Molière and Claudel. Diaghilev invaded the world of music. Having staged Debussy's *L'après-midi d'un faune* and Ravel's *Daphnis et Chloé* in 1912, he went on to give Paris the uproarious *première* of Stravinsky's *Sacre du printemps* with Nijinsky's inept choreography. Only lately brought out of retirement, Satie was composing again. *Annus mirabilis* of French literature, 1913 brought down a cloudburst of books: Proust's *Du côté de chez Swann*, Alain-Fournier's *Le grand Meaulnes*, Apollinaire's *Alcools*, Roger Martin du Gard's *Jean Barois*, Valery Larbaud's *A. O. Barnabooth*, Péguy's *L'argent*, Barrès' *La colline inspirée*, Colette's *L'entrave* and *L'envers du music-hall*. The Prix Goncourt went to an obscure novel by Marc Elder. Valéry began writing poetry again after a fifteen-year silence, and Gide finished his novel of *l'acte gratuit*, *Les caves du Vatican*. It is almost as if the war *had* to come in order to put an end to an extravaganza that could not have sustained itself at this level.

In its early demonstrations the avant-garde remained a true community, loyal to itself and to its time. To a greater extent than at any time since the Renaissance, painters, writers, and musicians lived and worked together and tried their hands at each other's arts in an atmosphere of perpetual collaboration. It was their task to contain and transform the teeming excitement, the corruption, and idealism of this stage-struck era. In their enthusiasm, the Banquet Years often sinned through excess—through lack of discrimination and mere bluster. Because of their desire to outrage the public by making innovations in life as well as art, the creative figures often went astray and lost touch with human values. But their vices lie so close to their virtues that they cannot be separated without careful scrutiny. Their feast was not the last celebration of a dying aristocracy but a lusty banquet of the arts.

[2]

FOUR MEN: FOUR TRAITS

Despite its vociferousness and agitation, the avant-garde remains one of the most elusive forces of the Banquet Years. One can easily separate and scrutinize the aristocracy, the politics, the technical progress, and the individual artistic schools. But the avant-garde, arising out of the relationship between the restless society of *la belle époque* and the arts it produced, was neither a place nor a class nor an activity nor a body of work. It was a way of life, both dedicated and frivolous. The question is where to look, where to concentrate one's attention in order to distinguish its form and details.* Neither a comprehensive survey nor concentration on one figure will secure the proper perspective. There is, however, an old reliable method of history, half systematic research and half intuitive game, which might be called "representative men"—the art of finding little families of personages whose mere association suggests an

* Two authors have devoted important works to these tendencies in literature. Edmund Wilson (*Axel's Castle*) interprets symbolism in a highly generalized sense as an extreme state of sensibility, which achieves either a flight from experience (Axel) or a fierce plunge into it (Rimbaud). Marcel Raymond (*De Baudelaire au surréalisme*) traces a dual continuity, comparable to Wilson's, stemming from Baudelaire and leading either to the "new order" of Mallarmé and Valéry, or to the adventuresome revolt of Rimbaud, Apollinaire, and surrealism. See also Hugo Friedrich, *Die Struktur der modernen Lyrik von Baudelaire bis zur Gegenwart*, Hamburg, 1956.

interpretation of the age. Properly used this method allows the age to speak in great part for itself. Among the great artistic figures of the Banquet Years, the game almost plays itself.

There is, for instance, the family group of Renoir, Ravel and Proust; their rich, beautifully orchestrated masterpieces portray *la belle époque* at its ripest and never lose control of its sensuous plenitude. But all three gaze fondly backward toward the waning century and tell us not so much what has changed since 1885 as what can be made to survive. Their very technical mastery makes them the old guard who will never die. Or there is the later group of Picasso, Stravinsky, and Gertrude Stein—three exiles who found lasting inspiration in the cosmopolitan provincialism of Paris and in one another's work. But their long careers vastly overrun the period of the *avant-guerre* and lead far afield from the origins of modernism. Debussy, Mallarmé, Cézanne, and Valéry—a number of other clusters come to mind. Yet no combination coheres for long. It is rare that three or four artists, in different disciplines and not belonging to an organized movement, reveal a profound and enduring affinity.

Only by cutting below the most prominent figures is one likely to find men both representative of the era and significant in their own right. Their artistic identities are most discernible against their background rather than removed from it into a new context of individual greatness. Henri Rousseau, Erik Satie, Alfred Jarry, Guillaume Apollinaire: is this grouping less arbitrary than any other? They make, in fact, a singular team. Rousseau, a true artisan, painted with a combination of insight and awkwardness that has earned for him double standing as both modern and primitive artist. Satie's music partakes of the same simplicity, yet he lived in a series of scandals on the forefront of the artistic scene in Paris. Jarry's play, *Ubu Roi*, made him notorious at twenty-three, and within ten years he put himself in the grave with overwork, poverty, and drink. Before he died during the closing hours of World War I, Apollinaire had written some of the finest lyric poetry of the century and had assumed leadership of the Paris avant-garde. All four had colorful, significant careers, careers that might separately be ranked in the second magnitude of the epoch. Why, then, do they convey, in combination, the interplay of forces that steadily pushed the arts toward what Apollinaire called the New Spirit?

The reasons are simple. Their entwined careers in Paris exactly span the period 1885-1918 and suggest a unity in artistic conviction and practice that is less clearly expressed in any single figure or in a general survey of the era. Chronologically and in spirit they set its limits. In addition, their originality and persistence worked upon more stable artists and obliged them to take into account the most audacious and sometimes foolish aspirations of the age.

Beyond the fortuitous, yet important, associations of age, temperament, and acquaintance, one further circumstance unites Rousseau, Satie, Jarry, and Apollinaire. They represent, collectively and individually, four traits that profoundly characterize the era. The traits and the men form a progression from the deceptive simple vision of Rousseau to the equally deceptive sophistication of Apollinaire. In that progression lies the vital principle of the Banquet Years.

The first of these traits grew out of the cult of childhood established by the romantics. Wordsworth and Jean-Jacques Rousseau, Blake and Nerval reasserted the virtue and happiness of childhood as something inevitably stifled by education and society. Later generations began to perceive where the true challenge lay: in a revaluation of the very idea of maturity. Who is the complete man? There has been a series of answers, from the Greek devotee of *arete* to the Christian ascetic to the Renaissance courtier to the seventeenth-century *honnête homme*. In all of them, adult qualities of self-control preponderate over those of the child. But after romanticism, and starting long before Freud, a mood developed which reexamined with a child's candor our most basic values: beauty, morality, reason, learning, religion, law. With Rimbaud a new personage emerges: the "child-man," the grownup who has refrained from putting off childish things. Artists became increasingly willing to accept the child's wonder and spontaneity and destructiveness as not inferior to adulthood.

Only an age that had begun to revise its concept of maturity could conceive of accepting the Douanier Rousseau as an artist. For, in the simplest and purest sense, Rousseau was a child. He expressed a childlike vision of the world, and his serious whimsey appeals to the child in us. Here lies the meaning of Rousseau's "primitivism," for the child-man lives according to a personal primitivism which cleaves to an early stage in his own development. The history of the modern movement begins with a reaffirmed innocence of all attitudes and techniques that have made the arts beautiful and instructive and adult. Rousseau, unconcernedly starting his career at the age of forty, painted himself back into the years he had lost; in that lies his greatness and his modernism. The atavistic-prophetic monstrosity of *Ubu Roi*, a play that Jarry wrote at fifteen, and Satie's limpid piano pieces "for tiny hands," composed when he was over fifty, show a similar response to an earlier self. But Rousseau's entire career was devoted to creating the universe of a grown-up child.

There is always a great temptation to laugh at what is childlike. Rousseau's labored "realism" occasionally leaves us chuckling, as much in appreciation as in ridicule. And it is just here that the childlike tendencies in the arts meet the second trait characteristic of the period: the pervading note of humor. (The French borrowed the word from the English in the eighteenth century.) After the fervor of the early romantics, the mid-nineteenth century brought an upsurge of painting and writing that provoked laughter or grimace. Masters of caricature like Henri Monnier, Daumier, and Forain and sardonic realists like Toulouse-Lautrec and Flaubert bridge the gap between romanticism and 1900. After them came the Chat Noir, the Lapin Agile, and the Banquet Years. Humor, a genre that can command both the directness of comedy and the subtler moods of irony, became a method and a style.

Theories of comedy and laughter are notoriously unsatisfactory. Aristotle's remarks about "imitation of men worse than the average" concern only low-grade comedy. Three millenniums later, Bergson did far better in his distinctions between irony and humor. Humor describes the world exhaustively and scientifically *just as it is*, as if that were the way things should be. Irony haughtily describes the world *as it should be*, as if that were just the way things are. Bergson calls them the two aspects of satire. According to this clear discrimination, Jarry, Satie, and Apollinaire did not assume the lofty tone of irony, but took the literal, earthy approach of humor. Humor in these terms consists in the development of techniques of realism which the nineteenth century evolved. The added element is exaggeration, a disproportion in detail that can, if skillfully executed, suggest both sympathy and mockery. The future of realism in the arts of the twentieth century may lie in the ease with which it can sustain the carefully timed commentary of humor.

Whereas Rousseau remained oblivious to the laughter he often provoked, Satie, who possessed an equally childlike temperament, was well aware of the effects of his work. He is a humorist as well as a "primitive," and nothing could be more calculated than the waggish directions which he sprinkles through his compositions. ("With profound respect." "Take off your glasses.") Much of his music builds up a fragile fabric of inanity, and his writings become more and more extreme in their humor. "Why attack God? He is as unhappy as we are. Since his son's death he has no appetite for anything and barely nibbles at his food." At this point we no longer know how to react, for we have been carried beyond both the childlike and the simple humor.

In Satie we begin to see clearly that the ultimate modern transformation of the comic may render it no longer laughable, for the comic has delivered itself into the hands of the *absurd*.* The method of absurdity in the arts is simple, arithmetical. The absence of a priori values in the world, of any given truths, is posed not as a negative but as an affirmative proposition. The sign merely changes from minus to plus. Absence of any value becomes in itself a value. Contradiction, relativity of knowledge, man's confusion before his own image—these are sufficient axioms and describe the essence of man's predicament. This refurbished mathematics of human values goes back to the Stoics, to Tertullian, to Kierkegaard, to Hegel. Yet for all its philosophic implications, the absurd, during *la belle époque*, still provokes laughter, a quality it loses in the later skirmishes of Kafka, for instance, André Breton, or Sartre. When the absurd loses touch with the humor that

---

* Logic long ago discovered in absurdity a method of proof (*reductio ad absurdum*), and for several decades now German and French existentialists have reinvoked absurdity as the essential human condition.

reared it, it has ceased to belong to the comic vision of the world. The escapades and outrages of Ubu, Rousseau's portraits and tiger hunts, Apollinaire's pornographic heroes, and Satie's deadpan pseudo lectures partake still of comic innocence. This is not so after 1918, when innocence seems to yield to something far more calculated in meaning and effect. Dada and surrealism and existentialism are seldom funny; they have lost the festivity of the Banquet Years. This history of the modern arts may one day be written from the standpoint of the transformations of the comic spirit into varieties of the absurd, a methodical changing of signs. The four men considered here delighted in the freshly reversed state of things; later, it became a serious matter.

One of the most searching examinations of how humor and the absurd can be raised to the level of a discipline was written by Apollinaire about Jarry.

> There is no term to apply to this particular elation [*allégresse*] in which lyricism becomes satirical in which satire, directed toward reality, so overreaches its object that it destroys it and rises to a level that poetry can scarcely attain. Meanwhile triviality turns out to be in perfect taste and even, by an inconceivable state of things, becomes necessary. The Renaissance alone allowed such orgies of intelligence in which sentiment plays no part, and by a miracle Jarry was the last of those sublime debauchees. (*Il y a*.)

In Jarry we confront a reversal of values in which the baseness and incongruity of life must be understood as a source not of disgust but of joy. The intelligence can feed on triviality and by persistence create the sublime. By clinging to this attitude, Jarry pushed systematic absurdity into the realm of hallucination, of violated consciousness. And this is the third trait of the arts of the period: the eruption of dream into waking experience. The tendency is already a commonplace for our century.

So far as we know, the human species has always dreamed and has always attached oracular and supernatural meaning to dreams. By the end of the nineteenth century, dream, overtaking occultism, stood for a whole visionary and mystical tradition in the arts. It was, in litera-

ture, the German romantics first, then Gérard de Nerval
and Rimbaud, who abandoned themselves most totally to
the "second life" of dream. Their revaluation of oneiric
experience was a necessary prelude to the Banquet Years.

All his life Jarry was haunted by the insistent reality of
dreaming consciousness. His earliest poetry uses conventional imagery of night and darkness to suggest dream
surroundings. The novel *Les jours et les nuits* goes much
further. He depicts the possibility of "true hallucination,"
as he calls it, the sustained waking dream in which there
is no distinguishing night from day. And Jarry's incredible
life takes place in the atmosphere of a self-inflicted nightmare. Dreaming and waking become a matter of illumination, like night and day. The employment of dream techniques in the arts implied an effort to reach beyond the
bounds of waking consciousness toward faculties that
could grapple with unrestricted intuitions of time and
space. These new realms of consciousness and expression
were pursued with something approaching religious conviction by Bergson and Proust, Redon and Gauguin. Without relying on the existence of a "higher" or spiritual world
apart from our own inner being, dream can endow
ordinary experience with an aura of ritual and the supernatural. In his underhanded fashion, Jarry was a devout
man.

The uncensored maturity of the child-man as seen in
Rousseau, humor pushed steadily toward the absurd as
achieved by Satie, and dream magnified into hallucination
as practiced by Jarry—these characteristics of modern art
are subsumed in a fourth, which is, in essence, a resource
common to the other three: a cast of ambiguity or equivocal interpretation which can shape the surface and structure of a work. Again it has become a commonplace. More
deliberately and astutely than the others, Apollinaire exploited the technique as a means of enlarging the scope of
his work. Ambiguity here means neither meaninglessness
nor obscurity—though both dangers are present. It means
simply the expression of two or more meanings in a single
symbol or sound. The awareness of ambiguity is far from
new. The Middle Ages came to read the Scripture on
several levels of interpretation, and Dante wrote the *Divine Comedy* in expectation of a similar method of ex-

egesis. But what has happened today is of a different nature.

True classical style in writing required that a word have one clear, logical meaning in each context.* The permissible exception was the pun, a deliberate witticism playing upon the chance similarity in sound of two or more different words. But the pun was considered familiar, even vulgar, and had no place in noble style. Except for comedy, it dropped out of use during the classical era until it came back from the dead transformed at the beginning of the nineteenth century. For the symbolists—Mallarmé, above all—language was endowed with a mystery of meaning that increased with the number of different directions in which each word could point. Jarry held a similarly advanced theory of poetic meaning, maintaining that all meanings that can be discovered in a text are equally legitimate. There is no single true meaning, banishing other faulty ones. The pun, then, with its Argus eyes, had been raised to the status of a legitimate literary method.

Beyond his simplified perspective and inimitable style of likeness through distortion, the ultimate ambiguity of Rousseau's work—and its profound appeal—is its manner of being at the same time ugly and beautiful. Modal harmonies and imperfect cadences became Satie's method of keeping himself always in the open. Apollinaire, coming after the other three and looking back on their search for a new style, used ambiguity as a means for embracing all the qualities they expressed. In his poetry, as in his roving Bohemian life, the childlike cannot be distinguished from superficial erudition, and esoteric allusions blend into figures contrived out of the most familiar objects of his surroundings. After abandoning punctuation and typographical conventions (of words following one another from left to right and top to bottom), Apollinaire experimented with a completely open system of word order, the supreme pun in which all meanings are possible.

All this embracing of ambiguity makes the arts difficult of access and occasionally irresponsible. It often renders the extraction of a single meaning infeasible. On the other

* For example, La Bruyère's dictum: "Among all the different expressions which can render one of our ideas, there is only one which is the right one, the true one."

hand, it permits the complexities and conflicts of mental operations to carry over into their products. This may seem an idle virtue, for clarity has long been one of the supreme artistic standards. Yet there are subjects about which one cannot be clear without fraud. Every emotion and conviction has its reverse side, and ambiguity can stand for a profound frankness, an acknowledgment of the essential ambivalence of truth and experience, of life itself. Striving to apply a rigorous and simultaneous attention to several meanings, ambiguity aims beyond vagueness at *inclusiveness*, for which the only other method is monumental size. In accomplishing a great economy of exposition, ambiguity parallels the process of "dream-work," as Freud called it, and of wit and humor. It is significant that he treats dream and wit as essentially one process. Economy and compression are Freud's basic terms to describe the operations of the unconscious in dream-work and wit-work. Ambiguity offers an ancient and refreshed technique for embedding these operations in the texture of a work of art. Apollinaire found a legitimate means of putting everything—absurdity, dream, and innocence—into his act. And he understood, as recent criticism has too often forgotten, that unstrained ambiguity is always tinctured with the comic. Its apparent confusion of meaning surprises us with a profound revelation of the inner mind.

Exactly here the four traits, and the four men who embody them, reveal a profound unity. They manifest an unrelenting desire to dredge up new material from within, from the subconscious, and in order to do so they attempt to forge a new and all-important mode of thought, the logic of the child, of dream, of humor, of ambiguity. Such a logic must be vitally different from traditional discourse, must be a method that will free the artist from the need to spin out his work into a single, explicit, discursive meaning. The arts have always plundered the subconscious, but around the turn of the century they began to resist the convention of arranging their findings in established patterns of consistency. Science had already challenged the principle of causation, on which the laws of logic had rested secure. Romanticism had introduced two new factors which prepared the ground for revolution: uninhibited subjectivity and interest in occult knowledge. The Banquet

Years began to search out a new canon of thought and a new structure of expression.*

The subconscious, with its demands for its own logic and the accompanying threat of the obscurity of artistic experience, is of little help in explaining the self-conscious and defiant public role assumed by many artists in the Banquet Years. Like voices for reform in government, the avant-garde had to make a spectacle of itself in order to be heard. Its behavior revived the attitudinizing of the dandies and decadents, and was reinforced by the theatrical and anarchic atmosphere of the period. Yet generalized historical interpretation does not illuminate the essential differences involved. We must reckon with the lofty

---

* Only one other equally far-reaching attempt to recast the operation of the human mind has been made within the central cultural tradition of the West. At the beginning of the Counter Reformation, *The Spiritual Exercises* (1548) of Ignatius Loyola gathered and restated in comprehensible form techniques of spiritual meditation which had been maturing since the Egyptians. Loyola's means of raising one's mind to God relies not at all on logic, but on a methodical alteration of attention between the degradation of man and the holiness of the Almighty. It is designed to release the mind into a state of spiritual suggestion, a free association of ideas and symbols leading to divine knowledge.

Loyola's treatise is in many respects an amazing document. The fifth exercise of the first week, for instance: "Let the preparatory prayer be the usual one. The first prelude is a composition of place, which is here to see with the eyes of the imagination the length, breadth and depth of hell." Jarry, following Lautréamont and Rimbaud, observed a similar technique of hallucination. In describing the methods of prayer, Loyola asserts the clearest transcendence of reasoning: "The second method of prayer consists in this, that the person . . . should say the word *Father,* and dwell on the consideration of this word so long as he finds meaning, comparisons, relish and consolation in thoughts pertaining to it; and let him act in the same way in regard to each word of the *Our Father* or of any other prayer. . . ." Satie frequently composed a piece around an obsession with a single interval or chord. Discursive logic is linear and moves from point to point. Art of the modern era, like religious meditation, is circular and revolves around a point whose location is limitless. Apollinaire wrote his first "calligraphic" poems literally in circles, the circles of expanding and contracting attention.

aspirations of certain creative figures, aspirations whose heretical character gives them the power both to attract and repel.

It comes to this: toward the middle of the nineteenth century a few artists began to "live up to" their art, to live on a level with it. Rimbaud spoke of flattening the barriers between art and life; Oscar Wilde maintained that he devoted his talent to writing and his true genius to living. Jarry took the final step and fused his life and his art through literary mimesis; he adopted in "real" life the fictional role of Ubu, his most horrendous creation. In writing a counterfeit journal-novel about the crossing of art and life, Gide used the artifice of introducing Jarry into the middle of a fictional action as if that were his true milieu. Satie's cult of youth and Apollinaire's alternate embracing and rejection of all humanity—all these different poses strive to manipulate the nature of individual identity, to enlarge it or abdicate it. If one pursues the tendency, one finally confronts the disturbing content of such statements as Max Jacob's *Art poétique:* "Personality is only a persistent error"; and Jarry's, at the very edge of the precipice: "The soul is a tic."

Conventionally, a work of art is considered to be the product of a different self from the one displayed in habitual action and ordinary living. A few courageous members of the avant-garde set out to extend the artistic, creative self until it displaced all guises of habit, social behavior, virtue, and vice. When our entire life stems from our one deepest self, the resulting personality is usually so startling and abnormal as to appear a mask or a pose. It is the ultimate paradox of human character. This was very much the case with Rousseau and Jarry, with Jacob and Satie; in each of their lives one feels a deep-seated force such as possesses a lunatic or a saint. Unity of personality is the most admired and the most victimized of all conditions, for it defies judgment.

In the attempt to fuse art and life as a means of forging a new personality, nothing could be *normal* any longer in the old sense. The norm to which art traditionally referred its products was average perception. From Leonardo to Courbet, painters painted a tree as everyone sees a tree— or thinks he does. Romanticism introduced the exceptional vision of the lonely genius. But today difference, the exception, has itself become a norm, the norm of originality in both art and life. The twentieth century, with its "experimental" arts pitted against growing social conformity, passionately believes that there can be something new under the sun. These are the very words of Apollinaire's seminal lecture on the New Spirit.*

One step, one proposition now carries the arts into the ultimate modern heresy: the belief that God no longer exists. It implies further that after God "died," man himself became the supreme person, the only divinity. It is a cliché of the history of ideas to trace from Nietzsche down to surrealism and existentialism the unseating of God in literature and the deification of man. The Catholic critic Michel Carrouges has done it exhaustively in *La mystique du surhomme* (1947). Jarry, who followed the snarling contests of Lautréamont and Baudelaire with a still lively divinity, could state bluntly in *La dragonne:* ". . . we have covered a few years in our evolution since the guinea pig. . . . God is dead." With the field thus cleared of supernatural encumbrances, the true approach to the divine came to consist in man's probing of his own innermost states. For this century everything, from dream analysis to the perception of relativity, became self-knowledge as the first stage in self-assumption. The ancient sin of *hubris,* man's too-great arrogance in the face of the cosmos, disappeared when divine powers no longer existed outside of man. Evil was confined to a failure in confronting oneself. The most challenging and systematic statement of this general position lies almost forgotten in a two-volume work by the British philosopher S. Alexander, who gave it the apt title *Space, Time, and Deity* (1920). He contends that

* A passage from Poe's *Marginalia* demands quotation. "Original characters, so called, can only be critically praised as such, either when presenting qualities known in real life, but never before depicted (a combination nearly impossible), or when presenting qualities (moral or physical, or both) which although unknown, or even known to be hypothetical, are so skilfully adapted to the circumstances which surround them, that our sense of fitness is not offended, and we find ourselves seeking a reason why those things might not have been, which we are still satisfied are not. The latter species of originality appertains to the loftier regions of the ideal." It was the French, already moving in this direction, who first perceived Poe's significance as a prophet for the arts.

"mind" is the highest level of existence that evolution (or "emergence") has produced so far: "Deity is the next higher empirical quality to the highest we know" (Vol. II, p. 345). God will come as an outgrowth or a construct of mind—man surpassing himself.

The four traits of the Banquet Years now take on further meaning. They do not merely describe four aspects of a deep preoccupation with the subconscious; they are symptoms of man's aspiration to divinity, of his belief that he can surpass himself. The childlike and absurd, dream and ambiguity are means of reaching into ourselves to extract what education and society may have buried. The blending of art and life represents an attempt to preserve spiritual meaning in a godless universe. In refusing a dualistic order of earthly and divine, the twentieth century has attempted to have its cake and eat it, too. This "spiritual revival," heresy in the eyes of both positivist materialism and revealed religion, undertook to slay the gods and insist that the realm of the spirit had not been lost. The seriousness of this latest Promethean endeavor can be measured by the intensity of its demonstrations and by the persistence of its ideas.*

This enlarged spirit of modernism, Apollinaire's New Spirit, emerged first in France and never seized any other country with equal urgency. One explanation of this urgency leads to a comment on the character of French civilization since the Revolution, on her rare hybrid of stability and constant upheaval. Like the anarchists, the artists of the avant-garde took liberties with the structure of life itself, defied convention and lethargy in order to assert a new order of things. This tendency to violent dissent is a prime attribute of the celebrated French critical

* Science has addressed itself to equally perilous schemes. There is the work of William James on "religious experience." More recently, science fiction indicates a tendency in the scientific mind to seek artistic expression for its more transcendent goals. Still far from a satisfactory art form, science fiction nevertheless comprises a compelling substitute for metaphysics and meditation. "The true 'hero' of a marvel tale," writes H. P. Lovecraft in his *Marginalia*, "is not any human being but simply a *set of phenomena*. Over and above everything else should tower the stark, outrageous monstrousness of one chosen departure from nature." The comment reaches beyond science fiction to catch a wide segment of modern art.

spirit. Now, active criticism normally bases its undertakings on the possibility of change, on the hope that it will produce efficacious reform. But here lies the incipient fallacy of the French critical spirit since the Revolution. The premise of all extreme protest and censure in France seems to be not change but permanence: nothing will change irretrievably or change faster. Therefore, one is free to go to any lengths to obtain a new order of things. Unconsciously or consciously everyone knows that the attempt is in part utopian and hypothetical, an activity cultivated for its own sake, *like an art.* Since Saint-Just the threat of insurrection carries an undertone of security, whispering that only a few individuals can venture so far afield. This is not to doubt the sincerity of the great political, moral, and artistic reformers; they have been totally dedicated. But they knew under what conditions they could operate. France tolerates extremes of heterodoxy and outrageous behavior because it knows that ultimately no one will be harmed: the life of the nation will scarcely be touched. The avant-garde formed first in France because there was an artistic tradition of defiance, and it has lasted longest there because the country as a whole has only reluctantly taken to heart the lessons of its own most venturesome talents. France is inoculated against itself. In the United States, any active avant-garde is so rapidly absorbed by the cultural market that it scarcely has time to form and find a name. Like the profound stability of the ocean beneath its waves and storms, there is a great reservoir of indifference and conservatism in the French which has sustained a dynamic culture. It becomes a paradox peculiar to France that the most significant aspect of a period can be discovered on its surface. The seething agitation in Paris during the Banquet Years was not mere local color but evidence of the most urgent aspirations. Whatever their separate significance, the careers of Rousseau, Satie, Jarry, and Apollinaire illustrate vividly in combination how the long banquet of 1885–1918 honored a special sort of rejuvenation and spiritual revival in the arts.

PART TWO

The Rejuvenation

PART TWO

The Reformation

Henri Rousseau, 1844-1910

[3]

OBJECT LESSON FOR MODERN ART

Modern painting, like Greek and Renaissance art, has its professional myths. Fortunately for us, Vasari was able to collect a wealth of stories from the Renaissance and tell them with gusto. He relates how Giotto, when asked by the Pope's emissary for proof of his skill, drew freehand a perfect circle. Uccello used to mutter in his sleep, "Oh, how delightful a thing is this perspective!" and Donatello whispered passionately to his statues while he worked over them, "Speak then! Why wilt thou not speak!" As vividly as any museum, real or imaginary, these stories set the Renaissance still living before us. We need such mythologies in order to understand the past.

The list of familiar tales on modern art runs from Van Gogh's severed ear to how Picasso could not paint a likeness of Gertrude Stein during eighty sittings—and then caught it months later from memory. But too few of these stories reveal, as Vasari's do for his time, the deepest aspirations and significance of art today. One of the most provoking of all modern legends is contained in the career of Henri Rousseau, called the Douanier. More fortunate than most, he attracted his Vasari in the person of Guillaume Apollinaire—less a biographer than an unexcelled forger of myth.

Rousseau had so strong a sense of reality that when he painted a fantastic subject, he sometimes took fright and, trembling all over, had to open the window.

When he did a portrait of someone, he was much calmer. Before anything else he carefully measured his model and inscribed on the canvas the measurements reduced in proper proportion. All the time, in order to keep his spirits up, the Douanier sang songs of his youth and of the time he had spent in the toll service. (*Il y a.*)

Rousseau had *no aesthetic sophistication*, Apollinaire implies; yet he painted unaccountably *modern* works. The cubists and surrealists were both disturbed and reassured to find that so ingenuous a sensibility could produce paintings as revolutionary as their own. Furthermore, Rousseau's life is outstanding in the martyrology of the Banquet Years. In both his life and his work, we can examine him as an object lesson in modern art.

It is natural that the edges of the myth should blur into extravagance. Rousseau has been called everything from the most patent fraud ever perpetrated on a doltish public to the artist who restored angelic themes to modern painting. Even his sobriquet is a misnomer, for he was never a *douanier* (customs inspector), but a *gabelou* (employee of the municipal toll service). Most of the lingering falsehood stems from Apollinaire. In many articles he stated that Rousseau went to Mexico with troops sent by Napoleon III to support Maximilian, and that it is the memory of the "forbidden" tropical fruits in Central America that obsessed him in his jungle paintings. Nearly every account of Rousseau's life repeats this information, but no evidence of such a trip has ever been found in public or family records. Rousseau's imagination was capable of its own voyages.

The most flamboyant of the Rousseau anecdotes attributes his entire career to a hoax perpetrated by Alfred Jarry. Crossing the Seine one morning on the Pont des Arts, Jarry is supposed to have found Rousseau at his post down on the quay. "My friend," Jarry told him earnestly, "I can see in your face that you're a painter. You must take up painting." Jarry immediately directed the composition of Rousseau's first canvas, *Adam et Eve*, and the escapade wound up in court with Rousseau, in tears, offering to do a portrait of the judge's "lady." A different version of this Pygmalion story has Gauguin, on a wager, teaching Rousseau to paint; still another implicates Félicien Rops.

The truth is far different. *No one discovered Rousseau.* At the beginning of his self-chosen career as a painter, he earned a curious and paradoxical recognition to which neither Jarry nor Apollinaire contributed. They had a hand in his later career. There exists only one fully objective account of his life—his obituary in the *Chronique des Arts* in 1910.

> The painter HENRI ROUSSEAU died last week in Paris, a retired employee of the toll service who for many years exhibited regularly at the Salon des Indépendants and the Salon d'Automne paintings whose naïve composition won him a certain notoriety.

To do justice to this notoriety we must begin at the beginning.

Henri Rousseau was born on May 21, 1844, in Laval, a town in the northwest of France where Jarry was born thirty years later. His father, Julien Rousseau, a tinsmith and hardware dealer, enjoyed bourgeois prosperity. According to Rousseau's granddaughter, the maternal line can be traced back through its military record to a colonel and Chevalier de Saint Louis under Napoleon. During the false calm of the Second Empire Rousseau lived with his parents in a fifteenth-century structure called the Beucheresse Gate. The ancient tower still stands in Laval and bears a plaque in memory of the tinsmith's son who became a painter.

When the time came for him to draw his number for military service, Rousseau, now living in Angers, was given deferment as a student. Then in December 1863 he enlisted for seven years in the infantry, an action whose explanation only recently came to light in the exhaustive biography by Henry Certigny. Working in an attorney's office, the young man was discovered in the petty theft of stamps and small sums totaling some 25 francs. By enlisting immediately and appearing at the trial in uniform, Rousseau apparently hoped to increase his chances for clemency. He received and served a month's sentence in the Pré Pigeon prison. Amazingly enough this early blot on his record was not unearthed when he was brought to trial forty years later on a similar charge. Once in the army, he was *not* (as Apollinaire reported) packed off as a regimental musician to Veracruz, nor did he become a sergeant in 1870 and "save the city of Dreux from the horrors of civil war." After two hitches in France between 1864 and 1871, Rousseau was discharged as a private.*

In 1869 Rousseau married a girl from Saint-Germain-en-Laye and took a job as clerk in a lawyer's office in Paris. Soon after, he entered the Paris Municipal Toll Service, and now began his fifteen years as *gabelou*. The city of Paris imposed duties on many articles, and inspectors were required to control smuggling. The long tranquil hours took him to the quays along the Seine, to the city gates, and to the still-rural suburbs. He enjoyed the secure position of a minor functionary with already considerable seniority, because military service was counted toward retirement. During this period we first hear of Rousseau's ingenuous personality. According to Apollinaire and Wilhelm Uhde, a dealer-critic in Paris and later a good friend of the painter, Rousseau believed in ghosts and spirits. He encountered them during his long watches in remote places and told the other *gabelous* how, when the ghosts mocked him with foul smells, he shot at them. His fellow workers rigged up a false ghost on strings between wine barrels; Rousseau confounded them by doffing his hat and asking if it would have a drink. These stories, even if apocryphal, indicate that his victimization as a naïf began before his artistic pretensions took shape.

The young couple produced a numerous family: nine children in rapid succession. All of them died in infancy except the fifth, Julia, and a younger brother, who lived only to the age of eighteen. The mother herself died at thirty-six. According to the granddaughter, "The Paris air and my grandmother's very delicate health were the causes of this blight." Rousseau was left with two young children,

* A description of Rousseau has recently been disinterred from military records: "Height 1 meter 63 centimeters, black eyes, oval face, normal nose, round cheeks, left ear scarred [*oreille gauche coupée*]." In self-portraits the left ear is usually hidden; much has been made of this disfigurement, recalling Van Gogh's.

his job, and an interest which may at first have resembled a hobby.

During these years, he had become a faithful "Sunday painter." Later in life he stated that he had always wanted to paint, but was long prevented from doing so by circumstances. His "Sunday" could fall on any day of the week, and beginning sometime in the seventies he devoted these days to painting in the suburbs and in his studio. The earliest of his dated works reads 1879.[1] The principal fact about these years as *gabelou* is that he gained enough confidence in his art and dedication to it to give up a secure job for the life of a painter with a tiny pension. The death of his wife, Clémence, was probably the final stroke that released him from the drudgery of making a living and started him in pursuit of new rewards. Soon after his retirement from the toll service in 1885, his two surviving children were taken in by their aunt and uncle in Angers; he was leading the promiscuous life of a bachelor and neglecting them for painting.

According to his own statements, he was given advice by the prominent painter Gérôme; he refers to another less-known painter, Félix Clément, as his "teacher," and a few years later cut out Clément's obituary to paste in his notebook. It has remained impossible to determine just how much formal training, if any, he received from these artists. He obtained a copying permit for the Louvre in 1884. In his own eyes, Rousseau had had sound academic instruction; his work shows that he assimilated it in a very limited fashion. (He had also studied music and had toyed with the idea of becoming a musician.)

In 1885 his first publicly exhibited works were hung at the official Salon des Champs-Elysées. The remarkable event is generally unknown or overlooked, yet it was of crucial importance for his future career. Rousseau's two paintings were slashed with knives by spectators, removed from the show, and put with the *refusés*. The year Rousseau sacrificed everything to start a new life as an artist, he met with public abuse of his paintings. We know of the event through the newspaper clippings he pasted without comment into his scrap book, and his imperturbability corroborates what we can already detect in his painting:

[1] Superior numbers refer to a partial list of Rousseau's works on page 361.

somewhere in his forty years he had learned the quality of perseverance. Seeing his hopes of academic recognition so violently flouted at the very outset, Rousseau associated himself henceforward with the newest tendencies in painting and was not again refused.

One important coincidence favored Rousseau's career and probably saved him from oblivion. His retirement was almost simultaneous with the foundation of the juryless Société des Artistes Indépendants. Rousseau clearly would have liked to continue in the official Salon, but, instead, his fate was closely linked to the seething early years of the Indépendants. For its first important exhibition in 1886, he trundled four paintings through the streets of Paris in a hand cart and hung *Un soir de carnaval*[7] among works by Seurat, Redon, and Signac. His other three canvases have disappeared. In 1887 Rousseau hung three paintings and five drawings, five the next year, three the following year, and then an average of five a year except for banner years like 1891, 1895, 1896, and 1902, when he exhibited nine or ten. His career was launched.

At the time of his "retirement" at forty-one, Rousseau was a handsome, robust, black-bearded man with wide-set intelligent eyes and a slight stoop. In his devotion to his work he scarcely paid attention to the social ferment around him—increasingly violent strikes, anarchism, and, finally, the Dreyfus case. After living in various parts of Paris he settled in the Plaisance section, a poor laboring quarter behind Montparnasse. He lived precariously, and we know little of his activities until 1899, when he shaved off his beard, married a second time, and took a new hold on life. His new wife, Rosalie-Joséphine Noury, opened a stationery shop and tried, with little success, to sell his paintings to the residents of the quarter. Never of good health, Joséphine died after a short time, and Rousseau was alone again. He looked for a job as copyist, and finally became an inspector for *Le Petit Parisien*, a daily paper. Like his old position as *gabelou*, the work took him long distances across Paris to check on distribution of the paper to *kiosques*. His material distress in these years is indicated by the fact that he exhibited no paintings in 1899 and 1900. He even fell back on his musical talents, and we hear of him playing the violin in the orchestra at the public concerts in the Tuileries Gardens. When his plight became severest he simply went out into the street and played for alms. Remy de Gourmont spoke of several times meeting him playing the fiddle for his next meal. Yet it was known in his quarter that Rousseau was always willing to share what little food he had with any derelict who came hungry to his studio.

Despite his poverty, Rousseau contributed his talents to a new privately sponsored adult-education project called the Philotechnic Association. The city helped by lending classrooms in the evenings. Rousseau taught music and drawing, and after a few years he was decorated with the *Palmes académiques* because of a confusion between his name and another Rousseau on the list. Though he soon learned of the error, Rousseau wore the little violet rosette in his lapel for the rest of his life and used the official wreath after his name. He gained enough prestige in his quarter to be commissioned to do a few portraits, principally of children and of formally composed family groups. But he remained miserably poor and asked very little for paintings over which he had labored several weeks.

The year 1889 brought the Universal Exposition to Paris and with it the Eiffel Tower. Little wonder Rousseau painted the miraculous structure into so many canvases. In honor of the gala year he wrote a play, *Une visite à l'exposition de 1889,* a comedy in three acts and ten scenes describing a country family seeing the Paris sights. He made uninhibited use of abrupt scenic change and telescoped action. There is a fine comic scene in the hotel, during which a country servant girl, quartered in the same room with her master and mistress in order to save money, objects to having to see Monsieur Lebozec in his underdrawers. Rousseau confidently sent his work to the Comédie-Française, where it was turned down as "too expensive to produce." Ten years later he wrote another play entitled *La vengeance d'une orpheline russe,* far inferior to his first effort.

Both plays (ultimately published in Switzerland in 1947) bear the name of a coauthor, Madame Barowski, whose identity is uncertain. Several people who knew Rousseau, principally Apollinaire and the Italian Soffici, have mentioned an affair with a Polish schoolteacher. Rousseau's granddaughter has discounted the story as a distorted version of the Czech origins of his first wife.

These confused tales corroborate what is already clear: Rousseau, very handsome in his mature years, did not suffer for lack of female companionship. Many years later, when the police had occasion to investigate Rousseau's past conduct, they reported:

> His habits and probity were of the most dubious sort, but he is not known to have frequented the masculine sex. He merely received fairly often visits from various women in whose company he spent wild nights, but the names and addresses of the women are unknown.

Uhde writes of his "various affairs" and his almost indiscriminate love of women, every one of whom he wished to make his wife. They did not, however, distract him from painting.

After the first debacle in the official Salon, Rousseau's works in the Salon des Indépendants were noticed favorably and watched from year to year. There is no evidence, except spurious legend, that the public maligned his work at this juncture. In his notebooks from 1886 on, Rousseau collected with great care the articles that discussed his work. During the first years, his painting received sympathetic attention as slightly out of the ordinary and worthy of encouragement. The adjectives "curious," "primitive," and "sincere" appear frequently, and other artists are accused of imitating his style.* In 1891 one critic stated bluntly that "the public has not yet reached the level of this genre." Yet at last the crowds were beginning to wonder or snicker, for that same year a dissident journalist cast the first stone: "Monsieur Rousseau paints with his feet with his eyes closed."

Not until 1894 did the punishment really begin. One article, printed in several papers, mentioned "the scoffing

---

* In spite of a faint suggestion of irony, the most perceptive notice appeared in the *Journal des Arts* (March 30, 1890): "But I am being slow in reaching M. Henri Rousseau whom I shall permit myself to call the 'cornerstone' [*clou*] of the Indépendants. M. Rousseau is an innovator in painting. It is he who invented the portrait-landscape, and I advise him to copyright his title, for there are unscrupulous characters who are capable of using it. But the misadventure would end there, and no one will appropriate M. Rousseau's manner. Before such vast compositions [*machines*] criticism is powerless."

public"; Rousseau is called a "preprimitive" and criticized
for painting hands without thumbs. From then on, the art
critics began to revel in such ready-made copy, and Rousseau became an "annual aberration," the victim they
waited for from year to year, advising their readers to go
and see his work if they wanted a good laugh. By 1902 he
was a "celebrity"; one of his jungle paintings was reproduced in a newspaper in the guise of a political cartoon.
The scandal reached the point where some members of the
Indépendants wanted to drop Rousseau. André Salmon
reported that his cause was defended by Toulouse-Lautrec.

This neglected background clearly demonstrates that no
one "discovered" Rousseau. He hung his work and it drew
notice. Gustave Coquiot, one of the organizers of the
Indépendants, maintained stoutly that, "Odilon Redon and
I were, around 1888, the first to glorify Rousseau." It is a
feeble claim, especially since it was advanced in 1920.
This much is true, however: just at the moment when the
public and the journalists turned against Rousseau, a few
writers and artists began to recognize his talents.

The first was Alfred Jarry. Several accounts say he found
the Douanier standing beside one of his paintings at the
Indépendants, but it is more likely that they encountered
one another as temporary neighbors on the Boulevard du
Port-Royal in 1893 and discovered they had a common
birthplace. At this time, Jarry was a precocious young poet
scarcely twenty, charming but eccentric and not yet called
up for military service. Rousseau was close to fifty, with a
long life of wars and loves and losses already behind him.
Hard as it is to imagine their friendship, they were close
enough so that three years later Jarry stayed with Rousseau
for several weeks when he was evicted from his own lodgings. Ten years passed before Rousseau knew anyone else
in the literary or artistic world so well. In 1894 Rousseau
painted Jarry's portrait with chameleon and parrot and
exhibited it at the Indépendants with an inscription in
verse that echoes Jarry's style. The portrait was mislabeled
Mme. A. J. because of Jarry's shoulder-length hair. That
year, in his art chronicle, *"Minutes d'art,"* Jarry devoted
precious space to the huge composition *La guerre*,[18] and
to his own portrait. ". . . some curious *Henri Rousseaus*:
the spirit of war on the bristling horizontality of its frightened horse riding across the translucent corpses of axolotls;

the portrait of a man with Chinese eyes and a little tuft of hair . . ." The two paintings have had contrasting histories. The Jarry portrait no longer exists. According to the several versions of the story, Jarry, having brought it to his room in the Rue Cassette, either burned it accidentally, or cut away the background and kept only the head, or cut out the head and kept only the background. André Salmon supplies the final refinement: "He liked to say that, afraid of piercing himself [*i.e.*, the portrait] in an awkward flourish of his umbrella, he cut himself out carefully and kept himself rolled up in the 'long central drawer of our white-wood Colbert desk.' " Whatever its fate in Jarry's hands, the portrait has been lost. *La guerre,* on the other hand, which had been lost, was found again in 1947. After its authenticity had been vehemently disputed by a few experts and the surrealist André Breton, the Louvre acquired it and hung it prominently.

The year after the Jarry portrait, a ripple of recognition began to form around Rousseau. Jarry and Gourmont commissioned him to do a lithograph for their magazine, *L'Ymagier.* Both Gauguin, who met him through Jarry, and Pissarro publicly admired his use of black. The *Mercure de France* devoted a laudatory notice to him (by an unremembered critic, L. Roy), which stated unequivocally: "Only bad faith could lead one to believe that the man capable of suggesting such ideas to us is a bad artist." But the years brought no true success.

Not far from where Rousseau lived at this period, the composer William Molnard had a studio in the Rue Vercingétorix. Gauguin, temporarily back from Tahiti, had his studio in the same street during the winter of 1894–1895. Molnard and Gauguin entertained every Saturday. The Douanier frequently appeared with or without invitation and moved unabashedly among such guests as Degas, Strindberg, and Mallarmé. Sometimes he brought his fiddle and gave a short concert. Several stories have come down about Rousseau and Degas, the eccentric old royalist who sketched laundresses and ballet girls with equal passion. At one of these Saturday gatherings, Rousseau overheard Degas making acid remarks about the difficulties of exhibiting in Paris. The Douanier, in a gesture that staggered the already famous artist, offered to use his "artistic connections" to "help" Degas. He was not joking.

Late in 1894 a volume appeared in Paris entitled *Portraits du prochain siècle*. It contained portraits and brief biographical sketches of such authors as Mallarmé, Léon Bloy, Verlaine, Henri de Régnier, and Jules Renard. Rousseau discovered the announcement of a similar volume on artists. He made an ink drawing of himself, with broad black beard, bushy eyebrows, and coat buttoned tight across his chest, and delivered his unsolicited entry in person to the publishers.*

HENRI ROUSSEAU
painter

Born in Laval in 1844. Compelled at first by his parents' lack of means to follow a career quite different from that to which his artistic tastes called him.

It was accordingly not until 1885 that he made his debut in Art after many disappointments, alone and without any master but nature and some advice from Gérôme and Clément. His first two creations shown were sent to the Salon des Champs-Elysées and were entitled: *Une danse italienne* and *Un coucher de soleil*. The following year he produced *Un soir de carnaval*,[7] *Un coup de tonnerre*. And then *Dans l'attente, Un pauvre diable, Après le festin, Le départ, Dîner sur l'herbe, Suicide, A mon père, Moi-même portrait-paysage de l'auteur*,[10] *Tigre poursuivant des explorateurs, Centenaire de l'indépendance*,[16] *La liberté, Le dernier du 51ème, La guerre*,[18] a genre portrait of the writer A[lfred]. J[arry]., about 200 pen and pencil drawings and a number of landscapes of Paris and environs. It is only after great hardships that he succeeded in making himself known to the numerous artists who now accompany him. He has perfected himself more and more in the original manner which he has adopted and he is in the process of becoming one of our best realist painters. As a characteristic feature he wears a bushy beard and has been a mem-

* Again the evidence points to Jarry as instigator. He had contributed an entry on Gerhart Hauptmann to the first volume and probably told Rousseau of the second—which never appeared.

ber of the Indépendants for many years, believing
that complete freedom of production should be
granted any initiator whose thoughts reach up toward the beautiful and the good. He will never forget the members of the press who have been able
to understand and support him in his moments of
discouragement, and who will have helped in the
end to make him into what he must become.

Paris, July 10, 1895

This note, the most important document we have from
Rousseau's hand, contains clues to many of his attitudes
toward painting and supplies a skeleton biography. The
first forty years of his life—army career, work in the toll
service, first wife, nine children—Rousseau dismisses in
two curt lines. The break has been complete; he did not,
like most men of fifty, look backward, but forward to what
he felt he was destined to become. We can believe his
granddaughter when she says that after his wife's death
"my grandfather threw himself desperately into painting."
It is almost as if he had set about to paint out his past.
Uhde and Apollinaire and the others invented a legendary
past to replace it. The general tone of the rest of the note,
suggesting he has succeeded as a painter and gained wide
recognition, is usually taken as evidence of Rousseau's
naïveté. In 1895, however, he had two notebooks full of
clippings on his work, and his public victimization had
barely begun. True, the artists that "accompanied" him
were probably amateur painter friends, but Redon and
Gauguin, Toulouse-Lautrec and Degas had already noticed
his work.

The note is written carefully, in clear anticipation of its
being published. (The anticipation was realized, if not
exactly in the manner Rousseau expected. It has been reproduced in close to ten monographs.) According to its
simple story, he happened to have started life amiss in
1844; *as an artist* he was born in 1885. Interpretation of
his life would be easier if one could consider him twenty
years old at his debut, instead of forty; his spirit was that
young. Yet long gestation produced an artist of full maturity in his earliest works. The only painting surviving
from his first group at the Indépendants in 1886, *Un soir
de carnaval*,[7] shows his characteristic style already perfected.

Rousseau's estimate of himself turns out to have been amazingly accurate. He speaks blithely of his "original manner" with the strange suggestion that he has struggled to perfect this style of painting. Can these words have been put into his mouth by Jarry? Admiring the most academic masters, did he nevertheless sense the nature of his unique style? He throws in a detail about his beard and in the same sentence makes a plea for artistic freedom. A subtle irony whispers through his remarks about the kindness of the press, which at that very moment was beginning to turn on him. Yet the future-perfect tense of the conclusion expresses the glorious destiny he foresees for himself. We are confounded if we smile, for the Douanier wrote true.

After the turn of the century, Rousseau's figure comes into clearer outline. We begin to know how he lived, what his personality was, and (it is the key to true biography) how he spent his time. He had been a Sunday painter who lived only for his Sundays. By retiring, he secured his dream: Sunday all week long. For certain solitary artisans and artists, every day holds a rare stillness and reverence which for the rest of the world comes only once a week. One of the haunting qualities in Rousseau's painting is that he conveys this Sabbath feeling of joyful rest. He never lived another weekday; he never painted a workaday picture. Living in a single-room studio in the Rue Perrel over a plasterer's shop, he painted himself forever into his Sunday world. He said that he did not mind living in one room because when he woke up in the morning he could "smile a little at his paintings." Then he would get up and go to the corner café for his breakfast. "If the weather was nice, he had a glass of white wine; if it was raining a cup of coffee; and on a gray day, some cognac." It makes little difference if Philippe Soupault's description is imaginary. There was Madame Bourges, the fruit seller on the corner, and Louis Leblond, the locksmith, and Monsieur Quéval, his landlord: they were all his friends. As it is still today, this was a quarter of small artisans and metal foundries; no wealth or Bohemianism made a show in the cobbled streets between the low ancient buildings. Rousseau worked calmly on; he believed in his work and loved it. That was enough for him. Seated on a stool in front of his canvas, he had a habit, as he grew older, of dozing off for a while and then continuing unperturbed from where he had stopped. Often his wife appeared to him in a dream and guided his brush. As Christian Zervos put it, "He lived like a monk of the Middle Ages among his enchantments."

Poverty afflicted him as grievously as it did the laborers who were his neighbors. He always needed money for paint and canvas, and he tramped across Paris, his violin under his arm, to give music lessons. After the experience of teaching in the Philotechnic Association and with the prestige of his *Palmes académiques*, he hit upon a solution that suited his status as artist. He opened a school. In his doorway, hidden away in one of the lowliest streets of Paris, was displayed the sign, "Courses in Diction, Music, Painting, Solfeggio." For eight francs a month, he instructed both the very young and the very old. Insubordination and doltishness in his pupils did not ruffle him. His art students have never achieved fame, yet a nice paradox lurks in the fact that he should have earned at least a meager living teaching a subject supposed ignorance of which made him famous.

Rousseau never lost the habit of walking great distances to remote suburbs. There he did rapid impressionistic sketches—Vanves, Passy, Bellevue, Ivry, Vincennes, Meudon, Charenton, Saint-Cloud, Alfortville, Nogent. To judge by his paintings, the world consisted of Paris and its still-pastoral outskirts, the strong angular people who inhabited these places, and, far far away, tropical jungles full of danger and beauty. The Jardin des Plantes, in those days one of the best botanical gardens in the world, frequently lured him into its cavernous humid greenhouses with palm trees reaching up toward the glass. And there was a zoo in the same park full of monkeys and snakes and antelopes. When the universal expositions were held in 1889 and 1900, he felt as if the world had come to his doorstep. "Let's go look," says each of the characters in his play, and they see Paris from one end to the other.

In appearance Rousseau was short and solidly built in his good years, with a full beard and a head of black hair. His complexion was light and his eyes a sparkling blue. He dressed in dark high-buttoned suits and carried a cane as he grew older. By preference, he wore a large artist's beret as the mark of his calling. With the years his hair turned white and he shaved off his beard, leaving only a fluffy white mustache. His steps became shorter and more puttering, yet his youthful spirit never died.

Descriptions of Rousseau's personality seldom fail to mention the extent to which he was "simple" and "innocent." Yet so great a simplicity, so great a purity of heart, often excites in others a desire to do hurt. We look for some flaw or vice, we scoff at what we cannot understand. That is just what happened. "Friends" and strangers who merely knew his reputation played a thousand tricks on him. The victimization which had started while he was in the toll service now became a standing joke. Gauguin told him once that he had been awarded a government commission for a painting. Rousseau went happily to the appropriate office to find out the details and was sent scornfully away. A stranger called on him and introduced himself as Puvis de Chavannes, the academic painter then at the peak of his fame. Rousseau, believing that such a tribute was natural and deserved, politely showed the impostor around his studio. Another time, a group of friends arrived with a man who resembled the Minister of Fine Arts; a ceremony was performed in which Rousseau was awarded a decoration while the concierge's daughter stood holding flowers. Obviously some of these stories are fictions, just as the idea of Rousseau's total innocence is partly a fiction. Perhaps he learned in time to hold up his end of the game. One of the cruelest jokes played on him was that of telling him that the President of the Republic had invited him to dinner; Rousseau went off in delight. After his rebuff, he came back with a story of his own. "I went up to the front door, but they told me I couldn't get in without a card of invitation. When I insisted, the president himself came out, patted me on the back and said, 'Sorry, Rousseau, but you see you're wearing an ordinary suit. Since everybody else is in formal dress, I can't very well receive you today. But come again some other time.' "

Though scarcely good biography, these tales drive home one fact which must remembered. Through all the pranks, Rousseau's childlike nature never soured. He never shrank back into himself in the face of a world that tossed him about like a mascot, praising and ridiculing him, feting and ignoring him. Perhaps his unshakable self-confidence partook of certain delusions about himself and the world, but he proved, after all, to be right. A letter he wrote to the mayor of his birthplace, Laval, reaffirms the assurance with which he regarded his work.

July 10, 1898

To Monsieur le Maire:

I have the honor of sending you these few lines as one of your countrymen who has become a self-taught artist and is desirous that his native city possess one of his works, proposing that you purchase from me a genre painting called *La bohémienne endormie*,[28] which measures 2.6 meters in width and 1.9 in height. A wandering Negress, playing her mandolin, with her jar beside her (a vase containing water), sleeps deeply, worn out by fatigue. A lion wanders by, detects her and doesn't devour her. There's an effect of moonlight, very poetic. The scene takes place in a completely arid desert. The Gypsy is dressed in oriental fashion.

I will let it go for 2,000 or 1,800 francs because I would be happy to let the city of Laval possess a remembrance of one of its children.

In the hope that my offer will be treated with favor, accept, Monsieur le Maire, the assurance of my distinguished consideration.

Henri Rousseau
Artiste-peintre

This is touching, almost pathetic. Yet even though he never made the sale, there is something very significant here. In the letter Rousseau asks a price far beyond anything he had received or would ever receive, for a painting. Was he trying to exploit local sentiment? Was he so confident of the picture's value?* Uhde tells us that, even with the ridiculously low rates he could command in Paris, Rousseau had the astuteness to sell his better work for higher prices. Occasionally such characteristics have been taken as proof that the Douanier was not so simple as he seemed. A professor of English in Paris, Charles Chassé, in his book on Jarry and Rousseau, belabors this evidence into the thesis that Rousseau really duped friends and ene-

---

* Today *La bohémienne endormie* is rightly considered one of Rousseau's greatest works and hangs in the permanent collection of the Museum of Modern Arts in New York City.

mies alike and made a name for himself through a highly knowledgeable fraud on public taste.

Rousseau was not so sly as that; there were simpler human flaws in his character. What usually showed itself as a kind of tranquil self-confidence sometimes took on the aspect of mulishness. When opposed, he could fall into frenzied moods like tantrums. Gustave Coquiot, who had frequent occasion to deal with him at the Indépendants, added this to his praises: "Rousseau could sometimes be as conceited and disagreeable as anyone . . . he was the kind of fellow who is insupportable some days, and then his beastliness beats anything. . . ." Fernande Olivier, who knew Rousseau through Picasso and observed him better than most, described the same characteristic. "His face turned purple the minute he was thwarted or bothered. He generally acquiesced to everything people told him, but one had the feeling that he held back and did not dare say what he thought." Stubbornness was his vice, his form of pride. Yet stubbornness was also the core of his genius, for without it he could never have started his singular career or persevered in it.

The tide began to turn in 1905. The Salon d'Automne, a new grouping of young and avant-garde artists formed two years before, accepted two of Rousseau's paintings. Works by Matisse, Derain, Braque, Rouault, Vlaminck, Friesz, Dufy, and other unabashed colorists were assembled in a large central room with Rousseau's *Le lion ayant faim*.[39] After a jeering article by the critic Louis Vauxcelles, the room was christened the *cage aux fauves* (wild-animal cage)—terminology probably inspired in part by Rousseau's subject. Thus for a season Rousseau was associated with the fauves and welcomed by them. The popular magazine *L'Illustration* (Nov. 4, 1905) published a two-page spread of reproductions of works in the salon, and Rousseau's painting appears prominently with a Cézanne, a Guérin, a Vuillard, a Matisse, a Rouault, and a Derain. The caption states that Rousseau, previously ridiculed at the Indépendants' shows, has been given a place of honor and respect in the Salon d'Automne. The next year, the new salon accepted one painting, in 1907 four, including two exotic landscapes and *La charmeuse de serpents*,[46] now in the Louvre.

Apollinaire probably made Rousseau's acquaintance in

1907 through Jarry, who died that year. It is very much as if just at the moment that Jarry disappeared from the scene, Apollinaire appeared, equipped with vast promotional capacities. He had become one of the well-known figures in the artistic and literary world of Paris, writing poetry and criticism and enjoying enormous prestige for a young man of twenty-seven who had not yet published a book. His first critical mention of Rousseau was scarcely flattering, yet he soon modified his tone. Rousseau kept a special notebook of clippings on Apollinaire, and through him rapidly made friends in new quarters. Unquestionably, Rousseau was "taken up," but he had been waiting for twenty years. He expected to be admired and sought after, just as he had expected a visit from Puvis de Chavannes. He met the artist Serge Férat, who became a loyal friend and began to buy a few of his paintings. He met Robert Delaunay, another painter who recognized and proclaimed Rousseau's talents and whose mother held a *salon* where Rousseau was welcomed. Ardengo Soffici, an Italian author and painter, paid his respects in person, bought some canvases, and in 1910 wrote the second full-length article on Rousseau. It appeared first in Rome and then in the *Mercure de France,* which had published the first article, L. Roy's, in 1895. Rousseau moved tranquilly in these new circles, his engaging manner unchanged, but old and stooped and white-haired now.

No one was distubed by his eccentricities. Ambroise Vollard (author, astute dealer, and publisher of, among other things, Jarry's *Almanach illustré du Père Ubu*) tells of a luncheon in his famous "cellar" where Rousseau sat silent throughout the meal barely listening to Vollard talk to an academician who had also been invited. At the end of the meal Rousseau produced a sketchbook and began to draw. "It's wonderful, Monsieur Vollard, the white walls and the figures in this light. If I could only catch the effect in a painting." Another time he tried to approach the Mexican ambassador in Paris in order to interest him in buying an exotic landscape.

Three dealers began buying his works: the German Wilhelm Uhde, Vollard, and Joseph Brummer, a Hungarian, who later opened a successful gallery in New York. "Rousseau carried his canvases to Vollard's place," wrote Vlaminck, "the way a baker delivers his bread." None of them paid Rousseau very much for his paintings. Rousseau kept accounts in a notebook meant for laundry lists: "Sold to Madame la Baronne Œttingen, my self-portrait for 300 fr. . . . Sold to Monsieur Delaunay, a lovely Mexican landscape, with monkeys, for 100 fr. . . ."* By 1910, when he had only a few months left to paint, he could write to Soffici, "I have orders on all sides, and I must make you wait."

Not to be outdone by the hospitality of his new friends, Rousseau began about 1907 to hold his own *soirées familiales et artistiques*. He loved to gather around him friends and students and local tradespeople to celebrate any occasion that could be invented. He sent out formally phrased invitations to these Saturday parties and prepared his studio with great care. His bed was folded in a corner, the floor was swept and covered with the cheap rug he had secured in exchange for three of his pictures, bottles of wine stood on a table, and the chairs were rigidly lined up facing the "stage" at one end of the room. Rousseau, the rosette in his buttonhole, greeted the guests with a bow at the door, like an usher, and seated them in strict order of arrival. The proceedings were held up until everyone appeared. The most regular guest was an ancient music student well over seventy, totally devoid of talent, of whose progress Rousseau would gravely remark, "He's coming along."

For the organized part of the party, Rousseau reproduced in multicolored inks from gelatin plates lists of the evening's events. Drawn up carefully like theater programs, with date and address, they told what marches the orchestra would play, "followed by Madame Fisher with her repertory," and "Monsieur Rousseau (violin solo) with his works and creations." The stage was offered to any guest who felt the urge to perform, and on the back of the program there was always publicity for the Academy and Rousseau's private lessons. Uhde's description reveals why

---

* In 1914 Rousseau's paintings sold for over 1,500 francs, and in the thirties the Museum of Prague bought *Moi-même*,[10] sold originally to Madame Œttingen for 300 francs, as shown above, for 140,000 francs. In its recent sale to the Museum of Modern Art in New York, *Le rêve*[53] bought over $100,000. There is faint indication that Rousseau had a loose contract for a time with one of these dealers.

the hospitable Douanier never caught up with his wine bills.

His soirees were supposed to be literary philo-sophical affairs, but there was always much drink-ing, laughter and horseplay. Whenever the atmos-phere became a trifle bacchantic one woman and her four daughters with flowers in their hair would make a ladylike exit. By midnight things were often bacchantic for fair—perhaps old Rousseau himself in the midst of the chaos, tootling a flute before the full-length portrait of his dead wife and dancing from foot to foot, tears streaming from his eyes.

Rousseau also invited friends to his pupils' Examination Days, occasions on which the young students invariably disrupted proceedings by making outrageous blunders, playing the wrong selections, and trying every schoolboy prank in the book. Rousseau, delighted to have people fill-ing his studio, was never perturbed. His soirees attained so wide a reputation that another trick was devised. Several strangers began showing up in the Rue Perrel one evening when Rousseau had not sent out any invitations. At first he was happy with the unexpected company, but more and more people came. After the tenth knock, he refused to open the door.

The list of people who attended these affairs is stag-gering. One friend brought another, beginning with Apol-linaire, Delaunay, Soffici, Férat, Baroness Œttingen. Soon half the young artists and writers in Paris were turning up: Picasso, Braque with his accordion, Max Jacob, Vla-minck, Georges Duhamel, Jules Romains, Brancusi, Marie Laurencin, Philippe Soupault, René Arcos, Charles Guérin, Félix Fénéon, Francis Carco, Maurice Cremnitz, An-dré Warnod, and many more. What was there to draw them to these evenings, especially in view of the fact that most of them were thirty years younger than Rousseau? Some of them undoubtedly saw a parody of their own lives and ambitions, and an almost Ubuesque version of the famous artist entertaining in style. But, more than this, there was Rousseau's personality, his desire to enjoy life to the full without the gaiety interfering with the seriousness of his work. This was the true spirit of the time, the spirit that associates Rousseau inseparably with the Banquet

Years. In spite of all his troubles, his still-unrealized ambitions, and his sixty-five years, his youth was perennial and unforced. Furthermore, people were beginning genuinely to admire his work and to want to know more about the man who produced it. Whatever the explanation, few *salons* or cafés in the marginal history of painting have matched the simple exuberance of Rousseau's *soirées familiales et artistiques.*

At this period, the young American painter Max Weber was in Paris. He became a close friend of Rousseau (who called all foreigners "Americans"), and when Weber left in December, 1908, Rousseau had a special soiree "in honor of the farewell to Monsieur Weber." Weber purchased as many Rousseau canvases as he could afford, and Rousseau gave him a number of drawings. These items made up the first one-man exhibition of Rousseau's work anywhere when they were put on display in 1910 in the Alfred Stieglitz Gallery in New York.* America and Germany vied for several years for leadership in appreciating Rousseau's work.

Max Weber's few published remarks on Rousseau make clear the immediate attraction people felt toward him. The two painters met at Madame Delaunay's *salon.* ". . . a round-shouldered genial old man, small of stature with a smiling face and bright eyes, carrying a cane, entered the room. He was warmly received, and one could see that he was pleased to find himself among so many friends and admirers." That day Weber walked back with Rousseau to his studio.

> On my way home from this first visit, which I shall never forget as long as I live, I felt I had been favored by the gods to meet one of the most inspiring and precious personalities of all Paris. . . . "Here," I said to myself, "is a man, an artist, a poet whose friendship and advice I must cultivate and

---

* Uhde reports an aborted show in 1908 or 1909. "A furniture dealer in the Faubourg Saint-Antoine asked me to hang a few pictures in a room in the Rue Notre-Dame-des-Champs where he was exhibiting his tables and chairs. My first thought was of Rousseau. He brought over a number of his works in a pushcart, and we hung them together. I sent out invitations but forgot to include the address of our little 'gallery,' so only a few visitors appeared."

cherish." . . . By a sacred sense of privacy he was shielded from the snobbery, pretense, and sophistication which was rife in the art circles of the time.

. . . There is nothing chameleon about him. (*Art News*, Feb. 15, 1942)

Rousseau's greatest moment—almost a transfiguration it seems to us now across the years, and it must have appeared so in the dizziness of that evening—came in 1908 at the *banquet Rousseau*. Its story, so often recounted, must here be told once more, for it epitomizes the combination of festivity and conviction that characterized the period. The gathering has been interpreted by some as a lampooning of Rousseau, as a magnificent farce organized for everyone's enjoyment at Rousseau's expense. Such a misconstruction of fact demands correction. It was a celebration of unpredictable new resources in the arts, a spontaneous display of high spirits to greet ideas being unearthed every day by Picasso and Apollinaire, by Max Jacob and Braque, by everyone present at the gathering, including Rousseau. Taking Rousseau as a unique pretext, the banquet celebrated a whole epoch.

Picasso organized the banquet and decided to have it in his own studio in the *bateau lavoir*. The immediate occasion is supposed to have been Picasso's discovery of a portrait by the Douanier in Père Soulier's secondhand shop opposite the Cirque Médrano.* The painting was the handsome full-length *Portrait de Mlle. M.* (1897),[28a] which Picasso bought for a song as old canvas and still owns. He later described the incident and its effect on him.

> Rousseau is not an accident [*cas*]. He represents the perfection of a certain order of thought. The first of the Douanier's works that I had the opportunity of acquiring took hold of me with the force of obsession. I was going along the Rue des Martyrs. A bric-a-brac dealer had piled up some canvases outside his shop. A portrait head protruded from the pile, the face of a woman wearing a stony look, with French penetration and decisiveness and clarity. The canvas was immense. I asked the price.

* Leo Stein has maintained that the banquet grew out of Rousseau's offer to play the violin for a few of Picasso's friends.

"Five francs [*cent sous*]," the man said. "You can paint on the back."

It is one of the most truthful of all French psychological portraits. (Fels, *Propos d'artistes*.)

The feting of Rousseau in the riotous Montmartre manner arose out of this serious artistic appraisal.

The details of the banquet, which are to be gleaned from a variety of written and remembered accounts, remain reasonably coherent until the festivities are well under way. After that, a curious optical effect sets in which has produced a wide spectrum of deviant versions of just what happened. Thirty guests were invited for eight o'clock, shortly after which time Apollinaire was to arrive escorting the guest of honor.* A huge barnlike room with thick beams and African masks on the wall, Picasso's studio was decorated with strings of Chinese lanterns. The newly acquired portrait was draped with banners, one of which read, "*Honneur à Rousseau.*" The place of honor consisted of a chair set on a crate at the head of a makeshift table of planks laid across trestles. The Restaurant Azon nearby loaned crockery and glassware, and part of the meal had been ordered from Félix Potin, a catering grocer. Among the guests invited for the meal were Maurice Raynal, André Salmon, Maurice Cremnitz, Gertrude and Leo Stein, Alice Toklas (who remembers wearing a new hat, but who was, according to conflicting reports, in evening dress), Max Jacob from the next studio, Jacques Vaillant, Georges Braque, Maurice de Vlaminck, René Dalize, and André Warnod. Most of the men brought lady companions; the rest of Montmartre, alerted to the event, was not due to show up until after dinner.

During the late afternoon things began in comparative quiet in Fauvet's corner bar a little way down the hill. Since the guests took a long while to assemble, however, during which time consumption of *apéritifs* never flagged, spirits rose rapidly. In the absence of Apollinaire, her watchful attendant, who was fetching Rousseau, Marie Laurencin ("Coco") departed from her normal demure

* Eyewitness accounts have been published by Fernande Olivier, Maurice Raynal, André Salmon, Gertrude Stein, and Leo Stein.

behavior and became delightfully tipsy. The males gave their full and intense attention to a new coin-operated and artistically decorated electric organ. It was after dark before they all straggled up the slope with snatches of song and laughter to the studio. Their arrival in the candlelit premises was like a descent of carousing gods. Two neighboring studios were requisitioned as ladies' and gents' coatrooms. A Gargantuan supply of wine and Fernande Olivier's heroic cooking prevented anyone from noticing a few irregularities about the arrival of food from Félix Potin. In the rented chairs they waited again with mounting enthusiasm and dwindling patience for Apollinaire to arrive with the guest of honor. Finally three knocks resounded through the room. The door opened to reveal Rousseau wearing his soft felt artist's cap, carrying his cane in one hand and his violin in the other, and Apollinaire behind urging him to enter. After struggling more than two decades for recognition and fellowship with other artists, Rousseau looked through a door in the *bateau lavoir* and saw Picasso's studio decked out as it would never be again and filled with artists and writers who had come to honor him. They had been reveling several hours without him, yet in an instant they all fell silent at the sight of this white-haired old man who was the reason for their merriment. Thirty years older than any of them, he turned out to be just their age. Maurice Raynal completes the scene.

> The appearance of the Douanier . . . made a tremor of emotion run through the gathering; it was, certainly, one of the most touching pictures of Rousseau. As he looked about, the gleaming Chinese lanterns charmed him, and his old face broke into a smile.

The guests were at first so saddened by their emotion that Rousseau had to set the tone of the evening by gaily taking his seat under the portrait and having a drink. After a few moments the festivities were again in full swing.

Cremnitz sang the first song in praise of the Douanier, rhyming *pinceau* (brush) with Rousseau. In reply the Douanier raised his fiddle, which he had not put aside, and played a song he had written. Before long he was playing one of his waltzes, *Clémence*, named for his first wife; people began to dance. Marie Laurencin lost her balance and fell on top of some pastries on the sofa. According to Fernande Olivier, Apollinaire sent her home to her mother after an argument; according to Gertrude Stein the two of them went downstairs for a short time, and when they returned Marie was a "little bruised but sober." Later in the evening Apollinaire took an opportunity to catch up on his correspondence on a corner of the table while the celebration raged around him. He also recited an elaborate toast in verse, referring to the Douanier's memory of the "Aztec landscape" and to the misfortunes that had overtaken his family. Everyone joined in the chorus of *"Vive! Vive* Rousseau!" Up on his unsteady platform, Rousseau was stoically enduring torture from one of the lanterns, which dripped hot wax on him all evening.

Now the next act began. People who had not been invited to dinner trooped through the studio, consuming what was left of the food and wine. Frédé, owner of the Lapin Agile, wandered in looking for a drink with Lolo, his donkey. Rousseau, who had been nodding for some time, fell asleep and awoke only at intervals. He was not accustomed to so much wine even at his own soirees. The highlight of the evening was a performance by Cremnitz and Salmon. The Stein version indicates that they "went off their heads with drink, began to fight, and had to be locked by force in the men's coatroom." The rival version has it that they faked an attack of delirium tremens for the benefit of the Americans present (*i.e.*, the Steins and Alice Toklas), who were apparently in evening clothes. The two young poets chewed soap to make foam and went through every violent antic they could think of. Fauvet, the barman from the corner, arrived to say that one of the lady guests had wandered—or rolled—down into the gutter outside his establishment. By this time no one turned a hair, and the party lasted till dawn, with the Steins taking Rousseau home well before the end. He wrote to thank Picasso for the banquet; after that he was seen a great deal in the studio in the *bateau lavoir*.

The Rousseau banquet remains one of the landmarks of the pre-World War I era, a sequence that has been told and retold until it is a cliché. The occasion lacked only the crowning presence of Jarry, who had died the year before; yet in a true sense his spirit of dedicated eccentricity presided—a lark in dead earnest. The years following 1907 saw the sudden burgeoning of cubism, a school of painting that toyed with the philosophical significance of its plastic investigations. The reversals of logic and challenges to reality which underlie its vociferations seem to take their cue from Jarry. "Dr. Faustroll, in the shape of Alfred Jarry, prowled in the shadows. Did he have a rôle in the birth of these new speculations?"* André Lhote, who knew the cubist period firsthand, adds to these observations that he "heard put forward theories strongly perfumed with 'Pataphysics."

The significance of the *banquet Rousseau* has by no means been allowed to lie dormant, especially since the rise of his reputation and his prices after 1918. Charles Chassé spoke of the banquet as a "miserable farce," an immense joke at Rousseau's expense. More than a decade later, the issue was so sensitive that André Salmon was impelled to take Gertrude Stein to task after the publication of her book *The Autobiography of Alice B. Toklas*. In it she described the event a little patronizingly but not without sympathy. Salmon's charges, and the charges of those who wrote with him in the 1935 supplement to *transition*, seem unjust. Yet the affirmative point he makes must not be forgotten. After explaining the act he and Cremnitz had put on, he defined the mood that prompted them to act that way.

> It is evident that Miss Stein understood little of the tendency we all had, Apollinaire, Max Jacob, myself and the others, frequently to play a rather burlesque role. We made continual fun of everything. . . .
> We invented an artificial world with countless jokes, rites, and expressions.

Miss Stein probably did understand this tendency, which was the very seed from which sprouted all the extravagances and innovations of the postwar years. What may have antagonized Salmon and his friends was that, living in its very midst, she held back from this tendency in her behavior while exploiting it to the full in her writing. The young men could not tolerate what they considered a false

---

* *Spéculations* is the name of a collection of Jarry's magazine pieces which reveal the particular twist of his mind.

position; they practiced in their lives the total attitude of their art. Salmon expresses their strength and their confidence.

Today, fifty years after the fact, the anecdotal riches of the Rousseau banquet have survived undiminished into legend. It was not a matter of public mockery that several of the most audacious young painters of modern times saw fit to honor a naïf artist of the people. The joke is, finally, not on the Douanier; the joke is on the journalists who found Rousseau such an easy victim, and on Chassé, who scrupulously collected documents that finally prove the opposite of his thesis. A title he chose in derision can today stand as a simple description of the event it was intended to ridicule: "The Ascension of Rousseau."

Rousseau's final years held a few such celebrations of the first magnitude, but they brought him only the most uncertain artistic recognition and no material security. In fact, the period began on a gloomy note despite the *bateau lavoir* party. A few months before the banquet, Rousseau had been jailed on a forgery and embezzlement charge and then released to await trial. He was ultimately found guilty on incontrovertible evidence. The fault lay in Rousseau's guilelessness and his willingness to do a favor for one of his former pupils. By 1909 the newspapers knew that Rousseau made good copy, and his trial drew smiling attention from all sides. Recently it has provided the materials for a full-dress scholarly volume by Maurice Garçon.

Gabriel Sauvaget, a former pupil, was an employee of the Meaux branch of the Bank of France. He had already embezzled 1,500 francs in 1903, but Rousseau knew nothing of his record. Sauvaget persuaded him to open an account at the Melun branch of the same bank under the name of Bailly and to have printed in Paris some false credit transfer forms. Sauvaget forged the signatures on a 2,100-franc transfer from Melun to Meaux. Rousseau, always helpful, consented to draw the money using forged identity papers which Sauvaget provided. Sauvaget let him have the odd one hundred francs for his pains. Rousseau seems to have been quite unaware that he was doing anything more than obliging an acquaintance. A few days later the crime was detected, and Sauvaget acknowledged full responsibility. Rousseau was held for the month of

December, 1907, in La Santé prison, when his imploring and eloquent letters to the *juge d'instruction* and to the *conseiller municipal* of his quarter secured his release until the trial in January, 1909. Of the several accounts of the trial, *Le Figaro*'s is the most concise.

> Severe toward Sauvaget, Monsieur Laurence, the attorney general, was more lenient toward Rousseau. Despite the moving pleas of the defense, the jury turned in a conviction. They were as hard on Rousseau as the jury of the National Society of Fine Arts could have been toward his painting. . . . Sauvaget was condemned to five years of imprisonment and Rousseau to two. The Court granted the painter suspended sentence. . . . Rousseau, gratified by the Court's pronouncement, spoke on his way out to the judge, Monsieur Bomboy. "Thank you, your honor, thank you, thank you! I shall paint the portrait of your lady." And there was not the least irony in his sincere thanks. The painter-Douanier still had faith in his art.

The defense had introduced two pieces of evidence to establish the innocence of Rousseau's character: his notebooks of press clippings with marginal comments, which, read aloud by the clerk, fulfilled the courtroom's expectations of entertainment; and one of his tropical paintings full of monkeys and bright oranges, which quickly set the jury grinning. Guilhermet, the defense lawyer, finished his summation with a swelling extra-legal coda. "This morning he [Rousseau] said to me: 'If I am condemned, it will not be an injustice for me, it will be a misfortune for art.' Well then, members of the jury, give Rousseau back to art; spare this exceptional creature. You do not have the right to condemn a primitive." After this plea, Rousseau leaned forward and said to Guilhermet in unhushed tones that everyone could hear, "Look, now that you've finished, can't I go along?" Afterward, he remained on friendly terms with Guilhermet, and with Ernest Raynaud, a lawyer-poet who had investigated the case. Both of them were frequent guests at his soirees.

As with the other misfortunes in his life, Rousseau makes little mention of the trial. His extant letters to friends, collected in a special number of Apollinaire's *Soirées de Paris* in 1914, say nothing of it, Apollinaire omits it entirely from his articles. Rousseau may never have understood that society considered his acts criminal, not charitable.*

Soon after the trial, at the age of sixty-four, Rousseau fell madly in love with an undistinguished widow of fifty-five named Léonie, a salesclerk in a Paris department store and daughter of a man he had known in the toll service. Protected by her still-sturdy parents as if she were a maid of seventeen, she scorned the near violence of his attentions. He hung about the store, bought presents with the small sums of money he was just beginning to earn, and went so far as to start action on a marriage license. Because Léonie and her parents doubted his professional standing, Rousseau secured written testimonials from Vollard, Uhde, Apollinaire, and Salmon. He drew up a will leaving everything to Léonie including the twenty-percent royalties on sales of his paintings already in the hands of dealers. She was only requested to give half of the money to his daughter. All Rousseau's friends testified to the genuiness of this late-flowering passion; he moped and sighed and could not be cheered up even by a ride in one of the new automobiles, which were becoming a common sight in Paris. The one surviving letter of many he wrote to Léonie is enough to convey the surge of his feelings. What some critics have called vulgar is, rather, a very moving directness.

August, 19, 1910

My beloved Léonie,
    All my thoughts are for you.
    Before going to bed, I must say a word about the observation you made at Vincennes while we were waiting on the bench for the trolley. You said that if I was no use to you, at least I served as your buffoon.

* A diverting item dug up at the time of the trial is the canard about one of Rousseau's paintings at the Indépendants having been seized two years before by the Bureau of Censorship. It had supposedly been a vast canvas representing the Czar and the Mikado, both nude, shaking hands (or having a jujitsu match as one writer interpreted it) while Kaiser Wilhelm wandered about in the background. A vaguely similar painting had once been censored, and the journalists had pinned the story on Rousseau. He angrily denies it in the notebook where he pasted the clippings.

Whose fault is it that I'm no use to you for cohabitation [*sic*]? Don't you think I suffer, don't you think that I would be happy to feel more often the sensations of love which come when two beings love each other as we do, natural sensations; and neither the woman nor the man must refuse the right, since nature has made us thus, has created us for one another. Christ said; "Every tree or every creature which beareth not fruit hath no use." Therefore we should procreate, but at our age we do not have to fear that. Yes, you do make me suffer, for fortunately I still have my feelings. Let us unite and you will see if I am incapable of serving you. For your part, be less cold with me, don't break my heart, when I want to caress you, by being sullen and responding reluctantly to my advances. And why act this way with me, since we understand each other on this point I believe, since we love each other. True, it is not only for that that people marry at our age, but we have not either of us had the final say yet. . . .

A thousand affectionate kisses.

Always your Henri.

H. Rousseau

Fortunately, these disappointments could not distract Rousseau from his work. All through the dismal months of 1909 he was working feverishly, on, among other things, the double portrait of Marie Laurencin and Apollinaire called *Le poète et sa muse.**[51, 52] He began a lengthy one-sided correspondence with Apollinaire, dealing mostly with hours for sittings and other arrangements. The letters reveal that the Douanier was troubled to the very last by grinding poverty. Letter after letter states that he has less than one franc left for dinner; can Apollinaire pay him something in advance for the portrait? He regrets having to set a price on the painting, "But I have had too many reverses to do otherwise. I have my pension, true enough; how would I do without it? But I have not been able to

---

* To satisfy himself, he finally had to do two versions. The first time, he painted a row of gillyflowers in the foreground instead of "poet's carnations," as he intended. The first version is now in Moscow with the Stchoukine collection; the second is in the Municipal Museum in Basel.

save anything unfortunately, and when I paint a picture which requires two or three months work, I must live somehow and furnish my time and my own materials." The critics continued to ridicule his work, taking exceptional advantage of his trial. It came to the point where he appealed to Apollinaire. "You will avenge the harm which is being done me, won't you?" His troubles never ceased. Léonie turned a deaf ear; he was an old man. Yet his talent did not decline. In 1908 he had tried the new subject of men in motion which led to *Les joueurs de football*,[45] during 1910 he finished one of his boldest and most magnificent works, *Le rêve*.[53] In public he kept up his good spirits, acting as if one day would follow the next without end and allow him to realize all his projected paintings.

Rousseau's last soiree was held on July 14, 1910. It was on this occasion that he asked Uhde the question "Do you love peace?" When Uhde said that he did, Rousseau led him to the window and showed him the German flag waving among the others in the flag-bedecked streets. A month later he cut himself inadvertently in the leg and ignored the wound until blood poisoning set in. His eyes sunken and yellowing, he lay on his tiny bed without the strength to chase the flies from his face. One of his most recent actions had been to write Léonie the letter just quoted, so full of strenuous passion, and now he spoke tenaciously of getting back on his feet very soon. Finally, he was taken to the Necker Hospital in a near coma, and the only one of his friends still in Paris, Uhde, came to his bedside. The young German dealer held the hand of the sixty-six-year-old Frenchman who had waited forty years before he could retire and devote himself to painting. The hospital provided the final irony by diagnosing this innocent primitive as an "alcoholic." He died in the ward, alone, on September 4, 1910, when most Parisians had still not returned from the provinces for another season. Rousseau, who knew no such seasons, never had to leave the city to find his landscapes, his inspiration, or a place to die.

Most of his friends received the announcement of his death in the country. The funeral service took place in the Church of Saint-Jean Baptiste de la Salle, and the body was buried in a pauper's grave in the Bagneux cemetery— where Jarry had already lain for three years. Only seven persons made up the cortege—members of the family who had come up from Angers and Paul Signac, president of the Société des Artistes Indépendants. Rousseau was one of the few early members who had remained active for twenty-five years.

The following year, Robert Delaunay and Quéval (Rousseau's landlord), contributed to buy a thirty-year plot in the cemetery and to erect a small tombstone with a bronze medallion of Rousseau. Apollinaire wrote in chalk an epitaph which immortalizes the legend of the Douanier. Brancusi, the Romanian sculptor who until 1957 had his studio of enchantments not far from the Rue Perrel in the Impasse Ronsin, chiseled the lines into the stone in 1913.

Gentle Rousseau you hear us
We salute you
Delaunay his wife Monsieur Quéval and I
Let our baggage through free at heaven's gate
We shall bring you brushes and paints and canvas
So that you can devote your sacred leisure in the light of truth
To painting the way you did my portrait
The face of the stars

In 1942 Rousseau's remains and the tombstone were moved to Laval, his native city, and placed in the Parc de la Perrin. About the same time, the Association of the Friends of the Douanier Rousseau was formed with the help of Monsieur Beck, former mayor of Laval. Relations were established with Rousseau's surviving family—his only daughter, her husband, and a granddaughter. During the transfer ceremonies Monsieur Beck made a singularly astute remark about the city's two famous sons, Jarry, the author, and Rousseau, the painter. "Now all we lack is a musician like Satie and a dramatist like Roussel. . . ."

Guilhermet, Rousseau's friend and lawyer and an authority on criminal psychology, made this statement about him many years later. "Rousseau always remained an enigma for me. Was he a man mystified by everything, or was there something of the mystifier in him?" The lawyer found reason to wonder if Rousseau had not made fun of his contemporaries, if he had not consciously assumed a mask of naïveté and innocence before the world. But the truth (and legend) of Rousseau's personality cannot be shaken by calling it a hoax. Any total simplicity can appear ambiguous, can assume the aspect of extreme cleverness. At times Rousseau's ingenuousness startlingly resembles Jarry's deliberate distortion of the world. Jarry, author of profoundly metaphysical and mystical works, rode about Paris on a bicycle with pistols in his belt and lived on fish he caught in the Seine. Rousseau, the great naïf artist of modern times, who talked one way and painted another, realized all the goals he set for himself in his "next century's portrait."

Part of his victory was over time. It is as if he grew younger during those long "months of Sundays." His world was the Paris he lived in and the luxuriant, dangerous, alluring jungle which grew behind the softness of his eyes. The miraculous nature of his accomplishment turned naturally into legend. It has been discovered that the owner of a side show in a traveling fair applied in 1930 to purchase the Douanier's mortal remains to show as a pious relic. But he was no angel and no saint. There was a simplicity about him which enabled him to express the most simple and heart-rending yearnings of popular art. His vision carried him unerringly to the very center of the strictly disciplined yet exuberant strivings of twentieth-century art.

{ 4 }

THE PAINTINGS

They [the primitive painters of 1300–1500] had in common a compact clear technique, and a still awkward command of form, movement, and light, although often more personal and moving than that of their successors.
——Charles Sterling, *Les peintres primitifs*

The initial question in dealing with Rousseau's work is immediately thrust upon us: Is he a modern "primitive"? The terms "primitive" and "naïf" were used very early to describe his work and found ready acceptance; recent estimates of his work have tended to treat him as a painter who cannot be separated from the evolution of modern art by such glib and arbitrary classifications. Now, more than fifty years after his death, we may well challenge the stock adjectives. Yet if its meaning is carefully restricted, the term "primitive" can be applied to Rousseau without misrepresention.

It is no slur to call Giotto and Cimabue "primitive"; it is a means of locating them within two centuries which prepare the formulation of the strict optical conventions of Renaissance art. Rousseau reveals a comparable primitivism, for he strove in his conscious thinking about art to achieve a naturalistic, academic style. He admired Bouguereau and Gérôme and Courtois. Twentieth-century Western art, however, the disgruntled offspring of a great naturalistic tradition culminating in impressionism, was seeking out the methods of primitives from Italy, Africa, and contemporary Paris. Like Picasso and Braque and Matisse and Delaunay, Rousseau worked not with the optical image (a rational transformation of what we see), but with his personal beholding of things. He stood beside them without having made the journey of styles which they had made in their development as artists. He is primitive in that, occupying the same ground as these men, he nevertheless looked yearningly toward a style they violently rejected. Robert Goldwater writes of this paradoxical situation in a sentence that is not so muddled as it seems.

> But it is important to realize that the style which he achieved was but a stopping place upon a road along which he would have travelled further if he could, and that the effect which he attains, seen from the point of view of the mechanics and psychology of its creation, is *because of* this intention, even if it is in spite of it from the point of view of the sophisticated observer. (*Primitivism in Modern Art.*)

In other words, Rousseau was primitive in performance but not in intention. The distinction is accurate yet dangerous.* What is usually described as his *intention* was really his *ambition*—the desire to show in official Salons. It was the only reward he could imagine after a life of obscurity and hardship. The ponderous *machine*-like titles for his paintings express this ambition without indicating the limited extent to which it influenced his actual painting. The patent disparity between his so-called aims and his accomplishments has bothered many critics, but never Rousseau. He learned what he needed from successful academic painters, their smooth brushwork and skillful color; then he went his own way. In considering his work we can distinguish artistic intentions from worldly ambitions only by looking at what he was willing to sign as the product of his hand.

Confused and irritated by these distinctions, many a critic reaches the point of speculating on how much of a simpleton Rousseau was—as if the greater his doltishness,

---

* Literary criticism has with good reason enunciated an "intentional fallacy" which condemns any final appeal to the artist's intentions in judging his work.

the better his painting, because the more miraculous. Following this line of reason, artistic fashion has tended to inflate Rousseau's reputation by calling him a talented ass. No comment should be necessary on this collapse of critical thinking. Rousseau's intelligence as a painter must be measured in his painting and not in his sentimentality or his ignorance of banking finance.

More than the complaint that Rousseau is a product of fashion, a related accusation goes to the heart of the *cas Rousseau*. He has been called—though not in these terms— the "sandwich man" of modern art, the down-and-out bum to whom a miserly wage of recognition was paid to perform the humiliating task of publicizing modern painting. In this interpretation his living or remembered figure becomes the pitiable dupe of cubism and surrealism and every other ism, the victim who earned only laughter for his efforts. The surface meaning of the accusation is, of course, wrong; Rousseau painted independently, carried advertising posters for no one, and was not ridiculed by other painters. But there is a latent content in this accusation, the implication that Rousseau represents a special case of modernism. It will require an entire chapter to reveal the truth beneath the falsehood.

There remains one last preliminary: the technical problems of dealing with Rousseau's work. First of all, forgeries. Soon after his death, a profusion of counterfeit Rousseaus appeared in Paris (and from as far away as Japan), perhaps because counterfeiters believed a "primitive" should be easy to imitate. The fact is that a forged Rousseau can usually be recognized very quickly. Yet as recently as 1943 a de luxe volume by Roch Grey appeared in Paris in which twenty-three out of 128 illustrations reproduce forgeries. Their obvious fraudulence pays backhanded tribute to the status of Rousseau as a painter, for he has turned out to be more difficult to forge than Picasso or Matisse.*

The other technical problem is dating. In general, all Rousseau's works should be dated earlier than the years

---

* I except the skillful *Portrait d'Homme*.[12] Very little known and never reproduced in early volumes, it has nevertheless been authenticated by Christian Zervos. Because of the modeling of the face and certain color combinations in background and detail, I classify it among the forgeries.

accepted today, even many works he dated himself. Rousseau could not possibly have painted so many works in his
four last years as are now assigned to the period 1907–
1910. The date of a painting's exhibition at the Salon des
Indépendants does not necessarily correspond to the date
of its completion. Attaining a certain notoriety at the close
of his life, Rousseau naturally drew upon a stock of earlier
works and ideas, and dated them—as did Bonnard and
Chagall—with the year of their public appearance. The
peculiar qualities of his style have produced a situation in
which many of his paintings must be dated loosely within
a period of ten years.

As an artist, Rousseau followed no steady evolution of
style, nor even a series of outwardly melodramatic reversals
like Picasso's. At his first Salon des Indépendants in 1886,
the year following his retirement at forty-one, Rousseau
hung *Un soir de carnaval*,[7] one of his masterpieces. Painted
large (almost four by three feet) and in limpid color, this
canvas shows him already in command of his mature style.
The brushwork and detail are immaculate, and he combines
in an astonishingly simple composition areas of pure color
with areas of an intricate fretwork in silhouette. Twelve
years later Rousseau painted an equally successful picture,
La bohémienne endormie.[28] It restricts treatment of detail
to the lion's mane and the robe of the gypsy and allows
areas of subtle color to glow in the same mysterious moonlight that filled *Un soir de carnaval*. A gradual simplifica-
tion of manner appears to have taken place. After a similar
interval came the final masterpiece, *Le rêve*,[53] almost his
largest picture.[*] Rousseau returned to the exploitation of
detail and unrolled a veritable tapestry of exotic foliage
with a few spaces of solid color; again, moonlight and
mystery. In none of these compositions did he explore
linear perspective; we feel space as accumulation. In *Le
rêve* he accumulated detail to create the physical presence
of the jungle; in *La bohémienne endormie* he accumulated
plain (and plane) color to imply depth; in *Un soir de carnaval*, the best of the three and the earliest, he employed
both methods. What can one tell of his "evolution" from

[*] It measures 80 x 118 inches—practically seven by ten feet.
Le lion ayant faim[39] (1905) is larger by a few inches.

these high points in his career? Only that he reached the fullness of his style very early and sustained it to the last.

Three portraits spaced at equal intervals across his years as a painter point to the same conclusion. Despite their miniature size and style, the pair of portraits of *Monsieur* and *Madame Stevenc*,[5,6] dated 1884 (not exhibited until 1906), have already developed the conventions and simplifications of the human face which Rousseau used in his *Autoportrait à la lampe*[8] (1890) and in the last of his portraits, *Joseph Brummer*[50] (1909). The treatment of nose, eyes, and hair—the fundamentals of Rousseau's portrait style—changed very little. The paintings imply no clear development in stages. One must accept the craftsman in Rousseau which made him approach every subject in a paradoxical manner: every painting was a totally fresh endeavor, a problem removed from previous experience and demanding no logical place in a regular progression of styles; and at the same time every painting called forth a number of conventional techniques and characteristic emblems which solved for him some of the more troublesome problems and marked it as his work. The pure craftsman thinks not so much of improvement and progress as of maintaining a high level of skill.

If there is a traceable progression in Rousseau's work, it has been described by the critics Daniel Catton Rich and Douglas Cooper. However, the chronological approach to his work is a misleading convenience. One stage does not grow logically out of the last, as we usually expect from an artist. Along with their similarities, the paintings have a discontinuous quality which suggests that the order of their execution is not a profoundly relevant factor. In addition, the uncertain dating of the bulk of Rousseau's canvases makes chronological classification difficult. The extreme irresponsibility is to date them in such a way as to demonstrate a preconceived scheme of progression.

A few points must be granted. Rousseau's earliest paintings—the few still extant—tend to be very small. The first sizable painting we know is *Un soir de carnaval*, a hint that he swiftly developed a kind of miniature style into very large compositions. Yet the smallness of the early work is explained in great part by his lack of time for painting until he retired. Then the dimensions enlarge suddenly.

Around the turn of the century, Rousseau appears to have experimented a little with atmospheric perspective in a tentative approach to impressionist technique. Many drawings, like the one belonging to Max Weber of the *Vue de Malakoff*,[56] and a few paintings like *Vue d'un coin du château de Bellevue*[31] (*c.* 1900), suggest the foliage of the background rather than depicting it in detail. The most remarkable shift in Rousseau's work, his turning to tropical and exotic scenes during the last five years of his life, grew as much out of the circumstances of his unorthodox career as out of any aesthetic conviction. The jungle scenes became popular when they were exhibited and sold better than his other works. His own need and a ready market impelled him to repeat tropical subjects to the verge of mechanical production.

Rousseau collected and read attentively everything that was written about him, and it is remotely possible that the early articles on his "primitive" manner helped produce the singular arrest in a highly personal style, and it is doing him no injustice to propose that he may have unconsciously understood that there were qualities in his work quite different from the traditional execution he admired. Whatever its origin, the singleness of Rousseau's style—the combination of stiffness and freshness in every painting—is the essence of his greatness; through thirty years and more than three hundred paintings he worked with the same fundamental insights.

Aside from still lifes, Rousseau painted only two subjects: landscape and the human figure. In itself the choice is neither original nor startling. Rousseau's work owes its distinct qualities not so much to his treatment of these separate subjects as to the manner in which he combined them. Through a widely shifting balance of components, his painting portrays *man occupying landscape*. Rousseau's genius, the secret of his art, can be best perceived in the naturalness and mystery of this relationship.

Thus, his production can be classified less satisfactorily by chronological periods than according to the way it yields to particular stresses and according to the completeness of the integration he makes between two basic ingredients. There are three obvious categories: straight landscapes, straight portraits, and a combination of the two for which, significantly, Rousseau had his own term, "portrait-land-scapes." Out of them grows a fourth category of paintings in which the balance is so subtly yet powerfully struck that they transcend both landscape and portrait to achieve a superior reality—his most haunting and inscrutable works. These categories serve to divide Rousseau's work for purposes of analysis and to suggest the meaning he found in the visible world.

The pure portraits, lacking any hint of landscape, are very few and early. The twin portraits of *Monsieur* and *Madame Stevenc*[5,6] are followed six years later by another pair, *Autoportrait à la lampe*[8] and *Portrait de la femme de l'artiste à la lampe*[9] (1890). The first pair (probably copied from photographs) immediately suggest miniatures by their size and by the oval space which Rousseau lay out to contain the figures. Using areas of even color in the background and clothes, he concentrates our attention on the faces, which are masklike in their rigidity. But they are still human—*intensifications* of the human face in the manner that Jarry insisted upon in advocating masks for stage use. The rigidity is caused by the absence of modeling and shadow and by the use of a kind of facial convention to portray features. It is the formula he used all his life: a prominent nose with flaring nostrils and a bridge which divides in two unbroken lines to form thick eyebrows; large eyes painted in heavy outline; and a straight expressionless mouth. The eyes stand out strongly because of the black contour which he invariably applied; they seem to stare out through a mask. The eyes of Madame Stevenc, by their shape and placement, resemble the cryptic pair of eyes that appear on one side of ancient Egyptian sarcophagi.

The two later portraits, of Rousseau and his wife, reaching the dimensions of a sheet of typewriter paper, present a considerable contrast. Without giving up his basic simplifications, Rousseau appears to have been concerned with both the idea of a good likeness and the inclusion of realistic detail. The faces are a complex structure of planes, not a single flat shape. He worked carefully this time with a rhythmic pattern of lines in the background and introduced the decorative-symbolic presence of the brass lamp. The wrinkles that he painted into the faces serve both as severe realism and as lines of stress and tension in the composition. Rousseau's later depictions of human features varied his original formula without elaborating it.*

The only other straight portrait is the little ink sketch that Rousseau drew of himself in 1895.[55] Fortunately, we can compare it with the excellent photograph of him as a young man from which it was copied. Rousseau observed the general pose and silhouette of the photograph and paid almost loving attention to the flowing of hair and beard. Then he boldly blackened the contours of nose and eyebrows and turned the shoulders, the coat, and even the face into direct frontality. What the figure loses in handsomeness it gains back in strength of line. The little drawing shows a characteristic blend of crudeness and skill.

In 1890, the year of the two portraits with lamp, Rousseau exhibited *Moi-même, portrait-paysage*.[10] From that year on with the exception of the sketch, all his portraits took the form of the human figure in a carefully arranged setting—usually full length. *Autoportrait à la lampe* already indicates that Rousseau felt the need of a rhythmical and decorative background to fill out the composition; his still lifes contain similar backgrounds. This early self-portrait also includes a domestic object, the brass lamp, the first of a whole repertory of accouterments which accompany the subjects of his portraiture. We never find Rousseau isolating human features as a form of pure beauty or expression. They appear in association with appropriate landscape or fragments of ordinary life. There was nothing casual about the name he gave this type of painting, which he considered his discovery. In 1907, writing the *juge d'instruction* before his trial, he stated flatly: "I am the inventor of the portrait-landscape." He gave it as a credential, an accomplishment for which he would be remembered.

In the *Moi-même* portrait of 1890, decorative and symbolic details surround and encroach on the standing figure of Rousseau. Their cumulative significance matches that of the human form. His palette, brush, and artist's beret

---

* His most brilliant variation comes not in a portrait, but in the face of *La bohémienne endormie*.[28] By emphasizing opposite pairs of features (eyes and nostrils) and carrying little shadow on the black skin, he portrays a face which seems to look into itself, to be divided into two halves turned inward upon the gypsy's dream. Many of Picasso's late cubist and surrealist heads exploit this same effect of introversion, of introspection.

establish his profession. Paris is intensely present in the bridge across the Seine and beyond it in a marvelously painted cluster of roofs and erect chimney pots, like organ pipes. The gala mood of 1889 smiles in the bright flags decorating a barge tied up at the quay,* in the Eiffel Tower rising half hidden in the background, and in a balloon and gondola rising in the sky. Rousseau's figure stands boldly and masterfully in the middle, except that he had some difficulty about length of leg and making the feet rest solidly on the ground. As a result—and also because Rousseau's head is just on the level of the free balloon—the figure seems itself to rise into the bright sky. He clearly intended to paint himself securely into a familiar scene which would identify him; in effect, he floats, gentle and unreal, in a world of vividly real details.

A few years later, Rousseau painted another portrait-landscape, *La première femme de l'artiste*.[19] Like *Moi-même*, it is a large composition (80 x 45 inches), and the bright background of foliage and flowers crowds the margins around the tall full-skirted woman.† One hand "rests" on her hip; the other holds a dainty parasol; a kitten plays with a ball of wool at her feet. The portrait effortlessly runs the gamut from playfulness in the kitten, through exoticism in the background, to calm elegance in the formalized yet handsome face. It was to be another fifteen years before Rousseau matched the magnificence of these two portraits. Without laboring over physical likeness, he expressed character in a pose, or *repose*, of the whole body, in a selection of significant objects attached to the figure, and in a meticulously painted background. He portrayed not an appearance but an environment.

In 1891 Rousseau exhibited a small portrait of *Pierre Loti*[11], which should probably be dated somewhat earlier. The painting assembles a number of parts related as much by composition as by an anecdotal meaning: an obsessive, masklike face with more than usual attention to shadow

---

* In the lower left-hand corner of his important painting *La ville de Paris* (1912), Robert Delaunay reproduces this typical fragment of Rousseau, whom he knew and admired.

† The flora of this portrait, in its stylization and thickness, is clearly "tropical." Rousseau had painted his earliest tropical landscapes[15] only a few years earlier.

and modeling; a red fez and dark-curled mustache; a staring tiger cat sitting in the foreground on a little table; a large hand with cigarette and ring—almost a separate creature—placed over the heart; a red and white collar arrangement like a cutout in the deep black of the coat; a large tree on one side balanced against a compact row of four chimneys on the other; and a single cauliflower ear (although the head is shown almost full face) protruding from the right side of the face like an artificial hearing device or a deformity. Yet for all the separateness of the parts, the painting does not fall apart. A slack area immediately appears if any detail is covered, and a strong, ironic personality is very much present in the portrait.

Rousseau continued the portrait-landscape approach in a series of children's portraits which span the years 1893 to 1905. As if a child's world were one of simplified reality, he reduces the *décor* in most of them to a flat area of grass and flowers on which the child neither sits nor stands, but hovers, as in *Portrait d'enfant*.[37] (One unfinished portrait shows a chair being brushed in around the child like a scaffolding.) The faces, heavily fleshed and sometimes almost bearded, resemble adult faces on stunted bodies.

L'enfant aux rochers,[24] with its bleak unearthly foreground of jagged rock, recalls the photographer's painted prop with comic scene and hole for the head. Despite their deformity, the paintings have a wistful beauty. Each child holds a flower and stares rigidly out of the frame, bold but lost. In the most ambitious child's portrait, *Pour fêter le bébé; l'enfant au polichinelle*[36] (1903), a sturdy blond child clothed in white occupies most of the large canvas and holds at arm's length a marionette figure of Punch. The marionette, costumed in brilliant motley, brings a strange reversal into the painting, for its dark features (aside from an enormous handlebar mustache) appear more human than those of the child. In fact, the angular Punch strung on his wires resembles Rousseau's conventional depiction of himself. We have crossed into the world of fairy stories and magical dances in which toys came to life and the child moves among them as an equal.

Three late paintings observe the balance of portrait-landscape: *Une noce à la campagne*[38] (1905), *Le poète et sa muse*[51,52] (1909), and the *Portrait de Joseph Brummer*[50] (1909). They employ what is almost a compositional for-

mula: the figure or figures are placed in the middle of the
canvas and surrounded by a pattern of sinuous branches
and foliage against a light sky. The dark or black clothing
is set off by one patch of color, and a small object is introduced at the bottom to keep the foreground alive. *Une noce
à la campagne* demonstrates the surprising range of facial
appearance the Douanier could express within the limita-
tions of his nose-eyebrow-eye scheme; he painted eight
figures as radically different as characters out of Dickens.
He also discovered a means, repeated in the Brummer portrait, of lightening the entire composition. He decreased the
amount of foliage from left to right across the canvas, so
that one feels free space surrounding the bare tree trunks
on the right side. In the Brummer portrait he achieved the
same effect by lightening the shade of green in the leaves
from left to right.

Ever since Rembrandt, the intense portrayal of human
character has tended to eliminate the natural world as a
distraction. The face should tell all. Even the romantics
hesitated to paint a formally commissioned portrait out of
doors. Rousseau set his highly formal compositions against
pastoral or semipastoral backgrounds. His refusal to separate portraiture from landscape and genre painting characterizes the "primitive" sensibility which sees a person and
the objects that surround him as a single entity. Rousseau
treated his canvas as a surface upon which to combine and
relate the material parts of a person's life, rather than as a
means of dramatically isolating a face from all incidentals.

Despite the significance of these portrait-landscapes, by
far the greatest number of Rousseau's paintings are landscapes—so called by him and frequently entitled *View
of* . . . with a place name. Probably because they keep to
small dimensions, seldom exceeding twenty inches in length
or breadth, he was able to produce several every year. He
found all the scenery he needed in and around Paris and in
postcards or engravings of more distant places. Before
1890 he began making free sketches in oil from nature,
which he elaborated in his studio. His transposition of
scenery into painting, although it was in many ways more
radical than that of either the impressionists or Cézanne
(and closer to the latter), did not carry out either the
decomposition of surface quality inherent in the one or
the decomposition of scenic integrity inherent in the other.

While recomposing a landscape within the confines of a frame, Rousseau preserved its appearance as landscape and also a simplified local color. He never practiced the obliteration of a scene by overexploiting its aspect of pure design or pure color. His fields are fields, not colored planes; his trees are trees, not simplified lines.

Landscape painting, then, proclaims Rousseau's steadfast sense of beauty and reality in nature, a sense of the true *picturesque*. That abused word is a guide to the second quality of his landscapes. In the process of beginning a picture, Rousseau used scenery as the material for a carefully thought-out composition within the imposed limits of the frame. His earliest dated work, *Petit moulin avec attelage*[1, 2] (1879), exists in two versions (and probably more), which show Rousseau changing the proportions of his picture area, omitting trees, narrowing the foreground, adding a woman's figure, and varying his tints in order to consolidate a composition that was originally too open. Yet it is indisputably the same scene. A few years later in *La falaise*[4] (c. 1885) he began to reduce everything to flat areas of color and sloping diagonals punctuated with small shapes—sails and men. Yet it remains a recognizable place. Before 1900 he returned to clarity of detail and settled upon what subsequently becomes the basic unit of design in his landscapes: the tree. Like Corot, the Douanier discovered the double soul of the tree: the clearly marked sinuous line of trunk and branches, and the massed rhythmic color area of foliage. For the most part he built up a tracery of trunks and branches in the foreground; behind it he spread thick, luminous foliage, which is picked out in detail only as it approaches the foreground. Between these two planes, not separated by any contrived feeling of depth, are placed a few small objects—usually men and women in highly stylized costumes and postures.

Three or four landscapes fit this scheme almost perfectly, for instance *Paysage*[32a] and *Bois de Vincennes*[33] (1901). In both, the arabesques of bare tree trunks in the foreground move across a nearly impressionist background of autumn color. The long tranquil horizontal of wall in the former divides the painting vertically and not in depth; in the latter the silhouette of one prominent evergreen adds horizontal and vertical emphasis. The tiny human beings, who move in terrible isolation across the scene, inhabit another universe from that of the bold figures in the portrait-landscapes. These little creatures wander, lost and anonymous, in the powerful presence of Nature. In the last tropical paintings, most of them of much greater size than the earlier landscapes, natural growth encroaches overwhelmingly on any human presence. The only surviving creatures are semilegendary dream figures, animals, and aboriginals. For Rousseau, landscape is not houses or mountains or virgin forest; it is man walking in wonder among the trees.

At intervals during his steady production of works that record the mutual attunement of landscape and the human figure, Rousseau painted canvasses that surpass both landscape and portraiture. All are large compositions in which a distinct feeling of awe and catastrophe has intensified his style without basically modifying it. Their thematic content is uniform: in either a totally barren or an unnaturally verdant countryside, a living creature confronts a mysterious presence. Rousseau did not himself separate these paintings from the rest of his production, yet in them he contrives to express an almost undefinable experience. They testify less to a special effort on his part to outdo himself than to a happy choice of subject which released latent powers. Chronologically they are distributed evenly through his entire career.

Un soir de carnaval[7] (1886)
Promenade dans la forêt[14] (1890)
La guerre[18] (1894)
La bohémienne endormie[28] (1897)
Mauvaise surprise[34] (1901)
Le lion ayant faim[39] (1905)
La charmeuse de serpents[46] (1907)
Nègre attaqué par un léopard[49] (1908)
Le rêve[53] (1910)

The list is a minimum. The enigmatic subjects range from the serene arm-in-arm pose of *Un soir de carnaval* to the savagely carnivorous attack of *Le lion ayant faim*. *La bohémienne endormie* owes its effectiveness to the fact that the encounter is unresolved: we cannot know whether the lion will devour the gypsy or respect her dark sleep. This picture, more than the others, provides the key to the mystery of these confrontations. In an arid desert scene of night sky and brown sand meeting in a clearly drawn horizon, a lion stares at a sleeping form clothed in brilliant colors. A still-life arrangement of mandolin and jar in the lower corner seems to hold the whole composition motionless until one suddenly notices the lion's tail, which is lashing wildly. Its savage movement creates a frightening challenge to the stillness. Robert Melville writes of this work:

> We can abstract from *The Sleeping Gypsy* a recipe
> for the enigma in painting: it is the situating of
> utterly still, imperturbably self-contained figures in
> a purely formal relationship which contrives never-
> theless to simulate the appearance of an encounter.

The stillness and formality of these paintings reside not so much in the lack of any portrayal of motion, but in the absence of normal motivation of the events taking place. What is the lone woman with her parasol doing out in the sinister-looking woods in *Promenade?* And what has startled her? Why does a sofa appear in the middle of the jungle in *Le rêve?* Each work has its riddle whose answer lies partly in the glib phrase that Rousseau "dreamed it all up." His tranquil consciousness could transpose directly onto canvas a waking dream. The dream aroused his full ca- pacities as an artist when it contained a feeling of doom, of fateful happenings not explicitly defined. The power of these inscrutable scenes rests on the simplicity and ease with which Rousseau the conscious craftsman could be attentive to Rousseau the dreamer.

The works have a few more points in common. In most of them there is a detail that corresponds to the discon- certing movement of the lion's tail. In *Un soir de carnaval,* below all the intricate pattern of foliage and behind the two costumed figures, a masked face peers out from a tiny window in the hut: some baleful presence lurks in the calm moonlight. In *Nègre attaqué par un léopard,* the small all- black figure of the Negro against the thick undergrowth looks more like the shadow of a man than like solid flesh. The leopard has locked its jaws on emptiness. In the manner of Uccello's battle and hunt paintings, several scenes gain in mystery by creating great depth of perspec-

tive without any atmospheric softening of line. Values of
near and far are partly suppressed. A distant line of mountains on the horizon in *La guerre* is etched as cleanly as
the tree trunk in the foreground. Space is at the same time
projected and flattened.* In the tropical composition, every
carefully painted leaf tends to come to rest in the front
plane, as in tapestry work. Behind the matted foliage one
imagines the watchfulness of creatures whose forms cannot
be clearly distinguished. Whatever their subject and treatment, all these paintings partake of an atmosphere of ritual
and formality. The emotional charge they communicate
resembles that which emanates from Egyptian hieratic art;
yet like Oedipus before the Sphinx, we find our awe mixed
with irreverence and defiance. For a detached observer,
sacred ritual can easily change in appearance into stylized
preposterousness, and one must acknowledge a realm of
art which is both disturbing and diverting. "The riddle,"
writes J. Huizinga in a sentence that fixes one of the
neglected cultural contexts of art, "was originally a sacred
game, and as such cut clear across any possible distinction
between play and seriousness." Rousseau's most haunting
paintings are riddles in this profound sense: true grotesques
which provoke apprehensive laughter followed by long
wonderment. Having seen them once, one never forgets
them.

These riddle paintings do not, however, form a compact
classification. They are all *hors série*, exceptional in the
sense that they stand apart from the rest of Rousseau's
work, from each other, and from the whole history of
painting. In order to give reality to each separate vision
of mystery, Rousseau labored over every inch of the huge
canvases and filled them with a sense of transformed reality.
Within their borders landscape, wild beast, and human
being partake of a single life. That life can be regarded
as the all-absorbing presence of Nature, or, better, as the
singleness of Rousseau's internal eye.

A classification of Rousseau's painting based on the
changing balance between landscape and human figure
omits the important series of still lifes, that he began

---

* Chirico and Dali, not insensitive to Rousseau's work, developed this technique to the full in the surrealist style of "magic
realism."

around 1890. In 1892 he painted a curious decorative panel of a hand holding three roses, called *Bonne fête*.[17] Probably of the same period is *Bouquet de poète*,[13] a simple arrangement of flowers in a bowl set against areas of solid color. It is difficult to date the subsequent works that, almost without exception, show a vase of flowers on a table against a plain background. A small painting belonging to Louis Stern,[25] with a pinkish-brown background and impasto technique, may well be the earliest of a series of four or five painted of the same white vase filled with different flowers in a variety of color combinations. Rousseau took the dominant color of whatever flowers he happened to have, used it in two different tints in the background, and developed it through contrast into a vibrant harmony of tones. One of the best of this series,[35] belonging to the Tate Gallery, is a study in shades of red and pink interspersed with green, dark brown, yellow, and blue. Confined by flat treatment to the front plane of the composition, the still lifes nevertheless gain movement from the subtle lines Rousseau wove into the background color. His literal vision had its own freedom. If he painted a vase so tall as to make the composition top-heavy, he placidly added a sprig of ivy in the lower foreground to readjust the balance.

These still lifes, by their directness and simplicity and by their sensitive color, go beyond elementary values of composition and decoration. Generally the smallest of his works and the most thickly painted, they carry an intensity of feeling—feeling about pure color and natural form— that often becomes diffuse in his larger canvases. Their intensity resembles that of Redon's flower paintings, a subdued passion which contrasts with the monochrome analyses of early cubism. The palpably objective existence on canvas of Rousseau's still lifes produces a set of subjective harmonies which can be conveyed only by those colors, those arabesques of stem and petal. The term "magic realism," a misnomer for most of Rousseau's paintings, partly describes his flower still lifes. The very plainness of their reality is mysterious.

Several of Rousseau's most ambitious paintings have not yet been discussed: *Le centenaire de l'indépendance*[16] (1892), *La liberté invitant les artistes*[40] (1906), *La ré-publique*[43] (1907), and *Les joueurs de football*[45] (1908). The first three are large paintings of festivity and celebration performed in the spirit of the professional artist in his public and civic role. The *Centenaire,* in fact, began as a project submitted to a jury for the decoration of a borough hall in Paris. Rousseau then revised his mural-like composition to include a gay circular dance similar to that of Breughel's peasant feasts and Matisse's *Joie de vivre.* It is a far more successful painting than either *La liberté invitant les artistes* or *La république,* both of which convey the stiffness of ceremony by a stiffness in the composition. They are saved from banality by their fine color.

Les joueurs de football is almost the only significant painting in which Rousseau concentrated on the human form in movement—focused on it as intently as on the stillness of a vase of flowers.* In a carefully laid-out clearing, four players in brightly striped costumes quite literally gambol. Rousseau is not concerned with an accurate documentary vision of the game. He turns it into a remarkably convincing dance. The figures move—for it is possible in a work of art—in total stillness. One partial explanation of the paradox can be discerned. Despite some obvious awkwardness in execution, the poses of raised hands and high-stepping legs imply vigorous movement; but in their dance these well-lit bodies cast no shadow. They appear to have no location, to float in air, as do many of Rousseau's subjects. Movement without location achieves a kind of abstraction of purity. Still, there is nothing ethereal about the strongly featured faces. Even a note of comedy appears when one notices that the two yellow-and-red-striped players are blond and the two pink-and-blue-striped players are dark. Around them stands a close frame of foliage; in the center background Rousseau marks off the field of action with the clean white ruling of a rail fence which jumps forward out of the blurred leaves. None of the anatomical inaccuracies can diminish the liveliness of the composition, which rates among Rousseau's best.

Considering the wide variety of works from his brush, one can hardly assign Rousseau to any restricting classification. The term "primitive" allows him as great a range as the term "modern." Aside, however, from certain of his

* More often, as in *Paysage exotique: l'orage*[15] or *La guerre,* he depicted movement in animals. The stilted rhythmic dance of the blessed in *Le paradis*[17a] multiplies itself into decoration rather than convincing movement.

still lifes and *Les joueurs de football,* the most interesting aspect of his work is its constant readjustment of the components of landscape and the human figure. The same could be said of the Sienese Sassetta, certain of whose paintings in the Saint Anthony series depend on the placement of the people within a studied arrangement of trees and rocks. And with all his mastery, Poussin devoted himself to the same problem. Poussin, however, setting his figures in lovely pastoral countryside, creates a feeling of Olympian nostalgia; Rousseau was content to paint familiar scenes within walking distance of Paris and people them with friends and neighbors. Toward the end of his career, he allowed a welter of foliage to overgrow the human form in several paintings. Yet in these same years he achieved an astonishing equilibrium of color and form, of people and things, in such works as *La carriole du père Juniet*[47] and the *Portrait de Brummer.*[50] Produced at intervals during thirty years' production, Rousseau's finest paintings convey the ominous and alluring atmosphere of the riddle and form a haunting image of the spiritual in art. They transfix a moment of ludicrous yet convincing mystery— a mystery that keeps two half-dancing carnival figures alone in the moonlight, that keeps a glaring lion poised over a Negroid gypsy in the desert, that keeps a festoon of snakes docile before the music of a flute player.

Artists have many signatures. Conventionally they supply name and date in lower corner, an indication that the painting is finished and ready for its public career. Another kind of signature, one that helps identify Rousseau's work, can be read not in a single painting but in the recurrence of certain objects or combinations of detail through a whole series of paintings. The category does not include the deliberate repetition of principal subject such as the Annunciation in Christian art or the façade of the Cathedral of Rouen in Monet's series. It applies, rather, to the unconscious tendency of the artist to include a few familiar items in painting after painting: the cupped candle in the best of Georges de la Tour's works, the smokestacks on the horizon of Degas's race-track paintings, the ubiquitous cow that wanders in and out of Chagall's dreams. Such a repeated detail can easily become a mannerism: for example, certain letter combinations in cubist collages, like *journal* and *vins*, went through such an evolution. Or, in the hands of a highly self-conscious artist, it can be incorporated into the normal signature: Whistler's butterfly. Used discreetly or unconsciously, these details are best described as *emblems*, objects whose recurrence gives them heightened significance. They are like tiny still lifes carried over into landscape and portraiture and noticeable only to the unhurried eye.

In Rousseau such emblems are reasonably frequent and remain unconscious. His two principal stylizations or formalizations, namely, of the human face and of trees and foliage, cannot be considered emblems. They constitute his principal and conscious subject matter. But when he reduces the human figure to miniatures in broad-brimmed hats walking through the park, then he is using these tiny black shapes differently. Are they casual people strolling through the *Vue de Malakoff*[48] or *Le parc Montsouris*[20]? There appears to be more to them than that. As a child does, Rousseau painted himself into every composition that he could; in the back row left of *Une noce à la campagne*,[38] out in front shaking hands with Redon in *La liberté invitant les artistes*,[40] to the right of Père Juniet in *La carriole du père Juniet*,[47] and so on. Correspondingly, the little men with canes that parade through the landscape take on the significance of Rousseau's emblematic presence in the scenes he paints. They do, in fact, look like him. He inhabits his paintings the way most of us inhabit our dreams.

In the middle ground of *Un soir de carnaval*[7] appears a curious object for that forlorn spot—a street lamp. It occurs with equal irrelevance in the isolated countryside of *Petit paysage*[32] (*c.* 1900) as if it had grown like the trees around it. In many paintings, like *L'octroi*[29] and *La passerelle de Passy*[21] and *Vue de Malakoff*,[48] the street lamp asserts itself in clear outline. Rousseau must have liked its stable convenient shape. It is doubtful if he ever thought of it as an urban symbol to be slyly introduced into pastoral scenes. Rather, he felt at ease with so totally familiar an object. When one occurs in the scene he is painting, he assimilates its simple lines into his composition; when he needs something to fill out a space in one of his landscapes, he often gratuitously supplies a street lamp, as if every corner of France had an equal claim to nocturnal illumination.

In several early canvases, Rousseau worked out a compact little shape to occupy part of the background. It consists of a village of red tile roofs clustered around the tall spire of a church. He used it as a point of color and a triangular shape—and also probably as the emblem of the village that exists just over the horizon of every French country landscape. But before long, this simple sign of man's habitation on earth bursts out into a far more dramatic shape—the Eiffel Tower. First in the portrait-landscape *Moi-même*[10] in 1890, Rousseau painted the tower that had risen high on the sky line the year before. Soon after, he painted *Tour Eiffel et Trocadéro*,[26] and from then on it becomes as familiar in his paintings as the street lamp. While cultivated people were complaining about this blemish on the Paris silhouette, Rousseau delighted in the marvelous structure which could be seen for miles around and displayed a flag so proudly. More than the occasional airplane or balloon that he set in his limpid skies, the Eiffel Tower functions in his paintings both as symbol of his whole environment and as compositional ingredient. For centuries the cross fulfilled the same basic functions in religious paintings.

Comparison of the painting *Tour Eiffel et Trocadéro* with the original sketch[54] reveals that Rousseau added one principal detail: the little man in the foreground fishing in the river. If there was a single human pose that Rousseau found appropriate to his scenes, it was that of the fisherman. He is both active and passive; his action consists in keeping still. He appears so regularly beside Rousseau's paintings of the Seine that he becomes an emblem far different from the other little figures, who walk under the trees. His patience defines the eternal time of painting. His diagonal rod and wide hat fit comfortably into the design. His unchanging stance in painting after painting comes to express the miracle of man's endurance, the persistence of his hope.

The emblems mentioned so far are sprinkled through Rousseau's landscapes. In the portraits, which tend to reduce the components to face, costume, and background, there is only one set of objects that asserts its presence as more than normally significant. The clue comes, perhaps, from the decorative panel *Bonne fête*[17] (1892), which represents a hand holding some roses. This severed hand with its clean cuff and distorted shape has already appeared holding a cigarette in the *Portrait de Loti*[11] (1891), reappears eerily foreshortened in *L'enfant aux rochers*[24] (1897), and takes its place in many subsequent portrait-landscapes. Rousseau makes one aware that our clothing leaves exposed only two areas of flesh, the face and the hands. They are our most sensitive centers of expression. In *Une noce à la campagne*[38] he keeps all hands hidden except those of two old grandparents in the front and the bride's holding the groom's. That awkward clasp, placed just where her white dress meets the jet black of the men's suits, is the most conjugal touch in the painting. In the Brummer portrait the relaxed hands hang from the arms of the chair and convey a repose that does not appear in the stark face. It is no great distance from Rousseau's independent treatment of hands to their removal from context in cubist and surrealist painting for display as suggestive or symbolic fragments.

The special significance of emblems in Rousseau's work lies in their double nature as arbitrary and appropriate. When he painted a street lamp into a landscape or placed a hand against a black coat in an anatomically impossible position, he was often arbitrarily adding to a composition for reasons of stress and balance. Occasionally he must have acted on pure whim. But the detail added is almost always appropriate to his entire vision. It is right that there should be fishermen along the Seine; the world now agrees with Rousseau that the Eiffel Tower is the supreme symbol of Paris. He painted them not as symbols to invoke a universe of expanded meaning, but as the most familiar natural objects in his world. Emblems are part of the sure and steady means by which he painted himself into the world he saw and by which he transformed that world through the act of painting it.

Rousseau's primitivism and his modernism finally come into focus most revealingly in his method—for he had a method. It involved a regular sequence of procedure, and rested, despite his estimate of himself, far more on plane composition and interplay of color than on conventions of optical representation.

Usually he began with a small rudimentary version of his subject; a photograph, sketch, or engraving. The subjects he chose were formal and (except for the tropical scenes, which he rapidly made his own) familiar.* His basic method was free copying, a technique that allows a painter to work quietly in his studio and avoid long hours before a model or landscape. Manet and Degas used photographs, often to produce a more literal transposition than any of Rousseau's copies. Blake's florid treatment of the classic human figure and drapery resulted from his having copied fragments of engravings and prints. For Rousseau, as his portraits show, the photograph or print served as a preliminary assembling of materials, out of which he composed the painting. The photograph of the Juniet family from which he painted the celebrated *La carriole du père Juniet*[47] shows how he selected and revised at will. The bleak snapshot is transformed into a study of red wheels and shafts penetrating masses of black. In the painting the people sit in a compact arrangement in the cart, with space around them, instead of standing formlessly on the curb. They have become, recognizably, creatures of Rousseau's vision.

His own sketches, even more than photographs, reveal the logic of his method. They range from fairly crude pen and ink drawings on paper to expert impressionist landscapes in oil. Few measure over twelve inches in either dimension. In at least nine instances we can compare the sketch and the completed painting based on it. There are

* Even in the paintings with lengthy description titles, literary and anecdotal content play a minor role. (See list of paintings, numbers 16, 18, 39, 40, 44, 53.) The elaborate titles closely resemble the explanatory texts included in popular prints and woodcuts. The crude decorative pattern and simplified color of these prints (Epinal is the best-known locality which produced them) doubtless provided Rousseau with one of his earliest artistic experiences. In the mid-nineteenth century a town like Laval was flooded with "religious" and "historical" series of these pictures. Furthermore, when Rousseau met Jarry in Paris, the latter was engaged in publishing specially selected Epinal prints as serious art.

no sketches of portraits or of tropical scenes, for in both cases he probably painted partly from photographs and partly out of his own imagination. It is for landscapes that he developed a shorthand technique comparable to that of Seurat in his *croquetons*. Again the problem of dating arises in the attempt to trace the maturing of his sketching style.* After the sensitive but somewhat uncertain ink drawings of 1885, Rousseau turned to rapidly brushed oil on cardboard and increased the terseness and suggestiveness of his line. In two outstanding sketches in this style, *Paysage avec pêcheur*[57] and *Tour Eiffel et Trocadéro*,[54] he painted with obvious ease, leaving areas of bare canvas to express mass and even line (the fishing rod) and employing only restrained tones of gray, green, and black. Out of these highly sophisticated drawings he formed the schemes of finished paintings which, totally different in style, insist upon precise detail, local color, evenly covered canvas, and balanced design. This transformation is the heart of his work. He taught himself an amazingly skillful technique in sketching, yet he refused to consider these sketches the final product of his talent. Considering this clear discrimination of purpose, we cannot call him a naïve painter.

Rousseau signed his sketches and in earlier years exhibited many of his drawings. In a letter to Apollinaire in 1908 he wrote, "Excuse me for not having answered your letter right away, I was working in the country and only came back yesterday." He considered sketching from nature an essential part of his work. Yet the size and scrupulousness of detail never leave the slightest doubt as to what is a sketch and what is a finished painting.

In his studio Rousseau went about laying out and filling in his canvases in a systematic manner. Contradictory reports of his work methods yield a general idea of how he proceeded. First he outlined the general scheme of the composition and indicated areas of color. Then, starting at the top and working toward the bottom, "like pulling down a window shade," he filled in color and detail. In huge paintings like the tropical scenes, he found it preferable to apply one color at a time, especially since these paintings

* In the only published study of the sketches, Ingeborg Eichmann has accepted the dates of the final paintings. I should place most of the drawings much earlier, but in general Miss Eichmann's observations are very pertinent.

were predominantly green.* At the end he frequently revised the position of a tree or a figure or a detail, as we
can see from a few ill-disguised patches of overpainting.
Yet in general the making of the finished work was a matter
of steadily applied craftsmanship during which he could
reckon the number of days or weeks required to complete
the task. We owe his unfailing meticulousness of detail to
an ability to sustain the craftsman's role throughout the
long labor of transferring onto canvas the complex image
in his imagination. Speed of execution is not the flavor of
his art, as it is of Frans Hals' or Toulouse-Lautrec's. Few
modern artists have succeeded so well in filling immense
canvases both with a massive composition and with detail
and color applied to every visible area.

The need for order resides in every aspect of Rousseau's
work, even in the places where his style verges on the un-
couth. His perspective strikes us as exceptionally awkward,
for he was reluctant to relinquish any *object* worth painting to the obliteration of distance. He never mastered the
rules of foreshortening, and painted such odd effects as the
shutters in *La fabrique de chaises*,[27] which appear to project into a dimension totally removed from the rest of the
scene. Yet his gawky treatments serve their purpose. He
sought no more from perspective than a bare minimum of
order in space; space in itself as an independent construct
did not interest him. He could never have played tricks
with it like Van Eyck and Velasquez, placing a mirror on
the back wall of a room to intensify and disrupt the illusion
of depth.

A much stronger order in Rousseau's painting is his
sense of pure form and his relating of forms within the
picture space. He did not generalize his forms as did Gris,
or, more extremely, Mondrian. Yet there are few more expert compositions than *L'octroi*,[29] in which various ob-
tuse, acute, elongated, and globular shapes embed the

* That Rousseau could paint in a somewhat different manner
is indicated in a letter to Apollinaire during the painting of his
portrait. "All the background of the Muse is finished, the second
and third planes of the middle ground also. Only the foreground
and the figures are left." The portrait in just this state, with the
figures merely sketched in, is shown in a photograph of Rousseau painting in his studio.

precise geometry of an iron grillwork gate. He seems to have painted the scene in order to set the regular lines of the gate against soft forms of shrubbery. And in *Les bords de l'Oise*²² four slender poplar trees in the left background contrast with a round bushy tree in the right foreground. Rousseau liked this arrangement so well that he kept it intact for another version²³ in which he changed only the position of some cows and incidental shrubbery. There are also two versions of *L'été*.⁴¹, ⁴²

But Rousseau's combination of forms cannot be separated arbitrarily from his principal means of ordering a composition: color. It expresses all relations of distance, value, and mood. He used color in broad areas of slightly changing intensity such as skies and backgrounds for still lifes; he used it in more rapid contrast in the greens and reds and yellows of his landscapes. The academic practice of muting color by adding black is rare in Rousseau's highly toned works. Yet, unlike the impressionists, who had introduced a scientifically based use of color, he did not hesitate to use pure black. In most paintings his color shows a remarkably high degree of saturation, and yet his tones convey a sense of repose and completeness that is absent from the rebellious clashes of fauve painting. He keeps the tensions in discreet balance. Richness of color suits the deceptive stillness of his work and is not intended to suggest movement and change.* On completing a work, he carefully chose the color as well as the dimensions of his signature: it forms part of the composition. He kept his palette immaculately clean and used a selection of paints that shows the economy and sureness of his technique.†
A few critics have tried to dismiss Rousseau's value as a painter by calling him "only" a colorist. However, that is already saying a great deal. He avoided the smothering

---

* By striping the men's costumes in *Les joueurs de football*,⁴⁵ Rousseau gives the necessary nervousness to his usually tranquil contrasts. It is proper that his color should have reacted to a new subject.

† Maximilien Gauthier states that analysis yields the following as the standard composition of his palette: white lead, ultramarine, cobalt blue, lake, yellow ocher, ivory black, Pozzuoli red, raw sienna, Italian earth, emerald green, vermilion; as accessory colors, Prussian blue, Naples and chrome yellow.

"brown sauce" of academic practice and preserved color as both a sensuous and an expressive property.

Rousseau's decorative sense is almost as sure as his sense of color and, like it, serves the luxury effect as well as the need for order. (The terms are Roger Fry's.) In both color and form, decorative styles fall into two general categories: repetition and variation (complication). The former tends toward simple rhythmical patterns, like a row of trees; the latter tends toward what Focillon called the "system of labyrinth"—Arabic decorative borders, baroque devices, and old-fashioned stencils. Most "primitive" art favors repetitive decoration; Rousseau employed both techniques. His love for forms in series can be seen in the row of pennons in *Centenaire de l'indépendance*[16] or the repeated shoulder straps of *Les artilleurs*.[21a] Yet the intertwined foliage of his tropical paintings illustrates the system of the labyrinth. In a painting like *Bois de Vincennes*,[33] the beautifully drawn trees in the front plane partake both of repetition and variation. The trunks rise at approximately regular intervals across the width of the canvas and then branch out in independent linear designs.

In several of Rousseau's early works, roads or paths run across the scene with so little adjustment to depth that they occupy the surface of the canvas more than the distances of landscape. As a result they divide the picture like a mosaic: *Le paradis*[17a] displays just such a "primitive" effect. The assertive diagonal and horizontal lines in paintings like *La carriole du père Juniet*[47] and *Pêcheur à la ligne avec aéroplane*[30] have a similar effect of throwing the composition forward into the front plane. No representation of three-dimensional space according to Renaissance tradition holds Rousseau's work together. It coheres according to a large-scale surface arrangement, similar to cloisonné. His scenes and portraits are not so treated as to have one focal point for our attention. Equal areas of canvas within the frame tend to be filled with passages of nearly equivalent significance. Even the wide spaces of blue sky are not merely areas of color. The craftsman in Rousseau could devote enormous patience to brushing his skies to a perfect tint and texture and add a cloud or balloon when a space was about to go dead. Surface tension carries the unity of his compositions to the edges of the canvas. The frontality or pull toward frontality of the portraits also favors the location of the composition in the front plane. Obliqueness would imply depth. The forward plane of many landscapes is established by a very close foreground painted in precise detail. In *Le rêve*[53] lush magnified leaves spring up in the foreground, and meet, as if in the same plane, other plants which are much farther away. All these devices prevent us from entering too easily into an expected illusion of space. He incarnates his universe by painting it exhaustively and palpably *close*.

We can enter his universe, then, because he "saw his paintings through to the end," as Apollinaire wrote. He meticulously created a smooth, varnished surface which draws no attention to itself as paint. In general he applied enough paint to cover the canvas and no more, though in still lifes he tended—almost as if he could create a leaf— to employ a technique more like impasto. (Accordingly, his paintings have kept well except for the canvas, which was, of necessity, the cheapest.) Wholeness of effect remained his technical and artistic ideal. The Douanier was once moved by a collection of Cézanne's work to say: "I'd like to finish all these." André Derain was talking about the same thing when he stated: "Compared to Rousseau, Cézanne is a trickster." Rousseau wanted to achieve "natural" appearances, which Cézanne strove long to surpass. No matter how one estimates the qualities of these two modern masters, one must admire the devotion with which Rousseau *finished* a painting, from the moment of choosing a subject, through sketching, composing, and executing, to the final stages of signing, varnishing, and framing. Method guided his hand always.

However, the ultimate qualities lie beyond method. Most subtly of all, the light that fills Rousseau's paintings from no apparent source or direction holds everything in peaceful equilibrium despite any difference in size. His titles lay claim to many variations in atmospheric effect, including many sunsets and "storm effects." Yet in spite of impressionist titles and occasionally impressionist touches, Rousseau painted only three lights: high noon, moonlight, and the uniform floodlighting of a photographer's studio. Even this division is precarious; they resolve into a single mysterious lighting from all sides, shadowless, without high lights, without any power to dissolve color. It is this steady emanation that lifts his human figures off the ground unless

their feet are actually buried in the grass, that isolates his
flowers in profound stillnes, that moves through all the in-
tricacies of his foliage. As Daniel Catton Rich points out,
the light in his paintings has, if any, a movement out of
the background into the foreground.* But essentially it is
static, as in *Les joueurs de football*.[45] It stills all movement,
not in the instantaneous seizure of a flash bulb, but in the
prolonged stillness of noon or night. Like his perspective,
Rousseau's even, undramatic use of light releases objects
to the voraciousness of surface design. Only color works
forcefully to preserve contrasting distances from the eye.
One of the revelations of black-and-white reproduction of
Rousseau paintings is that they flatten out and lose their
depth.

In dealing with light in Rousseau's work one finds oneself
moving already within the realm of his meaning. The
formal effects of his light guard the enigma of his work,
the feeling that we cannot fathom its sheer simplicity.
There is of course a level of significance in his canvases that
is easily accessible. The predominance of pastoral scenes
and the pastoral treatment of city and parks convey the
yearning of a creature of the city for the peace and space of
the country. Yet Rousseau could be satisfied with suburban
countryside and a few scattered people wandering among
the trees. Though he never painted a crowded city street,
he did not tire of describing a city of bridges, quays, and
one magnificent tower of steel. True "country" existed in
his studio.

The most singular quality of his work, however, arises
from the steady light that floods his compositions and
hushes them as the world can be hushed only by high noon
and by moonlight. The very steadfastness of his light,
denying the movement of the sun and the succession of day

---

* The whole paragraph is worth quoting: "His approach was
far from literal. Inspired by his vision he arbitrarily rewove the
appearance of nature to suit his purpose. The long series of
imaginative paintings show Rousseau obsessed by one repeated
scheme of composition. He imagines a strongly lighted distance
against which he silhouettes darker forms of tree or foliage.
Plane upon plane is piled up in intricate design, and usually
two small figures focus the eye on the foreground. This same
'dream picture' haunted him from the days of *Carnival Evening*
to the last jungle picture he painted."

and night, removes his paintings from time. It represents no dramatically pregnant moment of history and no fleeting instant of visual reality. Academic classicism and impressionism never affected him deeply. Steady illumination creates an expanded present which transfixes past and future in permanencies of composition and design. *The time of Rousseau's painting is the time of abstract art.* One finds the same effect in the "primitive" compositions of Giotto, in certain Dutch interiors of the seventeenth century, in Chardin, and then not again until the new literalness of cubism.

The timeless quality need not rob the paintings of movement, but it is movement within plastic space, not within elapsed time. The formalized figures of *Les joueurs de football*[45] and *Centenaire de l'indépendance*[16] move convincingly within the context of Rousseau's painting. On the other hand, his most colossal and ferocious attempt at realism, *Le lion ayant faim,*[39] which measures nearly seven by ten feet, has the repose of abstract art. More than his stylized anatomy and summary perspective, more than his sure color, it is a profoundly spiritual peace that confounds us in his work. High noon or moonlight—he painted the pure stilled time of eternal Sunday.

Classic art opened a window on reality. Modern art since impressionism has closed the window and treated painting as part of the wall, a segment of flat surface. The Renaissance, which miraculously survived until 1900, carried the former tradition to the logical yet almost unrecognizable extreme of impressionism. The latter tradition goes back as far as the Egyptians for its models and today pursues the double course of abstract and expressionist art.

The paradox of Rousseau's work is that although he tried to produce works in the lineage of the window-on-reality, he painted himself into the segment-of-wall tradition. He could not paint (except in his nearly monochrome sketches) the world as his eye saw it, but only as his mind reconstituted it. Instead of realism or verisimilitude, he achieved what was far more important for his epoch—a singularly stable vision and a poetry of light and color. His attempts at realism can be ludicrous, a fact that need not be concealed or excused. Some of his animals would enliven the comic strips. Others figures fully merit the words grace and beauty. His work can be associated with both abstract art and expressionism through its two principal strengths—design and emotionally significant color. To find a similar combination, critics have turned back to painters like Piero della Francesca and Poussin. After the revolts of German expressionism, Italian futurism, and Parisian fauvism and cubism, modern painting had to find a new balance. After bold assertions of independence, it needed verification. It found primitive art, it found child art, and it found Rousseau. René Huyghe has stated the point clearly. "For the cubists Rousseau was not only an antidote; he was, like the primitives and like Negro art, a justification by instinct of the searchings of their minds. . . ." He was the most unexpected object lesson.

In part, Rousseau turns out to be what he was accused of being: the sandwich man of modern art. The sandwich man carries his message on display and we lose sight of his figure between two placards hung back and front. When the chief figures of modern art found Rousseau in 1908 and gave him a banquet, they were also setting him before the world as an example. He was the extreme test. If the public could be made to understand the eminently plastic qualities beneath Rousseau's awkward realism, then it might come to accept the similar innovations of twentieth-century painting. Rousseau's true figure as man and artist was sandwiched between his twin public role as primitive and modern. His painting continues to be partly hidden by these two placards, which must ultimately be removed altogether.

Defenders of modern art have stood stoutly by the inherent value of Rousseau's painting despite its crudities. In much the same way, Jarry stood by *Ubu Roi*, the "primitive" work of his career. But more clearly than *Ubu Roi* among Jarry's other writings, Rousseau can hold his own among modern painters. At a time when, as André Malraux points out, popular art was beginning its death agony, Rousseau carried that declining tradition to new heights and delivered its best qualities into the hands of twentieth-century art. In this context we begin to understand Rousseau's staggering remark to Picasso about their respective styles, a remark often quoted as senseless but whose perceptiveness finally emerges: "We are the two great painters of this era, you in Egyptian style, I in modern style."

Picasso had seen and celebrated the modern aspects of Rousseau's work; Rousseau could perceive in Picasso's work primitive aspects he was blind to in his own.

Rousseau's influence has been surprisingly wide. Artists from Gauguin to Chirico have not been afraid to look long at his formalizations and grotesqueries. Owner of five Rousseau canvases,[5,6,20,28,40] Picasso experimented as late as 1938 with deformations of the human figure clearly related to Rousseau's portraits. In December, 1911, Rousseau and Delaunay were the only two French artists whose work hung in the first *Blaue Reiter* exhibition in Munich. It was at this early date that Kandinsky wrote perceptively of a "new realism" to which Rousseau pointed the way. After World War I, a whole doctrine of "magic realism" evolved, which appealed to the authority of Rousseau's practice. The reason, however, why so much can be read into his art is its freedom from theory and its utter submission to the total vision of a child. This does not mean photographic realism, a highly sophisticated development of the sensibility absent from children's drawings and which did not devour the art of the West until the sixteenth century. Rousseau's realism is that of the remembered or dream image set down directly in paint—an image seeking not to outrage the purely optical arrangement of the world, but to complete it. As a result, he paints a cow's head in profile with the same "twisted perspective" of the horns as one finds in the animal drawings of the Lascaux cave, themselves masterpieces of direct statement. The Douanier calmly applied his technique to every segment of the world he knew, and the very concentration of his craftsmanship created paintings with magical overtones. His realism is the product of patience plus the certainty that the world will understand his work. It contrasts with the other great realist of the mental image who also stands on the threshold of modern art: Van Gogh, whose style was the product of passion plus doubts about his own sanity. Their weaknesses spring from the basic character of their work: Van Gogh approaches frenzy, Rousseau approaches sentimentality. Rousseau's assurance that his work, different from anything that was being done in his day, was great painting, astonishes us by its innocence and its rightness. He had the imagination and faith of a child.

Rousseau's compositions relate not merely to modern art

in its manifold development today but also, in a tentative fashion, to another art form, the motion picture. When Rousseau scatters through a landscape several figures identical in size and shape, when he paints the figures of *Les joueurs de football*[45] so much alike that we can easily see the same man in four successive positions (and even those positions broken down into separate parts), and when he fills his tropical canvases so full of detail that it can only be taken in a little at a time as the eye moves across the surface—in all these cases he suggests the possibility of an unrolling in time as well as in space. It is cinematographic time (a succession of "stills"), not chronological time. These works ask for comparison with the sequential or panoramic style of temple friezes and medieval panels showing the same action in several stages, and with the episodic construction of the movies. A few almost abandon the instantaneous unity of one glance which distinguishes traditional art. *Le centenaire de l'indépendance*[16] breaks down into three arbitrarily combined scenes like a tryptich, and not even a homogeneous three-dimensional space is constructed to hold them together. On the right side in the immediate foreground stand three men and a woman; in the center the smaller figures of the dancers move with a lively disjointed rhythm under a spreading tree; on the left a drummer plays in the far background and some children watch the dancing. The three distinct groups are connected only by a line of banners which stretches across the upper part of the canvas. The eye moves over the scene not in a smooth line of flowing mass but in three jumps. Rousseau knew nothing of cinematic technique, but his work employs some of its organizing principles and would lend itself to film treatment in close-up such as has already been given to Hieronymus Bosch and Grandma Moses. But such an examination of art as a collection of fragments does not do justice to the whole, and Rousseau's wholeness, or wholesomeness, is what gives one the greatest difficulty in setting him into a category or a tradition.

Rousseau's place in the world of art today comes to resemble that of the "Indians" whom the earliest explorers and adventurers found already living in the New World. Columbus and Cartier discovered the descendants of travelers who had reached the American continents by a totally different route. The presence of these natives proved that the land was habitable and plenteous, and the new arrivals from Europe set about to conquer and exploit it. After a few centuries, reduced in numbers and living on reservations, the Indians became a subject of myth, and the new residents who had inherited the land looked back wistfully to the innocent, simple life the Indians must have lived before the white man's arrival. Yet today it is all one country, which Indians and foreigners inhabit together.

Rousseau was the native who turned up on the shore when the exploratory voyages of modern art arrived in the new world. He was taken up and exploited, kept apart on a reservation and disguised in myth. It is time to admit him to full citizenship. We have too long patronizingly called him *le Douanier* instead of by his true name, which is as good as any. He did not discover the new world; he was born into it.

In 1910 Rousseau exhibited his last painting at the Salon des Indépendants, a huge canvas entitled *Le rêve*.[53] An art critic wrote him to ask why he had placed the luminous red sofa in the middle of the jungle. Rousseau had already explained to André Salmon: "You shouldn't be surprised to find a sofa out in a virgin forest. It means nothing except for the richness of the red. You understand, the sofa is in a room; the rest is Yadwigha's dream." He went on to reply to the critic in the tranquil, confident tone of the biographical notice he had written fifteen years earlier. The simple power of dream, he says, dictated the scene to him; that is sufficient explanation. A child does not tell us of the originality and daring of his dream but only of its compelling *reality*. Rousseau assumed that the future would understand his doing what he considered the most natural thing in the world—to paint what he saw. It was one of his last letters, and written by no April fool.

April 1st, 1910

Dear Monsieur,

I reply immediately to your friendly letter in order to explain the motive for the location of the sofa in question. This woman sleeping on this sofa dreams that she is transported into the middle of this forest, hearing the notes of the charmer's pipe. This gives the motive for the sofa being in the picture. I thank you for your kind appreciation, and if I have kept my naïveté, it is because M. Gérôme, who was a professor at the Beaux-Arts, as well as M. Clément, director of Beaux-Arts at the Ecole de Lyon, always told me to keep it. You will no longer find that amazing in the future. And I have been told before that I was not of this century. I will not now be able to change my manner which I have acquired by stubborn application, believe me. I finish my note by thanking you in advance for the article you will write on me and pray you to accept my deepest sentiments, as well as a good cordial handshake.

Henri Rousseau
Artist-peintre
2 *bis, rue Perrel* (14°)

Erik Satie, 1866-1925

[5]

MONTMARTRE PIANO PLAYER

The wonder of Satie's fifty-nine years is that he contrived to live two complete careers: he was twice a composer. During the closing years of the century he attained notoriety as an extravagant Montmartre Bohemian, watched his best friend, Claude Debussy, begin a successful career, helped his first protégé, Maurice Ravel, pick his way safely around Wagner and César Franck, and himself composed a motley collection of works whose innovations were generally passed off as eccentricities. Suddenly, in 1898, he bowed out and retired into silence and oblivion. Twelve years later, at the age of forty-eight, Satie was rediscovered, dubbed a precursor, and, like a forgotten relative, was drawn back into circulation by Debussy and Ravel. Characteristically, he proceeded to confound everyone by composing works in a totally new style and fiercely refused to rest on his first and acknowledged career.

At this juncture, Satie wrote for his always reluctant publishers a blurb on himself and his music which, like Rousseau's autobiographical note, was not printed until many years later. And the resemblance goes further. Beneath the ironic grimace of Satie's style can be discerned the same tranquil self-confidence, the same dedication to his art, and the same accurate evaluation of his place on the contemporary scene that Rousseau displayed.

M. Erik Satie was born in Honfleur (Calvados) on May 17, 1866. He is considered to be the strangest musician of our time. He classes himself among the "fantasists" who are, in his opinion, "highly respectable people. . . ."

After having essayed the loftiest genres the eminent composer now presents some of his humoristic works. This is what he says about his humor: "My humor resembles that of Cromwell. I also owe much to Christopher Columbus, because the American spirit has occasionally tapped me on the shoulder and I have been delighted to feel its ironically glacial bite."

This is what the Master has to say about these pieces: "I wrote the *Descriptions automatiques* for my birthday. This work is a counterpart to the *Véritables préludes flasques*. It is clear that the Deflated, the Insignificant, and the Puffed-Up will not appreciate these works. Let them swallow their beards! Let them dance on their own stomachs!"

The beautiful and limpid *Aperçus désagréables* (piano for four hands)—Pastorale, Chorale, and Fugue—are written in the most superior style and enable us to understand why the subtle composer is justified in declaring: "Before writing a work I walk around it several times accompanied by myself."

Sarcasm came easily to him, yet it cannot here hide the completeness and willfulness of his break with the past, like Rousseau's retirement in order to paint. Satie dismisses everything he composed before 1910 in the condescending phrase, "loftiest genres"; Debussy, because he belonged to the earlier period, is passed over in silence. Satie began his second career by shedding forty years of his life, and he did so after having literally gone back to school to learn all over again. He came closer than most men to discovering a second youth.

Satie is today a musician more heard of than heard. Yet his two careers, because they associated him with successive generations of composers and yielded strongly contrasting bodies of work, testify to the shift of musical sensibility that took place in France during the Banquet Years. Many composers are greater or better known; few reveal more clearly than Satie the origins and early development of twentieth-century music. At the turn of the century France was still recovering its balance after the most recent wave of German domination. To resist the massive appeal of Wagner, the stout figures of Fauré, Chabrier, Debussy, and Ravel had to stand firm in their search for a music that could once again be recognized as French. It is more appropriate than surprising that among them there should have been one composer who was French to the point of eccentricity: part mascot, part primitive, part jester, part sage. Satie, his music and his career, could never have happened in Germany—or in Italy or in England. His music is of Paris; despite his origins, he knew no other city.

The critic Georges Auriol maintained that Satie was not even born in France. "In reality his arrival among us is from a more distant place. . . . Erik came to us from the North in a leather bark manned by a crew of trolls. . . . Satie is Puck in our midst." His blood was, in fact, mixed. His father came of a sturdy family of sailors and captains turned marine brokers in Honfleur, a port on the Normandy Coast. The *honfleurais* have long had a reputation for solid bourgeois spirit and a particular brand of dry humor attributed to their proximity to England. The mother, of Scottish stock, had come from London to Honfleur *en pension* for her vacations. For religious reasons, both families regarded the marriage with suspicion. Eric* Leslie Satie was born on May 17, 1866, soon followed by a sister, Olga, and a brother, Conrad. In 1870 the family moved to Paris, where the mother died two years later. The Satie grandparents took charge of the three young children, baptized them in the Catholic Church, and rebuffed all advances from the English relatives.

"I had an ordinary childhood and adolescence—" wrote Satie in *Mémoires d'un amnésique,* "no moments worth recounting in serious writing. So I shall pass them over." He attended the municipal school in Honfleur and studied piano with Monsieur Vinot, organist at the Church of St. Catherine, who developed Satie's taste for antique modes. The only relief from the bleakness of life with his grandparents came in the company of a black-sheep uncle who was called "Sea Bird." A bachelor of unconventional habits and easy morals, Sea Bird had sold the brokerage business

* The baptismal spelling was changed later.

his father had bought him for a bookstore which demanded little attention and devoted himself to horsemanship (with a gig so perfectly fitted out that it was never used for fear of damaging it) and boating (relaxing in an equally well-kept boat which remained moored in the harbor). Most important of all, Sea Bird often took Eric with him to see performances of traveling circuses and acting troupes, and the boy went along backstage while his uncle exchanged ritual amenities with the female performers. These early years revealed no exceptional brilliance in the boy. He was independent and a little wild, with clear questioning eyes, closely cropped hair, and prominent ears.

When Eric was twelve, his grandmother died and he rejoined his father in Paris. The next five years of adolescence and early maturity were even more lacking in love and happiness than the childhood in Honfleur. His father's second wife found little affection to offer her stepson, and his father was preoccupied with a succession of unprofitable enterprises and liberal ideas. Eric's formal education was rapidly abandoned except for music; accounts of his Conservatory training have until recently been unreliable or slanted to promote the image of a largely self-taught musician like Moussorgsky and Chabrier. A young English musicologist, Patrick Gower, has established that Satie was admitted in 1879 to the *classe préparatoire* in piano with Professor Decombes. On Satie's examination performance of Mendelssohn at the end of the second year this sympathetic young teacher noted: "The laziest student in the Conservatory—but gets a lovely sound." As required by regulations, Satie was dropped after failing three years in succession to be chosen for the public competition. In 1885, however, he passed the regular entrance examination and spent a full year in Mathias' piano class. His new professor listened to him play Mendelssohn again in June 1886: "Worthless. Three months just to learn the piece. Cannot read properly." Many years later Satie maintained that music as a career was thrust upon him, and up to this moment in his development the statement probably holds true. But at about the age of sixteen he discovered Bach and Chopin and was at the same time deeply drawn to the mystic doctrine and ritual of the Catholic faith. In literature he turned to Flaubert and Hans Christian Andersen, an unusual combination of tastes which suggests that he

discerned in both writers their veiled yet deep-seated religious preoccupation. It is what makes Flaubert at his most
earnest often read like an author of fairy tales, and Andersen like an author of stories not at all for children but for
unbelieving adults. Out of all these revelations of the
world of feeling grew a strong commitment to music, as if
it offered consolation for all he had missed in his cheerless
childhood. Yet outwardly the boy appeared idle and frivolous.

In 1885 Eric wrote two piano works which were to be
published two years later. His father, now a stationer,
printed a few of Eric's tunes. His first career had begun in
earnest, but still under the spiritual and moral influence of
his Uncle Sea Bird. With a literary friend, Contamine de
Latour, Satie spent a great deal of his time finding further
consolation among the Paris *midinettes,* who sewed dresses
until noon and had the rest of the day in which to seek
protection and companionship. At eighteen, Satie looked
austere and a little priggish in a high stiff collar and a
pince-nez on a ribbon. Yet he was ready to reject every
conformity.

Despite his poor record, Satie entered Mathias' class for
a second year in the fall of 1866. Contamine de Latour
writes that "his studies permitted him to volunteer for a
year of military service instead of serving the required five
years." Indeed, he dropped out of the Conservatory in
December and volunteered, but the infantry barracks at
Arras offered no advantages over life as a music student.
By deliberately exposing himself to the winter air, he contracted severe bronchitis and secured a discharge. During
convalescence he began work on what are still his best-
known works, the three *Gymnopédies.* A quarrel with his
parents over an amorous episode with the family maid then
provoked him into leaving home. Late in 1887 he moved
into a room in the Rue Condorcet at the foot of Montmartre close by the Cirque Médrano, to which he was instinctively attracted. When in 1888 Rodolphe Salis, the
patron of the Chat Noir, hired Satie as second pianist, the
young musician assumed full Bohemian regalia. He grew a
beard, adopted a flowing tie, velvet coat, and soft felt hat,
kept his pince-nez, and moved all the way up the hill to
the Rue Cortot behind the Place du Tertre. It was at this
time that he modified the spelling of his name from Eric

to Erik and addressed himself to the task of earning a double reputation as Montmartre eccentric and serious composer.

In 1887 Chabrier's *Le roi malgré lui* had its first performance at the Opéra-comique, and Fauré's *Requiem* was published, to be performed the following year. Chabrier and Fauré were the two most independent and original composers working in France. Satie was no one's disciple; he studied under no one, and idiosyncrasy was to be his refuge. But if any influences are detectable in his work, they are Chabrier for harmonic freedom and musical humor, and, to a lesser degree, Fauré for pianistic style and techniques of melodic accompaniment. Probably Satie became familiar a few years later with Chabrier's comical "natural history" songs of 1890 and the fine burlesque *Duo de l'ouvreuse del l'Opéra Comique et de l'employé du Bon Marché*. Like Glinka's in Russia, such compositions brought gay spirits back into the realm of serious music. After hearing *Le roi malgré lui*, Satie sent Chabrier one of his own magnificently copied and inscribed compositions (in red ink and Gothic script). There was no reply. The music may well have been one of the *Sarabandes* composed that year, and whose sonorities unmistakably echo the overture of Chabrier's opera. These three short piano works contain passages of seventh and ninth chords sounding without preparation or resolution or consistent tonal center. The insistently startling harmonies finally become as plodding and antique as the monotonous rhythm.

The three *Gymnopédies*, completed the following year, suspend a modal melodic line with a Gregorian ring over a swaying *ostinato* bass. The accompaniment, with its deceptive changes in key and mode, never runs exactly parallel to the melody, yet never abandons it. It is the fine adjustment of these two elements that makes the style of the *Gymnopédies* so hauntingly simple. (See illustration below.)

With its equivocal cadence the music seems to drift serenely as in a dead calm. Two years later the *Gnossiennes* (more oriental than Mediterranean despite the derivation of the title from King Knossos of Crete) revive the banished tritone as a means of giving the melody a foreign, semihumorous quality. At twenty-two, Satie had found his first original style, a blend of boldness and timidity which

Gymnopédie No. 3

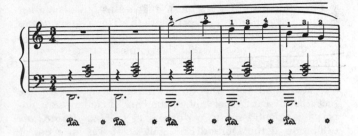

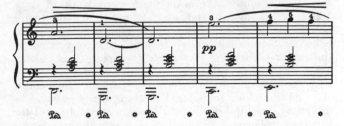

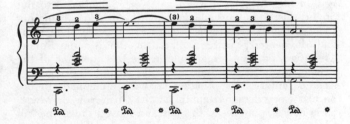

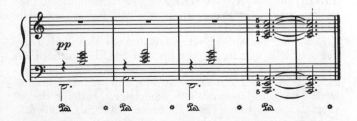

equalize each other so completely that the music seems to move at a standstill. These early piano compositions are contemporary with the late works of Brahms and Verdi, yet in comparison Satie's music reaches us out of another century—the ninth or the twentieth. The *Gymnopédies* and the *Gnossiennes* mix exoticism, innovation, and awkwardness in such a way that the simplest passages convey the greatest freshness.

After the *Gnossiennes* in 1890 Satie became semiofficially associated with the Rosicrucians. For a play of the sect's flamboyant chief cultist, the "Sâr" Péladan, he composed incidental music performed at the first Rose-Croix exhibition at the Durand Ruel gallery. It was an event of considerable importance in the *fin-de-siècle* world of 1892. Within a few months, however, he wrote a letter to the newspaper *Gil Blas* disavowing any influence on his music. Satie's adventure with this "Chaldean" sect corresponds to the contemporary Pre-Raphaelite movement in England; Yeats had joined the London Rosicrucians in 1887.

In those days, and in Satie's life, it was a conveniently short distance from esoteric religions to cabaret gaiety. The exuberant, worldly, profoundly Parisian atmosphere of the cabaret had become a cult all its own—an aesthetic and a way of life. In 1891 at the Chat Noir, Salis began to put on his justly famous shadow plays; in 1892 Toulouse-Lautrec had become a habitué of Montmartre night spots and discovered Yvette Guilbert at the Moulin Rouge. There was nothing remarkable in the fact that one of the piano players in this raucous world should also compose exalted fanfares for pseudo-Christian ceremonial. Before he had worked many months at the Chat Noir, however, Satie had a squabble with Salis and moved down the hill to a similar establishment, the Auberge du Clou (the Nail Tavern) in the Avenue Trudaine. He accompanied the singers, played waltzes, and improvised for an assorted clientele.

It was at the Auberge du Clou in 1891 that Satie met the man who was to become his best friend, the thorn in his flesh, and the source of his greatest sorrow. "The moment I saw him I felt drawn to him and wished I might live at his side forever," Satie said later. "And for thirty years I was fortunate enough to see my wish fulfilled." The man was Claude Debussy.

He was four years older than Satie and had held a Prix de Rome. He had visited Bayreuth and Moscow, knew the writings of symbolists and Pre-Raphaelites, and had already been associated with "impressionism."* He had a wide acquaintance among writers and painters, and his work soon found a hearing. Debussy inscribed a copy of his *Cinq poèmes de Charles Baudelaire:* "For Erik Satie, gentle medieval musician who strayed into this century to give joy to his best friend, Claude Debussy. October 27, 1892."

Frequently, Satie has been singled out as the crucial influence that turned Debussy away from the Wagnerianism that still worked strongly in his music. Such a description does not do justice to their friendship. The young men exchanged ideas, encouraged one another to define a point of view, and began operas on plays by the same author: Maurice Maeterlinck. Satie's *Princesse Maleine,* which apparently had precedence, was destroyed and never mentioned again; Debussy's *Pelléas et Mélisande,* after its first version had been thrown into the wastebasket, became the call to colors for new independence in French music. Many harmonic and dramatic ideas that governed its composition resulted from a collaboration between two mature musicians searching for a road that would lead away from Wagner.† Debussy continued to work with these ideas, whereas Satie later rejected most of them and began all over again. Today, *Pelléas* seems still under the shadow of Wagner.

After the Auberge du Clou, Satie became pianist at the Café de la Nouvelle Athènes, where Degas and Renoir and Pissarro had met and debated in the seventies and eighties, and where Gauguin fled from the stock market to buy paintings and talk with the impressionists. In the nineties the establishment still attracted a lively crowd of painters and

* In 1885 the Prix de Rome tribunal wrote of *Printemps* that it showed "forgetfulness of the importance of preciseness in line and form," and a "vague Impressionism" which endangered the "truthfulness" of a work of art.

† Jean Cocteau relates that Debussy was led to reject the leitmotiv by one of Satie's remarks: "There is no need for the orchestra to grimace when a character comes on stage. . . . What we have to do is create musical scenery . . . in which the characters move and talk."

writers—and such perceptive amateurs as an inventor by the namel of Ravel. He often brought his son Maurice, who was still in his teens. The young man found a kindred spirit in Satie, and Ravel later acknowledged the bread-and-butter piano player at the café as one of his masters, along with Chabrier and Gounod.[*]

Between his cabaret work and serious composition, and among his musical friends, like Debussy and Ravel, and several literary companions with whom he periodically attempted to collaborate on an opera, there was a life for Satie, possibly a fruitful one. Yet about 1892 he inherited a little money after his father's death and began to indulge his fantasies with fierce energy. At the age of twenty-seven he appears to have settled on a public role of heterodoxy and to have committed to it all his natural and spiritual resources. He already had a suitably fabled room in the Rue Cortot, a "closet," his friends called it, rigged up with a system of locks and transoms to allow light and air to enter from the landing and keep out prying looks. Though he had squeezed a piano into the room, he usually visited friends to "try out" his new compositions. He had a chair, a bed, a chest, and a bookshelf that served as both work-table and altar. Yet this was only the beginning. In the unfamiliar freedom of comparative affluence, Satie's behavior now took on the aspect of purposeful oddity. His actions became extravagant and a little mad, incoherent except as a vast, unsmiling parody of all human society

---

[*] Roland-Manuel, Ravel's biographer, describes their friendship at length. "Maurice Ravel never tired of emphasizing the decisive character of this meeting with Satie. The advice, the devilment, the artless audacity of that weird Socrates inspired, whether one likes it or not, very many of the technical achievements and triumphs of aesthetic judgment for which his successors justifiably gain credit. Such achievements could never have been brought about but for the astonishing man who for thirty-five years was the intimate advisor upon every type of bold and impudent experiment in French music, and whom Ravel was delighted to call, 'a clumsy but talented explorer.' At first Satie was surprised by his gratitude, which found expression not only in the dedication of the last of the *Poèmes de Stephane Mallarmé*, but, more especially, in the harmony of *Un grand sommeil noir* and *Sainte*, and the melodic and rhythmic structure of *La belle et la bête*, that delightful fourth *Gymnopédie*."

grafted onto unchecked natural eccentricity. The combination recognized no restraints and rapidly carried Montmartre humor into the sphere of the absurd.

Breaking with the Rosicrucians and their high priest, Satie undertook to found a religion of his own. He renamed his tiny closet "Our Abbatial," anticipating by a few years Jarry's "Our Great Chasublerie" on the other side of the Seine. Satie's resounding "Metropolitan Church of the Art of Jesus the Conductor" issued an official publication, *Le Cartulaire*, written, published, and paid for by Satie. The numbers for May and June, 1895 (the only two that appeared, numbered 1–63 and 2–63) are among the most bizarre documents of the epoch. Using a series of inflated ecclesiastical headings and pseudonyms, Satie began by excommunicating the young music critic Willy, with whom he had come to blows at a concert. Willy, pen name for Henri Gauthier-Villars, produced quantities of copy by his own talents and through the employment of ghost writers. The most famous of them, his wife, was trained and exploited like the rest. After breaking with him, she took her own name: Colette. Willy had attacked Wagner in the pages of the *Echo de Paris*. Himself strongly opposed to the German composer, Satie pompously pointed out that Willy did not have the authority to criticize Wagner and finished: "I command removal from My presence, sadness, silence and dolorous meditation." In the same number Satie condemned ex cathedra the latest theatrical and literary ventures of the Paris scene. "Christians who have complaints of an aesthetic nature about M. Lugné-Poe . . . must make them known to Our Abbatial. Our brothers will find in Us a rampart against the satanic works revealed in the *Mercure de France*, the *Revue Blanche*, and *La Plume*. . . ."* This was probably Satie's peculiar method of expressing approval of such avant-garde activities.

The inheritance also carried Satie direct from the lawyer's office to a tailor to buy a dozen identical suits of gray corduroy, which were his dress for many years. He published at his own expense in 1895 the synopsis of a "Chris-

* At Lugné-Poe's Théâtre de l'Œuvre or at the *Mercure*, Satie may have met Jarry as early as 1895. No record of a meeting exists, but their paths must have crossed in Montmartre and on the Left Bank.

tian Ballet," *Uspud,* which he had composed with Contamine de Latour. A huge visionary affair full of heavenly
and demonic presences, it was sent to the director of the
Opéra; he did not bother to acknowledge it. When the
director, Bertrand, finally agreed during a stormy inter-
view in his office to consider the work, Satie demanded
that it be submitted to a special commission of forty musicians, half of them to be chosen by the authors. In his
apocryphal account of Satie's life, the composer Florent
Schmitt describes a "benzoin duel" in which "the inhospit-
able director succumbed under the third friction."

In 1892 Satie began his most inspired and sustained
escapade: three times and with impenetrable seriousness
he presented himself as a candidate for the supreme honor
of election to the Institut de France, or the Academy. The
first time, he proposed himself for the vacancy left by
Ernest Giraud, Debussy's teacher, then, in 1894, to replace
Gounod, and finally in 1896 to replace Ambroise Thomas.
The little-known bearded Bohemian in his twenties made
protocol visits to dignified Academy members and submitted extravagantly inflated information about himself in
the applications. On the first round only Gustave Moreau,
the painter, received him with any kind of attention; the
second time, his rebuff provoked a pontifical letter addressed to Camille Saint-Saëns from the Master Chapel of
the Metropolitan Church of the Art of Jesus the Conductor. "I have acted not according to foolish presumption
but in response to a conscientious sense of duty. . . . Your
aberration can only arise from the feebleness of your ideas
about this Century and from your ignorance of God, the
direct cause of aesthetic degradation. I pardon You in
Jesus Christ and embrace You in God's grace." The paper
Le Menestrel published this outlandish communication,
and when Satie at the end of his life wrote the entertaining fragment "My Three Candidacies," he kept the pose by
speaking of the "great grief" these failures had brought
him.*

* In 1861 Baudelaire, best known because the public censor
had condemned several of his poems four years earlier, became
a candidate to the Academy in a somewhat comparable gesture.
But there was some basis for his pretensions, for Baudelaire was
forty, had published widely as poet and critic, and had the
sympathy of Sainte-Beuve and Vigny.

Satie plotted and carried out these skirmishes with a fine sense of dramatic gesture. He practiced the unconventionality that Montmartre flaunted before bourgeois prosperity and smugness, and, unabashed, carried it further than less dedicated Bohemians. His pranks seemed to originate from a serious, deeply pondered behavior. Doubtless he half accepted the mystic frumpery with which he surrounded his "church" and enjoyed its overblown pretensions; doubtless he half believed in the greatness of his own destiny and paid the calls for the Institut as Rousseau might have done. Yet he had not lost his sanity. One of the keys to Satie's humor is the fact that instead of repressing his illusions he asserted them—and turned out in the end to have a good hold on reality. "Don't part with your illusions," Mark Twain advises in *Pudd'nhead Wilson's New Calendar* with the wisdom of a fellow humorist. "When they have gone you may still exist but you have ceased to be alive." Satie was, above all, alive.

In accordance with the sensitive compensating mechanism that sustained Satie's character, this period of mock-heroic behavior coincided with the insistent religiosity of inspiration in his Rosicrucian works (1891–1895). Four years earlier, the *Sarabandes* already showed tendencies toward liturgical style, especially the third, which is divided into chordal passages and passages of runs and broken chords. In the Rosicrucian pieces this division often becomes a regular alternation of unaccompanied melody and rich harmonies—an arrangement probably borrowed from the medieval alternation of cantor and choir. Antiphonal style appears in many pieces of this period; their spiritual suggestiveness rests on ecclesiastical conventions of mode and structure and not on yearning Wagnerian harmonies. The pompous texts that accompany some of them have been interpreted as parodies of Wagner's aesthetic, yet we have no reason to doubt the sincerity of the music. It was necessary that Satie pass through this period of spiritual purge. Afterward, he was able to begin all over again with new freedom and humility.

The *Messe des pauvres* (1895), the last composition of the period, emphasizes verticality and unvarying dynamics. In reviewing a recording of the *Mass,* Virgil Thomson speaks of the "self-containment" of every sonority, the lack of voice leading and thorough bass, and of how this kind of writing "does not invoke the history of music. . . . Its inner life is as independent of you as a Siamese cat." Insofar as it is possible in Western music, Satie was approaching a style of disjunction, of separation rather than unity of parts.

Home-grown religion, academic aspirations, and music did not monopolize all of Satie's time and energy. The exiguous premises of the Abbatial became the arena of a major love affair between Satie and a turbulent young woman whose career as an acrobat had been interrupted by a trapeze accident. Suzanne Valadon had begun drawing at the age of nine and was now painting professionally after becoming friendly with some of the greatest artists of the time: Puvis de Chavannes, Lautrec, Renoir (she posed for all three), and Degas (her stoutest supporter and the first to buy her work). At seventeen she had had an illegitimate son, who, in his teens, was to begin a career of painting and alcoholism, and took the name Maurice Utrillo. Now twenty-eight and a year older than Satie, Suzanne Valadon moved into a studio next door to him in the Rue Cortot. In 1893 she painted his portrait as a handsome, bearded, shaggy-haired Bohemian; he wrote musical good-mornings to her as "Biqui" and sketched her portrait, in turn, with straight-hanging hair almost hiding her girlish face. Inevitably it was a stormy affair. To defend his position in their quarrels and ruptures, Francis Jourdain relates, Satie used to exhibit in the street window of his Abbatial "proclamations in which the virtue of Suzanne Valadon . . . was bitterly contested in concise terms." Only the two portraits have remained as evidence of this passionate interlude in the Rue Cortot.

Satie as fiery lover constitutes a very partial portrait. For one of the basic traits of this *bon vivant*, so addicted to farcical behavior as to appear exhibitionistic, was his timidity. Led on by temporary wealth, an erratic disposition, and the Montmartre surroundings, Satie began to drink steadily, as if in defiance of that timidity. In an increasing consumption of wine, pernod, and brandy, which dismayed his friends and began a slow attrition of his system, he found a means of exposing certain parts of himself and hiding others. But alcohol, unfortunately, tended to transform his high spirits into irascibility; as time went on, he quarreled with one after another of his friends over trivial or imagined slights, until he began to imagine himself surrounded by enemies. He was often goaded into towering rages, grown-up tantrums like Rousseau's, during which he refused to listen to anyone. Naturally, his relations with women were affected. After the affair with Suzanne Valadon he kept his attachments so private that even his best friends, excluded from his apartment, speculated on his domestic arrangements. Increasingly he treated women with politeness tinged with sarcasm. He told his sister-in-law, "You want to know why I'm not married? The fear of being cuckolded, just that. And I would deserve it. I'm a man women cannot understand." Yet in later years his songs still treat women and themes of love with sensitivity and tenderness.

In the realm of feeling, it is as if Satie lived a little distance ahead of his music. The verve of his temperament and the practical-joke tone of his private church anticipate a change in the esoteric and pseudo-mystical preoccupations he shared with the *fin-de-siècle*. Having advised Debussy to abandon the "sauerkraut" of Wagner's aesthetic, he had to lift the spell of Rosicrucianism and liturgical sequence from his own music. With glints of humor in the modulations and terse comments sprinkled through the score, *Pièces froides* (1897) finally broke through his fixations after the two-year silence following *Messe des pauvres*.

In the interval, his writing had thawed out miraculously, taken on new rhythmic interest, simplified its harmonies, and found a style more suited to his ebullient personality. The *Pièces froides* come in two sets of three each: "*Airs à faire fuire*" and "*Danses de travers*." Each of the "*Airs à faire fuire*" starts out like a liberated *Gnossienne*, with variations and surprises. A feeling for oriental scales still explains many of the accidentals, and Satie perfected the trick of writing carefully marked phrases long enough to establish a tonality, which he then drops completely in the next phrase. The compressed, comical cadence in the middle of *Airs I* (see illustration, p. 128) is characteristic of his treatment of the harmony. The second of these "airs" introduces a simple, tuneful, almost banal kind of writing, which revives the suppleness of the *Gymnopédies*. The only quirk is Satie's lowering of the seventh degree—a modal predilection he does not insist on this time.

Airs à faire fuire, I

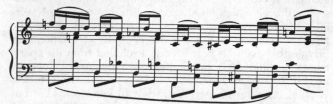

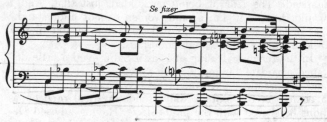

Airs à faire fuire, II

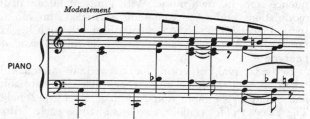

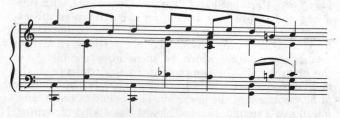

This unpretentious melody, alternated with a secondary theme in different keys but never developed in any other way, conveys a gay wistfulness. The very turn of the

phrases and the rhythm suggest that Satie distilled so
clear a line from the popular music he heard and played
in Montmartre cabarets. Nowhere in the classical music
of the nineties, except perhaps in Chabrier, could he have
learned this loosening of style. Religious aspirations sub-
side into mild sentiment, which is rescued from banality
by a strengthened sense of movement. The awkward
searching about for strange sonorities comes to an end, and
for the first time Satie sounds not medieval or Greek or
Javanese, but Parisian. He sounds like himself.

The *"Danses de travers"* are three slightly differing
treatments of one scheme of broken chords in ceaseless
modulation. A strong bass line in arpeggio—Satie restricts
himself to the root position—propels each section through
to the end without any rests or change in rhythm. The
soprano line scarcely forms a melody, but repeats unhurried groups of notes which lead the shifting harmonies and
function as suspensions and anticipations. The practice
became increasingly important in later work.

Danses de travers, III

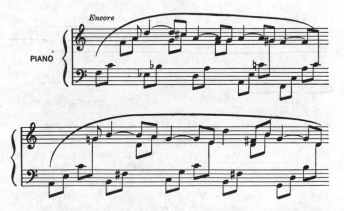

These highly pianistic passages recall Fauré's subtle
arpeggio accompaniments. In music like this, Satie's facetious directions and comments begin to take on meaning,
for they call attention to tiny variations in the dynamics of
an evenly flowing line. "Marvelously," he says when the
harmony comes clear, and "Be visible for a moment," for

the expansion of a fragment of melody. These "Crosswise Dances" use repetition and near repetition to create a feeling not of stillness but of controlled circular movement. It amounts to a folk element in Satie's music, something he found both in plain chant and in Montmartre chansons.

The last years of the century which produced the *Pièces froides* were still a formative period for Satie in more than a strictly musical sense. Templier, his French biographer, who knew him at the end of his career, states that "At the Auberge du Clou Satie found great pleasure in keeping company with painters. Through contact with them his sense of humor, his musical aesthetic, and his Bohemian spirit took shape." In a later lecture on Debussy, Satie spoke of how their ideas developed in those days of teeming life. "Why not make use of the means of representation which Claude Monet, Cézanne, Toulouse-Lautrec were showing us?" Chabrier, the friend of Villiers de l'Isle-Adam and Verlaine and Coppée, of Manet and Monet and Renoir, was the first modern French composer to work in close touch with the extramusical ideas of his time. Debussy showed the same inclinations. It is both the quality and the shortcoming of Satie's music that for long periods he subjected himself almost exclusively to nonmusical influences.* This explains in part the wealth of its innovation, the economy of its means, and its small scale. There are times when his music becomes as "white" ("blank") as some of Monet's last pictures, which seem to disappear on the canvas.

During these Montmartre years Satie developed a working habit whose products offer evidence both of the cross-fertilization of his talents and of the intimate details of his existence. Very early he began keeping notebooks, for the most part small *cahiers de musique* six to eight inches long, folded in the middle to fit in his pocket, and stained on the back from the café tables, on which he liked to work. On the covers he noted his cash accounts, with a specific sum for each cup of coffee, each glass of brandy, each course of a meal. In these neatly added figures (some-

---

* During the last ten years of his life, when he had fallen out with many of his musical companions, Satie spent most of his time with painters, who had become his best friends and with whom he collaborated on books and ballets: Braque, Derain, Picasso, Léger, and Brancusi.

times decorated with a comment or an exclamation point when his consumption had been excessive) one can read the years of ease followed soon by poverty and self-denial. He also noted down here in his fastidious Gothic script observations on any subject—fragments he assembled years later into lectures and articles. And he copied down a variety of odd items which caught his eye: strange words, squibs from the newspaper, street signs. His work in these same pages as a draftsman and caricaturist in miniature displays the precision essential to comic effect. In the end his calligraphy, lavished on such inanities as *"Non de chien"* and *"Un touriste est quelqu'un qui habite une tour,"* itself becomes ironic. All Satie's life—the circumstances of a precarious existence, tiny musical gems which came to nothing, a strong sense of the bizarre, an incisive eye for line—went into these notebooks. Beneath their waste-basket format they reveal the meticulousness of his work, the way he caught melodic and rhythmic ideas and worked them gradually into wholes, and the extent to which his music kept company with words and drawing. To the end of his life he gave himself exercises in harmony and counterpoint in these little books, wrote out positions of chords, and experimented with new tone groupings. Once the "lazy, worthless" musician began learning he never stopped. Appearances, however, show an interruption, an abrupt silence.

A dedicated and active artist who has, in ten years, succeeded in winning a small group of admirers in his field and who prefers Bohemian independence to respectability does not usually retire from the struggle in his early thirties. Satie found reasons for doing exactly that. Unlike his academic candidacies, this gesture removed him from the public eye. Apparently there was no warning. In 1898 Satie simply picked up and moved, not merely across the Seine, but south across Paris, beyond the fortifications, to the still-countrified suburb of Arcueil-Cachan (Arcachan, he called it). He found a room over a dreary café-restaurant called the Four Chimneys. In a wheelbarrow he carted his bench and chest and bed the arduous distance to the opposite side of the city and installed himself in waterless unheated quarters. He also transported his twelve corduroy suits and his eccentric habits. Slowly he settled into his new home and into the café downstairs, where he worked, and before long he became part of the uninspiring suburb where "one divines the mysterious presence of Our Lady of Lowliness."

Why this departure, this break? The decision remains partially inscrutable. After a few years of ease, he was penniless; in any large sense he was unknown. Already Debussy (soon it would be Ravel) was finding his stride and making a reputation. In 1897 the Chat Noir had closed, and old companions like Allais were appearing less and less in Montmartre. Years later Contamine de Latour saw the move as a natural reaction to the "forced gaiety" of Montmartre. "He felt the need to devote himself entirely to work and study. And at the same time his mystic bent . . . led him to seek solitude."

There followed twelve years—1898–1910—of partial hibernation and virtual silence compared to the frenetic activity that filled the years before and after. With the exception of one or two events which break through the stillness, the interlude constituted a kind of early death for Satie—a death in obscurity from which he wondrously returned. A comparable retreat into silence was undertaken at this same moment by the poet Paul Valéry. Long hibernation confirmed them both in highly condensed, personal styles.

There was, however, a living to make. He still had to spend part of his time in Montmartre, now six miles away. But he always came home to his apartment, and often, having missed the last horse-drawn omnibus or being too poor to pay the fare, he walked. His reputation for prowess in "footing" (walking) turned rapidly into legend. It was said he carried a hammer in his pocket to protect himself from attack on the two-hour nocturnal journey and composed on the way. He drank increasingly heavily—but he had always shown a singular capacity for both drink and food. His meager living was earned by accompanying singers and composing popular songs, plus the microscopic income from his published works.* With the popular *chansonnier* Vincent Hyspa, he played a few society engagements, for which he had to borrow suitable clothes from his brother.

Debussy continued to welcome him *en famille*, as sev-

* During the first quarter of 1903 he received seventy-six centimes from the Society of Composers for performance rights.

eral photographs of this epoch testify. Satie frequently used Debussy's piano, and came every week for dinner; yet their friendship, firmly rooted in the past, could rely less and less on any continuing sympathy and understanding. Satie also continued to see and write his brother, Conrad, to whom he sent this plaintive message: "I am having a poor time dying of sorrow; everything I timidly undertake fails with a boldness never before known." In 1899 he composed *Jack-in-the-Box*, a pantomime, and *Geneviève de Brabant*, an operetta for marionettes; after a few months he "lost" both scores—right in his room, as it later turned out. In 1905 he began work with Maurice de Faraudy on an operetta, but he soon walked out in a huff.

Publicly, Satie displayed his oddest behavior. Georges Auriol describes him going about with a lighted clay pipe stuck in his pocket, its stem reaching up to his ear. In cafés he insisted on being served specifically the bottom portion of cognac out of the graduated carafes that sat on all the tables. That quantity was slightly larger than the ones above it, he maintained, and he had the right to demand any one of the portions offered. Was there nothing better for him to do now that Debussy's *Pelléas* had been performed at the Opéra-comique in 1902 and Ravel had completed his astonishing *Quartet* the following year? The mask of humorous eccentricity fitted him only too well by now. His friends could not help thinking that his next move was merely another prank, this time overplayed.

In 1905, in his fortieth year, Satie went back to school. A notebook contains a draft of the letter he wrote to the director of the Schola Cantorum asking for a scholarship. "I am a poor artist up against the difficulties of life; therefore it is absolutely impossible for me to pay the tuition price required of students taking this course." He apparently obtained the necessary assistance. Debussy, at whose house Satie was becoming uncomfortable amid the influx of admirers, advised against it. "At our age you don't shed your skin again." And Satie replied with a simplicity that shows how much he was risking: "If I lose, too bad. It would mean I had no guts in the first place." Furthermore, it was not just any school. The Schola Cantorum, founded ten years before as a monument to César Franck, emphasized formal training, and as his principal course Satie chose counterpoint under Albert Roussel, a former naval officer who had given up a promising career at sea for music. The teacher was three years younger than his pupil. As Debussy and Satie had debated it and then practiced it in their different ways, so-called impressionism slighted contrapuntal resources of music for new harmonic riches. Now Satie worked for three years in what some men would consider humiliating circumstances to regain lost ground. He also took Vincent d'Indy's course in analysis and a course in orchestration.

Many of his exercises and analyses have been preserved in the notebooks. "The beginning of your canon modulates too much," Roussel notes in a spidery hand on one of them. By 1908 Satie was himself again, entitling his exercises "Irksome Example" and "Agreeable Despair." He was given a piano piece by Ravel to analyze, and a Palestrina motet. Of the latter he wrote:

> The religiosity of this passage is immense. However each part is of very simple musical inspiration. I believe that the ecstatic charm revealed here is the consequence of the crossings of the vocal lines. . . . The seraphic musician must have been one of the greatest believers that ever lived.

Roussel, who had at first tried to dissuade Satie from studying because he already had a mature and original style, was not disappointed in the end. He wrote:

> . . . it seemed to me that his ironic smile signified "Oh, oh! So that's not allowed professor? Really? Well, that correction is just what I wanted. Here's some counterpoint without a wrinkle."
>
> But no, no irony at all; Satie brought me, with an utterly serious and convinced air, impeccable counterpoint exercises in an astonishing calligraphy, and his enthusiasm for Bach chorales would have set him apart even in an organ class.

In 1908 the Schola gave Satie a diploma which granted him the right "to devote himself exclusively to the study of composition." After that his silence became complete. He even stopped composing popular songs.

Photographs of Satie at this time show him with graying beard and short hair revealing Mephistophelean ears. His half-smiling eyes glinting behind his pince-nez gave him a goatlike, puckish look. He now wore a derby hat, high stiff collar, and dark suit, like a distinguished professor considerably older than his forty-four years. A respectable exterior was the best frame for his character.

In the winter of 1908–1909 he threw himself into local affairs in Arcueil. He became a member of the Radical-Socialist party and the local *patronage laïque* which performed various benevolent services. He took children of the neighborhood on outings to the country. His affections turned by natural inclination toward the young, and the young befriended him with enthusiasm and loyalty. He organized concerts and celebrations in Arcueil by inviting his Montmartre friends, and his activity was sufficiently outstanding to reach the attention of municipal authorities. Like Rousseau some twenty years earlier, but without any confusion over names, he was decorated in 1909 with the *Palmes académiques* during a ceremony complete with speeches and toasts. The people of Arcueil offered him a *Vin d'honneur* on the occasion, and afterward, the local paper reported, there was dancing until three in the morning. Before long Satie began giving courses in *solfège* every Sunday morning at ten: the shadow of Rousseau deepens. He contributed to the local paper a characteristic column called "A Fortnight in Society." Its sly humor must have puzzled suburban readers. The following year he resigned his duties and turned his attention back to music. Twelve years had passed and his second career was soon to begin.

Musically there is only one major event during these twelve long years. Debussy is reported to have told Satie in 1903 that his works did not observe a strict enough form; a few weeks later, according to this widely accepted version, Satie turned up with the sardonic title, *3 Morceaux en forme de poire,* followed by a more formless composition than ever which had nothing to do with pears or the number three. Whether or not Debussy ever offered such advice, we now know that *3 Morceaux* is an amalgam of short compositions, some of which date back as far as fifteen years, others of which he borrowed from the café concert songs he was producing in considerable number at the time. Satie's letters to Debussy that year, as well as the manuscript preserved in the Bibliothèque de l'Opéra, reveal that he worked through the summer of 1903 on what had begun as a shorter work with the title *2 Morceaux en forme de poire*.

Satie's most ambitious piano composition, *3 Morceaux* is also in many respects his most successful. The music (for four hands) calls for very competent performance without virtuoso technique. Phrasing and the proper emphasis of dissonance present the greatest difficulty. Thumbing his nose at the title, Satie really divided the piece into seven parts, to four of which he gave names used in the conservatory to designate parts of composition exercises.

After a playful double opening, the first "piece" consists of only thirty-six simple measures in 2/4 time, yet its construction shows as much originality as any section of the work. Starting with a tranquil melody in C minor, the harmony descends by thirds until everything is stopped dead by a fortissimo cadence in D minor which cancels all previous harmony. For once Satie uses the leading tone and lets us feel the full tonal finality of the V-I progression. Then he goes serenely on.

3 Morceaux, I
PRIMA

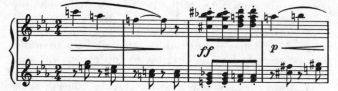

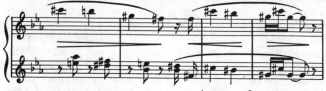

(continued on next page)

The arbitrary break occurs three times in the easily flowing line, as if such pure movement could not be left unmolested.

The heart of the work is in section II—the longest and the only one that falls into the ABA form. All of it, in its melodic and rhythmic characteristics, shows the influence of cabaret music. Between the brisk opening and closing parts lies a slow, lightly contrapuntal passage which introduces one of the most sustained melodic phrases Satie ever

SECONDA

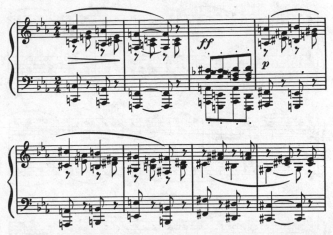

wrote. The progressions and melody are truly classic in their simplicity, with only a few chromatics toward the end. After a third "piece" full of syncopations, Satie wrote an *En plus* very much like another *Gymnopédie* in 4/4 time and not dressed up for four hands. Its almost motionless tilting between the first and second degrees instead of a conventional cadence has the effect of suspending the music in mid-air. The concluding *Redite* with its wandering tonal center and another unemphatic cadence provide a mere flattening out at the end rather than a recapitulation.

3 Morceaux contains everything Satie had learned up to 1903—and more. It surpasses such works as *Pièces froides* in rhythmic variety and sureness of melodic line. He showed surprising skill in assembling heterogeneous materials and coupling the pieces in a whole. The very fact of a sustained composition running twenty minutes in performance implies his growing confidence; up to that point his longest work had been the highly repetitive *Messe des pauvres*. Most important of all, he now reunited a seriously split musical career. Along with the semireligious, experi-

3 Morceaux, II
PRIMA

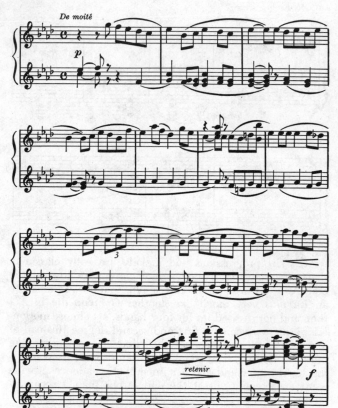

mental, and frequently heavy-handed music written between 1887 and 1900, Satie was also composing popular waltzes and songs for the cabaret artists he accompanied, pieces in which his fascination with sonority had to give

SECONDA

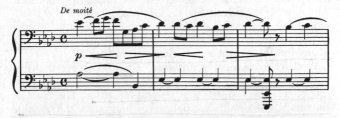

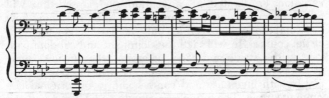

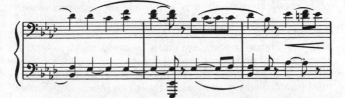

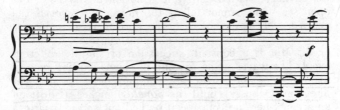

way to horizontal movement and melody. *La diva de l'empire* (1900–1903) begins to feel its way toward uninhibited exploitation of syncopations and ragtime rhythms. "Jazz," Satie observed in one of his notebooks, "shouts its sorrows at us, and we don't give a damn. That's why it's fine, real." In *3 Morceaux* the popular side of Satie's work makes its presence felt alongside his sonorous, "serious" style. Without this coupling, both styles might have declined into a fixed pattern of composition. But in

1903 cabaret sprightliness blended constructively with the modal and harmonic tendencies of the Rose-Croix manner. The new style revived early accomplishments of the *Gymnopédies* and the *Gnossiennes* and opened a path into the future. One can now ask the pertinent question: Is this in any but the loosest sense "classical" music?

A strictly classical symphony, a work of symmetrical movement and proportion, lays out its course in the first few pages—even in the first several measures. The themes, the tempi, the tonality are defined or suggested; the possible variations are limited by convention; the elapsed time will fall between ten and thirty minutes. We do not know how the composer will cover it, but we have a general idea of the course. He will take the dominant and subdominant keys in this stride and carry us around the outside course of the slow movement. Above all, he will develop certain motifs with ingenuity and come home to his original key running strong. The miracle of Haydn and Mozart and the great classical composers is a miracle of performance on famous courses—the symphony, the quartet, the variation, the suite. Increasingly with Beethoven, Brahms, and Wagner, the course opens out into a cross-country—travel across unexplored areas where the terrain cannot be predicted. Yet one feels the reality of their progress across solid ground, where musical analysis can follow and survey the advance. With Debussy it is no longer dry land, but open sea. One cannot tell if the music moves or if the ocean merely flows about it; the horizon is so remote as to offer no point of reference. What one feels in *Pelléas* or *La Mer* is a constant succession of slightly different events like waves going by, and of slowly shifting moods, like the moods of a seascape. The movement has no clear direction. Debussy (until the *Sonatas*) makes us drift on an ocean where no course can be laid out and no bearings taken. Like Wagner

Satie, too, abandoned dry land, but not to drift like Debussy. It is as if he spent his life watching the waves breaking on a tiny section of shore, fascinated by both the monotony and the variety of their fall. Form in Satie means neither a course nor a drifting. It is a fascination with a series of points which turn out to be one point. His music progresses by standing still. The *ostinato* bass suggests permanent movement and permanent rest. It can be heard to mean that all parts are different or that all are the same. Fragmentary mosaic construction, approaching extreme brevity, and experiments with pure sonority exclude development. Without it all parts of a work can be simultaneously present with no need for recapitulation. The simplest of Satie's pieces, some of the humoristic works and children's pieces built out of a handful of notes and rhythms are the most enigmatic for this very reason: they have no beginning, middle, and end. They exist simultaneously. Form ceases to be an ordering in time like ABA and reduces to a single brief image, an instantaneous whole both fixed and moving. Satie's form can be extended only by reiteration or "endurance."

There is a trivial feature of Satie's music that takes on significance in this context. His first major sets of pieces all contain three parts: three *Sarabandes,* three *Gymnopédies,* three *Gnossiennes.* Of the fifty-odd works that followed, almost half are similarly threefold. This trinitarian obsession was a quirk which became part of his musical pose. But in about eight works—clearly in the three mentioned above—the arrangement stands for a formal approach to his material. Satie takes one musical idea and, instead of developing it at length and working variations on it, regards it briefly from three different directions. He varies only the bare contour, the notes in the melody but not its general shape, the chords in the accompaniment but not its dominant mood. An artist drawing a head from three different sides could obtain the same effect. There are obvious grounds for comparison of this procedure with that of the cubists. They investigated the complexity in time and space of a simple object studied simultaneously from several points of view. Satie frequently scrutinizes a very simple musical object: a short, unchanging *ostinato* accompaniment plus a fragmentary melody. Out of this sameness comes subtle variety. Far from being a mere trick, this serial construction illustrates one of Satie's principal resources—brevity as pure form. So used, it is surprising and humorous. Only Anton Webern has gone as far in exploring the art of brevity in music, with his *Five Pieces for Orchestra* (Op. 10, 1911–1913). Even the most intense of conductors cannot play these thirty-second fragments of tone color without smiling. Brevity in music is inescapably comic and, as Satie employed it by threes, inescapably plastic.

Satie was not alone in this readjustment of formal values. Ravel achieved a contrasting effect in the monotony of *Boléro*. Its development is restricted to dynamics, tempo, and pitch. The initial musical idea never budges. Where Satie abandoned traditional unity through reducing the dimensions of his work to those of a miniature, Debussy and Mahler (differently) go in the opposite direction.* Their music swells and overflows the confines of musical expression on every side. It has no beginning or end, not because they come too close together to be distinguished, as in Satie, but because they lie too immensely far apart. Extreme brevity and extreme length both exist outside of conventional form in art. In his revision of the classical set-course attitude toward musical composition, Satie was discovering the possibility of telescoping time, of planting the whole world in an instant. These are the strivings of a new sensibility.

In the last analysis, Satie seems to combine experiment and inertia. The earmarks of his later work were already visible at the turn of the century. From the *Sarabandes* to the last ballets, he never abandoned parallel fourths and fifths. Transposition and modulation did not concern him. Was he incapable of writing proper voice leading, or did he choose to ignore it? The question has no answer. There are passages in Daumier where caricature cannot be distinguished from systematic exploration of positions of the human body. We can easily come to regard Satie as a children's composer, putting together small musical objects and enjoying the unexpected and refreshing effects he could obtain. Through brevity and open construction he kept his works free of any inexorable unraveling in time. They establish a pattern of sound as delicate and surprising as that of an aeolian harp.

* Debussy admired Satie's *Sarabandes* so much that he wrote one on the same pattern in *Pour le piano* (1901). He also orchestrated two of the *Gymnopédies* and did so with Satie's entire approval, according to the conductor, Gustave Douet, who first performed them. Yet an aesthetic distance separated the two friends, and Satie stated it incisively when he produced the lively acerbities of *3 Morceaux*.

If the *Sarabandes* foretell the course of French music to 1914, the *Gymnopédies* and the *Gnossiennes* foretell the turn it was to take after the war. Satie may, indeed, have confounded himself a little with these contrasting styles. That would explain his long silences, his bold return to the starting point, and the slow crystallization of his late manner. After *3 Morceaux*, it was seven more years before he broke his silence again.

{ *6* }

SCANDAL, BOREDOM,
AND CLOSET MUSIC

Satie's career after 1910, his second coming, has frequently
been recounted, for it lies within the memory of many
people who are still living. The time came to "discover" his
disconcerting genius, yet it was the same personality
whose antics had startled Montmartre twenty years earlier.
The century had taken its first steps. Fauvism and then
cubism had replaced impressionism as the artistic avant-
garde; the principal figures of the "New Spirit" in literature,
Apollinaire and Jacob, were working in close touch with
painters; the Ballets Russes would soon shock Paris with
the distinctly fauve rhythms of Stravinsky's *Sacre de printemps;* Debussy was attracting disciples and imitators. It
turned out that Satie himself had been changing and could
not be relied on to act as if he had been dead for twelve
years. His new works belied all preconceived ideas about
his style. It was for these pieces that Satie wrote the publisher's blurb (quoted on pages 113–14).

Not unlike Rousseau being feted by the cubists, Satie
was "taken up" in the years 1910–14 by his old friends
Ravel and Debussy. Since these two composers were no
longer on amicable terms, they appeared to vie for the
rights to rediscover Monsieur le Pauvre, as Satie came to
be called. In January, 1911, at the recently formed Société
Indépendante Musicale (S.I.M.), sponsored by Fauré,
Ravel performed three of Satie's works composed more
than twenty years earlier. The program spoke warmly of

"a prescience of the modernist vocabulary" and "the quasi-prophetic character of certain harmonic discoveries." A few months later, at the Cercle Musical, Debussy conducted two *Gymnopédies*, which he had orchestrated in 1897. Roland-Manuel, who had been an enthusiastic young class-mate of Satie's at the Schola, orchestrated the prelude of *La porte héroïque du ciel* (1894) for the S.I.M. in 1912. The critics Calvocoressi, Ecorcheville, and others wrote increasingly sympathetic notices. The publication of 3 *Morceaux*, eight years after its composition, left no room for doubt abut his talents.

At first he was as delighted as a child, yet he quickly tired of people turning invariably to his earliest works. Publishers, sniffing a fashion, requested his music, but Durand nevertheless rejected in succession *Préludes flasques (pour un chien)* and *Véritables préludes flasques* (1912), the "real" version. Satie wrote them in a new style of which he had given notice in 1897 with *Pièces froides* and in 1903 with 3 *Morceaux*. Bare, linear, abrupt piano pieces with coy comments were not what people wanted to "rediscover."

As he made clear in a lecture, Satie was disappointed. "I wrote my *Sarabandes* at twenty-one in 1887; my *Gym-nopédies* at twenty-two in 1888. They are my only works that my detractors admire—my detractors in their fifties of course. Logically they might equally well like the works of my maturity, of their companion in Age. But no." And he wrote with the same bitterness to his brother, telling of how he came out of d'Indy's Schola full of hope and confidence in his new knowledge.

> My first work in this direction is a choral and fugue for four hands. I have had a good share of heckling in my life, but I was never so scorned. What had I been up to with d'Indy? I used to write such charm-ing things. And now! What a show off! what cheek! . . .
>   That's life, my boy. You can't make head nor tail of it.

His dander up, Satie ignored his reputation as the precursor of impressionism and turned out the best of his so-called "humoristic" piano works: *Croquis et agaceries d'un gros bonhomme en bois* (1913), *Chapitres tournés en tous sens* (1913), *Sports et divertissements* (1914). These amount to a new genre, a style that resists performance and partakes of the elusive personality of the composer. The most faithful of his followers did not know what to make of the change.

The title "humoristic" for the years 1908 to 1916 has ample justification but scarcely describes the shift in his style. Except for an occasional disconcerting harmony, he now abandoned vertically stressed construction and wrote spare, two-part counterpoint. These works, most of them for piano solo, demonstrate with what paucity of materials he could form a complete musical composition. By 1912 Satie had achieved an individual keyboard style of great economy and flexibility. The "humor" in the works of this period resides to a great measure in the titles and in the gnomic texts which pepper the scores. He concocted ironic instructions on interpretation (the famous "Like a nightingale with a toothache"), ludicrous dreamlike scenarios ("The man who carried huge rocks"), and parodies on the current fad of Spanish themes (a Hispano-Parisian *"Espagna"* about the *"Puerta Maillot"* and the *"Rue de Madrid"*).* In addition to this, Satie's melodies allude with mock innocence to every genre of music: nursery rhymes, operettas, Chopin (deliberately labeled Schumann), and Gregorian chant.

By its characteristic eccentricity, one composition in 1914 begs for comment and quotation. It is *Sports et divertissements,* a large (almost two feet square) sumptuous publication in facsimile which reproduces the meticulousness of Satie's calligraphy in black ink on a red staff.† These twenty snatches of music, never over a page long and each

---

* The score of *Heures séculaires et instantanées* (1914) contains Satie's ultimatum about written texts: "I prohibit any person to read the texts aloud during the period of musical performance. Every infraction will arouse my just indignation against the culprit. He will be granted no mercy." Satie understood that the literary side of his music was beginning to become a distraction, yet he could not suppress it.

† The story is that the publishers originally commissioned Stravinsky to compose a work. He declined, maintaining that the fee was too small. When the same proposal was made to the poverty-stricken Satie, he also declined at first, maintaining that the fee was insultingly large.

accompanied by an amazing illustration by Charles Martin,
remain almost unknown. The text is seminarrative, the tone
blithely ironic, and Satie obviously wrote with close attention to the appearance of the notes and rests on the page.
After some opening comments exhorting readers to turn
the pages of the score with "an amiable and smiling finger,"
the "*Chorale inappétissant*" (reproduced) continues the
cross grain of absurdity through the clear lines of its logic.
It might almost be an exercise in appoggiaturas and sonorities built up by fourths. Without fail the dissonances
resolve in an unexpected manner, and the Chorale sneaks
slyly back to C major. These twenty seconds of music
seem both obvious and perverse. "*Water-Chute*" (reproduced) starts off with an enticing waltz in D major, again
with chromatic effects and nonharmonic tones introduced
by constant appoggiaturas. The water slide is clearly visible
on the page, and the harmony wanders off at the end in
a seventh chord in first inversion. Others of these pieces
show different characteristics: bitonality ("*La Pêche*"),
facetious "spelling" of chords ("*Bain de mer*"), a poly-
chordal arpeggio with the tonic and dominant seventh
chords sounding together to replace a cadence ("*Le
Golf*"*), inversions of the accompaniment ("*Le Pieuvre*"),
and a travesty of the *Marseillaise* ("*Les Courses*"). *Sports
et divertissements* has been compared to Japanese haikai,
and it does indeed relate to the oriental tradition that iden-
tifies calligraphy and poetry. In the formal history of
Western music, *Sports et divertissements* cannot hold anything but a peripheral place. But it remains perhaps the
sole example of a modern work that combines, precariously
but successfully, calligraphy, painting, poetry and music.

Brevity, harmonic bareness and even cliché, increasing
rhythmic interest, a fondness for two-part variations and
for a single line over an insistent *ostinato* bass, a tendency
to mold music to a descriptive text—these characteristics
of the humoristic period were rooted both in the direct
appeal of the cabaret music and in the counterpoint that
Satie studied at the Schola. These keen-edged pieces start

---

* The text is typical and defies translation. "*Le colonel est
vêtu de 'Scotch Tweed' d'un vert violent. Il sera victorieux. Son
'caddie' portant les 'bags.' Les nuages sont étonnés. Les 'holes'
sont tout tremblants: le colonel est là! Le voici qui assure le
coup: son 'club' vole en éclats!*"

Préface

Cette publication est constituée de deux éléments artistiques : Thème, musique.

La partie thématique est figurée par des Traits — Des Traits à l'esprit ; la partie musicale est représentée par des points — Des points noirs. Ces deux parties réunies — en un seul volume — forment un Tout : un album.

Je conseille de feuilleter ce livre, d'un doigt aimable & souriant ; car c'est ici une œuvre de fantaisie. Que l'on n'y voie pas autre chose.

Pour les "Recroquevillés" & les "Abâtardis", j'ai écrit un choral grave & convenable. Ce choral est une sorte de préambule amer, une manière d'introduction austère & infonde. J'y ai mis tout ce que je connais sur l'Ennui.

Je dédie ce choral à ceux qui ne m'aiment pas.

Je me retire.

Erik SATIE

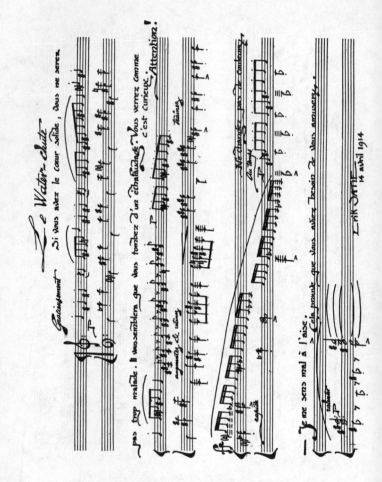

from scratch in that they take no musical tradition for granted, and that meant rejecting some of the most convenient and tyrannical elements of musical notation. All Satie's works from 1910 to 1915 except his songs appear in published form without bar lines and key signatures, and the scheme now seems fully appropriate to his droll and limpid style. (At this time Apollinaire was proceeding almost identically in respect to punctuation and typography of poetry.)

Some forms of the comic in music are fairly obvious— undisguised mimicry in certain Renaissance madrigals, Mozart's and Weber's bitonal jokes, the humorous quoting in Debussy's *Général Lavine—eccentric*. Of all musical compositions, the raucous contrivings of Prokofiev (*Scherzo humoristique*, Op. 12, *Sarcasmes*, Op. 17) come closest to Satie's mood. The comic strain in Satie's music, however, never leaves pathos far behind. It mixes our feelings much the way a puppet theater provokes laughter compounded of sympathy and sadism. *Sports et divertissements* and the other successful humoristic pieces have the tiny dimensions and the vast appeal of a guignol performance. They demand not the perfection of a single performance, but the familiarity of frequent repetition.

Recognition in musical circles brought Satie the opportunity to enter the world of fashionable *salons* in Paris. With his distinguished appearance, puckish behavior, and refusal to speak about his private affairs and troubles, he was quickly accepted. Several hostesses asked him to perform his works in their drawing rooms, and this kind of lionizing permitted him to supplement his practically nonexistent finances. In 1916 one of the select events of the season was a Granados-Satie concert sponsored by Picasso and Matisse and attended by the most fashionable of cultivated audiences. But social success did not make him change his ways. After his discovery by Paris audiences, after the generalized outrage of his humoristic period, it is as if Satie turned his career into a series of scandals in order to complete the record of escapades that had distinguished his Montmartre days. For him scandal was both deliberate and inevitable in that it sprang from his uncompromising manner of following his own bent, of ignoring what was expected of him, and of burning his bridges behind him. He was, in the words of the Irish saying, "dead, but he won't lie down." To many of his contemporaries, the fifty-year-old composer seemed merely to be involving himself in one noisy demonstration after another. In all, there were five, beginning with the historic performance of *Parade* by Diaghilev's Ballets Russes in 1917.

In 1915 Satie, who at forty-eight was behaving like a happy schoolboy helping to organize the militia of Arcueil, met Jean Cocteau, the spirited young poet of twenty-six who had seen action by volunteering his services in two private ambulance corps organized by friends of his. Cocteau heard Satie and Viñes play 3 *Morceaux* and immediately proposed to Diaghilev that he and Satie collaborate on a ballet.* Cocteau left a sheaf of notes with Satie. Picasso was later brought in for the sets—his first venture in the theater. Diaghilev approved. Cocteau, Picasso, and Massine began work in Rome while Satie, in Paris, laid out a straightforward score decorated with parts for typewriters, sirens, airplane propellers, Morse tickers, and lottery wheels. (Because of crowding in the orchestra pit and lack of equipment, many of them were omitted in the performance.) In a letter to Madame Edwards,† to whom he apparently intended to dedicate it, he revealed that work on his new *truc* (number) had obliged him to put aside a setting of some La Fontaine fables. La Fontaine never reappeared.

Picasso designed sets and costumes that combined his harlequin and geometric-cubist periods. Rehearsals in Paris

---

* In an earlier aborted collaboration of Cocteau and Edgard Varèse, several composers, including Debussy, Stravinsky, Roussel, Ravel, Florent Schmitt, and Satie, were asked to contribute incidental music for a circus version of *A Midsummer Night's Dream*. Oberon was to have made his entrance into the ring of the Cirque Médrano to the strains of *Tipperary*.

† Nee Misia Godebska, this irresistible female became, successively, Madame Thadée Natanson and therefore hostess to the Revue Blanche group including Jarry and Apollinaire, Mallarmé and Renoir; then Madame Alfred Edwards, wife of one of the most powerful and wealthy newspaper publishers in Paris; and finally Madame Sert, wife of the Spanish muralist and famous for her *salon* of artistic celebrities. Her memoirs, modestly entitled *Misia*, are unavoidably fascinating. Satie, through Ravel, knew her as a young woman.

were stormy, with Satie protesting against Cocteau's un-
manageable "libretto," which in fact barely survived. It
was probably Diaghilev himself, then living in Rome and
hobnobbing with the futurists, who tossed in the idea of
sound effects. Apollinaire wrote an enthusiastic statement
for the program pronouncing on the "New Spirit" and (it
was the first use of the word anywhere) the "surrealism"
of the venture. *Les Sylphides* and *Petrouchka* were on the
same program at the *générale* for the benefit of the War
Fund, May 18, 1917. Ansermet conducted.

The Paris public, starved for distraction during the long
crises of the war, at last found something to vociferate
about. Ignoring the music, they heard only the seasoning
of sound effects and called it a "din." On stage they saw
not a ballet but a road show. According to plan, the
incidental racket and the manager's costumes (built ten
feet high into "moving scenery") seemed to overwhelm the
essentially modest music and dance movements. Though
the occasion could not rival the *première* of *Ubu Roi*, whistling and clapping intermingled in the auditorium, and a
few fists were raised. Satie was delighted and, according
to one witness, joined in the whistling from the front row
of the balcony. The conservative critics reacted scornfully
to Picasso's designs and to the music, several of them using
the epithet *Boche*. It was not difficult in those days of
heightened emotions to persuade people that such antics,
supposedly aimed at a new aesthetic, were in reality a
German-engineered attempt to undermine the solidarity
of French culture. One of the critics so outraged Satie
with his account that the composer sent him an insulting
post card and found himself involved in a damage suit.*
Cocteau waxed eloquent in Satie's defense before an un-
comprehending magistrate and was himself taken into
custody for insulting the opposing lawyer. Satie was sentenced to a week in prison and ordered to pay one thousand
francs' damages. Max Jacob describes Satie's condition in
a letter to Jacques Doucet, wealthy *couturier* and patron
of the arts.

> Satie will have a court record and will no longer be
> played in any national theatre. He will be refused

* The card, to Jean Poueigh of the *Carnet de la Semaine*,
read: "*Monsieur et cher ami, Vous n'êtes qu'un cul, mais un
cul sans musique.* Erik Satie."

the right to travel, America will be closed to him, and Spain, and what have you . . . so he thinks his life is ruined, annihilated.

It required several months of appeal and agitation by friends before the sentence was lightened.

This was not the only misfortune caused by *Parade*, for its performance helped precipitate the final break between Satie and Debussy. When Satie's persistence in his new career had won him recognition as the opponent of impressionism and the champion of younger schools, Debussy was puzzled. The author of *Pelléas* had now become an invalid and was modifying his style in the last *Sonatas*. But if Debussy felt out of touch and neglected by his friend, Satie, in turn, felt that Debussy begrudged him a tardy rise to fame. After the storm over *Parade*, Satie was hurt that he received no word of congratulation from the man whose early works had seemed to immobilize Satie and leave him no direction in which to move. Finally, in 1918, Satie wrote a letter of bitter reproach to his friend and caused him one of the most miserable moments during the year of his death. Later Satie was filled with remorse over his gesture. The often-quoted appraisal by Louis Laloy (whom Satie treated as a deadly enemy) gives a good picture of their friendship.

They were like two brothers, the one rich, the other poor, the one generous but conscious of his superiority; the other unhappy beneath his jester's mask, hiding his feeling of inferiority, but keeping up his jokes in order to amuse his host; each on guard against the other, but all the time bound by ties of genuine affection.

If Satie's intransigence enabled him to survive, it also lost him his best friend.

Though pursued by ill luck in later performances, and rarely seen, *Parade* had done its work. More than any single event at that time, it set the tone for the postwar years— the tone defined by Jarry, promoted by the Rousseau banquet, and now offered to a wider public. It was a serious-humorous exploitation of popular elements in art, a turning to jazz and music hall and to all the paraphernalia of modern life, not in a spirit of realism, but with a sense of

exhilaration in the absurd.* At the end of their collaboration, the authors understood the importance of what they
had accomplished. Also, a few others did. Carl Van Vechten, one of Satie's early admirers, wrote back to the United
States about it. Auric called *Parade* "the work of which I
would be the first to say that in pure emotion it equals the
noblest pages of Boris." The scandal of *Parade* made Satie's
reputation at fifty, as *Ubu Roi* made Jarry's at twenty-three.

"*Grosse action toute simple qui groupe les charmes du
cirque et du Music-Hall,*" wrote Cocteau in the notebook
he left with Satie. "A simple roughly outlined action which
combines the attractions of circus and music hall." Cocteau
had begun by setting down the Larousse definition of
parade ("a comic act, put on at the entrance of a traveling
theater to attract a crowd") and went on to elaborate a
scheme (it was not used) of delivering lines through holes
in the scenery. The rest of Cocteau's rich flow of ideas
about modern properties and movements simmered down
into what was finally called a *ballet réaliste*. The action revolves around the fact that the crowd, mistaking the
parade for the real act, never enters the tent despite increasingly hysterical persuasions. With this "book" Satie
labored long—over a year—to write a suitably impersonal
score. Fourteen years after *3 Morceaux*, it stands as his
second summation.

Eight notebooks full of *brouillons* for the music, kept
with the Conservatory collection of manuscripts, and a fair
copy of the score in Cocteau's notebook make several revelations. Satie worked first to find his themes, and then laid
out his times and keys. Often it is the bass line that he

* Jazz reached Paris the year after *Parade*, when a Negro
orchestra from America played at the Casino de Paris. It became fashionable in the twenties, when Cocteau and *les Six*
adopted the Bar Gaya as their haunt. Here the enterprising
pianist Jean Wiener, who had helped make Satie's music known
before the war, earned his keep by playing jazz with a Negro
saxophonist by the name of Vance Lowry. The Bar Gaya lost
out to another fashionable *boîte de nuit*, Le Boeuf sur le Toit,
made famous by Milhaud's and Cocteau's ballet-mime of the
same title. After Stravinsky had introduced its most primitive
African rhythms in *Sacre du printemps* (1913), Satie discovered the contemporary mood of jazz ("it shouts its sorrows") and wrote into *Parade* its first concert treatment in
French music.

completes before the rest. At the very beginning he decides on the conclusion, for immediately after the opening "Prelude of the Red Curtain" he notes, "to finish the ballet," and composes the recapitulation of the fugue and its final cadence. In several instances, having set down the parts with only accidentals, he indicates a key and reminds himself, "Put in the signature." Satie understood the totally different demands of solo piano music with humorous insinuations, and of a full-length ballet involving the collaboration of a hundred-odd artists and stage crew. This time, therefore, he constructed as an architect, with a concern for clear usable space rather than for the gemlike effects of *Sports et divertissements.*

After an unhurried "Choral" comes the "Prelude of the Red Curtain," inscribed in manuscript to Picasso, who designed and painted for the performance a quiet scene of circus performers. The action opens with the "First Manager" (really a barker or hawker) in a vibrant yet pathetic dance to a simple rhythmic theme endlessly repeated.

Parade, First Manager theme

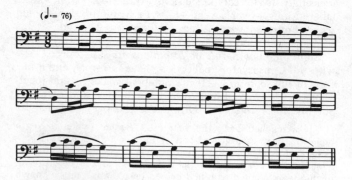

The effect is of compulsive, half-comical activity as the manager, in Picasso's "costume" of ponderous cubist constructions, attempts to attract people's attention. The "Chinese Prestidigitator," in his celebrated garb of vermilion, yellow, and black, enters to a relentless *ostinato* accompaniment in both high treble and bass. Massine took the enigmatic role himself, with pigtail, much bowing and fire-eating, and a vanishing and reappearing egg. Afterward, "a mime with an organ point" brings in the second or "American Manager," who wears a "skyscraper" on his back and stamps like "an organized accident . . . with the strictness of a fugue." The "Little American Girl" introduces the "Steamship Rag" (*Ragtime du paquebot*). Despite humorous syncopations and an exaggerated climax, these jazz passages bear the direction "Sad." In rapid succession the girl mimes the action of catching a train, driving a car, swimming, acting in a movie, and foiling a holdup— with sound effects for each. The third manager, on horseback, performs without music and presents the next act, the two "Acrobats," who tumble to a fast waltz accented with xylophones.

In a sudden change of pace, the managers return and try desperately to keep the crowd from dispersing. They fail. A "Finale" recalls a bare minimum of themes, and the ballet is drawing to a close. The managers fall exhausted, the Little American Girl is in tears, the Chinese Prestidigitator remains impassive. On the last page seven slow measures bring us full circle back to the opening theme and end in a wistful cadence sidling off into C major.

An enumerative description of *Parade* leaves the impression that the ballet is composed of a great number of small units following one another rapidly and with little preparation. Part of the quality of *Parade* does reside in just such a nervous shifting of mood and theme and in the avoidance of any long development section. But Satie framed the mosaic-like texture of his music within a double portal: the fugue, which provides a continuity for the scattered action by returning at the end; and the managers' theme, whose rugged musical structure is also repeated during the final moments. The principal numbers of the ballet achieve a different sort of existence—a self-sufficiency comparable to that of objects in cubist paintings. Satie's quoting of popular themes amounts to a form of musical collage; his economical orchestration corresponds to the cubists' restraint in using color; and his raucous noise effects correspond to their experiments with new surface textures.

But such correlations are never entirely valid. *Parade* belongs as much to the tradition of tuneful, rhythmic French dance music as to the new cubist aesthetic. What stands out as eminently "modern" about *Parade*—modern in the sense of expressing the whole artistic attitude of the

twenties even though written in 1916–1917—is its use of
popular themes and jazz, its festive mood, and the clear
lines of its organization. Debussy's ballet *Jeux,* composed
only four years earlier, still offered a shimmering surface,
wispy, evanescent melody, and tennis players lost in a
Watteau-like *décor.* Satie, on the other hand, making sure
of his melody and rhythm, took liberties which establish
him unmistakably in the twentieth century.

The novelty and success of *Parade* naturally inspired
young composers to seek out Satie, especially men of an
independent bent who admired Satie's unstifled freedom.
The first composers to associate themselves with him were
Auric, Durey, Honegger, and, later, Germaine Tailleferre
("our Marie Laurencin"). In June, 1917, Blaise Cendrars
helped organize their first concert in a painter's studio.
Satie, referring loosely to *les Nouveaux Jeunes,* introduced
them to the public the following year at the Vieux Colombier Theater. Milhaud, recently returned from South
America, and then Poulenc joined the group, as well as
Cocteau, whose contribution was the brilliant pamphlet
Coq et Arlequin. Milhaud best describes their feelings.

> It was then that Erik Satie let us hear, intact and
> discovered afresh, enriched with a new simplicity
> and poverty, the voice which belongs to French
> music freed of every foreign influence. The art of
> Erik Satie was a veritable Renaissance. . . . Dur-
> ing all that time he was content to sniff out a move-
> ment, to indicate a direction; then he stepped back,
> leaving to others the task of committing all their
> strength along the path he had indicated. (*Etudes.*)

Not until 1920, however, did Henri Collet's designation,
les Six, fasten itself to this diverse group at the moment of
the first public performance of Satie's *Socrate.** Meanwhile,
Cocteau began publishing his lively broadside *Le Coq,*
which championed the movement and included much of
Satie's laconic writing. *Les Six* collaborated on only one
work, *Les mariés de la tour Eiffel,* and then went their

* Collet's lengthy article appeared in two successive issues of
the weekly paper *Comœdia* (Jan. 16 and 23, 1920), and bore
the title, "*Un livre de Rimsky et un livre de Cocteau—les cinq
Russes et les six Français.*"

separate ways. Satie later quarreled with Poulenc over the *Mercure*, and with Auric on the same account plus a torn umbrella. Despite his proneness to squabbling, however, it was Satie's personality that attracted the young as much as his music. Ambition and fashion left him untouched. When Auric, before they had met, wrote a laudatory article on Satie, the older composer paid a personal call on the beginner and expressed his amazement that anyone could admire his work so unreservedly. Refusing the title and role of *maître*, he showed his work to his "disciples" and asked their advice. And he had their interest genuinely at heart. Once, after a towering and apparently final quarrel with Sauguet, Satie abandoned his intransigence and made up with him through a characteristic exchange of *pneumatiques*. The opportunity had arisen to introduce Sauguet to Diaghilev at a luncheon and possibly to arrange the commissioning of a ballet by the young composer. Beneath Satie's crusty unpredictableness lay a gentleness as true as Rousseau's and a loyalty which few could mistake.

The fact that *Parade* brought the beginning of Satie's fame as a composer had its inevitable result: he abandoned that line of attack. As his next partners in scandal, he picked Plato and Socrates instead of any contemporaries. "Plato," he wrote to Valentine Hugo, "is a perfect collaborator, very mild and never importunate." The thought of a musical setting for the *Dialogues* is disturbing enough; that the composer of *Parade* should attempt to write one looked like ignorance or bravado. Yet he was not alone in his reorientation toward a classic line. At this same moment, his recent collaborator, Picasso, without abandoning his cubist style, was beginning a series of magnificent, limpid, figure drawings of classical subjects. Stravinsky had just completed *Pulcinella*.

After having had the idea for more than two years, Satie was commissioned in 1919 by the Princess Edmond de Polignac to set the Death of Socrates to music. The American-born princess and Singer sewing-machine heiress had one of the most brilliant musical *salons* in Paris. Stravinsky had composed *Renard* for her three years earlier. Satie now produced *Socrate*, a *drame symphonique* for voice and orchestra using Victor Cousin's translation, which he rewrote as he went along. It was performed in the princess's *salon*, and soon after at Adrienne Monnier's book-

store, Les Amis du Livre, in the Rue de l'Odéon. Claudel,
Gide, Jammes, Sylvia Beach, Milhaud, and Cocteau were
present at the latter performance. In January, 1920, the full
orchestral version of the work was presented at the Société
Nationale. Some of the audience giggled at the surface monotony of the work; the critics disagreed violently among
themselves. Jean Marnold of the *Mercure de France* called
it a "nullity" and a steal from *Boris* and *Pelléas;* Charles
Kœchlin thought highly of it. For *les Six* it became their
first rallying point.

But why Socrates? It is not easy to understand how the
humoristic period led to Plato's dialogues. Yet Satie had
begun work on *Socrate* in 1917, before the performance of
Parade. Probably there was some identification—Satie, the
sage of music, associating with the young and playing the
role of gadfly and midwife, fancying his life and the injustice of his treatment by the world as similar to Socrates'
career. He rose to the occasion.

Constant Lambert, after a sympathetic discussion of
Satie's earlier music, suggests that in *Socrate* "rigor mortis"
is beginning to set in. André Cœuroy wonders if *Socrate* is
not a work of supreme irony, intended to dupe or affront
its audiences. Alfred Cortot classifies it as "furniture music."
For the first performance, Satie himself printed the following statement in the *Guide du concert:* "Those who do not
understand [*Socrate*] are requested to assume an attitude of
submissiveness and inferiority." Most people, of course,
have not understood—including many of those who have
glibly called it his masterpiece. *Socrate* is that rare phenomenon, utterly *white* music, which denies its own existence as it goes along by an absolute refusal of development. Both rhythm and melody in Western tradition rely
on a fine balance between repetition and variation. Satie
wrote *Socrate* in figures that are endlessly repeated and
scarcely varied at all. Yet the music never stands still. At
a time when the ingredients of musical composition were
being measured out afresh by Stravinsky in *Les noces*
(1914-23) and by Berg in *Wozzeck* (1914-1920), Satie
attempted in *Socrate* a new balance between monotony
and variety.

Drame symphonique—symphonic drama—reads the subtitle. Satie's irony confined itself to this description. *Socrate*
is neither dramatic nor symphonic except insofar as Soc-

rates' life and death provide a dramatic subject. Satie works like a good printer, who would never add exclamation marks to a sentence or put a black border around the death scene. His instrumentation* calls for a chamber, not a symphony, orchestra. "Symphonic drama" inflates to Mahler-like proportions what should be called a "chamber oratorio."

Plato came first. Victor Cousin's translation carries a more Gallic flavor than Greek, but it has the virtue of bareness. Satie prepared the text like a surgeon grafting flesh. He detached sentences and paragraphs so skillfully that the *Phaedo*, one hundred and forty pages in the original French, reduces to a supple narrative of a few hundred words for Part Three of *Socrate*. He made additional changes by dropping unnecessary adjectives and modifying phrases. The manuscript shows him changing *"du reste"* to *"en fait"* to *"en vérité"* and then rejecting all of them. Satie did not linger over the philosophical sections except to skim off one or two poetic images—the song of the dying swan, for instance. He portrayed Socrates the man, first in daily life, then facing death.

There is none of the stolid proportion of a Greek temple in the music of *Socrate*. It has, rather, the decorative quality of a well-shaped and well-painted vase. The music is flat and monochrome, and any changes in tension occur without fanfare, like shifts to a new band of decoration. His treatment of the text demands these musical qualities. Debussy's great revision of vocal technique in *Pelléas* consisted in writing according to the emotional pressure of the words and in allowing a single pitch to carry a number of syllables without forming any melodic line. Satie followed not so much the poetic line of the text as its purely prose rhythms, its quality as speech. Thus he directs the performers: *"Récit (en lisant)."* The phrasing and the note values of the melodic line rarely conflict with the breath and syllable stress of normal speech. Words like death and love and soul are not prolonged or embroidered.

Once started, the vocal line scarcely pauses. The absence of chromatics, sudden rhythmic changes, and strong dynamics precludes any interruption or emphasis. The singers have no chance to project musical values more strongly

* Flute, oboe, English horn, clarinet, bassoon, trumpet, French horn, harp, tympani, and strings.

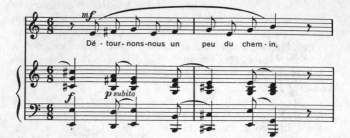

Dé - tour - nons-nous un peu du chem - in,

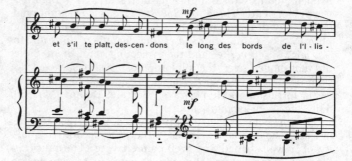

et s'il te plaît, des - cen - dons le long des bords de l'I - lis -

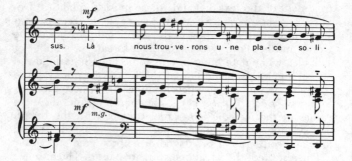

sus. Là nous trou - ve - rons u - ne pla - ce so - li -

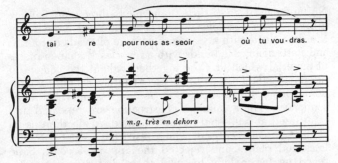

than the text. It flows on and on in stepwise movement without the motiv structure which characterizes Western melody until Wagner. There is melody, but no "tune." The second section, "Banks of the Ilissus," opens with a characteristic passage. (See illustration pages 162–63.) The music, like the text, never raises its voice. The quarter and eighth notes do not cluster together in rhythmic patterns but spread out in slow undulations, always modal, never cadencing with finality.

The accompaniment has a different scheme, not unlike that of the movie music he composed a few years later. For each section, Satie finds an *ostinato* phrase or a short sequence in the orchestra. It is repeated many times and then moves up or down a small interval.

Socrate, III

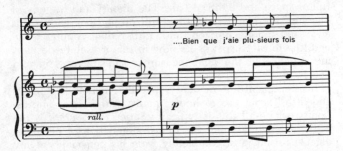

No modulation gives these movements direction; they are arbitrary transpositions which continue until Satie wipes the slate clean with a scalewise passage of triads or fourths and starts again. He builds with a few clearly shaped pieces of material which fit close together without the cement of harmonic relationships. The pieces rarely contain a clear dominant or follow a traditional progression even in the sequences. These units of construction are repeated and transposed at will—but never extended. Again there is an analogy to early cubism, which restricted itself to straight lines and planes and rejected the appeal of color. Satie relied on his melody to weld these disparate pieces together. His melody was made up not of memorable phrases, but of one unbroken succession of notes. A similar superposition of limpid melody and static accompaniment had produced the works of 1888 and 1890.

The marble-smooth surface can seem impervious, exasperating. *Socrate* represents such an extreme form of music, so much an attempt at perfection within a narrow area, that part of its humanity has drained away. It scorns the excitement of a fugue, the dramatic appeal of a sonata, and (except possibly in the first section) the sensuous beauty of song. One instant follows another until we have heard the whole; no smaller structures intervene which we can label A or B or subject and countersubject. The inhabitant of a richly varied landscape finds it boring or repellent to travel day after day across a desert or a flat sea. *Socrate* is deliberately arid and flat—but also, like sea and desert, it is full of space and light and air. The dignity and tragedy of Socrates' life can assume their full proportions within this clear and infinite horizon, and, rather than coming to an end, the music suspends its flow in this irresolute despairing cadence in the final measures. (See pages 165 and 166.)

Insistent, shifting modality, parallel motion in fourths and fifths, strict use of linear quality rather than impressionist color—all this is typically Satie. Yet *Socrate* is the work that, while being the fullest summation of his style, detaches itself most completely from his personality. Only Satie could have written it, but it no longer expresses an eccentric character, as do most of his other writings. Possibly because of the exceptional text, Satie produced a work that must be considered apart from his life, as a self-

Socrate, III (end)

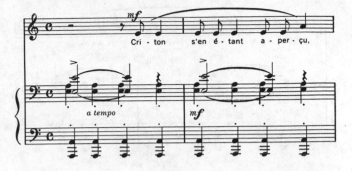

Cri - ton s'en é - tant a - per - çu,

a tempo

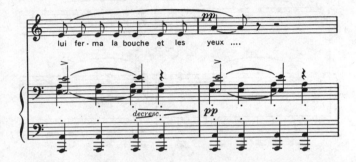

lui fer - ma la bouche et les yeux ....

decresc.

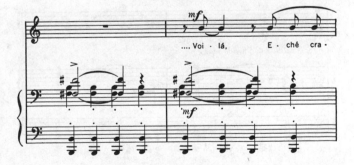

.... Voi - là, E - ché cra -

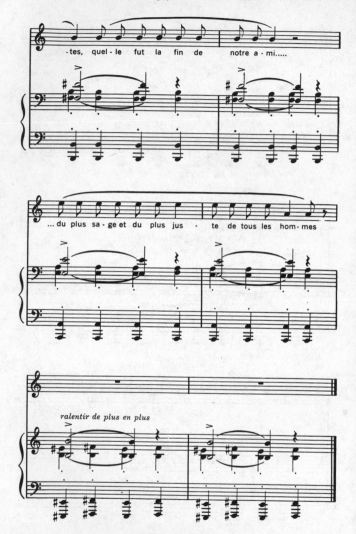

sufficient creation. Its very whiteness makes it one of the most satisfying of all musical attempts to recapture the Greek spirit apart from any academic authenticity. Monteverdi, Purcell, Handel, Gluck, Berlioz, and Debussy produced important works on Greek themes, but without adapting their style. (None of them used Plato or any similar prose text.) Satie, though he could not avoid drawing on his experience as a composer, completely abdicated his personal mannerisms. The rigor mortis of *Socrate* is the absence of Satie and the presence of Plato and Socrates.

The significance of this work in Satie's evolution is further indicated by the fact that his most noteworthy attempt at musical theory occurs in a long note he wrote in a *brouillon* for *Socrate*. It establishes the continuity of his ideas on several subjects—principally on the melodic structure of music.

> Material (Idea) and craftsmanship (sewing). The craftsmanship is often superior to the material.
>
> To have a feeling for harmony is to have a feeling for tonality. The serious examination of a melody will always constitute for the student an excellent exercise in harmony.
>
> A melody does not have *its harmony,* any more than a landscape has *its color.* The harmonic *situation* of a melody is infinite, for melody is only one means of expression in the whole realm of Expression.
>
> Do not forget that the melody is the Idea, the contour just as much as it is the form and content of a work.
>
> Harmony is lighting, an exhibition of the object, its reflection.
>
> In composition the parts no longer follow "school" rules. "School" has a gymnastic purpose and no more; composition has an aesthetic purpose in which taste alone plays a part.
>
> Don't be deceived: the knowledge of grammar alone does not imply literary knowledge; it can either contribute or be set aside by the writer without his responsibility. Musical grammar is neither more nor less than a grammar.

Satie addressed these observations to himself; they are published here for the first time.* His "classicism" shows in the

---

* Unfortunately, the notebook containing this text was stolen from the Conservatory before the collection was catalogued in 1950.

use of words like "idea" and "reflection," which may reveal the extent of his reading in Plato. But he rejects school rules without a qualm and uses the literary example of grammar to make his point. Twenty-five years earlier, Jarry, as a young poet, had explored this same idea of the openness of all expression. "The relation of the verbal sentence to every meaning that can be found in it is constant." (See p. 240.) Harmony was to Satie an adaptable semantic applied to melody not by rules, but by taste alone—Debussy's *plaisir*, Mallarmé's *hasard*.

The most important statement concerns melody. Satie assigns all functions to it: idea, contour, form, content. Everything else is the "expression" of melody. Although most of his later melodies tend to resemble popular song, *Socrate* develops a unique, nonrepeating, unpausing, timeless melody. As "idea" this melodic line sets *Socrate* apart from all his other music as limitless, perpetually moving. Despite his statement, melody provided Satie with his primary form only in the case of *Socrate*—where it really amounts to an absence of form. The music has been called "abstract," and like much abstract art it may not please immediately. But the durable quality of the work, the way it takes on new meaning after many hearings, makes it the one composition of Satie's that pretends to, and achieves, true greatness. The rest of his music is diversion, serious play, "worldly," in the best sense of the word, and often successful in those aims. In *Socrate* Satie took his eyes off the world and looked out of time toward eternity. It was a strange role for him. In 1920 the audience snickered at his setting of a timeless story: a man unjustly condemned who dies peacefully. Satie's only comment about this reception: "*Etrange, n'est-ce pas?*"

In March, 1920, a few months after *Socrate*, the actor Pierre Bertin organized at Paul Poiret's fashionable Barbazange gallery a concert of music by *les Six*, songs by Stravinsky, and a play by Max Jacob. The walls were covered by a show of children's paintings entitled, "*Les Belles Promesses.*" At the start of the first intermission in the play, Bertin presented Satie's and Milhaud's new discovery: "*musique d'ameublement*" or furniture music.

We urgently beg you not to attach any importance to it and to act during the intermission as if the music did not exist. Specially written for Max Jacob's play (always the ruffian; never a bum), it hopes to contribute to life the way a casual conversation does, or a picture in the gallery, or a chair in which one is or is not seated.

When the audience began getting up for the break, a piano and three clarinets, placed in the four corners of the room, plus a trombone, on the mezzanine, struck up what sounded like popular ditties played over and over again in close rhythmical patterns. The audience began to take seats again. Satie rushed around the gallery exhorting them to appropriate behavior. "Talk, keep on talking. And move around. Whatever you do, don't listen!"

Since that day jukeboxes, radios, television, music while you work, canned music, audiotherapy—a whole race of creatures—have sprung into existence to fill the aural background of our lives the way interior decoration fills the visual background.* In a prospectus he sketched out and sent to Cocteau for comment, Satie left no doubt about his intentions.

We want to establish a music designed to satisfy "useful" needs. Art has no part in such needs. Furniture music creates a vibration; it has no other goal; it fills the same role as light and heat—as *comfort* in every form. . . .

Furniture music for law offices, banks, etc.

No marriage ceremony complete without furniture music. . . .

Don't enter a house which does not have furniture music. (Reprinted in *Empreintes,* May, 1950.)

All music, of course, can be traced back to forms of furniture music: rhythmic dance patterns, devotional and inspirational atmosphere for worship, background sounds for courtly gatherings, carnival tunes, the cultivated pretext for a social evening in an undarkened opera house, and so on. Concert performance with lights lowered and admission by

* Henri Matisse associated himself with the furniture tradition in a remark very similar to Bertin's presentation: "What I dream of is an art without any disquieting or preoccupying subject, which would be . . . something analogous to a good armchair."

ticket brought about highly self-conscious habits of "listen-ing" to music instead of just living with it. Did Satie take the matter seriously? We can scarcely know. He worked scrupulously over a few pieces and humbled his art in a manner that was half penance, half gag.

Satie published no works specifically entitled "furniture music." It was enough that he elaborate the principle, illus-trate it once or twice in practice, and then leave it to fend for itself. Among his manuscripts there are only two note-books labeled *"musique d'ameublement,"* and those not even partially filled. Nevertheless, the principle of *moblier musical* inhabits far more music than merely what Satie composed in 1920 for a few performances intended to startle the public. He anticipated the functional conception of music well before the turn of the century and came back to it from time to time until 1919. Not until then did he realize the possibility of integrating it into his "serious" style—a style that already carried within it unconcealed borrowings from the music halls.

The transparent simplicity of *Geneviève de Brabant,* a miniature marionette opera, and *Jack-in-the-Box,* a short ballet (both 1899) led to an even further reduction in Satie's style in 1913. The three sets of children's pieces, *Enfantines,* using five adjoining notes in each hand and an open linear style, remain far more central to his musical evolution than Stravinsky's very similar *Les cinq doigts* (1921) to his. *Trois petites pièces montées* (1919), scored for small orchestra, are as facile and as much like a cliché as a hurdy-gurdy, and as touching. In 1919 Milhaud and Auric were adopting a comparable artlessness to produce the musical counterpart of Dada. This same year, on the other hand, Satie drew from the flatness of functional music some of the most effective characteristics of *Socrate.*

In 1924 the opportunity arose to write a significant piece of furniture music as background for the film sequence René Clair had made for the Picabia-Satie ballet *Relâche. Entr'acte* or *Cinéma,* as the film score was alternately called, conforms absolutely to the contour of Clair's fast-moving montage. The film, a joyous freehand anticipation of all the nightmare farces the surrealists would later pro-duce, includes as its climatic scene a hearse being hauled around the Eiffel Tower by a camel. The construction of the music could not be more primitive. Satie merely used eight measures, as the unit that most closely matches the average length of a single shot in the film. He fills each of these units with one stereotyped phrase repeated eight times. Between the units he inserts a double line, a new signature, and frequently a change in tempo. The transitions are as abrupt and as arbitrary as the cuts in the film. Typical measures lend themselves to infinite repetition and do not establish any strong tonal feeling.

Cinéma

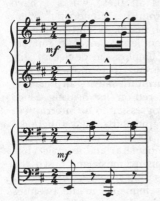
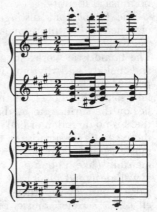
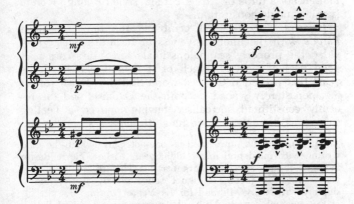

It makes excellent unassertive film music. Satie counted and timed and trimmed it to fit the movie exactly, and it reinforces the effect of the visual image without ever demanding conscious attention. *Entr'acte*, one of the earliest examples of pure movie music, satisfies the artistic demands of a new medium and the technical demands of live performance. It was a significant step toward finding a satisfactory method of film accompaniment. But removed from its proper context and played alone, the score has no form, no musical identity.

The factor that distinguishes all these works I have classified as "furniture music" from the "humoristic" piano pieces lies deeper than traits of simplicity and repetition. The humoristic works suggest endless nuances in tonality and melody and rhythm. They employ the device of surprise in order to change an apparently trite musical design into something novel. In the furniture music, all meaning lies on the surface, to be discovered on first hearing. Since there is no direction or line of progression to be interrupted, there can be no surprise in the rapid shifts. Such functional music cannot claim great value for itself except as workmanship (like a good pair of binoculars) and as style (like a well-designed chair). It led many musicians down the garden path of superficial composing in order to avoid at all costs "serious" music. Satie's influence in the twenties played a considerable role in the diversion. But he was himself not a dupe of "street-corner" style for long; *Socrate* is sufficient demonstration.

Relâche, a ballet that combined the braggadocio of *Parade* with the unobtrusiveness of furniture music, provided the properly scandalous finale for Satie's career. A good deal of activity, much of it nonmusical, filled the years that preceded this last work. Still the "fetish" of *les Six*, persistently wooed by both the Dadaists and the recently constituted surrealists, having enjoyed a fleeting success as dramatic,* Satie now attracted a second group

---

* In 1921 Satie unearthed a one-act play which he had written with incidental music eight years earlier. Pierre Bertin included it in a special program at his Théâtre Bouffe among works by Max Jacob, Radiguet songs set by Auric, and a shimmy written by Milhaud for *Le Nègre Gratin*. "But the hit of the evening," wrote Milhaud, "was without a doubt Satie's extraordinary play, *Le piège de Méduse* in which his wit sput-

of musicians, most of them brought by Milhaud. The four composers. Henri Cliquet-Pleyel, Roger Désormière, Maxime-Jacob, and Henri Sauguet, took the name "Arcueil School," after Satie's surburb. Admiring their music and their youth, he presented them in 1923 to the Collège de France and then to the public at the Théâtre de l'Atelier. A less outstanding group than *les Six,* the Arcueil School has nevertheless been remembered through Désormière's excellence as a conductor and Sauguet's ballet and operatic works.

Early the following year Satie delivered to the Comte de Beaumont, who was startling the city with his avant-garde programs called *Les Soirées de Paris,* the book and music for a ballet on classic themes, *Mercure.* Again Picasso contributed costumes and sets, Massine the choreography. It is not Satie's best work. The surrealists tried to exploit the occasion to woo Picasso to their cause by publishing a long manifesto praising his work and deploring his collaboration with Satie. The composer was already at work on *Relâche.*

At the age of fifty-eight Satie joined the Dada painter and author Francis Picabia and Jean Borlin of the Swedish Ballet to undertake the ultimate *clownerie* of his career. The critic René Dumesnil describes the performance with relish.

> In November, 1924, *Relâche** was the occasion of an uproar which has since remained legendary. . . .
> The opening night had been set for Thursday. But the theater remained shut, and so tightly that many of those invited wondered if *Relâche,* instead of

tered in every line; the unbridled fantasy of the play bordered on the absurd. Bertin, in the part of Baron Medusa, made himself up to look like Satie; he seemed to incarnate the man. A stuffed monkey on a pedestal interrupted the action from time to time to do little dance numbers." Parts of it are superb burlesque. The liveried domestic, Polycarp, treats the baron with a disdainful familiarity. The baron has a lengthy adventure on the telephone (still a novelty then) and winds up talking to a horse. When his future son-in-law comes in, he uses a magnifying glass to examine him. The play was published in 1922 with handsome cubist engravings by Braque.

* *Relâche* in ordinary usage means "no performance," referring to a theater's schedule.

just a title, were not a state of affairs. The company
manager appeared and stated that the indisposition
of Jean Borlin required postponing *Relâche* for a
week. People consoled themselves with a few drinks.
Many believed it all another prank of Satie's, and
when, a week later, the orchestra sounded the prelude to *Relâche* based on the student song, "The
Turnip Vendor," the audience howled. They roared
out the scandalous chorus; heckling and laughter
interrupted the performance. The music moreover
was affectedly, almost showily plain. The only entertaining moment was the René Clair film; but it
served principally to make the ballet the more overwhelming afterward. It finished in indescribable
tumult. However the curtain came up for the usual
bows. Driving a midget five-horsepower Citroën,
Erik Satie popped out on stage, took a turn around
the track, and ironically greeted the worthy audience whom he had just ridiculed magnificently. . . .
Beneath these mad eccentricities there was a strain
of melancholy. (*La musique en France entre deux
guerres.*)

"It amounts," said Picabia, "to a lot of kicks in a lot of rears,
sacred and otherwise." During this "instantaneous ballet"
the dancers smoke incessantly, a fireman wanders through
the modernistic set, constructed out of rows of metal disks,
and costume changes take place on stage. It was the first
time a film was ever included as part of a ballet.

Satie was roundly whipped for his naughtiness by the
press, outraged that an old man, a friend of Debussy and
Ravel, could lend himself to such antics. One critic began
his column, "*Adieu,* Satie . . . ," and many of his friends
followed public opinion. Milhaud, Sauguet, Désormière,
and Wiener remained faithful, as well as his friends among
painters and writers. By now he needed them, for age and
poverty were catching up with him. He had lived through
a full program of scandals since *Parade,* and—most scandalous of all—had held on to the spark of his youth and
refused to be confined by any of his works. He had less
than a year to live.

Considering his participation in contemporary artistic
upheavals, one might well expect Satie's work to have been
affected. Yet he held a singularly steady course despite

apparent reversals. In its simplicity and brevity, Satie's music tends toward self-effacement, and at times it seems to disappear like the lines of a very lightly traced drawing. His musical modesty, reaching its extreme expression in furniture music, is also a form of pride. If he never appropriated to himself the vast resources of musical expression, he also never abdicated the area he considered his own. His idiom became increasingly personal, especially through two extramusical characteristics which come very close to defining his originality as an artist.

Most of Satie's work associates itself with an external subject and does not isolate itself in a purely musical realm. The earliest works are dance forms which take the movements of the human body as text. In the Rose-Croix period he sometimes employed liturgical models. Next came the humoristic texts, laconic marginalia at first, but soon threatening to usurp control of his music. In the final period Satie returned to dance and theatrical subjects. Thus he almost always worked with a text, be it a Platonic dialogue, a Cocteau ballet, a medieval legend, a Picasso set, or his own fanciful-grotesque lyrics. He attuned his music to other arts, including the unexplored realm of the movies.

The second, and closely related, quality he gave his music was its carefully designed appearance on the page—beautifully drawn scores which visually express both lyric and humorous meaning. Since it alone reproduces Satie's manuscript, the published score of *Sports et divertissements* is the best example. By removing bar lines and signatures, Satie gave many of his works a visual purity which matches their musical aspirations. A comparable tendency in poetry had evolved before the turn of the century in the work of Mallarmé, who treated the printed form of *Un coup de dés* (1897) not as a script for oral performance or silent reading, but as the final stage of creation. A trained musician can "read" music in a conventional score, but Satie's childlike temperament never ceased to marvel that marks on paper can stand for musical sounds in time. He could not imagine innovations in one without the other, and his "hand" speaks for him as much as his melody.

In certain compositions these extramusical elements of text and calligraphy fuse with the music itself in an unexpected unity. At that point there seems to come into being a new art form, a genre of Satie's creation.* It comprises certain short compositions, as self-contained as droplets of mercury, in which the balance between elements is perfectly controlled. They require a new kind of listening, for they are too brief and tenuous for concert performance. One must play them oneself on the piano, murmuring the texts which punctuate the spaces in the staff, watching the visible pattern of notation, and listening to that same pattern become melody. Among these three aspects of the work, one cannot distinguish which is frame and which is framed.

Such is the singular and precarious nature of *Trois poèmes d'amour, Enfantines,* most of the humoristic pieces, and, above all, *Sports et divertissements.* The marriage of text, format, and music makes them miniature masterpieces. But in what genre? Ernest Newman's "small poem in music" describes some of Chopin and Scriabin, but not Satie. A suitable designation finally comes to mind only in French: *musique de placard* (*placard* means both closet and poster), in the double sense of extreme intimacy and deliberate publicity. The works find their proper setting among two or three friends around a piano who participate in the music as they would to sing a madrigal or a Christmas carol. Closet music is one degree more private than chamber music. Yet in thus restricting the dimensions of his work, Satie also made his reputation. The intimate works attained a special notoriety, like that of his private religious publication, *Le Cartulaire.* When he threw his little closet pieces in the face of traditional concert music, they assumed the proportions of manifestos: poster music. Thus intimacy becomes a public act. Satie's *musique de placard* conveys the same public privacy or private publicity as the drawings of Paul Klee and poems of e. e. cummings.

It is unlikely that Satie consciously envisaged a new genre any more than Rousseau imagined himself the sandwich man of modern art. Nevertheless, his historical significance—never far from his personal role on the Paris scene

---

* There is no intention here to demonstrate that Satie wrote "impure" music—a perilous contention in any context. If "pure" music is that whose subject is itself musical, *i.e.*, melodic phrase, rhythmic pattern, sonority, et cetera—then *3 Morceaux, Cinq nocturnes,* and a few other works easily fulfill the conditions.

—arises out of the compatibility of his deliberate choices with his natural gifts. At a time when French music was bewitched by German opera, he chose a music-hall style; when instrumental music leaned toward symphonic forms and exotic Russian sonorities, he contrived *la musique de placard*. It is entirely just that most of his works have been neglected in concert performance, where they do not belong; it is equally just that the inaccessibility of his music is beginning to be dispelled by new recording media whose vast distribution does not necessarily abolish the private act of listening. As technology has produced more and improved devices for sound reproduction, music has become increasingly divided between a public-passive activity and a personal-active one: floating in background sounds versus true listening. Satie's furniture music approaches the limit of the first evolution toward fatuity. His *musique de placard*, on the other hand, reaffirms a private and active participation in musical forms and insists on their kinship with words and drawings. Such a double-edged aesthetic may be confusing but it remains profoundly symptomatic of the twentieth century.

The essential simplicity of all Satie's work, trivial and serious, bears witness to an era of his life that he never relinquished. The more one learns about Satie, the more one comes to see him as a man who performed every contortion in order to keep sight of his childhood. Like a child who twists his body as he walks in order not to lose sight of his shadow, Satie made sure that the most treasured part of his past was always at his side. Some of his contortions were far from lovely, but they were wrenchings required to keep his eye on an elusive shadow. "I came into the world very young in a time which is very old." This motto stands beside his observation to Milhaud: "I should like to know the kind of music a one-year-old child would compose." Like many contemporary artists, he found out by composing it himself.*

Because of his refusal to abandon a childlike naïveté, Satie has often been described, like Rousseau, as a primitive.

---

* Satie's aversion to growing old assumed the proportions of an obsession. In his later notebooks he made lists of composers, kings, and historical figures with their dates. He carefully calculated their ages and appears to have consoled himself with the fact that many of them flourished at an advanced age.

His primitivism, however, leads directly into his sophistication. Satie had developed a keen critical sense of the culture in which he lived, an awareness that allowed him to persevere in his separate path despite the legend, scandal, and critical furor which rose around him.*

Sophistication resides in his deliberate clinging to the childlike elements of his music and personality in the knowledge that they would leave their imprint on modern music. After the exaggerated praise and ridicule heaped on his name, Satie needed a fine discrimination to strain out of his earliest years a few truly original elements—immaculate, modal melodies and detached harmonies—and then to add just those qualities for which we know him today —strict contrapuntal construction, jazz rhythms, and music-hall atmosphere. "Such musical qualities as I have," he wrote, "I owe to study and a native application of good sense."

It is hardly surprising that this simple sophisticated mind should have come to rely on humor both as a mask for the boldness of his innovations and as a deliberate method of making his work contemporary in spirit. In the manuscript (but not retained in the published score) of *Embryons desséchés* he wrote: "This work is absolutely incomprehensible, even to me. Perhaps I wanted to be humorous. That would not surprise me and be pretty much in my manner." There is a whole collection of shrewd texts which fill his notebooks and which he never intended to set to music. "The center of Paris is France—with its colonies of course." Satie shared with Rousseau a joyous childlike vision of the world in which distortion is at the same time comic and deeply revealing. But Satie, who was, above all, astute, went further than Rousseau and cultivated humor as an end in itself. Just as furniture music was the

* An intelligent article by Rudhyar Chennevière on Satie's irony makes this judgment: "Satie's work represents originality only, like the major part of the tentatives of this terminal part of our civilization. It is full of strange individual traits, it surpasses itself in exploiting these particularisms, formulating a doctrine and an art upon their psychological anomalies. . . . In Erik Satie's pieces there is only—Erik Satie; the really human element is missing." Chennevière regards the man as excessively idiosyncratic and avant-garde and never considers any awkwardness in his style. It is possible for Satie to be attacked with equal force as primitive and as sophisticate.

reductio ad absurdum of mood music, so certain writings show Satie finding huge enjoyment in the very absurdity of living. Without putting aside his gravity of statement he could lead a sensible opening sentence into utter preposterousness.

A Musician's Day

An artist must regulate his life. Here is my precise daily schedule. I rise at 7:18; am inspired from 10:30 to 11:47. I lunch at 12:11 and leave the table at 12:14. A healthy horse-back ride on my property from 1:19 to 2:35. Another round of inspiration from 3:12 to 4:07.

From 5:00 to 6:47 various occupations (fencing, reflection, immobility, visits, contemplation, dexterity, swimming, etc.).

Dinner is served at 7:16 and finished at 7:20. Afterward from 8:09 to 9:59 symphonic readings out loud.

I go to bed regularly at 10:37. Once a week I wake up with a start at 3:14 A.M. (Tuesdays.)

I eat only white foods: eggs, sugar, shredded bones, the fat of dead animals, rice, turnips, sausages in camphor, pastry, cheese (the white varieties), cotton salad, and certain kinds of fish (skinned).

I boil my wine and drink it cold mixed with fuchsia juice. I have a good appetite but never talk when eating for fear of strangling.

I breathe carefully (a little at a time) and dance very rarely. When walking I hold my sides and look steadily behind me.

Being of serious demeanor, it is unintentional when I laugh. I always apologize very affably.

I sleep with only one eye closed; I sleep very hard. My bed is round with a hole in it for my head to go through. Every hour a servant takes my temperature and gives me another.

For a long time I have subscribed to a fashion magazine. I wear a white cap, white socks, and a white vest.

My doctor has always told me to smoke. He even

explains himself: "Smoke, my friend. Otherwise someone else will smoke in your place." (*Mémoires d'un amnésique*.)

Irony, spite, and fantasy combine into a skillful fairy story about a nonsense world not less but *more* ordered than ours.* Satie's entire career represents an effort to confound, to provoke laughter, to give pause, and then to disappear —and least of all to entertain or edify. Since the absurd cannot be prolonged without itself becoming reasonable and systematic (witness *Through the Looking Glass*), Satie's talents revealed themselves best, as Paul Rosenfeld wrote, in "sudden visitations." The scale of his works expresses their essence, not their insignificance.

Satie managed to die with as much courage and eccentricity as he had lived. His first "death" had been the grim retreat to Arcueil; his second life required something more dramatic to end it. Now he had his own legend to contend with. When he had emerged from retirement in 1910, his Montmartre notoriety had been revived, also. He had fraternized with princesses and lectured to academies. In Arcueil his philanthropic activities had been accompanied by an elaborate set of political feints. He deserted the Radical Socialists for the local Communist soviet and began writing for *L'Humanité*. But before long he was complaining that in respect to art his Communist friends were "disconcerting bourgeois." On a concert-lecture tour in

* Some of the "texts" for his musical compositions can stand as near parodies of Rimbaud's prose poems:

Venomous Obstacles

"This vast section of the world is inhabited only by one man: a Negro. He is getting bored with laughing himself to death.

"The shadows of millennial trees indicate seventeen minutes after nine.

"The frogs are calling each other by their first names.

"In order to think better, the Negro holds his cerebellum in the spread fingers of his right hand. From afar he has the appearance of a distinguished physiologist. Four anonymous serpents hold him captive, hung from the lapels of his uniform which the combination of sorrow and solitude deforms. On the river bank an old mango tree slowly washes its roots which are repulsively dirty. This is no lovers' tryst [*l'heure du berger*]."

Belgium he told Milhaud to introduce him to a cabinet minister's wife as follows: "Erik Satie of the Arcueil Soviet greets her, his belly to the ground." By 1918 the *Mercure de France* was writing in its gossip columns that Satie's musical production had been drastically reduced because nine out of ten street lamps (at which he stopped to jot down notes during his nightly walk home) had been turned off under war restrictions. In 1924, after the ballet *Mercure*, Boris de Schlœzer discussed "The Satie Case" in the influential *Revue Musicale*: "Satie is a legend today, a password, a battle cry; he is also a philosophy of taste, an aesthetic, a credo. . . ." Yet all the time Satie kept part of his life absolutely separate—the room in which he slept and worked and from which he emerged into the world as an actor steps out of the wings. He came before the public with his role fully assumed, his part learned, and returned to the wings to catch his breath and apply himself intermittently to the music which was the other half of his life. His legend must include this self-protection and this devotion.

He fell ill soon after the wild caper of *Relâche*, lost his appetite, and was told he had cirrhosis of the liver. Pleurisy soon set in and kept him in constant pain. He spent entire days in Braque's studio, at Milhaud's, and at Derain's, lunching without his customary gusto and then sitting slumped by the fire with his overcoat still on, his umbrella in his hands, his spirits gone. Finally, the pianist Jean Wiener obtained a room for him in the Grand Hôtel on the Place de l'Opéra, to spare him the daily trip to Paris; he sat for weeks on end in a chair facing a mirror, cursing the telephone which always played tricks on him, receiving his friends with a smile, and unlocking the door for them without leaving his chair by an ingenious string and pulley rig, a throwback to his Montmartre "closet."

The Place de l'Opéra soon palled and he moved to the Hôtel Istria in Montparnasse, then the tumultuous headquarters of the avant-garde and the expatriates of a dozen nations. He developed a phobia on handkerchiefs; when Madame Milhaud fetched his laundry one week from the concierge in Arcueil, the bundle contained eighty-nine of them. Finally, he became too sick to stay in a hotel. Braque and the Milhauds accompanied him in the ambulance to the St. Joseph hospital where the Comte de Beaumont had

endowed a private room. Jacques Maritain, whom Satie
had seen frequently through Cocteau, brought a priest;
Satie described the young man the next day: "He looked
like a Modigliani, black on a blue ground." Maritain spoke
of Satie as a "really astonishing theologian," while Satie
took pleasure in whispering dark things about his Communist affiliations and what would his friends say? He was
in frightful pain but he kept up a jocular manner for
Brancusi, Wiener, and Roger Désormière, and for Robert
Caby and Yves Dautun, two more young musicians drawn
to his side in the last months.

To the rest—to all the friends with whom he had quarreled at one time or another—Satie refused admittance.
His integrity permitted no compromise. ". . . they have
said good-by to me already, and I prefer to hold them to
it. You've got to be intransigent to the very end." When
the editor of *Relâche* came to discuss publication, Satie
demanded immediate payment in cash, and put the money
away between sheets of newspaper in a suitcase.

For six months his illness dragged on, yet his spirit was
not broken. The Sisters in the hospital were devoted to him.
After long sessions with the *abbé* he took the last sacra-
ment—to please the Sisters, some said. He died July 1,
1925. André Cœuroy wrote the most balanced of the
obituaries.

> This musician, whose influence on the evolution of
> contemporary French music has been considerable,
> has not always been fully understood; but at the
> same time he did everything he could to produce
> that situation.

When Conrad Satie (who had been found through notices in the papers), Milhaud, Wiener, and Caby entered
the Arcueil apartment where no one had ever been allowed,
they felt strong apprehension—as if some secret would
leap out at them to betray the figure who had charmed
and dismayed them all. But Satie had obliterated his foot-
prints; there was no private life, no hidden chapter whose
discovery unmasked him, merely a comfortless room with
bed, chair, table, wardrobe, and piano. The arrangement
of the place showed an incredible combination of meticulous order and sordid disarray. His dozen corduroy suits
were piled on top of the empty wardrobe, canes and um-

brellas leaned in the corners, the piano pedals had been repaired with string, and behind the instrument were found the long-lost manuscripts of *Geneviève de Brabant* and *Jack-in-the-Box*. Everything was deep in filth. However, Satie had kept his notebooks and all the letters he had received as well as drafts of his replies. In cigar boxes he had filed away more than four thousand scraps of paper the size of calling cards with his ink drawings and cryptic inscriptions. Braque bought the piano. Milhaud tells us that he found on the wall of the house opposite a chalk inscription: "This house is haunted by the devil."

After the funeral, Diaghilev put on a memorial evening of Satie ballets: *Parade, Mercure,* and the newly found *Jack-in-the-Box,* which Milhaud orchestrated and which had sets by Derain and choreography by Balanchine. The Comte de Beaumont organized a concert program in which Désormière directed his own orchestration of *Geneviève de Brabant.* In 1929 a plaque was placed on the building in Arcueil, with speeches by the Communist mayor and Milhaud and, afterward, a concert at the town hall with Marya Freund performing *Socrate.* As always, Satie's personality was invoked as often as his music. The longest and most telling tribute to his character had already appeared in Cocteau's *Coq et Arlequin,* which reads like a sermon on the example of Satie's life and good works. "Satie teaches our epoch the greatest audacity of all: to be simple. . . . Raymond Radiguet, from 15 to 20, and Erik Satie, from 54 to 59, were the same age and traveled together." Other friends speak in similar terms. Stravinsky, who had met him first at Debussy's house, put it with apt brevity. "I liked him right away. He was a crafty fox [*fine mouche*], full of slyness and intelligently naughty." Satie did not allow his mask to freeze or his youth to wither. His bearded features remained kindly and whimsical to the end.

Comprehending that eccentricity is a strenuous form of anonymity and that music is a strenuous form of living, Satie established himself as an artist far different from the "sweet medieval" musician to whom Debussy inscribed a volume of his songs in 1892. Satie pushed the boundaries of his art out into the adjoining countries of literature, theater, and painting. His songs resemble musical self-denials before a text; his compositions for the stage scrupulously follow the demands of performance; many of his "descriptive" piano pieces are as much studies in immobility and secret movement as is still-life painting. The central problem of his music is not its "purity" but the steadiness with which it points to one of the sources of modern sensibility.

Ultimately Satie teaches a lesson which we can today read better than his contemporaries could. Men like Cocteau, Milhaud, Poulenc, and Auric took what they wanted most: the example of his simplicity and honesty. The deeper lesson can only be described as a demonstration in provocation and boredom. Both the music and the legend Satie left with us are so cast as to bore us or provoke us. Stripped of all inessentials, they can do nothing else. Provocation has begun to pall, for scandal has been employed as a method for over a century. For almost twenty years it has been impossible to *épater le bourgeois* in any lasting way. Dadaists and surrealists drove provocation to its violent agony and discovered Satie as one of the few musicians outrageous enough to suit their purpose. But they read only one side of the page. On the back is a text of greater significance for us today. "The public venerates boredom," Satie wrote. "For boredom is mysterious and profound." And elsewhere: "The listener is defenseless against boredom. Boredom subdues him." Satie's need for self-effacement springs from his fascination with boredom—fear of it and knowledge of its power. When Jean Wiener defends Satie as incapable of boring us because he could always "sprinkle his works with Honfleur jokes," Wiener is arguing off the point. For, with the simple resources of his musical style, Satie did steer perilously close to boredom and occasionally went aground. Yet is it a damning or a redeeming comment on our civilization that it can produce an art that is part exasperation and part tedium? Ralph Linton, one of the most perceptive of modern anthropologists, suggests an answer that breathes meaning into Satie's career.

> This tendency toward the unnecessary and in some cases even injurious elaboration of culture is one of the most significant phenomena of human life. It proves that the development of culture has become an end in itself. Man may be a rational being, but he certainly is not a utilitarian one. The

constant revision and expansion of his social hered-
ity is a result of some inner drive, not of necessity.
. . . It seems possible that the human capacity for
being bored, rather than man's social or natural
needs lies at the root of man's cultural advance.
(*The Study of Man.*)

With the inanity of furniture music, the intimacy of *la musique de placard,* and the stripped line of *Socrate,* Satie
challenges us not to be impressed but to be bored. He says
in effect: Here are the naked features of our world. If they
provoke you or bore, you will have reacted constructively,
for either way you will be forced to move. This is the
meaning of a staggering sentence contained in one of his
late notebooks, a sentence that describes his entire being:
"Experience is one of the forms of paralysis." The child, like
the true Bohemian, has not yet defined his life by excluding
alternate ways of behaving. The "lessons" of experience can
begin to cripple our freedom. There remains one form of
paralysis which is even more devastating. In Satie's world
the supreme heresy would have been the honeyed advertising slogan "They satisfy." If experience is a form of
paralysis, satisfaction is a form of death. In his hands music
never became an exercise in self-contentment. It was a
means of upholding our freedom.

Greatness was not a quality Satie valued, and he was not
a "great" musician. For being singular, for being humble
and joyous and wise, both man and work are unforgettable.

Alfred Jarry, 1873-1907

[7]

SUICIDE BY HALLUCINATION

> After us the Savage God.
> —W. B. Yeats

In respectful mockery, Alfred-Henri Jarry always boasted of his birth exactly on the feast of the Nativity of the Holy Virgin, September 8, 1873. He contrived to die with equal precision on All Saints' Day, 1907. His parents lived, like Rousseau's, in Laval, close enough to the ancient lands of Brittany for Jarry to call himself a Breton. The picturesque and stifling town was known best for the dogged devoutness of its population and for a high incidence of alcoholism. After his own fashion, Jarry was a true son of Laval in both respects.

The father, Anselm Jarry, born of a long line of masons and carpenters in Laval, had worked up to be traveling salesman for a wool factory and then manager. His business acumen was not great, however, and severe reverses obliged him to go on the road again. Neither his person nor his fortunes satisfied his wife, Caroline Quernest, daughter of a judge in Brittany and boasting noble ancestors. Both her mother and her brother were confined part of their lives for insanity. Caroline herself had been well educated and was convinced of her own artistic gifts. She indulged her stifled ambitions by wearing eccentric clothes, interfering in her husband's business, treating her first child, Charlotte, like a domestic servant, and spoiling Alfred. This parental combination of hard-working artisan father and unstable romantic mother produced an offspring endowed with both strains. Jarry was always something of a sensible maniac.

He made his own pronouncement on his parents some years later when he had adopted the regal speech of Père Ubu.

> Our father was a worthless joker—what you call a nice old fellow. He no doubt made our older sister, a girl of the 1830 period who liked to put ribbons in her hair, but he cannot have played much of a role in the confection of our precious person. Our mother was a lady of Coutouly ancestry, short and sturdy, willful and full of whimsey, of whom we had to approve before we had a voice in the matter.

From the beginning, Jarry scorned his father and showed a deep affection for his mother. Virtually deserting her husband, Madame Jarry took the two children away with her to Saint-Brieuc on the Brittany coast, where her father had retired. The boy took to roaming the open country. His earliest writings date from this period—poems and skits in the style of Victor Hugo and Florian. For a boy of twelve they show unusual precociousness and a merciless observation of the local residents and his schoolmates. In Brittany the young Jarry was already showing a characteristic blend of wickedness, charm, and savagery. He spent three years in the town where, forty years earlier, Tristan Corbière had spent the youth he grievously recalled in the poems of *Les amours jaunes,* and Villiers de l'Isle-Adam had learned the keen irony of *Contes cruels.*

In the fall of 1888, while Paris excitedly cheered General Boulanger, Madame Jarry and her children moved to the ancient town of Rennes. It is forty miles from Laval, where the father remained, trying to rescue his failing fortunes in the wool business. Jarry entered the *lycée,* and one of his schoolmates, Henri Hertz, describes how he immediately made his presence felt.

> In the *lycée* and in the town he had a reputation which, in family circles and among professors, provoked sudden silences and obvious embarrassment. He was a brilliant student with all the marks of the worst kind of troublemaker. He excelled in his studies but without trying. At any mention of his

irregularities, his escapades, and to tell the whole truth his vices, parents lowered their voices and children their eyes. . . . He delighted in attacks on our modesty. He loved to see our cheeks redden with shame and envy. Since he was already way ahead of the rest of us in his impatient maturity, we knew that everything which he had in common with us took on another meaning for him.

Madame Jarry had brought to Rennes a mixture of vice and virtue, half brat, half prodigy—a *potache*. (This familiar French word for schoolboy connotes mild toleration for the frenzied play acting of adolescence.) His companions admired him, haltingly followed his lead, and hated him a little for being able to flaunt an unpunished arrogance. His conduct, which alternated between virtuosity and effrontery, revealed a terrible wrenching of personality in which an aggressive imagination struggled with an almost invincible timidity. The other *potache* of French literature, Rimbaud, could not sustain the role. He abandoned his career as poet at the age of nineteen to become an ill-starred adventurer; Jarry, completing his best work between the ages of fifteen and twenty-five, refused ever to come to terms with the world. His life and his work united in a single threat to the equilibrium of human nature. He died at thirty-four in a gradual suicide by poverty, drink, and violated identity.

At Rennes the pupil Jarry was far from handsome. His stature was close to that of a midget. He had a scrunched-up little face which was further twisted by a racking cough, as if violent excesses had very early undermined his health. "With his steep brow, keen eyes, and grating voice," writes Hertz, "he hewed his own path through the wilderness, running any risk, rebuffing people fearlessly, his squat torso planted firmly on bandy legs." It is reported, too, that he had surprisingly soft eyes. Despite his abrupt manner, he had a charm which always disarmed his enemies. Casual friendship did not come easily to him, but he formed bonds of extreme intimacy with a few schoolmates—principally with one, Henri Morin, and his brother Charles.

In the provincial *lycée* Jarry's encounter with the physics teacher was destined to make literary history. Professor

Hébert was a well-meaning, obese, helplessly incompetent teacher such as boys immediately recognize as their prey. In 1888 the man was already an established institution, baited almost to death by the students, who brought frogs and grasshoppers into the ancient classroom (in a converted monastery), talked openly, and threw things at the blackboard while he was writing on it. His demonstrations in "my science of physics" always met with disaster; his classes were pandemonium for the whole hour—a circumstance which the *lycée* authorities seem to have blinked at. The name Hébert became legendary and underwent transformations into Heb and Hébé. The pupils of the school stole time from their lessons to compose extravagant plays and narratives of the adventures of Père Heb. In his own catastrophic versions he relived *Gil Blas* and *Don Quixote*. For years Monsieur Hébert suffered before his charges, trying not to hear their taunts, dropping capillary tubes and thermometers from trembling hands.

Jarry carried the attack to a new level. Before the expectant class, this brazen new student asked questions so cunning and paradoxical that Heb was reduced to confusion. And Jarry began to collaborate with the Morin brothers on the various cycles of Heb epics and plays. In a well-documented work on this period of Jarry's career, Charles Chassé summarizes the plots of some of these literary incunabula. "Père Heb's behavior consists of two movements: translation and rotation about a vertical axis. When he moves in a straight line, each of his extremes describes a cycloid." In the fifteenth century Père Heb turned into a fish in order to enjoy the warmth of the Gulf Stream. He swam up the Seine, was pulled out on the end of a line, and resumed his human form.

> Shortly afterward, Père Heb came up for his oral exams before several terrified professors. His sole baggage of learning was composed of two or three Cuneiform letters which he tried his haphazard best to reproduce.

The principal characteristics of Père Heb were physical: a *gidouille*, or belly, of immense proportions; three teeth, one of stone, one of iron, one of wood; a single, retractable ear; and a body so misshapen that he could not pick himself up if he fell down—as he often did. And so it went, according to the vagaries of the schoolboy mind. Everything the boys read and recited was burlesqued. No author existed who would not yield a new chapter of tribulations for Père Heb to survive.

All this savage scholarship was Jarry's meat, and, within a few months of his arrival, he took the initiative of staging some of the plays. Charlotte Jarry, the two Morin brothers, and several other students produced *Les Polonais* in the Morin attic with Jarry as impresario, scene painter, and star. This was the ur-text of *Ubu Roi,* the play that shocked Paris eight years later. In the Jarry attic marionettes were the specialty, a medium for which Jarry never lost his passion. His theatrical experience, however, was not confined to attics. He and Henri Morin dressed up and impersonated monks in the streets of Rennes; they became brave courtiers and attacked people in the marketplace with sabers; they raised havoc indoors and out with fearless chemical experiments; they canoed and boxed and fenced; they were tireless enthusiasts of the newest means of transportation, the bicycle, and the thirty-mile trip to Mont-Saint-Michel scarcely taxed their endurance. Yet in the early morning hours Jarry was studying and writing, surrounded by his dictionaries, stuffed animals, and collection of musical instruments. Before he left the *lycée* he had accumulated a prodigious knowledge—not all of it from books however. Occasionally he came late to school looking disheveled and exhausted, as if he had been up all night. To those who asked him where he had been, he answered unchallengeably, "In-the-bro-thels."

Jarry stayed three years in Rennes, distrusted by his teachers and untouched by the discipline of the school. He became a *bachelier* with an excellent record in Greek, Latin, German, and drawing. He very nearly chose to attempt the engineering training of the Ecole Polytechnique, but he finally decided to go to Paris and prepare at the Lycée Henri IV for the Ecole Normale. In 1891, at the age of seventeen, Jarry arrived in the capital—doubtless by bicycle.

Paris did not intimidate Jarry—at least not on the surface. He remained the *potache,* astonishing his companions in the vast halls of the Henri IV with his buffooneries. When the classics professor congratulated Jarry on his style in Latin and asked him what author he had used as a model, Jarry replied, "Aristophanes." The class guffawed, thinking he had confused the classical languages, and Jarry explained haughtily that he meant the footnoted translations into discreet Latin of the many obscene passages in the original Greek.

During initiation rites at the recess hour, new students were required to improvise a speech on the most unlikely topic that could be dreamed up. Jarry's performance became celebrated; the subject assigned him was Turkistan. Again a schoolmate, C. G. Gens-d'Armes, has recalled the incident.

> "Turkistan—just the subject I know best. The Orient my friends, the unfathomable Orient . . ." In a minute he was talking about the Turks, Istanbul, Pierre Loti, Aziyadé. He was recalled to the subject. "The subject!" he said. "What else am I talking about? Since when is a digression out of order? Cicero himself in *Pro Milone* . . ." The audience was submerged. The bell rang and Jarry concluded, "My friends, we have treated as best we could the first part of this vast subject. We shall take it up again tomorrow at the point where this idiot bell is forcing us to stop."
>
> He did not take it up again. But from that day on Jarry's mental mechanism disturbed me. When he opened the valve of his wit, he seemed to follow after the stream of his words without any control over them. It was no longer a person speaking but a machine driven by some demon. His jerky voice, metallic and nasal, his abrupt puppet-like gestures, his fixed expression, his torrential and incoherent flow of language, his grotesque or brilliant images, this synchronism which today we should compare to the movies or the phonograph—all this astonished me, amused me, irritated me, and ended by upsetting me.
>
> He was informed, intelligent, and discriminating; he was good, even sweet-tempered, and perhaps timid beneath it all. But he lacked that something which prevents people from putting the cart al-

ways before the horse and from ruining their lives.
His originality was too much like some mental
anomaly.

It was not long before this originality almost eclipsed the
engaging young man who sought protection behind it.

These were fervid times for the young men who had
reached the *lycée*. From Professor Bourdon in Rennes Jarry
had already heard the revolutionary doctrines of Nietzsche
before his works were translated into French; at the Henri
IV Professor Henri Bergson soberly developed his theories
of comedy and laughter; the Russian novel, anarchism,
occultism, and symbolism were in the air; and Jarry had
his own special interests in Rabelais, Shakespeare, Poe,
De Quincey, Coleridge, Greek and Latin texts, heraldry,
and the cabala. "That was the period," Jarry wrote years
later, "when a revelation took place; even a verse from the
Apocalypse is not too grandiloquent: 'The sky opened
and rolled back like a scroll.' " Gradually he abandoned his
schooling and the hopes of Ecole Normale for the tempting
career of an *homme de lettres*.

Jarry's closest friend at this time was Léon-Paul Fargue,
who was also writing verses and looking for a place in the
literary world. According to Fargue, Jarry "created a sensation with his hooded provincial cape and his stovepipe hat
which was taller than he was and glistened like burnished
metal." In 1893 they made friends with an auctioneer and
horse dealer by the name of Louis Lormel, who published
a small literary review, *L'Art Littéraire*, and with Marcel
Schwob, author of *La croisade des enfants* and editor of
the literary supplement of *L'Echo de Paris*.* Schwob
quickly recognized Jarry's talent, as did the writers Octave
Mirbeau and Catulle Mendès, who worked on the same
paper, and Félix Fénéon, one of the most perceptive defenders of symbolism and impressionism. Jarry attended
several of Mallarmé's last Tuesday soirees in the Rue de

* In 1896 Jarry dedicated *Ubu Roi* to Schwob and inscribed
a copy to him thus: "Just as the book is dedicated to him, this
copy is offered to Marcel Schwob because his writings are
among those I have admired the longest." A little over a year
earlier, Paul Valéry dedicated *Introduction à la méthode de
Léonard de Vinci* to Schwob, evidence of the range of the
older author's fascination over the young. He is today a singularly neglected figure.

Rome and often finished the evening alone with the poet of silence and the sonnet form. And now Jarry met Alfred Vallette, editor of the *Mercure de France*, and his handsome spirited wife, Madame Rachilde, a prolific novelist. These two became his lifelong friends, publishing his work, receiving him in their home, and caring for him in his last poverty-stricken years. The *Mercure* held regular Tuesday receptions whose habitués included the entire general staff of symbolism: the critic-novelist Remy de Gourmont, the poets Henri de Régnier, Albert Samain, Pierre Louÿs, Gustave Kahn, Charles-Henri Hirsch, Franc-Nohain, and many others. Among them moved a few unknowns like Paul Valéry, André Gide, Maurice Ravel, and Alfred Jarry. None caused such a sensation in the circle as Jarry. Madame Rachilde describes how he first appeared at the *Mercure* receptions with a strikingly pale face, straight black hair, bright red lips, a vague mustache, and dark phosphorescent eyes "like those of a night bird." He made his literary debut "like a wild animal entering the ring."

Despite his fearsome behavior, and because of it, Jarry was well received at the *Mercure* and on the café terraces. He was soon on friendly terms with Régnier and Gourmont, Valéry and—with wariness on both sides—Gide. On April 23, 1893, Marcel Schwob's *L'Echo de Paris* supplement published a brief text by Jarry which won a prize for the best prose work by a young author. These fragmentary dialogues, entitled *Guignol,* present publicly for the first time Père Ubu (changed from Hébé), his Conscience, and his science of " 'Pataphysics." A month later Jarry won the poetry prize in the same paper with three prose poems. Along with Mallarmé, Gide, Remy de Gourmont, and Fargue, Jarry became a contributor to Lormel's *L'Art Littéraire,* where he published two articles, two perceptive art chronicles which mention Gauguin and Rousseau, and the drama *César-Antéchrist.* The *Mercure de France* then brought out his first book, *Les minutes de sable mémorial.** The foreword, entitled *"Linteau,"* prepares one for the dense, highly aural writing.

* The title defeats translation because of the triple meaning of "sable": *sand, sable* (the animal), and *sable* (the color in heraldry).

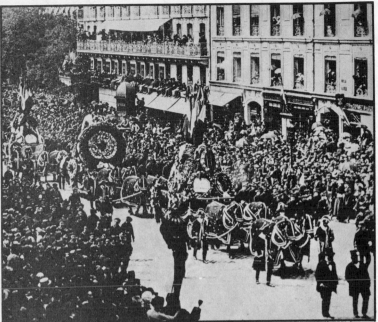

PLATE I   Victor Hugo's state funeral in May 1885 (1)
brought Paris to a standstill and marked the end of an era.
An unidentified banquet scene of the period (2) shows
not a clean-shaven face in the hall.

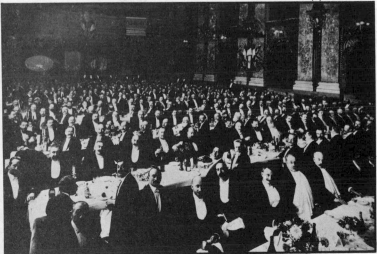

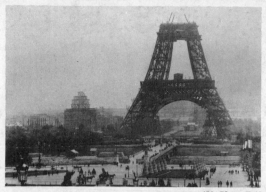

(1) Photo B.N.

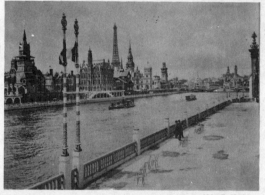

(2) Coll. Sirot

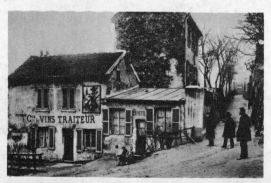

(3) Musée Carnavalet: Cliché Bulloz

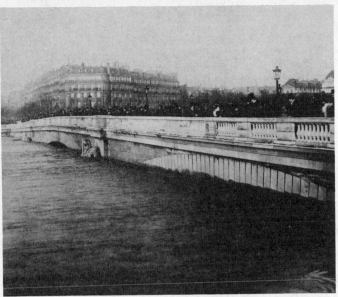

PLATE II The Eiffel Tower was still unfinished in July 1888 (1) as Paris prepared for the great Exposition of 1889. The 1900 Exposition erected Venetian façades along the Seine (2) but did not touch Montmartre, where cabarets like Le Lapin Agile (3) were in their heyday. Ten years later, when the Seine flooded, citizens kept a careful watch on the Zouave of the Pont de l'Alma (4), and Venice came without façade to the Avenue Montaigne (5).

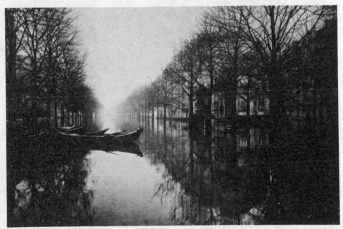

PLATE III At the turn of the century, manly histrionics of the right arm could serve to denounce the established church when Aristide Briand orated at a banquet in the provinces (1), to wield a sword in a journalists' duel in the Bois (2), to dispute a favored spot at the Salon des Indépendents (3), and to represent Dreyfus' innocence in the version Méliès re-enacted in a film studio while the events were taking place (4).

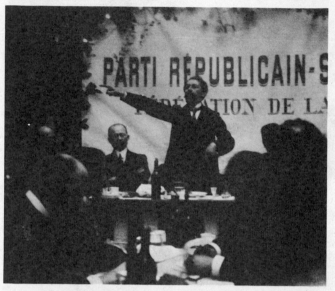

(1) Coll. Sirot

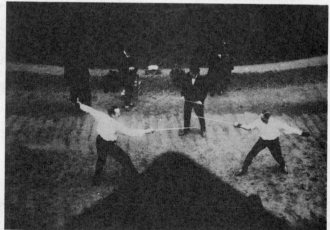

(2) Coll. Sirot

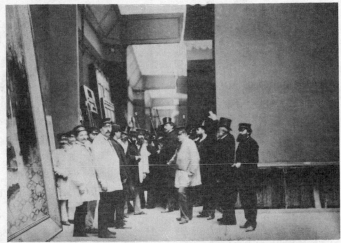

(3) Coll. Sirot

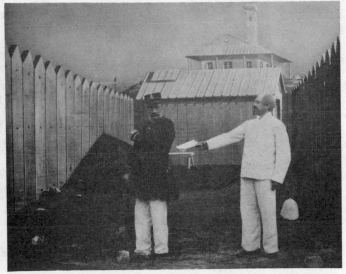

(4) Courtesy of the Museum of Modern Art, N. Y.

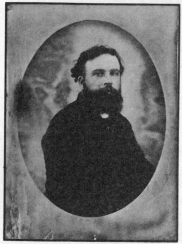

*(1) Courtesy of the Estate of
Tristan Tzara*

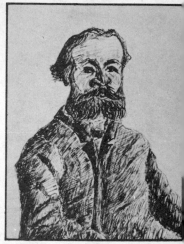

*(2) Collection Santamarina,
Buenos Aires*

PLATE IV   His friends referred to him, not as the "douanier," but as "gentil
Rousseau." It was from a photograph of himself as a young man (1) that
Rousseau drew his self-portrait (2) twenty years later, in 1895. But long
before that he had shaved off his beard and adopted an artist's beret.
The photograph of him in his studio (3) dates from after 1900.

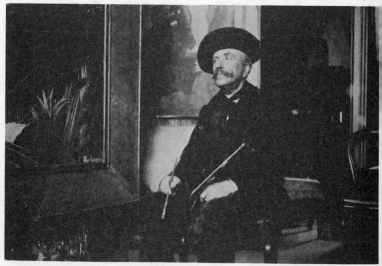

(3) Courtesy of René Char

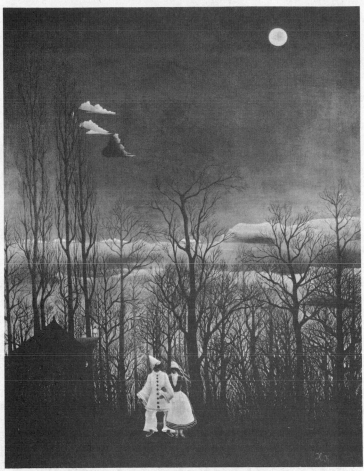

PLATE V *Un soir de carnaval,*[7] 1886. One of Rousseau's first paintings exhibited at the Salon des Indépendents and one of the greatest of his career. Barely distinguishable, a malevolent face peers out of a round window of the little house on the left.

—⁜ PLATE VI In *Un centenaire de l'indépendence*[16] (1), 1892, Rousseau expresses his stout republicanism in the movement of the dance and the rhythm of the pennons. His earliest known painting, *Petit moulin avec attelage*[1] (2), 1879, confines movement to the foreground and sets it against a carefully balanced composition.

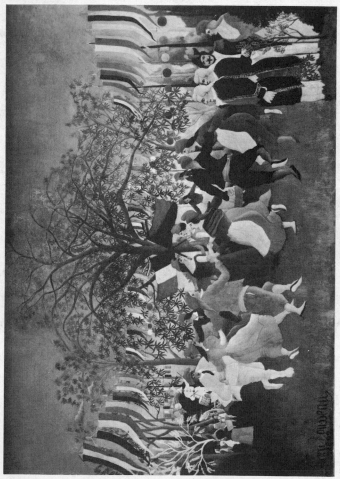

Cliché Bing

(1) *Formerly Düsseldorf; whereabouts unknown:*

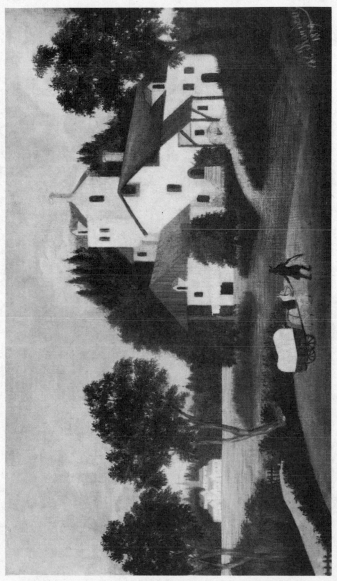

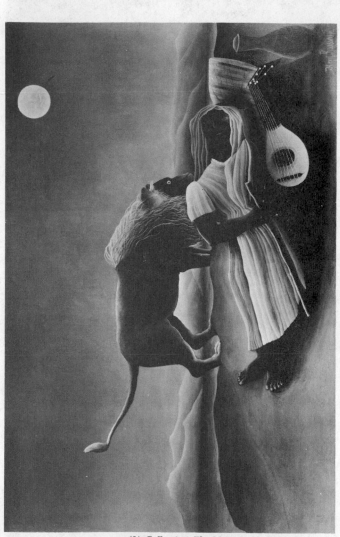

(1) Collection, The Museum of Modern Art, N.Y.:
Gift of Mrs. Simon Guggenheim

PLATE VII *La bohémienne endormie*[28] (1), 1897, anticipates several schools of modern painting, including cubism (the whole lower right-hand quarter) and magic realism. Rousseau could make his trees particularly eloquent: *L'été, le pâturage*[41] (2), 1906, should be compared to Plate X.

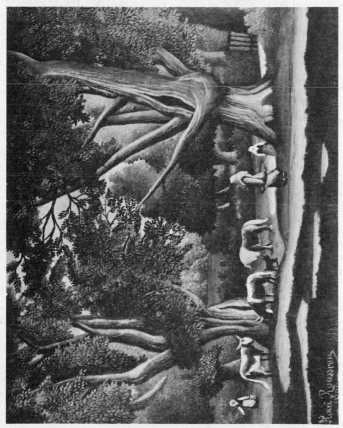

(2) Courtesy of the McNay Art Institute, San Antonio

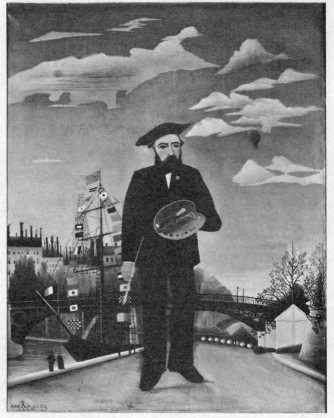

PLATE VIII In *Moi-même, portrait-paysage*[10] (1), 1890, Rousseau
floats serenely over Paris complete with chimney pots, decorated
barge, Eiffel Tower, and balloon. His portrait of Marie Laurencin
and Apollinaire, *Le poète et sa muse*[52] (2), 1909, looks like a studio
photograph and keeps the quiet dignity of all his portraits.

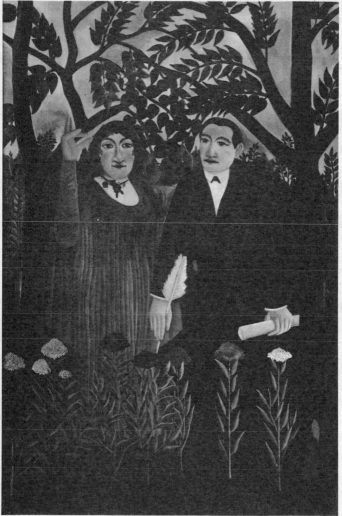

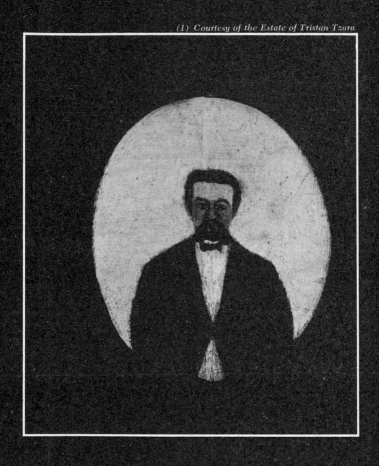

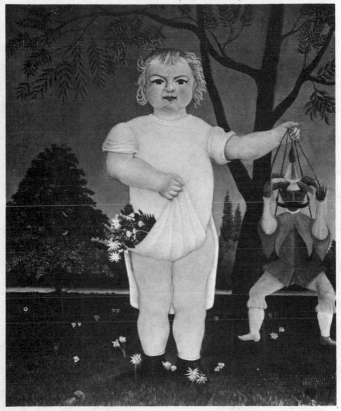

PLATE IX   The earliest known portrait by Rousseau, *Monsieur
Stevenc*[5] (1), 1884, shows miniature technique and photography
transformed into painting. In *Pour fêter le bébé*[36] (2), 1903,
Rousseau came very close to overt symbolism—the sturdy child
holding a puny clown of a man.

PLATE X   *Bois de Vincennes*,[33] 1901.

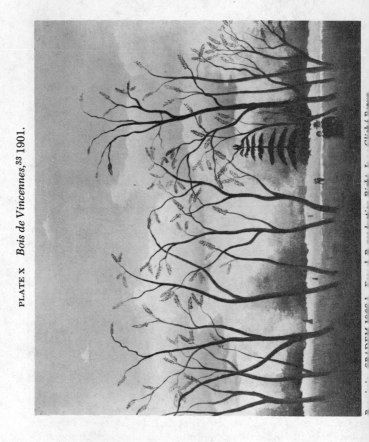

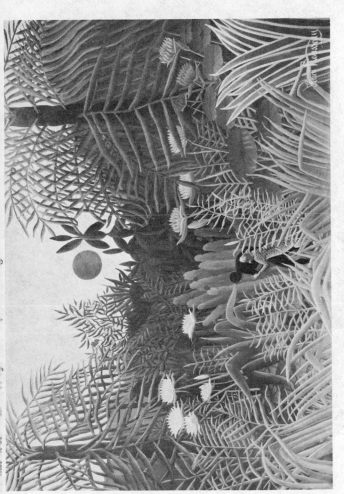

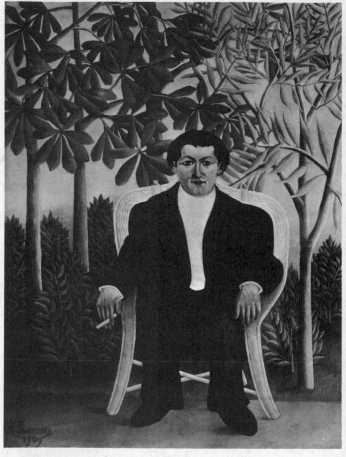

PLATE XII   *Portrait de Joseph Brummer,*[50] 1909.

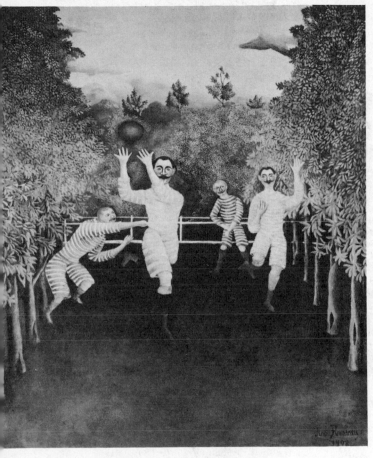

PLATE XIII *Les joueurs de football,*[45] 1908.

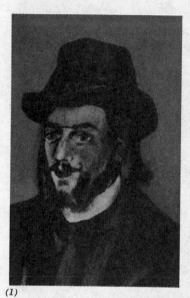

(1)

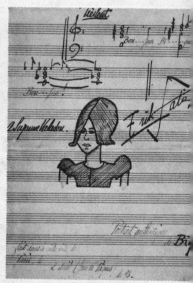

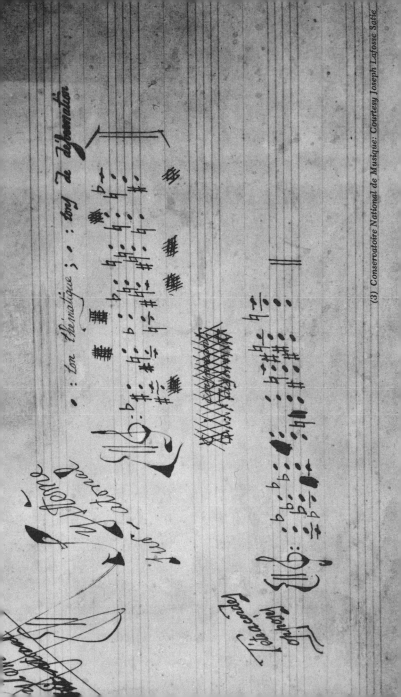

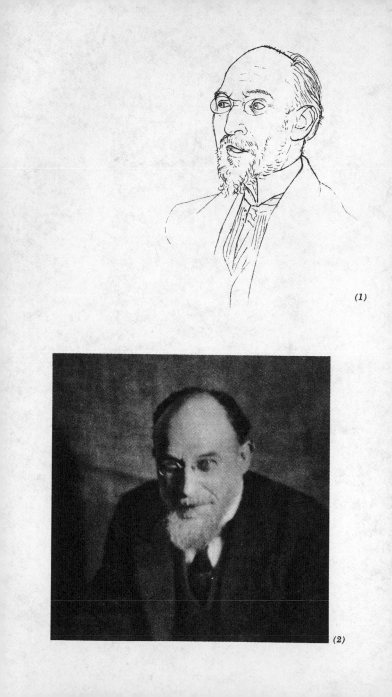

(1)

(2)

(3)

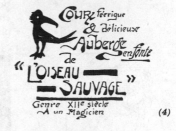

(4)

PLATE XV Picasso sketched Satie (1) during rehearsals for *Parade* (1917). Man Ray caught him with equal incisiveness a few years later (2). All his life Satie drew and inscribed whimsical texts on little cards (3, 4, 5) which he kept in cigar boxes.

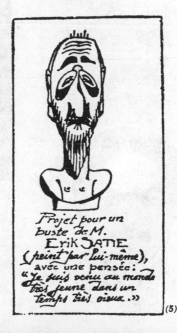

(5)

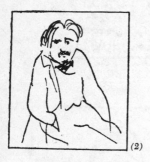

(1)

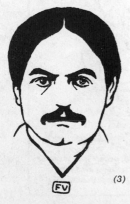

(2)

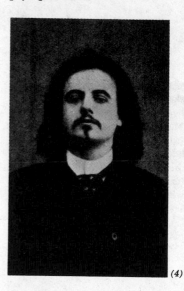

(4)

PLATE XVI Undersized and flamboyant, Jarry was photographed by Nadar (4) at the time of the *Ubu Roi* scandal. Later he was sketched by Bonnard (1), Picasso (2), and Félix Vallotton (3). The full-length photograph (8) shows him in boating costume in 1898. Bonnard also drew Père Ubu (5) trundling about Paris, but the definitive versions of Ubu are Jarry's own woodcut illustrations (6, 7). (Illustrations by courtesy of Le Collège de 'Pataphysique, Paris.)

FV

(3)

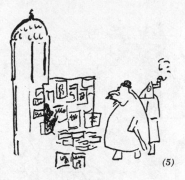

(5)

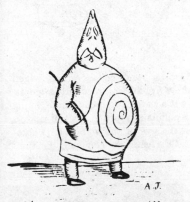

Véritable portrait de Monsieur Ubu. (6)

(7)

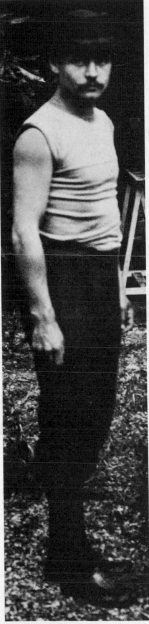

(8)

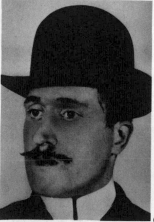

(1)

PLATE XVII During their early friendship and collaboration, which finally gave birth to cubism, Picasso drew Apollinaire in countless guises, from physical culturist to Pope-with-wrist-watch (1). An intense young man at twenty-one in Cologne (2), Apollinaire reached his full powers as poet and impresario of the arts on the eve of the war (3). (Photographs from *Apollinaire par lui-même,* "Ecrivains de Toujours," Editions du Seuil, 1954.)

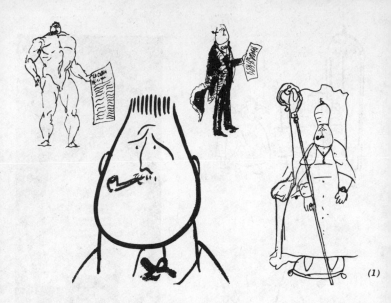

(2)

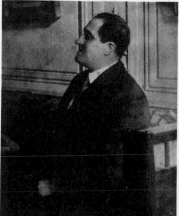

(3)

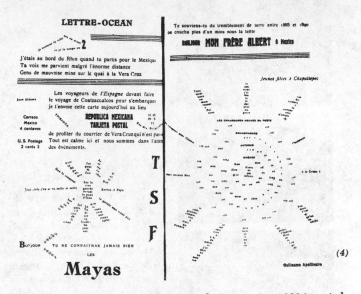

The next-to-last number of *Les Soirées de Paris* in June 1914 carried Apollinaire's most advanced esthetic pronouncement, *Simultanisme-librettisme*. Its principles were crudely but boldly applied by him in the first calligram, *Lettre-océan* (4). Marie Laurencin, Apollinaire's mistress for six years, commemorated the *bateau lavoir* era (1905-9) with a group portrait (5) of Picasso, Fernande Olivier, Apollinaire, and herself.

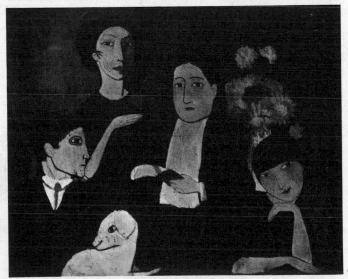

(5)

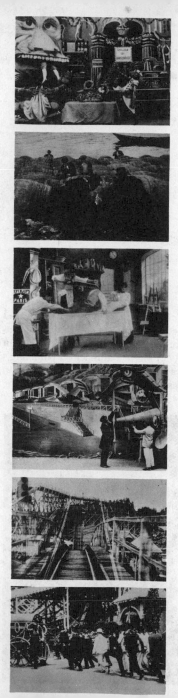

PLATE XVIII Ultimately the impact of the Banquet Years is the explosive and spectacular unity of montage, of juxtaposition. Here everything is happening at once, construction and destruction, serious endeavor and farce. The items shown: stills from films by Clair, Méliès, Zecca, and Feuillade (reproduced by courtesy of the Museum of Modern Art, New York); a page from Apollinaire's manifesto, *Antitradition futuriste;* Picasso's cubist frontispiece for Apollinaire's *Alcools;* La Décuplette, or ten-man bicycle; *(continued on next spread)*

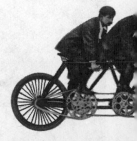

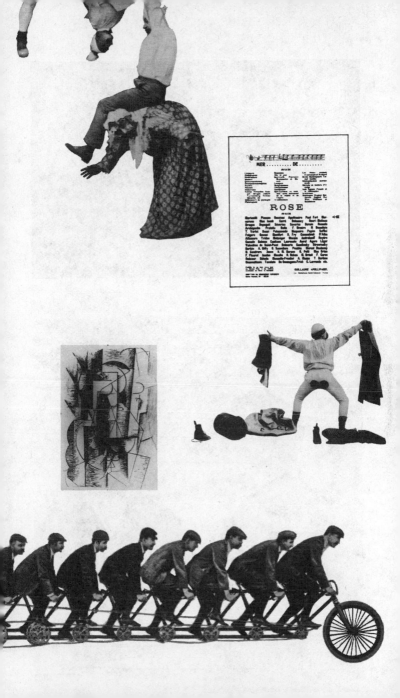

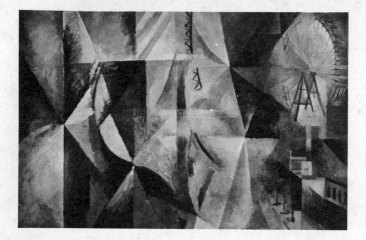

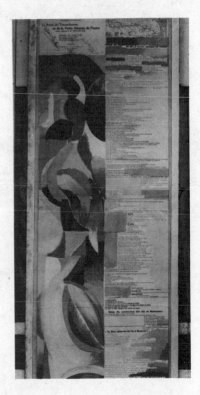

(Plusieurs goûtent et tombent empoisonnés.)

a simultanist painting by Delaunay in 1913; the anarchist Ravachol's police card; a drawing by Jarry from the manuscript of *Ubu Roi;* and the opening of *La prose du transsibérien* (1913) by Blaise Cendrars, colors by Sonia Delaunay-Terk. Complete with railroad map and standing over two meters high unfolded, this "simultaneous book" was advertised as "approaching the height of the Eiffel Tower."

PLATE XIX There is as much movement in this "still" of early flight as could be caught by a moving picture of the same scene. In the French countryside as in the streets of Paris, the Banquet Years appear to have been staged at the right place and in the perfect costume for a still camera.

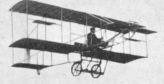

In all likelihood many people will not perceive that what follows is beautiful (without superlative: to start); and even if we assume that one or two things interest them, they may never believe those things were intended. For they will half see a few half-disclosed ideas, not embroidered with the usual trim. . . .

As with diamonds, one must weigh one's words, polyhedron of ideas, by scruples in the ear's scale, without asking why this and that. For one has only to look: it's written right on them.

Published when he was barely twenty, this selection of poetry and prose (illustrated with his own woodcuts) is probably the most important single volume of his work. It reveals the influence of symbolism, the durability of Heb-Ubu, and Jarry's first attempts to integrate the two contrasting strains.

During these years Jarry lived off the Boulevard de Port-Royal, at the foot of a dead-end alley so narrow two people could not walk abreast. Handprints in blood decorated the walls of the spiral stairway, and in the tiny room he hung censers and crucifixes and kept owls, which he admired for the absurd shape of their beaks and their nocturnal habits, resembling his own. His mother visited him frequently in this cell, which he called his "Dead Man's Calvary," the first of his legendary lodgings. For a time Rousseau was a neighbor, a coincidence which probably led to the meeting of these two sons of Laval. In March, 1893, began a series of events scantily recorded in his sister's terse words. "Paris . . . He takes long walks, falls ill, summons his mother and sister. His mother cares for him through forty wintry days, brings him through, then dies herself nine days later." The same influenza epidemic carried off his father within a week—"exactly on schedule," Jarry observed.

Jarry inherited a little money and the house in Laval with its imaginary tower, which he described as rotating very deliberately on its axis "once every century." He moved from Dead Man's Calvary to an apartment on the Boulevard Saint-Germain, where he installed a little marionette theater to entertain his guests, and invented the sport of bouncing chickpeas off the stovepipe hats of gentlemen on the boulevard below. Straightway he began spending his tiny fortune. With Remy de Gourmont as coeditor, he founded in October, 1894, a superbly presented review, *L'Ymagier,* devoted to popular and religious prints, Dürer engravings, Jarry's and Gourmont's woodcuts, and their comments on this material. The second number contained Rousseau's only known lithograph, entitled *La guerre.* After the fifth number Jarry broke with Gourmont, and in 1896 started another magazine entirely his own, *Perhinderion,* named from a Breton word meaning pilgrimage. He set about to print "the complete engraved work of Dürer plate by plate"; a special hand-set type face was cast for the text; he commissioned the original Pellerin firm in Epinal to do separate printings for him of old woodcuts by Géorgin; and in all this he was far ahead of his time, as was Gourmont, in recognizing the qualities of popular and primitive art. Small wonder that *Perhinderion* exhausted his fortune after only two issues.

The break with Gourmont early in 1896 came as the result of a ludicrous but significant incident in Jarry's life. Gourmont had been one of his most sympathetic admirers, reviewed his first book favorably in the *Mercure,* and planned an article on him for *Le livre des masques.* Gourmont's mistress was Madame Berthe de Courrière, who had lived previously with Huysmans (some say she also converted him and inspired the novel *Là-bas*), and now cared for Gourmont, who suffered from a disfiguring skin disease. An aging, lecherous, ambitious woman, who chased priests, the "old lady," as she was called, met Jarry at the *Mercure* receptions. The twenty-year-old poet had a fierce youthful spirit which in her eyes made up for his short stature and odd appearance. When one of the local wags, Jean de Tinan, told her that Jarry was burning with a secret passion for her, she swallowed the bait whole and made overtures to him in a lyrical and openly salacious letter—adding that he must need someone to "mend his socks." Possibly he tried her companionship for a short time; in any case he soon decided to live with his socks unmended and made no secret of the incident. It cost him Gourmont's friendship, and Jarry took Madame Rachilde to task for not having interfered in the hoax. The experience seems to have shaken him, for when he based a story on it some years later, he treats the matter savagely. "The old lady is old, as her name indicates," he begins. The story, which transcribes her correspondence verbatim, almost landed Jarry in prison. Beneath the bitterness of this section of *L'amour en visites* lies a note of real disillusionment, and the affair sheds light on his violently contracted private life.

One wonders, indeed, where it disappeared to. The only facts we have form a paltry debris. There is Jarry's schoolboy boast about visiting the brothels; there is one tale of his visiting card having been found by the police in the apartment of a fashionable Paris prostitute; Lugné-Poe states without comment that Jarry came to the theater several times in the company of friends of Oscar Wilde and Lord Douglas; and there is further evidence of homosexual proclivities. His writings refer to every variety of sexual behavior; from the beginning he flaunts a violent misogyny and portrays women in the role of courtesans. In the various texts of *Les minutes de sable mémorial,* he wrote of homosexual love in a tone of dark meditation and distaste. There is some imbalance here, a wavering of emotional states which has its roots deep in the turmoil of Jarry's life. It is possible that he fell victim to psychological impotency in the presence of any woman he might have loved, and that he was at the same time drawn toward sexual inversion and solitary vice. This would partly illuminate the compulsive manner in which he exploited erotic themes in several of his books.

The nearest Jarry came to intimacy—one hesitates to say "romance"—was in his steady attachment to Madame Rachilde. To her he paid a rare compliment veiled in the bombastic style he came to affect: "Ma-da-me, your character is nothing to shout about, and like all of us you are a negligible assemblage of atoms. But we will grant you one quality: you don't cling." Possibly there was an affair between the two; it is more likely that they understood each other beneath their braggart exteriors and enjoyed one another's company. Jarry's most revealing correspondence is addressed to Madame Rachilde, and he writes to her with a compelling directness that implies the sympathy of friendship more than sentimental or physical attachment.

In November, 1894, a month after starting *L'Ymagier,* Jarry had been called up for military service; but nothing could interfere with his literary activity. There was to be no obedient submission of civilian to military. The first day in the Laval barracks, he was assigned to a half-human corporal by the name of Bouilly, who made a fetish of discipline and set out to break this stunted long-haired recruit to army life. Jarry was always polite and attentive, though he persisted in calling all his superiors "Monsieur." He seemed to be trying. But he was a born comic with a gun and in his inevitably outsized uniform. His presence in the company finally became so demoralizing to the other troops that he was excused from parades and from most drill and training. He struck up an acquaintance with the first drummer, apparently the only man who could match Jarry's already growing capacity for drink. He boasted of his privileges and soon found himself assigned all the worst details: policing the area, K.P., and latrine duty. His last defense consisted in pompous statements about his work. "It is no mere bow to rhetoric to designate with the word 'brush' these objects generally known in the civilian world as brooms. They are, in reality, exceptionally suited for sketching decorative designs on the ground and for roughing out the possible boundaries of a future sweeping project—one which remains highly improbable."

Jarry's rebellion was too well conducted for the army to quell; he even swallowed a strong dose of acid, which landed him in the hospital for some weeks. After only a few months Jarry was "reformed" out of the army for chronic lithiasis (gallstones). But the story gained credence, probably with Jarry's blessing, that his medical discharge records carried the classification "precocious imbecility." By now one can understand how apt the fictitious designation must have sounded. Just where was he going, this unregenerate misfit? What drove him? Is there any answer short of attributing his behavior to permanent psychosis? The questions are especially urgent in dealing with a career that skirts close to lunacy. The answers begin to emerge slowly from these first adult years around 1895.

Jarry's nonconformity, his resolute role of the *potache*, tends to obscure the human being he remained in spite of himself. In his twenties he had a proud but not unattractive face with heavy-lidded eyes and unsmiling lips. As time went on he let his hair grow down to his shoulders and assumed increasingly outlandish dress—hooded cape, crook-handled umbrella, and women's blouses instead of shirts because "men's linen is too confining." But the people who knew him never lost sight of him and testify without exception to his goodness and charm. His most faithful friend was Vallette, the busy, levelheaded editor of the *Mercure*, with whom Jarry fished and canoed and bicycled. In an obituary note Vallette caught Jarry's flickering personality. "Extraordinarily comprehending, he was surprisingly ignorant of life; often sensitive, discreet, tactful under many circumstances, he liked to assume a cynical attitude. He was charming, unbearable, and sympathetic." Vallette is not alone in perceiving a fundamental innocence beneath Jarry's naughtiness. Dr. Saltas, who tried to restore Jarry's health in the final years, insists at length on his scrupulousness in paying debts when possible and calls him "noble." Paul Fort, the prolific author of *Les ballades*, sees him even more clearly. ". . . one of the most curious figures of the second generation of symbolists. He was popular with all of us, this sensitive witty young man, so pale and muscular. Popular? Not only himself but his manner of living among his owls and chameleons."

The longest tribute to Jarry's character comes in Madame Rachilde's romping biography, which reaches its climax in a scene of pure melodrama. One day Jarry was pulling her along country roads in a little trailer attached by ropes to his bicycle, and they started down a long hill with a hairpin turn under a viaduct at the bottom. The little team rapidly picked up speed, with the trailer overtaking the bicycle the minute Jarry attempted to apply his brakes. Madame Rachilde told Jarry not to go so fast. "Not so fast yourself, Ma-da-me," he retorted between his teeth. "*You're* pushing us now." The danger was suddenly upon them.

When it became apparent that they would not make the turn at the bottom and would smash into the stone viaduct, Jarry drew a knife and began to cut the ropes which prevented him from controlling the bicycle. Madame Rachilde closed her eyes in resignation. With a fiendish laugh he threw the knife away, lunged off his seat, and let himself be dragged with the bicycle until the trailer came to a stop. "Well, Ma-da-me," he muttered when he found himself only bruised and cut, "we believe we were a little frightened. . . . And never have we wanted so desperately to take leave of a woman." Madame Rachilde cites the incident as typical of his character—half criminal, half noble.

Jarry was in effect the extreme embodiment of his era. The *fin-de-siècle* world of Paris was topsy-turvy, rollicking on through corruption and optimism toward a still undefined New Spirit. Jarry reveled in the waggishness and was not alone in his innocent zest. The time came, however, when he could no longer be merely the *potache,* the moment when most young Frenchmen return to their families or settle into a secure career. Jarry's circumstances were exceptional. No one had been so close to him as his mother, and her death removed the only stabilizing force in his already unruly life.* At that moment he was tasting his first literary success, protecting himself from Gourmont's mistress, and suffering from a break in his intimacy with Léon-Paul Fargue. Drafted into the army, he discovered that total eccentricity escaped even that ancient tradition of conformity. The events of 1893–1896 appear to have confirmed him in a slow and probably reasoned decision not to abandon his *potachisme,* but to carry it to a new level, to devote to it the effort of imagination which he applied to his writing. These years contain a true conversion which compounded into one rash and unflagging exploit both his art and his life.

In his first published work, in 1893, Jarry used a near pun which changes "magnificent gesture" into "manifest imposture." From then on the magnificent gesture of his temperamental oddity became something deliberate and systematic, the manifest imposture that monopolized his total being. Henceforth he was hard to recognize; his "act" became a literary version of originality imposed upon the externals of his life.

The division in Jarry's work between obscure, intensely personal poetry and the extroverted monstrosity of Ubu now began to disappear. The novel *Les jours et les nuits* (1897) relates the story of Sengle, a misfit recruit, whose days are military fiascoes and whose nights bring escape

---

* A few years later he devoted one of his most passionately moving books, *L'amour absolu,* to the theme of maternal love multiplied and transformed into an all-encompassing religious experience.

to writing and reverie. In solitude at night he writes "curiously and precisely balanced" works, the products of his mind during sleep. In his daily life he has learned that by abandoning himself to external circumstances he can learn the secret of controlling them. For example, Sengle discovers he is able to will the fall of the dice.

> As a result of these reciprocal relations with Things, which he could direct with his thought (but all of us can, and it is not at all certain that there is a difference, even in time, between thought, will, and act: cf. the Holy Trinity), he did not in the least distinguish his thoughts from his acts or his dreaming from his waking; and perfecting the Leibnizean definition that perception is a true hallucination, he saw no reason against saying: hallucination is a false perception, or more precisely, a feeble one, or better yet, an anticipated perception (remembered sometimes, which is the same thing). And he thought above all that there were only hallucinations, or perceptions, and that there is neither day nor night (in spite of the title of this book, which is why it is chosen) and that life is continuous. . . .

The paragraph is crucial. The book reveals itself as a demonstration of how the barriers between sleeping and waking break down to render life "continuous." Jarry stands in the tradition of Jean-Paul Richter and Rimbaud and especially Gérard de Nerval, whose professed end was to "direct his dream." The opposition in his work between personal lyric and horrendous farce dissolves before this single view of life as sustained hallucination.

At this point then, Jarry's work intersects his possessed, hallucinatory life—the virtual incarnation of a dream. And at this point, also, he races past both the tranquil innocence of Rousseau in his child-man vision of the world, and the genuine sense of the absurd with which Satie prolonged his youth. Jarry's writing expressed an almost unthinkable code of conduct, which he did not shrink from applying to his own life. Dream must invade every waking moment to become the element in which we exist. The conscious and the unconscious fuse into a continuum which coincides with the fusion of thought and action, art and life, childhood and maturity.

Still human in spite of all, Jarry could not in every respect "live up to" these ambitious ideas. But they shed light on almost everything he did and reveal its purpose. He set about to upset the balance of waking (rational) logic and developed the elements of 'Pataphysics, a kind of reasonable unreason similar to the workings of our dreaming minds. He held out to our conscious attention the hideous figure of Ubu instead of repressing it along with other childish images. He forced his life into a mold closer to literary fiction than biological survival. And as a symbol of this total abandonment to the hallucinatory world of dream, he advocated and practiced the use of alcohol.

It was in these years that, in addition to everything else, Jarry began drinking. This explains in part the rapid disappearance of his inheritance. An unbelievable consumption of absinthe (and ether at the end) helped him do violence to his identity until his own personality dropped away. Like Rabelais, he proclaimed his faith in alcohol, calling it "holy water," the "essence of life," and "my sacred herb." "Antialcoholics are unfortunates in the grip of water, that terrible poison, so solvent and corrosive that out of all substances it has been chosen for washings and scourings, and a drop of water, added to a clear liquid like absinthe, muddies it." And elsewhere he wrote: "We thought we had done once and for all with this question of alcoholism, and that all sensible people understood that the use, and even more the abuse, of fermented beverages is what distinguishes men from beasts." He drank defiantly and triumphantly. De Quincey had a comparable addiction and equal boldness in calling his vice a virtue. Verlaine drank in secret; Nerval did not have to induce his intervals of insanity. Baudelaire, describing Poe and how he raised memory to the power of a "periodic dream," wrote a profoundly significant passage on the subconscious functioning of the human mind.

> But incontestably . . . there exist in drunkenness not only dream associations but patterns of reasoning which, in order to recur, require the circumstances which originally provoked them. . . . I believe that in many cases . . . Poe's drinking was a mnemonic method, a technique of work, a method both ener-

getic and mortal, yet appropriate to his passionate
nature. The poet had learned to drink the way an
author takes pain over his notebooks.

Alcohol helped Jarry achieve his fierce antic and sent him
early to his grave. He must have foreseen the results.

So it was that through drink and hallucination Jarry
converted himself into a new person physically and mentally devoted to an artistic goal—a person in whom Jarry,
the man, spent the rest of his days dying. The questions
about the basic intentions of his life now begin to find their
answers. He unlived his life. He abdicated his self in
order to become another, and the culminating event of
the process, which began with the loss of his mother,
looks suspiciously like a perverse father identification.
Jarry's public behavior began to crystallize around a single
figure whose presence had haunted him since the *lycée*
at Rennes, stayed with him in the army, and now usurped
his speech and bearing. It was old Père Heb, rechristened
with the infantile and immortal name of Ubu, in English,
Ooboo. By 1896 he had published six different fragments
of Ubu texts, all modeled on the original schoolboy farces
at Rennes. His systematic promotion of the character was
well under way. In the spring of 1896 Paul Fort virtually
commandeered from Jarry a full-length play called *Ubu
Roi* and published it in the review, *Le Livre d'Art*. At
about the same time, Jarry read parts of the play to Gustave Kahn, the self-styled inventor of vers libre, and
several of his friends. Their enthusiastic reaction fired his
secret ambitions. Ubu obsessed and possessed him totally,
swallowed him whole. Thereafter it was as if, like Jonah,
he could communicate only from inside the whale. He
had found his Other, the flesh of his hallucination.

The first edition of the play in book form, in June, 1896,
was greeted by a number of impassioned reviews, mostly
favorable. The subtitle gave an honest authentication:
"Drama in five acts restored in its entirety as performed
at the Théâtre des Phynances in 1888"—meaning the
puppets in the attic at Rennes. Jarry fixed on the idea of a
Paris production. When Lugné-Poe, the young director of
the Théâtre de l'Œuvre, asked Jarry to become *secrétaire-
régisseur* of the company, Jarry's hopes increased enormously. This group, which grew out of Paul Fort's Théâ-

tre d'Art and thus inherited a reputation for both symbolist and anarchist leanings, was the most active and forward-looking in Paris. Jarry had followed it from the beginning and offered the support of his growing fame. He accepted the position and worked hard through the long summer while Lugné-Poe (who let it be supposed he was related to Edgar Allan Poe) vacationed in the country. Jarry forwarded manuscripts, made plans for the coming season, and carefully insinuated into the program his two pet projects: Ibsen's *Peer Gynt* and *Ubu Roi*.

Since he ran the publicity and had a hand in everything, Jarry made certain that his play was not neglected. Posters, announcements, articles, and Jarry's own woodcuts appeared in a steady stream. *Peer Gynt*, partly adapted by Jarry, had only a minor success in the fall—despite Jane Avril, brought in to do Anitra's dance, Munch's work on the sets and program, and Jarry himself in the cast. The play was not the kind of Ibsen Paris expected. In November Lugné-Poe still hesitated over the prospect of *Ubu*. "I didn't know which way to take hold of the thing." A letter from the loyal Rachilde persuaded him to go ahead and stage the play as Jarry wished, *"en guignol"*—slapstick.

Jarry had expressed his ideas in a letter to Lugné-Poe, which was later printed as a preface to the play.

> Dear Sir,
>   . . . It would be curious, I believe, to produce this play (and at little expense really) in the following manner.
>   1. A mask for the principal role, Ubu, which I could do for you if necessary. But then I believe you have yourself been involved with this business of masks.
>   2. A horse's head of cardboard, which he could hang around his neck as in the old English theater, for the only two equestrian scenes—both these suggestions being in the spirit of the play, since I intended to write a "Guignol."
>   3. Only one set, or better yet, one catchall backdrop, eliminating raising and lowering the curtain. A suitably costumed person would come in, as in puppet shows, to put up signs indicating the scene.

(You see, I am sure that written signs are more "suggestive" than sets. No set or contrivance could portray the Polish army on the march in the Ukraine.)

4. The elimination of crowds, which are often bad on stage and have no intelligible effect. Thus, a single soldier in the review scene, and only one in the great scuffle when Ubu says: "What a horde of people, what a flight, etc."

5. The adoption of an "accent" or better yet, a special "tone of voice" for the principal character.

6. Costumes with as little local color and historical accuracy as possible (it gives the best idea of something eternal); modern ones preferably, since satire is modern; and sordid costumes because they make the action more wretched and repugnant. . . .

In a subsequent article in the *Mercure*, Jarry came out bluntly for the elimination of sets (*"décor* is hybrid, neither entirely naturalistic nor entirely artificial") and of acting in the usual sense. He reasserted his belief in masks, which convey "a character's eternal quality" and which can be made to express variations in mood by a few basic movements using the full effects of lighting and shadow. Jarry carefully defined "universal gesture" as opposed to ordinary pantomime, which cries out for words. Lines are to be delivered in a conventionalized manner "as if the mask itself were speaking." He continued to advance ideas on the production of *Ubu Roi,* including the unheard-of suggestion in 1896 that the role of Bougrelas, aged fourteen, be played by a boy of that age. Again he cited the Elizabethan stage for support. It was neither the prevailing realism of the time nor the essentially antidramatic theories of symbolism that determined his theatre. Its stylized comic earthiness stemmed from medieval theater, Rabelais, and the schoolboy experiments at Rennes.

Jarry finally had his way about the production, after carrying Ubu like a cancer inside him for eight years. Two excellent actors were found for the roles: Firmin Gémier, borrowed from the Comédie-Française, and Louise France. All literary Paris was primed for the event. Jarry's friends saw to it that every critic was present at the *première*. (The dress rehearsal had been fairly quiet.) The old Théâtre Nouveau in the Rue Blanche was filled to the last seat with partisans and enemies, with symbolists, decadents, naturists, independents, and the *Mercure* faithful, to hear the enormity Jarry had perpetrated. Loyal subscribers scarcely knew what they were in for. December 11, 1896, the opening night, is worth describing in detail. There had been nothing like it since the wild *première* of Victor Hugo's *Hernani* in 1830, when Théophile Gautier and Gérard de Nerval carried the day for romanticism by highly organized demonstrations.

Before the curtain went up, a crude table was brought out, covered with a piece of old sacking. Jarry appeared, looking dead white, for he had made himself up like a streetwalker to face the footlights. Nervously sipping from a glass, he spoke in his flattest, most clipped tones. For ten minutes, he sat in front of the explosive crowd, thanking the people who had helped in the production, referring briefly to the traditions of the Guignol theater, and mentioning the masks the actors would wear and the fact that the first three acts would be performed without intermission. He concluded in a more properly Ubuesque vein.

> In any case we have a perfect *décor,* for just as one good way of setting a play in Eternity is to have revolvers shot off in the year 1000, you will see doors open on fields of snow under blue skies, fireplaces furnished with clocks and swinging wide to serve as doors, and palm trees growing at the foot of a bed so that little elephants standing on bookshelves can browse on them.
>
> As to the orchestra, there is none. Only its volume and timbre will be missed, for various pianos and percussion will execute Ubuesque themes from backstage. The action, which is about to begin, takes place in Poland, that is to say: Nowhere.

In these earnest nonsense lines Jarry was already insinuating that the play is more than it appears, that the true setting of farce is (like Poland, a country long condemned to the nonexistence of partition) an Eternity of Nowhere, and that contradiction is the mode of its logic. The speech did not exactly insure a sympathetic reception.

Jarry vanished with his table; the curtain went up on the set—the handiwork of Jarry himself, aided by Pierre

Bonnard, Vuillard, Toulouse-Lautrec, and Sérusier. Like every other feature of this performance, the set has been described countless times. Arthur Symons, one of the few Englishmen present at this "symbolist farce," as he calls it, recalled every detail.

> . . . the scenery was painted to represent, by a child's conventions, indoors and out of doors, and even the torrid, temperate, and arctic zones at once. Opposite you, at the back of the stage, you saw apple trees in bloom, under a blue sky, and against the sky a small closed window and a fireplace . . . through the very midst of which . . . trooped in and out the clamorous and sanguinary persons of the drama. On the left was painted a bed, and at the foot of the bed a bare tree and snow falling. On the right there were palm trees . . . a door opened against the sky, and beside the door a skeleton dangled. A venerable gentleman in evening dress . . . trotted across the stage on the points of his toes between every scene and hung the new placard on its nail. (*Studies in Seven Arts.*)

Gémier, swollen and commanding in his pear-shaped costume (but without a mask, despite Jarry's campaign), stepped forward to speak the opening line—a single word. He had not known how to interpret the role until Lugné-Poe had suggested he imitate the author's own voice and jerky stylized gestures. The midget Jarry truly sired the monster Ubu. In a voice like a hammer, Gémier pronounced an obscenity which Jarry had appropriated to himself by adding one letter.

"*Merdre,*" Gémier said. "Shite."

It was fifteen minutes before the house could be silenced. The *mot de Cambronne** had done its work; the house was pandemonium. Those who had been lulled by Jarry's opening speech were shocked awake; several peo-

---

* One of Napoléon's officers at the Battle of Waterloo, General Cambronne, heard a report that one of his companies of guards was surrounded. His heroic response of *"Merde"* became the *mot de Cambronne*. Subsequently, the word achieved a paradoxical existence as an acceptable talisman of good luck said to a friend going on a journey. Still, public utterance of the word was, in 1896, unthinkable.

ple walked out without hearing any more. The rest separated into two camps of desperately clapping enthusiasts
and whistling scoffers. Fist fights started in the orchestra.
The critics were on the spot, their reactions observed by
both sides. Edmond Rostand smiled indulgently; Henry
Fouquier and Sarcey, representing the old guard, almost
jumped out of their seats. A few demonstrators simultaneously clapped and whistled in divided sentiments. Mallarmé sat quiet, waiting to see more of the "prodigious
personage" to whose author he addressed a letter the
following day. Jarry's supporters shouted, "You wouldn't
understand Shakespeare either." Their opponents replied
with variations on the *mot* of the evening. Fernand Hérold
in the wings startled the audience into silence for a moment by turning up the house lights and catching people
with their fists raised and standing on their seats. The
actors waited patiently, beginning to believe that the roles
had been reversed and they had come to watch a performance out front.

Finally, Gémier improvised a jig and sprawled out on
the prompter's box. His diversion restored enough order to
allow the action to proceed to the next "*merdre,*" when the
audience took over once more. The interruptions continued
for the rest of the evening, while Père Ubu murdered his
way to the throne of Poland, pillaged the country, was
defeated by the king's son aided by the czar's army, and
fled cravenly to France, where he promised to perpetrate
further enormities on the population. The story of *Ubu Roi*
is no more than this.[*] Père Ubu and Mère Ubu use language more scatological than erotic, and Rachilde maintains that the audience whistled because they "expected

[*] One obvious and neglected source of the action is the
libretto of Chabrier's comic opera *Le roi malgré lui,* which
concerns a fictitious king of Poland, Laski, his *grand palatin*
(out of which title Jarry & Co. forged the three *palotins* or
"palatoons"), and a generally farcical sequence of events. The
opera had its widely discussed *première* in 1887, just the year
before Jarry entered the *lycée* in Rennes. The circumstances of
the rout of Ubu may well have been lifted from Brillat-Savarin,
one of whose "Examples of Obesity" in *Physiologie du goût*
relates the scene perfectly. "In the case of the King of Poland,
his obesity came close to causing his death, for having fallen
among the Turkish cavalry before whom he had been obliged
to flee, he was saved by his attendants."

this Punch and Judy of an Ubu to function sexually" and were disappointed. The curtain rang down that night and the next on the only two performances of *Ubu Roi* until it was revived by Gémier in 1908. For the Théâtre de l'Œuvre it was the catastrophe that made it famous.

Also present in the house was a young Irishman by the name of William Butler Yeats. Despite a very limited knowledge of the language, his description of the performance is worth repeating.

> I go to the 1st performance of Jarry's Ubu Roi, at the Theatre de l'Oeuvre, with Rhymer who had been so attractive to the girl in the bicycling costume. The audience shake their fists at one another, and Rhymer whispers to me, "There are often duels after these performances," and explains to me what is happening on the stage. The players are supposed to be dolls, toys, marionettes, and now they are all hopping like wooden frogs, and I can see for myself that the chief personage, who is some kind of king, carries for a sceptre a brush of of the kind that we use to clean a closet. Feeling bound to support the most spirited party, we have shouted for the play, but that night at the Hotel Corneille I am very sad, for comedy, objectivity, has displayed its growing power once more. I say, After S. Mallarmé, after Verlaine, after G. Moreau, after Puvis de Chavannes, after our own verse, after the faint mixed tints of Conder, what more is possible? After us the Savage God. (*Autobiography*.)

No event marks more clearly than this the close of one era and the imminence of another. Yeats did not have to understand French to perceive the significance of Ubu, natural offspring of the turbulence of the nineties.

This single performance assured Jarry's celebrity far beyond literary circles. The following morning, and for weeks after, the papers discussed the play. Five critics wrote favorable reviews—the five whom Jarry mentioned in his introductory speech. Ten-odd conservative critics, led by the ponderous Sarcey of *Le Temps*, denounced it as the limit of folly. One of them started his article, "Despite the late hour, I have just taken a shower." A critics' battle royal soon developed between Henry Bauer, defending Jarry and wielding great power from his post on the *Echo de Paris,* and Henry Fouquier of *Le Figaro,* an elegant Marseillais with a loyal bourgeois following. After *Ubu Roi* he was determined to crush Bauer. Because he knew how to write better bombast than Bauer, Fouquier finally won and his rival lost his column in the *Echo de Paris.*

It is to Fouquier's credit that he came up with one fruitful idea.

> It strikes me that his performance brought a kind of release, a literary *Neuf Thermidor.* At least it has begun to put an end to the Terror which has been reigning over our literature.

Considering the prewar and postwar years to come, his terminology was pat and his prediction wrong. Ubu, the Savage God, arrived on the scene to inaugurate the Reign of Terror in literature. He was born full-fledged—belly, obscenity, ridiculousness, and all. The schoolboy imagination had succeeded in throwing dung in the public eye. Some laughed and some were incensed, but no one could deny that it had been cunningly thrown and that one performance of the play was enough to assure its fame. Catulle Mendès in *Le Journal* the following day wrote in a kind of frenzy.

> . . . in spite of the idiotic action and mediocre structure, a new type has emerged, created by an extravagant and brutal imagination, more a child's than a man's.
>
> Père Ubu exists.
>
> Compounded of Pulcinella and Polichinelle, of Punch and Judy . . . of Monsieur Thiers and the Catholic Torquemada and the Jew Deutz, of a Sûreté policeman and the anarchist Vaillant, an enormous parody of Macbeth and Napoléon, a flunky become king, he nevertheless exists unforgettably. . . . He will become a popular legend of base instincts, rapacious and violent; and Monsieur Jarry, who I hope is destined for a more worthy celebrity, will have created an infamous mask.

Amid all the heated exchange of opinion, Jarry appeared indifferent. He had to be persuaded to write a polite note to Mendès acknowledging the article, and twenty-three is not an age at which to be sophisticated about public acclaim. But Jarry was already engaged in redoubling the extravagance of his behavior and in completing his identification with Ubu. This scandalous performance gave him the final impetus to attempt a resolutely fabricated personality.

There are virtually no standards by which to judge the role Jarry created and the *décors* with which he surrounded himself in order to sustain it. He left behind every standard, ethic, maxim, golden rule, and secret of success. In the end his role implies new, almost nonhuman standards, and its most immediately significant aspect is the completeness of the transformation he wrought. Everything in his universe had to yield to his power to change it. Nothing escaped, neither the conventions of eating, which he destroyed by the simple expedient of devouring meals backward from pastry to peasant soup, nor common sense itself, which he stalked with the brilliant antireason of 'Pataphysics.

The transformation began with elemental personal considerations of dress and speech. His usual costume was that of a bicycle racer: tight sweater, short coat, and old trousers tucked into his socks. (As a symbol of great respect at Marcel Schwob's funeral, he pulled them out, something he neglected to do at Mallarmé's funeral, for which he borrowed a pair of Madame Rachilde's bright yellow shoes.) However, the variations were manifold. One night Jarry and his friend Demolder presented themselves at the box office of a light-opera company with a note from the composer entitling them to complimentary seats. Demolder wore a fur cap and carried a shepherd's crook; Jarry wore a dirty white canvas suit and a makeshift paper shirt with the tie painted on in India ink.* When the apprehensive house manager seated them in the balcony instead of the orchestra, Jarry took his revenge by complaining, just as the curtain was going up and in a rasping voice audible to the entire house: "I don't see why they allow

---

* This is not the last time we hear of the painted cravat. Apollinaire inherited the fashion.

the audience in the first three rows to come in carrying musical instruments."

Ever since the Lycée Henri IV, Jarry's inflexible staccato speech was even better remembered than his dress. André Gide has written the most vivid description of Jarry around 1895, when the repersonification was almost complete.

> It was the best period of Jarry's life. He was an incredible figure whom I also met at Marcel Schwob's, and always with tremendous enjoyment, before he became a victim of frightful attacks of delirium tremens. This plaster-faced Kobold, gotten up like a circus clown and acting a fantastic, strenuously contrived role which showed no human characteristic, exercised a remarkable fascination at the *Mercure.* Almost everyone there attempted, some more successfully than others, to imitate him, to adopt his humor; and above all his bizarre implacable accent—no inflection or nuance and equal stress on every syllable, even the silent ones. A nutcracker, if it could talk, would do no differently. He asserted himself without the least reticence and in perfect disdain of good manners. Afterward the Surrealists invented nothing better, and they had good reason to recognize him as a forerunner.

In conversation he adopted a periphrastic style, after Homer: the wind became "that which blows," and a bird "that which chirps."* The lofty role of King Ooboo required that he assume the royal *we* and pompous ceremoniousness. The result was a new form of speech, which still flourishes in Parisian literary quarters, a coarse inverted preciousness called *le parler Ubu.*

What surrounded the person of Jarry, or Père Ubu, as his friends soon called him, underwent an equally thorough transformation. His lodgings after the Dead Man's Calvary have become legendary. In 1897 he exhausted his inherit-

---

* In the first *Père Ubu Almanach* of 1899, Jarry applied the device with untranslatable refinements: *"Valette, celui qui Mercure; Allais (Alphonse), celui qui ira; Debussy, celui qui Pelle (et as et Mélisande); Degas, celui qui bec; Becque, celui qui gaz. . . ."* Twenty years later the Dadaists and surrealists reveled in the technique.

ance and left his apartment on the Boulevard Saint-Germain for temporary refuge in the studio of his fellow Lavalois, Henri Rousseau. (That year Rousseau hung the portrait of Jarry at the Salon des Indépendants.) Then he found a dingy room at 7 Rue Cassette, where he lived the rest of his life and which he dignified with the name of "Our Grand Chasublerie" because a manufacturer of ecclesiastical vestments occupied the second floor. Apollinaire's description is classic—though he places the room one floor too high by the French count.

"Monsieur Jarry?"

"On the third floor and a half," answered the concierge.

The answer astonished me. But I climbed up to where Jarry lived—actually on the third floor and a half. The ceilings of the building had appeared wastefully high to the owner and he had doubled the number of stories by cutting them in half horizontally. This building, which is still standing, had therefore about fifteen floors; but since it rose no higher than the other buildings in the quarter, it amounted to merely the reduction of a skyscraper.

It turned out that Jarry's place was filled with reductions. This half-floor room was the reduction of an apartment in which its occupant was quite comfortable standing up. But being taller than he, I had to stay in a stoop. The bed was the reduction of a bed; that is to say, a mere pallet. Jarry said that low beds were coming back into fashion. The writing table was the reduction of a table, for Jarry wrote flat on his stomach on the floor. The furniture was the reduction of furniture—there was only the bed. On the wall hung the reduction of a picture. It was a portrait [of Jarry by the Douanier Rousseau], most of which he had burned away, leaving only the head, which resembled a certain lithograph I know of Balzac. The library was the reduction of a library, and that is saying a lot for it. It was composed of a cheap edition of Rabelais and two or three volumes of the *Bibliothèque rose*. On the mantel stood a large stone phallus, a gift from Félicien Rops. Jarry kept this member, which was considerably larger than life

size, always covered with a violet skullcap of velvet, ever since the day the exotic monolith had
frightened a certain literary lady who was all out
of breath from climbing three and a half floors
and at a loss how to act in this unfurnished cell.

"Is that a cast?" the lady asked.

"No," said Jarry. "It's a reduction." (*Il y a.*)

The ceiling of the room was so low that the top of even
Jarry's head brushed against it as he walked about, and he
collected the flaky plaster like a severe case of dandruff.
It was said that the only food that could be eaten conveniently in the place was flounder.

For a year or two around the turn of the century Père
Ubu held court in an equally lowly summer residence—
an old stable for barge mules at the Coudray locks south
of Paris. In these drafty dirt-floored premises he decided
to repay his social obligations by throwing a banquet of
his own. The guests consisted of artists and writers from
Paris, the literate sub-prefect from Corbeil (at whose
house one rainy day Jarry had arrived barefoot for dinner),
and the local café keeper and tradesmen. Jarry had caught
a fish for every plate, and had laid in on credit enough
wine and absinthe for a regiment. Madame Rachilde, despairing of the Ubuesque preparations, labored long to
contribute an immense chocolate mousse molded in a salad
bowl. The banquet ran its intemperate course from general
conversation to demonstrations of how mightily the guests
could make the river resound with shouted commands of
"forward march." When the dessert arrived, the host rose
for a royal speech.

"This," he said in solemn machine-gun accents, pointing
first to the mousse and then to the wife of the café
keeper, "this represents the left breast of the giant Negress
of the carnival in the Place du Tôrn. Ma-da-me-Ra-chil-
de copied it from life in chocolate and vanilla, using
Mother Fontaine's milk, who, as the whole countryside
knows, sleeps with her goat. . . ."

The rest of his speech was lost in applause. Policemen
broke the party up; they had come to the locks to fish out
a body that had drifted in, and half the guests fled, thinking that Père Ubu's gala had exceeded the bounds of
decorum. The rest went to see the body.

Toward the end of his life the penniless Ubu attempted to have a "medieval dungeon" built on a shabby piece of property near the old stable. The resulting shack, which rose on four supports, he dubbed by ineluctable logic his "Tripod," and the architecture of this reduction of a castle deceived a few observers into calling it an abandoned freight car. The place was flooded regularly twice a year, and he had to hang his bicycle from the ceiling to save the tires from the rats.

In addition to being royally robed and lodged, Père Ubu had to be suitably accoutered. The bicycle, of course, became the royal vehicle, "that which rolls." He called it an "external skeleton" which permits mankind to outstrip biological evolution in developing new modes of locomotion. Then there were his weapons. In those days of anarchist assassinations Jarry made free with firearms, and often sallied forth at night in Paris with a carbine over his shoulder and two pistols in his belt. Beneath the bravado lay the knowledge that "there is no prohibition on arms openly displayed." A pedestrian who asked him one night for a light (*du feu*) suddenly saw a gun belch red flame in front of his nose while Jarry murmured politely "*Voilà.*" His marksmanship with a stubby *bouledogue* or revolver, was excellent, and he made a specialty of hunting spiders, frogs, and grasshoppers. The closest he came to injuring anyone was at the "Phalanstery," a summer house in Corbeil, rented co-operatively by the Vallettes, Jarry, and several friends. One day Jarry began shooting off the tops of champagne bottles lined up against the wall that protected the landlady's neighboring garden and that was scarcely designed to stop bullets. The landlady came knocking in great perturbation to see Madame Rachilde and complain that the shots endangered her children, who played in the garden. Père Ubu, overhearing, replied in full pomp. "If that should ever happen, Madame, we should ourselves be delighted to get some new ones with you." The following year the residents of the Phalanstery had to found their community elsewhere. No such incidents were provoked by the most functional item of Jarry's equipment, his fishing line, on which he relied heavily for nourishment. He caught fish where no one else had any luck and lived in a miraculous world of true fish stories. A design by the sculptor Zadkine for a monument

to Jarry shows him simultaneously riding a bicycle, pointing a gun, writing in a notebook on the handlebars, and
looking off into the sky—the whole thing lit from within.
He met the world fully equipped.

That part of his surroundings which Jarry could not
physically transform into Ubu's kingdom did not, therefore,
escape intact. So high a mental metabolism as his can alter
things by merely seeing them afresh. In a combination of
profound erudition and farce, he destroys our conventional
vision and sets things as systematically askew as his dress
and his lodgings. His magazine pieces called "*Spéculations*"
invent the voice of another civilization commenting on
ours.

> It is a human superstition that, when one wishes
> to communicate with dear ones temporarily at a
> distance, one should toss into the appropriate
> orifices (which might easily be sewer holes) the
> written expression of one's feelings, after having
> encouraged the postmaster with a small pittance
> and received in return some little pictures, no
> doubt blessed, which one devoutly kisses on the
> back. This is not the place to criticize the incoher-
> ence of these maneuvers; it is beyond argument
> that they make possible communication across great
> distances.

He can sustain it for several pages, and he wrote with the
same wry logic about microbes and buses and squaring
the circle. Everything in the world became a toy to him,
as much as his bicycle and his pistols. The moment never
comes in either his writing or his life when he had to
clear his throat and say, "But seriously . . ." He was always
serious and always discovering a humor that is closer to
metaphysics than to silliness. We can laugh with him and
at him, but it is not easy to laugh him off. He rejected no
part of himself or of his environment and methodically
transformed it all into an artificial world, the inverted
dignity of Père Ubu.

Such a transformation presupposes one absolute principle: the totality of human freedom. I can choose the
color of my coat; I can choose not to wear a coat; *I can
choose* (yet few men venture so far) *not to be I*. But: for
such absolute freedom there is retribution. Like the sorc-

erer's apprentice, Jarry was overwhelmed by his own power. Ubu acknowledges no affections, no damnation; for him nothing is sacred, not even, as in Faust, the clutch of his own mind. A distorted image of Faust, Ubu-Jarry is engaged in the only act logically left for him to perform: self-destruction. Elevation by alcohol became his form of protracted suicide; *yet while he was dying he was at liberty*. No worldly restraint could touch him.

One clue to Jarry's intentions in sustaining this role finally offers the possibility of interpreting an otherwise incomprehensible life. After his most outrageous escapades, he frequently commented, *"N'est-ce pas beau comme la littérature?"* ("Isn't it lovely as literature?") At certain moments, he implies, he effected a mutation of life into a work of art, something already in the realm of literature. His droll and occasionally abject "act" contained his highest ambitions: the sacrifice of his life to a literary ideal. "We maintain," writes the surrealist André Breton, "that beginning with Jarry, much more than with Wilde, the differentiation long considered necessary between art and life has been challenged, to wind up annihilated as a principle." It means that Jarry, if we glimpse him cursorily and with no willingness to measure his intentions, seems to live in foolish competition with his own work. Why run so wildly after Ubu once the personage had been created and staged? Why try to practice the preposterous theories of 'Pataphysics? It is enough that the books exist. On the other hand, the total career of Jarry, the accumulation of inaccurate and distorted and fabricated stories about him, creates a perspective in which Jarry becomes consubstantial with his work. Montaigne, who represents the complementary tendency, molded his essays so closely to his person as to consider them his own flesh; Jarry molded himself so closely to the lineaments of his literary creation that none of his own flesh remained. One gives the "truth" of confession; the other, the "truth" of hallucination.

Of course something of Jarry was left, unless one goes so far as to say that it was Père Ubu who wrote his books after 1896. He continued to eat and sleep and see his friends, and to be a welcome participant in the literary life of Paris. But his public personage was established. After a typical escapade in a café (he broke a mirror shooting at a customer's pipe), the account in *L'Illustration* the next day referred to "*le Père Ubu en personne.*" Since neither vanity nor true arrogance, but deliberate artifice caused the inflatedness of his behavior, most acquaintances tried to act as if it were all in the order of things. Something of the awkwardly personable, generous young man from Brittany still peeked through the chinks of the façade, but in Jarry's terms such revelations of the inner man meant weakness or failure. Soon even the chinks were filled. He was not the only eccentric in Paris, but he was by far the most rigorous.

This public form of privacy began by stimulating his work, and the years before 1900 were his most productive. After the best of his novels, *Les jours et les nuits* (1897), he finished the Rabelaisian *Gestes et opinions du docteur Faustroll* in 1898. It was followed by *L'amour en visites* (1898), the semimystical *L'amour absolu* (1899), and two successive numbers of an *Almanach du Père Ubu*, the second illustrated by Jarry and Pierre Bonnard, with whom Jarry collaborated for several months on a puppet theater. Only *Faustroll* had to wait for publication until after Jarry's death. But despite a favorable reception, these volumes scarcely supported him. Then in 1900 Jarry's frequent periodical writings and reviews bore fruit in an arrangement that he contribute a regular humorous chronicle, "*Gestes*," to the wealthy Natanson brothers' *Revue Blanche*. For three years Jarry lived on this income, and wrote two uneven novels, *Messaline*, "Novel of Ancient Rome," and *Le surmâle*, "A Modern Novel." After the *Revue Blanche* ceased publication in 1903, Jarry spent the winter in the Dauphiné with his loyal friend Demolder collaborating on a libretto of *Pantagruel*.

At thirty Jarry had completed his best years, enjoyed a unique notoriety in the literary world of Paris, and was already looked up to by a new generation. Most important among them were several young writers just beginning to publish: Guillaume Apollinaire, André Salmon, and Max Jacob. They sought out Jarry in his Grand Chasublerie, drew him into their revelries and discussions, and saw much of him at a time when the New Spirit was finally beginning to take the shape of frank modernism in opposition to the classical-eclectic tendency which led to the foundation of the *Nouvelle Revue Française* five years later. Jarry was a frequent visitor in Montmartre during the earliest years of the *bateau lavoir* and exercised a special fascination over Picasso. The painter adopted his eccentric, pistol-carrying habits and later acquired a valuable collection of Jarry's manuscripts. Among these youthful champions of the twentieth century, in the cubist doctrine they devised, and in the other isms that followed, Jarry found his progeny.

From this time on, Jarry's health suffered, above all from the ether which was the only intoxicant he could afford. He started work on a series of marionette plays and attempted a few magazine pieces. After surviving the winter of 1904–1905, he did not eat regularly the following year, and went without heat. Dr. Saltas, a friend who helped Jarry and at the same time exploited his talents, began collaborating with him on a translation of a Greek novel by Emmanuel Rhoïdes. But Jarry collapsed and had to return to Laval, where his sister could care for him. At this grim moment Jarry began a long-projected novel, *La dragonne*. It kept him working through periods of fever and exhaustion, and certain scenes of the unfinished work indicate that his powers were undiminished. But he discovered that his health was too severely impaired to be regained more than temporarily. When he reached the point of total physical enfeeblement and extreme unction (for Père Ubu was apparently willing to die a Christian), he still wrote frequently to Dr. Saltas predicting recovery and explaining at length how he had been brought so low. "We must rectify the legend—for Père Ubu, as I am called, is dying not of having done too much drinking, but of not having always had enough to eat."

In what seemed his last moments, he addressed to Madame Rachilde a letter in which the façade begins to crack. The maudlin pomposity of Père Ubu struggles openly with Jarry's own dwindling voice: he does not know whether to refer to himself as *he* or *I* or *we*.

Laval, May 28, 1906

Dear Madame R.

    This time Père Ubu does not write with a fever. (This is beginning like a last will and testament, but that is taken care of.) I think you understand by now that he is not dying (excuse me! the word slipped out) because of drink and other orgies.

He didn't have that Passion, and he has been so immodest as to have himself examined all over by *merdcins* [doctors]. He is without blemish, either in the liver or in the heart or in the kidneys. He is simply run down (a curious end for the man who wrote *Le surmâle;* his furnace is not going to blow up but simply go out). He will quietly stop running, like a tired motor. . . . And no cure known to man, no matter how closely he follows it (while laughing at it inside) will do any good. His fever comes perhaps from his heart trying to save him by sending his pulse up to 150. No human being has held on that long. For two days he has been of the Lord's Anointed, and as such feels like Kipling's trunkless elephant, "full of an insatiable curiosity." He will fall back a little further in the darkness of time. Just as he used to carry his revolver in his back pocket, he has put a gold chain around his neck, solely because that metal does not oxidize and will last as long as his bones, with medals in which he believes, just in case he should meet any devils. It's all as much fun as going fishing. . . .

[Jarry asks that his debts be paid—above all, to Vallette—with the revenue on his books.]

Père Ubu is shaved and has laid out a mauve shirt just by accident. He will disappear in the color scheme of the *Mercure* . . . and he will start out, still consumed with curiosity. He has a feeling that it will be tonight at five. . . . If he is wrong he will be ridiculous and that's that. Ghosts were always ridiculous.

With this Père Ubu, who has earned his rest, is going to sleep. He believes that the brain, during decomposition, continues to function after death, and that its dreams are our Paradise.

Père Ubu conditionally (he would so like to return to his Tripod) is perhaps going to sleep forever.

Alfred Jarry

P.S. I open this letter to say the doctor has just come by and thinks he can save me. A.J.

Jarry dragged himself through another miserable year, interrupted by increasingly serious relapses which made him return to Laval. His friends on the *Mercure* raised money with a subscribed edition of a mediocre operetta, *Le moutardier du pape*. Back in Paris in April, 1907, he wrote to an old friend, Victor Gastilleur.

> Please come by today. I've had some money orders from Laval and I don't have the strength to go cash them; they must be cashed or I'm done for. I've been in bed five days without being able to go out and get anything. You'll save my life if you come.

The willfulness with which he kept himself saturated with ether was no longer a form of drinking or alcoholism; he was simply killing himself. In writing the letter a year before to Rachilde, he had almost flinched before his chosen end; this time nothing shook his purpose. One of his last writings, a chapter called *"Descendit ad infernos"* intended for *La dragonne*, contains this visionary description of the hero's approaching death: "But soon he could drink no more, for there was no more darkness for him and, no doubt like Adam before the fall . . . he could see in the dark."

In the fall of 1907 Jarry dropped out of sight almost completely, making a last written appeal in October to Thadée Natanson for a louis d'or. Dr. Saltas and Vallette became so disturbed over his prolonged absence from normal haunts that they paid a visit to the Grand Chasublerie. They knocked for a long time before they heard Jarry feebly reply that he was coming. He never came. Knocking again and again to rouse him, they asked if they should send for a locksmith. From inside Jarry answered at last in barely audible tones that "it might not be such a bad idea after all." They found him in a state of complete paralysis from the waist down, lying helpless in his reduction of a room. At the hospital (he worried immediately about who would pay expenses) no hope was offered for his life. He revived enough to receive visits from a few friends. But Jarry's memory and his lucidity declined rapidly. One friend was so distressed to see his frightful condition that he had to turn away from the bed to hide his emotion. For the last time, Père Ubu rose with august dignity out of the ashes of Jarry and said gruffly: "Well, Polti, aren't you feeling well today?" Paul Léautaud relates that he spent several of his last days in a semicoma muttering over and over the never-completed phrase, *"Je*

cherche . . . je cherche . . . j'ch . . . j'ch . . ." He became
lucid for a brief time at the end and asked for—a tooth-
pick. Dr. Saltas hurried out to buy a box. When Jarry
finally had one in his fingers, Saltas writes, "It seems as if
he were suddenly filled with a great joy as on the days he
went off fishing or on a canoe or bicycle trip. I barely
stepped aside to speak to the nurse when she signaled
me to turn around. He was drawing his last breath."

As he had predicted to one of his ward neighbors, Jarry
died on November 1, 1907. An autopsy revealed that he
had suffered from acute meningeal tuberculosis, a condition his drinking had severely aggravated but not caused.
A cortege of fifty accompanied the body to the Bagneux
cemetery. Apollinaire relates that just as Père Ubu would
have wished, there was more eating and drinking after
the burial than weeping during it. His friends subscribed
for a monument for his grave, among them Octave Mirbeau, Alexandre Natanson, Alfred Vallette, Félix Fénéon,
Vuillard, Pierre Bonnard, Mère Ubu (*i.e.,* Louise France,
who had taken the role at the first performance), Gémier,
Léon-Paul Fargue, Eugène Fasquelle (a publisher), Odilon Redon, Paul Léautaud, Stuart Merrill, Paul Valéry.

In the unstable compound of fable and fact that must
pass as his life, the "real" Jarry is as much a pretense as a
personality. Because of the violent fusion he attempted of
life and literature, we shall find him equally present in his
writings. A biography of Jarry ends by being about someone else, the inside-out person he created. In an almost
frightening seizure, he became his pose. Jarry offers one
of the extreme cases in history of literary mimesis—of an
author becoming one of his own characters. Early in life
he compensated for his small stature and crippling timidity
by a profession of eccentricity. Within a few years he
found himself defying the prosperous smugness of the
fin-de-siècle with a resounding *merdre*. To live up to this
beginning he resorted to extreme measures which amount
to a modern form of self-scarification. His dedication to an
artistic end exceeded Rousseau's and Satie's in savagery
and exclusiveness. Through a prolonged suicide, Jarry
clung to the moment of total freedom that precedes death.
The wonder is that he could graft upon his diminutive
figure the huge blundering monstrosity of Ubu, whose
name has entered the language.

[8]

POET AND PATAPHYSICIAN

Jarry's death resembled nothing so much as drowning. "According to our observations," he wrote in *Spéculations,* "a drowned man is not a person killed by submersion. He is a being apart." In the beginning his memory left little trace, with Gémier giving one brief revival of *Ubu Roi* in 1908 and a few posthumous works coming out almost unnoticed. Several writers—Apollinaire, Salmon, Jacob, Cocteau, Breton, Artaud—never forgot Jarry's example, but, without Jarry to do his own publicity, the time was not ripe to bring him out of the depths. It was the repercussions of World War I that began to jar him back to the surface in 1921–1922 during the height of the Dadaist demonstrations. Two new volumes were issued (one of them edited by the youthful André Malraux), and Charles Chassé published a book violently contesting Jarry's authorship of *Ubu Roi* in favor of one of the surviving Morin brothers, an artillery officer. Chassé as much as accused Jarry of plagiarism and, to boot, challenged the literary merit of the supposedly purloined text. The mixed outburst of protest and welcome which greeted this attack resounded through every literary quarter, until the critic Pierre de Saint Prix declared: "More ink has been spilled about whether or not Jarry is the author of *Ubu Roi* than on investigating the question of Naundorff's being the son of Louis XIV. M. Chassé's book touched off a powder keg." The truth, however, had been clear all along. A play originally written in collaboration had become Jarry's by default. His new title and revisions made it indisputably his.

This lengthy debate, far from deflating Jarry's reputation, blew it up to new greatness. Cocteau's fantasy-novel *Le Potomak* (1919) had already started mutterings about Jarry's influence on the younger generation. The surrealists, setting up shop in 1924, named him one of their patron saints. Three biographies appeared in rapid succession including Rachilde's. In 1925 in *Les faux-monnayeurs*, the only one of his books he was ever willing to call a novel, André Gide included a brilliant banquet scene in which Jarry, the one explicitly "real" person among the fictional characters, stands up on a chair and fires a blank shot at another poet. The original incident had taken place at one of the *Mercure* banquets and involved Gide's and Jarry's friend Christian Beck, whom Jarry saw fit to shoot *à blanc*. In his keen sensitivity to shades of personality and identity, Gide realized that Jarry was *already* a fictional personage and could, in this novel of mirrors, dead ends, and false scents, represent the mysterious creature to be found at the heart of the labyrinth. By implication, the passage is one of the most unstinting tributes to the success of Jarry's repersonification of himself.

In 1927 Antonin Artaud and Roger Vitrac founded the *Théâtre Alfred Jarry,* which favored the film medium and proposed "to contribute by strictly theatrical means to the ruin of the theater as it exists today in France. . . . As to the spirit which directs [the company], it partakes of the unsurpassed humoristic teachings of *Ubu Roi* and of the rigorously positivist method of Raymond Roussel." Through Artaud and his pupil Jean-Louis Barrault, Jarry's dramatic theories survived into the theater of the thirties and forties after earlier plays by Apollinaire, Jules Romains, Tristan Tzara, and Cocteau had celebrated the continuing tradition of *Ubu Roi*. In 1945 Cyril Connolly dubbed Poppa Ubu the "Santa Claus of the Atomic Age," and two years later a Swiss firm published eight volumes of Jarry's *Œuvres complètes,* so incomplete that uncollected and unpublished works have been appearing regularly ever since.

The most fitting memorial to Jarry's teachings came into existence in 1949 with the foundation of the Collège de 'Pataphysique, a group of earnest and joyful spirits dedicated to disseminating the new "science" they consider central to all Jarry's work. Drowned rather than buried, Jarry has long remained just below the surface of the literary tradition in France and has bobbed up often enough to keep his reputation alive.

Jarry's literary work, which alone can today justify that reputation, may appear on first examination to break in half. The extreme points seem to lie so far apart that one end will not lift the other. At one extreme, occupied principally by the enormity of Ubu, one finds scandal and coarse humor; at the other one finds a very personal manner of lyric and hermetic writing. A random sampling of his poetry may easily disclose texts that seem to come from two different authors, two different countries of the mind. Yet both in the idiom of popular balladry and in a style of contorted symbolism, Jarry used internal rhyme, alliteration, and refrain to build up a monotonous rhythm. The lullaby effect serves to throw into relief the boldness of certain images and to prepare the way for comic effects. With its roots deep in a childhood spent in the French countryside, Jarry's "symbolist" poetry never departs far from the aural, jocose, yet moving manner of the popular ditty. Not versatility but singleness of vision produced the variety of his writings.

Because of the contradictions in his work, however, critics have tended to recognize Jarry either as an important and influential poet who later squandered his gifts on novels and farces, or as a humorist on a new level of seriousness, or as a talented psychotic. None of these estimates is entirely wrong; they are partial. Jarry remains a humorist who surpassed laughter, a poet with a double feeling for symbolist tracery and argot, and a visionary in the tradition of Poe, Lautréamont, and Rimbaud. Nevertheless, his work must be taken whole despite its disparity at first glance. Carefully read with an open mind, his writings do not break in half. On the contrary, they turn and turn constantly away from a straight line, modulating from grossness to subtle irony to sentiment to metaphysical speculation to blasphemy to anarchism—and come full circle back to grossness. His work shows the circular structuring of a ring which can be held at any point to test its strength. There is no "end" beyond which one falls off into vacancy. For Jarry, truculent indecorum reaches round by visible paths to lyric intensity. The unity, the center, is the same as for his life: hallucination accepted as reality: In that vividly lit universe all products, base and elevated, of his fertile mind demand equal standing. His writings elude criticism as stubbornly as his life confounds biography.

Aptly enough, Jarry constructed his two earliest books on a cyclic scheme: they contain all his styles. *Minutes de sable mémorial* begins and ends with the refinements of symbolism, yet it holds some of Ubu's coarsest escapades. Even more patently, the four acts of *César-Antéchrist*, Jarry's second volume, display a circular development. The drama recounts the collapse of the divine realm ("God is sleepy") into the second "Heraldic Act," during which Antichrist rules, descends further into the third "Terrestrial Act," where Père Ubu, the ubiquitous, dominates the scene with his oaths and outrages, and then rises again in final judgment of it all. In this short play Jarry carries us literally from the sublime to the ridiculous. Better than any statement of values or elaborate cosmology, it expresses his concept of how the universe is arranged. He presents Ubu as the representative of primitive earthly conduct, unrelieved by any insight into his own monstrosity, uncontrollable as an elephant on the rampage, earnest in his blundering. He is what he is because God has existed and has died both ritually and actually, because Antichrist has had his reign on earth, and because the powers of true deity will ultimately triumph. Meanwhile, mankind in the shape of Ubu dredges the depths of its nature. It is consistent with an almost teleological scheme of things, then, that Ubu-Jarry should never encounter a convention or a common-sense precept or a belief that need be held sacred. Jarry molested and destroyed, for in the end he knew that his function would be constructive. It is the meaning of the inscription that prefaces *Ubu enchaîné:*

> Père Ubu: Hornsboodle, we should never have knocked everything down if we hadn't meant to destroy the ruins too. But the only way we see of doing that is to put up some handsome buildings.

Only new construction can ultimately destroy the old. Beyond Jarry's nihilism there is a positive side to his work. Creating in Ubu a one-man demolition squad twenty years before Dada, he incorporated this figure into works that go on to broach transcendental values. A single facet of his work does not represent Jarry as an author and fails to show his desperate effort to renovate human sensibility. His method of hallucination constitutes an attempt to destroy and create simultaneously: to transform.

One work which stands midway between the apparent extremes of Jarry's styles is the third of the full-length Ubu plays, *Ubu enchaîné*, written and published in 1900.* A few selections from it will carry us deep into Jarry's seemingly jumbled sensibility. In the opening scene Père Ubu steps forward and fails dramatically to pronounce the famous "*merdre*" which set the audience agog at *Ubu Roi*. He and Mère Ubu have returned to France from Poland, and briefly they recall their earlier adventures. In answer to Mère Ubu's question about what he is going to do now, Père Ubu says magnificently: "Since we are in a country where liberty means fraternity and fraternity means equality under the law, and since I am incapable of acting like everyone else, and since this business about being equal to everyone else means nothing at all to me—I'm going to become a slave, Mère Ubu." She answers that he is too fat. They exit, clearing the stage for the entrance of the "free men" engaged in their "disobedience drill." They are soldiers in a highly (un-)disciplined anarchist army in which every order is scrupulously disobeyed. "Blind disobedience at all times is the strength of free men," the corporal tells his recruits. They drill. Père Ubu re-enters.

> (*The Corporal and the Three Free Men march around for a time; Père Ubu falls in behind and keeps treading on their heels.*)
> CORPORAL: Shoulder arms!
> PERE UBU: Long live the army [*armerdre*].
> CORPORAL: Stop, stop! No, I mean disobey. Don't stop!
> (*The Free Men stop; Père Ubu stands by himself.*)
> Who is thus ultra-free recruit who has invented a new manual of arms which I've never seen in seven years of giving the command: shoulder arms?
> PERE UBU: We have obeyed, sir, to fulfill our duties as a slave. I did just that: shoulder arms.
> CORPORAL: I've explained that movement a thousand

* The title parodies Aeschylus, whose play is called in French *Prométhée enchaîné*.

times but this is the first time I've seen it executed.
You seem to know the theory of liberty better than I
do. You even do what's commanded. Are you a very
important Free Man, sir?

PÈRE UBU: Monsieur Ubu, ex-King of Poland and Aragon, Count of Mondragon, Count of Sandormir, Marquis of St. Gregory. At the moment in slavery and
at your service, Monsieur?

CORPORAL: Pissweet, Corporal of Free Men. But when
there are ladies present, call me the Marquis of
Meadowfield. Remember, please, it's best to give
my full title even if you should have to command
me, for I'd say by your learning you were at least a
sergeant.

PÈRE UBU: Corporal Pissweet, I shall remember. But I
have come to this country to be a slave, not to give
orders, although I have been a sergeant as you say
when I was little, and even a Captain of Dragoons.
Good-by, Corporal Pissweet. (*Exit.*)

CORPORAL: Good-by, Marquis of St. Gregory. Squad
halt!

(*The Free Men start off and go out the other side.*)

By the time the play is over, as one might foresee, the Free
Men have "revolted" in order to try to win the servile
privileges of Ubu, including the easy security of prison
life—for Ubu spends his happiest days there. All that is
lacking is a gun which discharges in reverse like the back-
firing dialogue. In the unaccustomed atmosphere of absurdity we laugh apprehensively. Yet the comic theme of slavish
disobedience is merely a rear view with political commentary of the theme of confinement (solitude) and release
(active living) which haunts Jarry's most personal and
obscure works. The first performance of the play came in
1937 during the civil war in Spain. The incoherence of
Ubu enchaîné resembles the incoherence—and significance
—of that other great monstrosity: Picasso's *Guernica*.

What has Jarry left us after he has pulled all values out
from under our feet? There is only the preposterous figure
of Ubu, who somehow muddles through to survival. Mallarmé, sensitive to more than words alone, wrote to Jarry
after the first performance of *Ubu Roi:* "You have launched,
along with his tribe, a prodigious personage of rare and
resistant texture, and you have done it as a sure, sober,

dramatic sculptor. He has joined the repertory of the best taste and already haunts me." Jarry was sure of the power of Ubu the way Rabelais was sure of Panurge and Cervantes of Don Quixote. This certainly permitted his first great successful transformation: the incarnation of an adolescent phantasm as hero-villain of all mankind. Ubu is Jarry's vision of the second coming, a comic Apocalypse. He stands as the reverse image of Valéry's Monsieur Teste, delivered to the public the same year and dedicated to the same man. Instead of a head (*tête*) Ubu has only his "boodle" or belly. The "mystic without a faith" and the "ignorant mule," as their respective wives state the case, serenely divide the world between them.

The motto inscribed on the dedication page of *Ubu Roi* begins thus in fraudulent archaic French: *"Adonc le Père Ubu hoscha la poire, dont fut depuis nommé par les Anglois Shakespeare. . . ."* *Hoscha la poire* translates loosely into "shook (his) pear (head)"—namely Shakespeare.* It comes as no surprise, then, that Ubu enacts a schoolboy travesty of King Lear's fate, and instead of losing a kingdom usurps one. Like Macbeth, Ubu is tempted to his first crime by his wife, who fires his ambitions. The assassination parodies Brutus's plot against Julius Caesar, including the queen's dream of evil foreboding. Most obviously, Ubu derives from Falstaff, whose benignly corrupt personality could never be confined to one play or action. Jarry and his schoolmates did with Ubu what Shakespeare must have been tempted to do with Falstaff—give him free rein. Having placed Ubu at the center and not on the periphery of their plays, they could reconstruct the rest of the world around this gross being with an incontrovertible logic of his own. He had also absorbed the comic verve of Aristophanes and the semi-magical extravagance that characterizes *Peer Gynt*. When listing the books he prized most, Jarry cited *Ubu Roi* among the other classics.† He treats it with the respect due a text from which he learned as

---

* This deformation is doubtless modeled on Poe's waggishness in *Eureka*, where he speaks of "Aries Tottle."

† The list appears in *Faustroll* and includes work by Homer, St. Luke, Baudelaire, Bloy, Coleridge, Cyrano, Darien, Elskamp, Christian Dietrich Grabbe, Lautréamont, Maeterlinck, Mallarmé, the Sâr Péladan, Rabelais, Rimbaud, Verlaine, and Verne.

much as he contributed to it. This is, in effect, the long and short of the controversy over authorship of the play.

A few years later, having shouldered the burden of Ubu, Jarry wrote without collaboration passages that show a devastating insight into human nature.

> UBU: Are we right to act like this? Hornsboodle, by our great green candle, we'll take counsel with our Conscience. It's right here in this suitcase, covered with cobwebs. It's easy to see we don't use it often. (*He opens the suitcase. His Conscience comes out, a big fellow in a shirt.*)
>
> CONSCIENCE: (*It has the voice of Bahis, as Ubu has that of Macroton.*) Sir, and all that, please get ready to take notes.
>
> UBU: No thanks.We don't like to write, even though we don't doubt that you'll have interesting things to tell us. And by the way, I'd like to ask how you have the nerve to appear before us in shirt sleeves.
>
> CONSCIENCE: Sir, and all that, Conscience, like Truth, usually goes naked. If I have gotten myself up in a shirt, it is in honor of the august company.
>
> UBU: Well now, Mr. and Mrs. Conscience, you're making a lot of unnecessary racket. Answer this question instead: how would it be if I killed Mr. Achras, who has dared to insult me in my house?
>
> CONSCIENCE: Sir, and all that, it is unworthy of a civilized man to return evil for good. Mr. Achras has sheltered you; Mr. Achras has opened his arms to you as well as his collection of polyhedra; Mr. Achras, and all that, is a good and totally harmless man. It would be a cowardly deed, and all that, to kill a poor old man who cannot defend himself.
>
> UBU: Hornsboodle, Mr. Conscience, are you sure he can't defend himself?
>
> CONSCIENCE: Absolutely. It would be a cowardly deed to kill him.
>
> UBU: Thank you very much. That'll do for today. We'll kill Mr. Achras since there's no danger in it, and we'll consult you more often, for you give better advice than we expected. Into the suitcase with you.

Ubu has indeed "consulted his conscience," a faculty which enumerates not only ethical considerations but also the one circumstance Ubu wants to be sure of. Now he can proceed to murder Achras "in good conscience." The pompous manner of address inflates and deflates itself as it goes along. In the end there can be no disputing Jarry's claim to Ubu.

The figure of Ubu inhabits the segment of Jarry's work that lies opposite the writings in which he wrestled with the theme of love. His precocious and introverted emotional nature produced a number of difficult works which embody clear strains of narcissism and sexual inversion. *Haldern-ablou*, his earliest poetic drama about a noble and his page, is full of butterflies and chameleons and other symbols of change in nature. The crucial scene takes place on "the same avenue going in the opposite direction," and in the course of the action Haldern says: "I like the servility of women . . . but they must be dumb. . . . Love exists only outside of sex." But Jarry's misogyny arises from an even more central attitude—a shrinking before any physical act that attempts to express the fullness of love. He explicitly speaks in *L'amour absolu* of "the dregs of Love which is Fear," and in *L'amour en visites* he includes a revealing dialogue between Fear and Love.

Dissatisfaction with the flesh does not leave a man relieved of his passions. From the very beginning, Jarry's works portray man's struggle with his appetites. He quotes on two occasions a phrase from Song V of Lautréamont's *Les chants de Maldoror*: "Don't jump around so," or, better, "Don't make such a fuss." (*"Ne fais pas de pareils bonds!"*) In Lautréamont the phrase is addressed to a single hair left behind by God Himself after a wild night in a brothel. Jarry appropriates the passage by simply adding two words: "Uprooted phallus, don't make such a fuss." The sexual instinct, snatched from its normal context, threatens to go on the rampage. Exactly such a scene is described in the Prolegomena (*Prolégomènes*) to *Haldernablou*, where a sacred Phallus ravages a crumbling temple. We are already deep in the private symbolism of Jarry—much of it adapted from Lautréamont—and at the starting point of his long task of transforming love into a force by which man can surpass himself.

In 1897, four years after *Haldernablou*, Jarry published the novel *Les jours et les nuits*, which, implicitly in its style and explicitly in its action, approaches the state of sustained hallucination. In the course of his dreams, which alone release him from the confinement of army life, Sengle (from *singulum*) discovers the nature of his love for his friend Valens. He recalls a walk he took long ago with Valens when he was in an inspired mood "as if he had taken hashish." His soul seems to be flying three hundred meters above him in the sky and connected to him only by a thread, like a kite.

> And he had read in a Chinese book about the customs of a foreign people whose heads could fly up to the trees to seize their prey, always attached by a red thread, and afterward returned to fit themselves into the bloody collar. But if a certain wind blew the thread would break and the head would fly away beyond the seas.

The kite provides a dizzying image of solitude. Sengle has rejected any physical contact with his friend Valens; what, then, is the tenuous meaning of their relationship? It is that Sengle sees his past over again as present in Valens's memory—sees himself prolonged in another mind.

> Sengle was discovering the true metaphysical cause of the happiness of loving: not the communion of two beings become one . . . but the enjoyment of anachronism and of communicating with one's own past. . . . Sengle, in love with the Remembrance of himself, needed a living and visible friend, because he could not remember, being without memory.

Love cannot become much more refined than this. Jarry has pursued narcissism until it requires a second presence as witness. These semimystical passages on love glow with astonishing poetic beauty, yet they are hardly convincing out of context.

Even after this distillation of sentiments, Jarry's quest is not finished. He went on to write the most difficult and personal of all his texts, *L'amour absolu*. The hero, Emmanuel Dieu, is both man and God, the son, lover, and husband of Maria, who has an equal number of persons. The totally plastic identity of the two main characters allows the action to take place from a constantly shifting point of view, and the effects are as breath-taking as those of Joyce or Virginia

Woolf or Jean Genet, who use comparable techniques. Jarry creates "the thirty-seventh dramatic situation" (his friend Georges Polti had published an analysis of thirty-six): "*To perceive that one's mother is a virgin.*" Before Freud named the complex, Jarry explicitly compares his love for his mother, who had died only two years earlier, with the Oedipus story: "I am the Son, I am your son, I am the Spirit, I am your husband, in all eternity, your husband and your son, oh pure Jocasta." The combination of divine and human elements has an unmistakable mystical ring, closely related to the cabala, medieval Latin texts honoring the Virgin, and the controversy following the dogma of the Immaculate Conception (1864).* The dazzlingly rich yet simply written text succeeds in conveying a fullness of love that is indeed "absolute."

Subsequently, Jarry turned back to love as the world knows it and treated it as a magnificent game, a sport in which great performers strive for a record. Both *Messaline*, a novel of the debauches and customs of ancient Rome, and *Le surmâle* have a strong dramatic side—man pitted against his own human limits. "Love is an act of no importance; it can be repeated indefinitely." After this first utterance, Marcueil, the supermale, proceeds to prove that even without recourse to "perpetual-motion food" (compounded on a base of strychnine and alcohol) he can exceed the physical limits of man in both locomotion and love. Marcueil breaks all records and dies only when an electric "Love-inspiring Machine" yields to his superior powers, falls in love with him, shorts out, and kills him in an apotheosis of strength. In *Messaline*, the female counterpart of *Le surmâle*, the antique cult of Priapus replaces science and a similar triumph in death is achieved. The total narrative freedom of these stories, sustained by scrupulous scientific description, makes Jarry the principal heir in France of Poe, Verne, and Villiers de l'Isle-Adam. His early preoccupation with inward states of emotion reversed itself and found release in extraordinary adventure. Jarry ended

---

* Jarry may also have read the dream that Nerval relates in *Aurélia*. A goddess appears to him and says: "I am the same woman as Mary, the same as your mother, the same one also you have always loved in different forms. With each of your misfortunes I have dropped one of the masks which cover my face, and soon you will see me as I am. . . ."

by turning love into a physical exploit like bicycle riding. After *L'amour absolu* there was no further pitch of intensity available to him, and the two novels, in the frankness with which they dissect the act of love, suggest detachment from it. Misogyny and inversion no longer have the upper hand. The chameleon world of *Haldernablou* evolved gradually into the delightful farce of a work like *L'objet aimé*. This verse libretto, based on comic text and drawings by the Swiss artist Rodolphe Töpffer, laughs at love as no different from other human delusions and pretenses. Jarry's "cure" is complete and has been accomplished, moreover, by his literary method of simultaneous destruction and creation, like Ubu building on the ruins.

In a career as truncated as Jarry's, it is difficult to detect any clear evolution. Though he seemed to seek liberation from certain emotional states of love by converting them into comedy, there is another segment of his work which cannot be so tidily described. For in it he is concerned not with a type of emotion, but with transforming literature itself and quickening the human mind that produces it. Starting once more, however, from the irreducible figure of Ubu, one can work gradually through Jarry's themes and methods into his style.

The nature of Ubu might be explained by saying, in Bergson's terms, that he ignores with wonderful obliviousness the disparity of what is and what should be. Ubu is never aware of his own enormity; he keeps his conscience locked away in a suitcase. After his outrages, no effective judgment is ever asserted; one hears only weak protest from Mère Ubu and other hangers-on, who cannot challenge his authority. Ubu is always king. Yet is obliviousness enough to explain his comic nature?

Baudelaire had a theory of the comic which took as its premise that an angel tripping over its wings would not be funny in the manner of a man slipping on a banana peel.

> . . . Human laughter is intimately linked to the circumstance of our ancient fall, of our physical and moral degradation. . . .
>
> Let us try, since the comic is an element of damnation and of diabolic origin, to consider an absolutely primitive soul, one which so to speak has escaped nature's hands. (*De l'essence du rire.*)

Baudelaire takes as his example Virginie from Bernardin de Saint Pierre's romantic novel *Paul et Virginie*. Yet the innocence of Virginie's virtue is as nothing beside the innocence of Ubu's evil. Both are oblivious of human values. Ubu has only his appetites, which he displays like virtues. When we try to injure him with our laughter ("satanic" laughter, Baudelaire would call it), we discover that his behavior is so abject that we cannot reach him. He does not have traits of either a great hero or a great villain; he never deliberates. Can we really laugh at Ubu, at his character? It is doubtful, for he lacks the necessary vulnerability, the vestiges of original sin. Not without dread, we mock, rather, his childish innocence and primitive soul and cannot harm him. He remains a threat because he can destroy at will, and the political horrors of the twentieth century make the lesson disturbingly real.

In his innocent obliviousness, however, Ubu cannot blaspheme. It is too sophisticated an activity for his elemental existence. Blasphemy indicates a further stage in Jarry's literary development, for it presupposes something held sacred and therefore open to defilement. Strictly brought up as a Catholic, Jarry goaded his faith to the limits of survival in writings that mix irreverence and devoutness. In 1895 *L'Ymagier* published an article entitled "The Nails of Our Lord" in which, after examining the most abstruse sources and paintings, Jarry weightily concluded that Christ was attached to the cross with three nails (only one to pierce both feet) rather than four. Ten years later, in *La dragonne*, he succeeded in writing a passage that departs from Catholic doctrine in pure speculative inventiveness. During the great Battle of Morsang, a kind of second Armageddon, the young engineer Sacqueville single-handedly annihilates an army by drawing it into circular deployment and letting the units decimate one another. At dead center, he is himself invulnerable. One other survivor appears, the Abbé Rayphusce. In the silence of the vast battlefield he offers to hear Sacqueville's confession. Sacqueville counters by asking for a bottle—an empty one. His confession is a manuscript which he does not wish to entrust to any mortal; "an empty wine bottle is sturdy and travels quickly on the surface of the water." The priest's theological disquisition, which follows, reads like the creed of a new heresy.

. . . there is no Father except in the Spirit; the
Father is soluble in the Spirit, which is the ark of the
Father upon the waters. . . .

The Spirit is the future and eternal God, the same
which gets virgins with child and dwelt in the beginning upon the waters, and in whose kind man
will communicate when he no longer needs com-
munion or when God, left behind, communicates
of man . . . that is, from the moment that man has
"broken God's record."

The two men end up fighting a great sword duel to the
death. Sacqueville wins, throws the Abbé and the bottle together into the river, and watches in satisfaction as the
former sinks and the latter floats.

The entire passage implies man's usurpation of God's
place and dignity. Emmanuel Dieu, the hero of *L'amour
absolu,* anticipates this Promethean theme by his supernatural powers as well as his name. Jarry does not flatly reject
Christian dogma, but strives to apply its mysteries and
powers to human creatures who must replace an expiring
divinity. This Nietzschean and prophetic strain in Jarry's
writing is deliberately combined with such semicomic circumstances as the wine bottle and elaborately described
fencing positions.

One does not have to look far in Jarry's work for some
of the most gleeful and ingenious blasphemy produced in
modern times. The volume of *Spéculations* devotes many
pages to the Abbé Prout, a tippling priest of irrepressible
imagination who specializes in "canonical innovations"
such as the "Virgin and Mannekin-Pis" and the "Supposi-
tory Virgin." In "The Passion Considered as an Uphill
Bicycle Race" Jarry wrote a detailed travesty of the Cru-
cifixion.

Barrabus, slated to race, was scratched.
Pilate, the starter, pulling out his clepsydra or
water clock, an operation which wet his hands unless he had merely spit on them—Pilate gave the
send-off.
Jesus got away like a flash. . . .

And at the end:

The deplorable accident familiar to us all took place at the twelfth turn. Jesus was in a dead heat at the time with the thieves. We know that he continued the race as an aviator—but this is another story.

Blasphemy is the manner in which Jarry transformed religion into a sport, just as the mechanical idea of the athletic record gave him the opportunity to victimize romantic love. The objection one might sustain to both these procedures would be in the name of "good taste," and Jarry had his gruff answer to that. He said categorically, "Screw good taste."*

Ubu's innocent evil and its rudimentary development into blasphemy belong to the world of the child-man and represent a primitive attitude which first established Jarry's reputation as a literary delinquent. Ubu and even l'Abbé Prout would not have outraged Rousseau. Applied systematically to all things, including literature, the attitude became a method of humor based on logic perpetually reversing its terms. Alphonse Allais, Capus, Fagus, Fénéon, and Charles-Louis Philippe exploited similar methods, but never so strenuously as Jarry. A Negro fled from a bar in Paris without paying for his drinks; in his account Jarry affirms that, not at all a criminal, the man must have been an explorer from Africa investigating European civilization and caught without "native" currency. It is all a matter of point of view. When the army announced that it was about to equip its troops with a new rifle, Jarry rose to the occasion in pompous opinion.

We disapprove of the innocuousness of the military rifle for several reasons: a range exceeding our range of vision; such a high bullet velocity and small caliber as to produce no real wound but only an unimpressive puncture; inability to produce smoke, etc.

Needless to say there has been no need to change the Gras rifle. For it is a known fact that in the Lebel 86 the repeating mechanism, if anyone is so

* Baudelaire is long-winded in comparison. "The enticing thing about bad taste is the aristocratic pleasure of displeasing." *(Fusées.)*

foolish to try it, invariably jams, putting the rifle
totally out of service. We assume that the inventor
perfected this feature in order to render the arm
useless to the enemy in event of our defeat. (*Spéculations.*)

Of course there is more here than logical reversal. After
reading a hundred pages of such stuff, what strikes one is
the attitude, the pose Jarry holds. He writes deadpan. The
solemn tone of his observations never cracks; no matter
how hard he wants us to laugh, he never laughs with us.
The true humorist—and here Jarry is closer to Swift than to
Rabelais—never participates in the immediate effects of his
behavior. Jarry's method of describing the world becomes
more and more an exhaustive examination of a restricted
subject, taking every detail into account. According to his
own statement, we know that we heard Bergson at the
Lycée Henri IV elaborate his theory of laughter; Jarry's
practice fully illustrates the "scientific" nature of humor.

"Laughter," Jarry wrote, "is born out of the discovery of
the contradictory." The statement implies a distinguishing
between opposites which underlies all forms of the comic.
But Jarry could not be long content with observing this
neat division of things. One of the ever-present tendencies
in men of highly trained intellect has been that of travesty-
ing the very discipline by which they live. Dodgson, mathematician and logician, has been easily survived by Lewis
Carroll, who made playthings out of logic and common
sense. A somewhat different kind of mind, which feels that
its creative powers have not been fully explored, falls prey
to drugs: De Quincey and Coleridge, Poe and Baudelaire.

Jarry seized both tendencies and through them attempted to convert his career into a sustained pattern of
thought and behavior beyond literature and beyond laughter. He refused the contradictions of which he was so
keenly aware and asserted the equivalence of all things.
"God is the point tangent to zero and infinity," he argued
earnestly. No state of being excludes its opposite; everything is not only possible but real. He was learned, and his
learning came out backward to prove the preposterous and
establish the paradoxical. He was semi-devout, and he
blasphemed mightily. He was not clowning merely; he was
observing a relentless method. At the same time, he prod-
ded his imagination by constant drinking and by keeping

himself in a semiexalted state until there was no line between soberness and inebriation. *"Soyez toujours ivre,"* exhorted Baudelaire; Jarry obeyed literally. He was incapable of doing anything in moderation, just as verbal restraint is not characteristic of his literary style. What astonished his contemporaries, who never tired of describing his personality and his extravagant actions, was the very refusal to observe limits, his consistent inconsistency.

The universe of total hallucination ultimately absorbed all Jarry's life and writing. Primitive destructiveness was converted into absurd humor, was converted into an extravagant vision which contains both the crudeness and the subtlety of the former attitudes. In *Le surmâle*, for instance, we read of the death of one member of a five-man team racing ten thousand miles across Asia on a five-seater bicycle (plus a coxswain-feeder) against a locomotive. Like the rest of the men, he has been wired to his seat and pedals. The nonstop pedaling of his teammates breaks his *rigor mortis* and he begins to move again. Then, still dead, his frenetic strength surpasses anything he possessed alive. Jarry matches Poe in producing a reasoned scientific atmosphere for his extravaganzas; he jumps on our backs like an evil imp and will force us to see that there is meaning beyond the easy reach of comedy, as there is life beyond death. This kind of writing fixes tenaciously on an "absurd" situation until the first comic impression has been left far behind. His transformations finally obliterate the categories of literature and the frontiers of life.

What distinguishes Jarry's career from an entire tradition of visionary writers, from Plotinus to Rimbaud, is, first of all, his quasi-suicidal attempt to achieve a new level of existence through literary mimesis, fusing his life and his art. Of almost equal importance is the fact that he pretended (in both senses) to express his experience in the form of a science. In the Western world only established religious sects and their most perceptive initiates have usually been willing to suggest a systematization in the realm of supernatural experience. Jarry simply created a new discipline: 'Pataphysics.

Its principles are implicit in all his writing, and one of the most central found expression when he was only twenty, in an article for *L'Ymagier*. "It is conventional to call 'monster' any blending of dissonant elements; the Centaur and Chimera are defined this way to people who do not know them. I call 'monster' every original inexhaustible beauty." He refuses to reject contradiction as a mode of existence. The definition links the inhuman humanity of Ubu with the supernatural sexual exploits of the Supermale and with the spiritual depravity of Emmanuel Dieu and Sengle. They are all monsters—composed of dissonant elements, yet not so much fictional as immanent. Monstrosity may well revolt us at first, but it envisages both a new form of beauty and a new form of humor. Jarry deliberately transformed himself into a monster breeding monsters by a process of literary mutation. Ten years later Jarry modified his terminology slightly in a letter addressed to Marinetti, the animator of futurism. He wrote more revealingly of himself than of Marinetti. "It is true that in your works surprise aims less at laughter than at the beauty of the horrible [*l'horrifiquement beau*]." The refusal to drop a contradiction in logic or a raw dissonance in music is "horrible" to the ordinary sensibility; in just such circumstances Jarry found inspiration. Monstrosity, horrible beauty—the words connote the blend of repulsion and fascination that Jarry's writings arouse. The only relief takes the form of humor.

But how can the principle of monstrosity draw together objects and feelings that seem to inhibit several different universes? The answer involves a further principle, more fundamental, and once again defined very early by Jarry in explicit terms. "Lintel," the foreword to *Les minutes de sable mémorial* and his most significant statement on stylistics, contains the following passage.

> . . . and insofar as style is abrupt and irregular because ignorant of regularity, any unexpected regularity shines out, a gem, orbit, peacock's eye, candelabra, final harmony. But here is the criterion for distinguishing this . . . condensed simplicity,* the diamond formed of carbon . . . : *the relation of the verbal sentence to every meaning that can be found in it is constant.* . . .

* Simplicity does not have to be simple; rather, complexity drawn taut and synthesized. (*cf.`Pataph.*) [Jarry's note and italics.]

The traditional or common-sense meaning of a text, then, has no more exclusive claim to be the *true* meaning than any other that can be found in the same words. All interpretations are on a par, are equivalent. There exists no more rigorous statement than this of the belief and practice of ambiguity. Freudians, surrealists, and semanticists have claimed various significance for ambiguity; Jarry treated ambiguity as the stylistic manifestation of a universal principle of convertibility. A text means all things equivocally; anything may be(come) its opposite; not literature, but living is the supreme pun; writing is a slip of the tongue. Such total literary promiscuity is bound to yield the monstrous.

In the middle of the passage from *Les jours et les nuits* on Sengle's discovery of love there occurs the tricky phrase "the enjoyment of anachronism." Anachronism, the crossing of different times, produces *eternity* according to the dramatic theories Jarry invoked in describing the *décors* for *Ubu Roi*. When "revolvers are fired in the year 1000," time surpasses itself, just as contraries combine to produce not zero but infinity. Infinity of time and infinity of meaning determine the same visionary universe. Only the principle of conversion or hallucination can guide us through all the manifestations of Jarry's mind and relate his life to his art, Emmanuel Dieu to Ubu, beauty to monstrosity, eternity to anarchism, absolute love to obscenity, spiritual grace to drunkenness, day to night, and humor to seriousness. It is this equivalence of opposites that molded his writings into a circular shape, enclosing the human with the divine. A circle, everywhere identical to itself, contains no opposites.

Out of such slippery ideas Jarry forged his "science of 'Pataphysics," which, like Ubu, appeared in his earliest work. It can be directly linked to Professor Hébert's ponderous expression "my science of physics." Later, in *Gestes et opinions du docteur Faustroll* (1898; published in 1911) Jarry began to elaborate it into a full system.[*]

> 'Pataphysics is the science of the realm beyond metaphysics. . . . It will study the laws which govern exceptions and will explain the universe supple-

---

[*] Faustroll combines *Faust* and *troll,* a Scandinavian word for imp or gnome. (Ibsen calls for a chorus of trolls in *Peer Gynt.*) Thus Faustroll is the imp of science.

mentary to this one; or, less ambitiously, it will describe a universe which one can see—must see perhaps—instead of the traditional one, for the laws discovered in the traditional universe are themselves correlated exceptions, even though frequent, or in any case accidental facts which, reduced to scarcely exceptional exceptions, don't even have the advantage of singularity.

Definition: 'Pataphysics is the science of imaginary solutions, which symbolically attributes the properties of objects, described by their virtuality, to their lineaments.

Behind the double talk, Jarry is aiming not merely at the limit, but beyond the limit of man's conceptual powers, and this without ever abandoning the pretense of reason. He applied the resulting science to the "practical construction of a time machine" after H. G. Wells, and explained his conclusions in a brilliant article in the *Mercure* which inspired Valéry to write on the same questions of time and duration.[*] But 'Pataphysics finds its best expression in the deeply Rabelaisian *Faustroll*. Today, Rabelais' sense of the fullness and excitement of life usually disappears in the face of the organized solitude of contemporary life. Jarry's good doctor is born full-grown at the age of sixty-three, navigates unendingly across dry land in a sieve, and travels everywhere with a summons server who is trying to collect some hundred thousand francs of back rent from him. Faustroll has the verve to live beyond his means, and ours. But is it, one must ask again, literature?

The manuscript, of which only fragments had appeared in *La Plume* and the *Mercure* before Jarry's death, bears an inscription on the last page which seems to pose that very question. "This book will be published in its entirety

[*] Valéry's text broaches the problems of contradiction as a vital principle, a geometry of consciousness. In seven laconic pages Valéry looks deep into the structure of the universe and of the mind, and only at the end does he return to aesthetics via Wells. "The symbol is to some extent a time machine. It is an inconceivable shortening of the duration of mental operations, to the point where one might almost define the world of mind as the world in which one can use symbols." None of Valéry's later writings explore further than this text produced at the age of twenty-eight and provoked by Wells and Jarry.

only when the author has acquired sufficient experience to savor all its beauties." Such a statement attached to an unpublished text, and the pains Jarry took to put his manuscripts into safe hands, make it clear that he was perfectly convinced not only of his own originality and importance, but also of the particular significance of 'Pataphysics. He never did much more than name it and sketch in its outlines. Yet it stands as the final expression of all his attitudes, for it subsumes the principles of innocence and blasphemy, ambiguity and the absurd, and universal convertibility. They constitute the world within which he violated his own identity and exceeded the limits of literature. The disciplines of drink and 'Pataphysics, however, were finally not enough to sustain total hallucination. Unlike Rousseau and Satie, who could live to a ripe old age in a world of devotion and candor, Jarry had to die in order to find the beauties of a "universe supplementary to this one." His death at thirty-four put an end to a deliberately monstrous life which, having transformed everything else, had no recourse but to transport itself elsewhere.

No one style could suffice to convey the visionary realm out of which Jarry wrote his works. As he turned from the poetry and plays of his early years to novels and semi-humorous magazine pieces, his manner shifted not so much in essence as in emphasis. In the early poetry he made wide use of the ambiguity and open structure suggested in "Lintel." Often the tiniest jolt or change of lighting will totally alter the image, as in a kaleidoscope.

> *A l'horizon, par les brouillards*
> *Les tintamarres des hasards,*
> *Vagues, nous armons nos démons*
> *Dans l'entre-deux sournois des monts.*
>
> *("L'Homme à la hache," Minutes)*

On the horizon, through the mist,
Hazard's pandemonium,
Vague, we arm our demon host
In the shifty inbetween of hills.

By using a simple series in which we do not know what stands in apposition to what, he leaves the way open to several combinations of terms. At the same time *vagues* is an (untranslatable) instance of compound ambiguity, being an adjective of alternative gender modifying any of a number of nouns, and/or a noun in its own right. This kind of writing forms the basis of Jarry's best serious poetry, profoundly symbolist in origin, dense, but often very close to verbal excess.

Ambiguity is best suited to poetry. At the swifter pace of prose Jarry exploited two principal styles: enumerative visual description laden with metaphor, and deft flexible dialogue. His narrative consists of series of descriptions seldom speeded up to the point where we can forget the purely sensuous content of each scene. The description frequently verges on lushness, but a lushness which at its best arises not so much from the verbiage as from the elaborateness of the imagery.

> *Le fleuve a une grosse face molle, pour les gifles des rames, un cou à nombreux plis, la peau bleue au duvet vert. Entre ses bras, sur son coeur, il tient la petite Ile en forme de chrysalide. La Prairie à la robe verte s'endort, la tête au creux de son épaule et de sa nuque.*

> The river has a soft fat face under the slapping of oars, a wrinkled neck, a clear blue skin touched with greenish down. It holds in its arms against its heart the little Island which has the shape of a chrysalid. The green-clad Prairie goes to sleep, its head in the hollow between its shoulder and neck.

This fragment from *Dr. Faustroll* partakes of fantasy and even humor; the colors and textures recall Gauguin, the vision is Jarry's. He depicts people in a comparable style.

> *. . . ces agents moraux correctement vêtus de noir, cravatés de favoris blancs, le crâne privé de cheveux comme leur conscience, les écarts de leur nez subtil gouvernés par ce jockey: une paire de bésicles d'or. (Gestes.)*

> . . . those members of the morals squad correctly dressed in black, cravatted in white side whiskers, their heads as clean of hair as their consciences of any scruple, the swervings of each thin nose held in check by a tense jockey: a pair of gold-rimmed spectacles.

The passage reads like the transcriptions of a satirical cartoon by Forain or Gavarni, and now one can begin to discern the roots of Jarry's descriptive style. It reveals the profound influence of works of art he studied and wrote about in *L'Art Littéraire* and his own two reviews. The Gothic-surrealist accumulation of detail in Dürer, the crude passionate effectiveness of Epinal prints, blazonry and its inexhaustible symbolism, the particular manners of Rousseau, Redon, Bonnard, and Gauguin—the source of Jarry's visual inspiration lies here. He wrote poems about works by Gauguin* and the Norwegian Munthe. The panoramic description of the Battle of Morsang in *La dragonne* bears a remarkable likeness to Rousseau's enormous painting *La guerre*—horse, flames, barren trees, and apocalyptic mood.

The fact that Jarry was himself a talented painter-draftsman now takes on significance. After schoolboy prizes for "imitative drawing," he worked principally in highly stylized and visionary woodcuts, illustrating the original editions of his books: *Minutes de sable, Ubu Roi,* and *César-Antéchrist.* Later he turned to oils, and produced a series of small impressionist landscapes. Jarry's accomplishments as a graphic artist deserve revaluation†; his drawings can be compared to Daumier's and Töpffer's, and show characteristic leanings toward expressive and semicomic distortion. Painting and drawing, as he practiced them and studied them in the work of others, taught Jarry an essentially plastic vision. Often the apparently static nature of

---

* Jarry met Gauguin in 1893 when the painter returned from Tahiti for the Durand-Ruel show. They published side by side in *Essais d'Art Libre,* and Jarry joined him in Pont-Aven in 1894 and probably introduced him to Rousseau in the course of that year. Back in Tahiti in 1897, Gauguin wrote of Ubu as ". . . a new type . . . From now on Ubu belongs in the Academy dictionary; he'll designate the man who has a human body and the soul of a wood louse." *(Le Sourire.)*

† In a recent history of woodcuts, Imre Reiner comments on the *Ymagier* group, including Gauguin and Gourmont. "I mention . . . Alfred Jarry as their most important representative, more especially for historical reasons. Even if no immediate influence of this movement upon wood engraving can be traced, the desire for something higher in graphic arts had been roused and stimulated."

his descriptions betrays the unexpected detail and dynamics of a print or a planned composition.

Alternating with this highly personal descriptive style, Jarry employed a contrasting method of portrayal: dialogue, his most compressed and therefore most explosive writing. His plays are nothing else. The brisk exchange between Ubu and his conscience could not exist without this stylized manner of presenting abruptness of thought. In much the same way, marionettes stylize action into mimicry. Unless it is very formal and polite, speech moves without perfunctory connectives and transitions. *Therefore, although, notwithstanding* and the like have no place in dialogue pared down to the quick.

FEAR: Your watch has three hands. Why?

LOVE: That's the way it is here.

FEAR: My god, why three hands? Somehow it disturbs me. . . .

LOVE: Nothing more natural and simple. Don't be upset. The first hand tells the hour, the second drags the minutes along, and the third, never moving, points to the eternity of my indifference.

FEAR: You're joking. I don't think you'd dare pretend that. . . . Oh no, you wouldn't dare to. . . .

LOVE: To put my heart on stop position?

FEAR: I don't understand what you're saying.

LOVE: And when I say nothing?

FEAR: Oh . . . I catch on much better then.

LOVE: There, that's exactly the explanation.

FEAR: What explanation?

LOVE: The one I don't want to give you.

(*L'amour en visites.*)

And then at the end:

FEAR: So . . . you don't love me.

LOVE: You have only that to fear, Madame.

This perversely circular conversation reaches into some of the most intimate turmoils of Jarry's life, and at the same time grazes laughter. Between the two speakers, equal forces of attraction and repulsion, comprehension and incomprehension sustain a formal verbal dance like two pith balls with opposite charges hanging from the same hook.

Ultimately, Jarry lampooned the very nature of dialogue and human speech, as he did everything else. The principal instance is Bosse-de-Nage ("Bottom-Face"), the monkey who accompanies Dr. Faustroll on his Rabelaisian voyages. Jarry writes that Bosse-de-Nage could "pronounce correctly a few words in Belgian" but that usually he preferred to use the "tautological French monosyllable, 'Ha-ha,' and add nothing further."

> This personage will be very useful in the course of this narrative, serving at intervals to break the long speeches—just as Victor Hugo used to do (*les Burgraves,* I, II):
> "Is that all?"
> "No, just listen to this."

The monkey's meaningless and all-meaning "ha-ha" brings out the principle of true dialogue: that each speech must actively outstrip the last and not merely acknowledge what has gone before.

At his best Jarry combines description and dialogue into an intermittent *scenic* style. Even his novels are constructed scenically, with the action developing through an alternation of styles and moods, not through sustained narrative. One feels in his writing a great visual richness, which derives from the plastic arts, and it is thus that he gives reality and immediacy to his imagination. The dramatic discipline of dialogue afforded him the further virtue of *timing*—the capacity to manipulate sudden reversals of meaning and comprehension. Most of the infantile-comic side of his work comes through in this fashion—until the illusory realism of dialogue collapses and reveals itself as part of the same hallucinatory world. The burden of Jarry's art, from humor and obscenity to near-mystic visionary writing, rested on this blend of styles. Separately, their effectiveness is diminished; in combination, they achieve a great flexibility which conveys Jarry's flickering, comic, and ominous sensibility.

How better define Jarry after all this than as a great 'Pataphysician? The word suggests both scientific rigor and farcical wand-waving and permits him the combined qualities of comedian and wizard. His violated life is as much implicated in the word as his writings. Yet it is not quite enough to accept his own bizarre term and attempt no further interpretation. Jarry is so elusive a figure, despite the roughness of his exterior, that we need several means of grasping him. Two can now be suggested without supplying any new facts. The first of them is best approached through what has been somewhat precariously called his "humor."

Jarry's humor was an enormous, unsparing thing. One must be careful not to look for the psychological veracity of satire in his writing. He did not proceed like Molière or Aristophanes or Mark Twain, in whose works we find an intensification of familiar human characteristics; he abandoned the conventions of optical perspective. "It doesn't resemble anything," he said gruffly of his writing. Jarry's humor may, rather, be regarded as a psychological refusal to repress distasteful images. He laughed and invited us to laugh at Ubu's most monstrous behavior, not because we are immune—we are, in fact, deathly afraid of the "truth" of Ubu—but because it is a means of domesticating fear and pain. Jarry bore poverty and scandal and loneliness by laughing at them, and one lesson of his life is that humor offers both a form of wisdom and a means of survival in a threatening world. It demands that we reckon with the realities of human nature and the world without falling into into grimness and despair. The best comment on the attitude occurs in a nontechnical passage of Freud's essay on wit, where he has been discussing the "gallows-humor" of a condemned man who makes his last request on the scaffold for a kerchief to keep his neck warm.

> We must say that there is something like greatness of soul in this *blague*, in this clinging to his usual nature and in deviating from that which would overthrow and drive this nature into despair.

The jokester in Jarry did not shrink before the questions that disturbed him most deeply and may well have destroyed his personality. He laughed at sex in the form of erotic adventures, and he mercilessly parodied the Catholic Church. Yet his own sexual nature and the reality of spiritual experience were the two problems that haunted him constantly. The abject figure of Ubu and the uninhibited absurdity of Dr. Faustroll testify alike to Jarry's courage in confronting the most distorted or extreme images of humanity. All of us can take fright, but it requires greatness of soul to laugh at the moment when not merely life, but humanity itself is endangered. Endangered not because Jarry behaved scandalously, but because his behavior is latent in all of us.*

The second interpretation of Jarry's significance arises out of a detail that appears with increasing frequency in his work and sheds light on all his undertakings. Its nature is such that it becomes a symbol almost before it can establish itself as an object: the mask. Very early Jarry worked out theories of theater technique and staging in which he insists on the mask as the device best suited to displaying eternal attitudes of human character. "The truth of masks" is the truth of the particular released into universal (im)posture. His affection for marionettes and puppets can be explained by the fact that they are pure mask, without any distracting face peering out from behind. As time goes on, Jarry treats the mask as a falsity vital to survival. Emmanuel Dieu in *L'amour absolu* comprehends the paradox from his supreme pinnacle of meditation: "Since he is certain that, in order to be understood he must lie, every falsehood is indifferent to him. It is a way of reaching people." During her profligacy in the brothels of Rome, Messaline wears the "decorum" of a wig; Miss Elson, the American girl in *Le surmâle*, remains masked during her prolonged love encounter with the hero, Marcueil. And Marcueil himself has been obliged to mask his superhuman powers through "mimetism" in imitating the crowd. "Why did Marcueil feel the need to hide and at the same time reveal himself? To deny his powers and prove them? No doubt in order to verify that his mask was still on straight." In other words, the mask becomes a protection for one's reticence, an essential lie. We are dealing with a symbol not so much of falsehood as of release from inhibition.

Jarry treats the question of masks most searchingly in discussing the "inverse mimesis" of the characters in a novel by Henri de Régnier. Rather than imitate their surround-

---

* Jarry's greatness of soul is given exaggerated expression by the converted painter-poet Max Jacob, who saw in his friend's life a species of modern martyrdom of the spirit. "Isn't his [Jarry's] image that of Our Lord on Earth, but turned inside out? . . . Didn't God wish His Son to enact here below in the eyes of men the role of a kind of Ubu?" Sanctification goes too far. Jarry was courageous but not holy.

ings they "mold their surroundings to their own image and make themselves a palace out of the space around them."

> That each hero brings his *décor* with him, that we never see Prince Pranzig without his military coat or Mme. de Vitry without her glowing cheeks . . . proves that the author has turned his characters inside out and put their soul on the outside: the soul is a tic.
>
> . . . If the characters show themselves to us behind masks, we must remember that character has no other sense but mask, and that it is the "false face" which is true because personal. That author is very skillful who needs only a detail of the mask for his depiction . . . with Cleopatra, the nose is enough; we know that the rest is not far behind.

In the reversible world he had reached, Jarry's early dramatic theories about universal "type" characters find their conversion into the theory of the "tic" which constitutes our only soul. It was inevitable that under Jarry's merciless treatment the utterly typical should turn out to be totally exceptional, and vice versa. Jarry applied these theatrical principles not only to Ubu—a man turned inside out with his basest appetites hung on the outside—but to himself also. He lived a contortion and twisted himself inside out. His soul was, after all, an assemblage of tics. Mask, eccentricity, gallows humor, and greatness of soul are merely different names for his chosen attitude. The two guiding principles of his career, the absurd ideas systematized in 'Pataphysics and the theatrical ideas about formalized gesture and masks, led to a single principle of conversion: anything can be its opposite. He demonstrates that outrageous truth with the robustness of Rabelais, the spiritual truculence of Lautréamont, and the cool rationality of Poe. The world is his hallucination.

Having ventured so far, Jarry frequently becomes inaccessible. That is to be expected. The true source of astonishment is that the apparently disparate elements of his career should finally mesh. His biography, his legend, and his literary work are so organically combined that, strange to say, no sustained effort to isolate one from another aids in explaining him. Like the plates of a battery pulled apart, they cannot carry separately the charge which they accumulate when they almost touch. Jarry is a devilishly modern figure, unbearable and engaging, who transformed his life into something as "lovely as literature" and attempted to strike a new balance between seriousness and humor. Apollinaire wrote wisely when he called him "the last sublime debauchee of the Renaissance."

[9]

THE IMPRESARIO OF
THE AVANT-GARDE

I love men, not for what unites them, but for what divides
them, and I want to know most of all what gnaws at their
hearts.

—*Anecdotiques*

In his thirty-eight years Guillaume Apollinaire contrived to
leave a lasting mark on the poetry and painting of the
twentieth century. Yet the welter of material that has appeared on his life and personality makes a discouraging
confusion out of his career. What one acquaintance took
for amiability and good humor, another took for fawning
or deliberate inconsistency. He excelled, in fact, in balanc-
ing natural charm against intentional outrage. The different
sides of his temperament complemented each other and
produced an impression, unlike the one Jarry left, of eva-
siveness. Many acquaintances wondered how much of him
showed above the surface. He was not Bohemian in the
sense of scorning recognized channels of accomplishment.
Yet there was in him a distinct gift for sustaining an
unusual form of conduct and speech, in the knowledge
that it would be noticed and remembered. Whereas Jarry
by a tremendous tour de force created his role and lived
up to it, Apollinaire exploited his expansive personality,
celebrated it in his writing, and ran the constant risk of
turning his private life into a public performance. Jarry left
himself behind for a fiction; Apollinaire tried to carry

everything along with him willy-nilly—fact and legend, gossip and falsehood.

Barely turned twenty, Apollinaire put words of extravagant prophecy into the mouth of Dr. Cornelius Hans Peter of Prague, a character in the serial novel *Que faire?*

> On my arrival on earth I found humanity on its last legs, devoted to fetishes, bigoted, barely capable of distinguishing good from evil—and I shall leave it intelligent, enlightened, regenerated, knowing there is neither good nor evil nor God nor devil nor spirit nor matter in distinct separateness.

Ten years later, this hortatory, messianic tone had become his own, asserting itself in much of his poetry and more insistently in his critical writing. Apollinaire could not withhold himself from his enthusiasms, nor did he ever feel doubts about his sincerity. Ambition and material circumstances played their part in his conduct, but at bottom it was a rare combination of understanding and flair that turned Apollinaire into a champion of the arts. He became an impresario, and presented to Paris—ultimately to the world—the first new schools of painting to appear in the twentieth century. Or it might be more apt to call him a ringmaster of the arts, for, far from remaining backstage, he appeared in person and performed along with his troupe in the cafés and banquets, galleries and editorial offices of Paris. Rousseau, Satie, and Jarry represent the qualities of the Banquet Years that Apollinaire had the skill to exploit and appropriate to himself as promoter and poet. His spirited persistence helped engineer the triumph of the avant-garde, of which he was a part. Like Dr. Cornelius Hans Peter of Prague, Apollinaire sometimes sounded like a quack. But when his mercurial mind seized on a new trend in the arts, he spoke for his era with more authority than Gide or Gertrude Stein or Diaghilev. One of the surest approaches to his poetry is through his work as critic and impresario, for he was his own most avid interpreter.

An illegitimate child, knowing no father and no true home or family life, learning the realities of life very early and unperturbed by them, Apollinaire began with his roots more in the air than in the ground. In the end they buried themselves in a variety of soils. As a youth at the turn of the century, he absorbed the contrasting backgrounds of the French Midi and the gothic north in Belgium and Germany, of eighteenth-century licentious texts and the latest symbolist theories from Paris. His travels made him a cosmopolitan and his reading a semi-erudite man. He revealed a penetrating knowledge of himself when he wrote to André Billy, "My erudition is no doubt an aspect of my ignorance," for, despite all his experience of life, he felt an unrelieved incompleteness in himself which drove him constantly forward. His spiritual nature hides beyond countless oblique paths of eroticism, pursuit of the marvelous, and love of mystery. The loyalty of his friendship for men like Salmon and Picasso and Jacob and Billy was exceeded in strength only by the passion of his love for a few women, from whom he reluctantly separated himself. Despite differences in their temperaments and sympathies, he steadfastly stood by his mother and tried to win her approval. These bonds, which attached him to certain places and people, constituted the beginnings of identity he forged for himself as man and poet.

Henri Rousseau was one of the few friends who ever attempted a simple likeness of Apollinaire's Neronian figure, and Rousseau immediately encountered one of his most characteristic traits: Apollinaire rarely showed up for portrait sittings. Among the scores of literary sketches that have been written about him, we find only fleeting glimpses of a poet always behind in his correspondence, always threatened by a deadline, and always escaping to another appointment. The resulting composite portrait perpetuates several distortions, which demand correction. Even in his peak years of manifestoes and dislocated typography, he was never the total rebel. Having struggled hard to send down his roots, he was not prepared to tear them up indiscriminately. Nor was he simply a poet who chanced to write a surprisingly sensitive book about cubism in 1913 and then gave a lecture in 1917 that anticipated surrealism. From 1907 on, he was a working critic of the arts, obliged not only to keep himself informed but to choose those movements to which he would give his full support. The power of his influence during his lifetime and after his death can be explained only by a long record of vociferous and partisan activity. He showed simultaneous tendencies toward unrestrained fantasy and toward crude realism, toward religious faith bordering on superstition and toward reveling in blasphemy and evil. The men he most admired in the preceding generation had displayed equally para-doxical temperaments—Remy de Gourmont, Marcel Schwob, Jarry. Apollinaire prolonged their erudition and their "decadence" and refreshed it with a new youthfulness and robustness. He was not a great solitary, not an *illuminé* in the line of Nerval, not a *poète maudit* in the line of Baudelaire and Rimbaud. He stood, rather, at the center of a magnificent collaboration.

It was a fortunate day for the arts when the rich Spanish genius of Picasso, the steady French logic of Braque, the mystical Jewish intensity of Jacob, and the all-encompass-ing cosmopolitan lyricism of Apollinaire joined forces in the "central laboratory" of Montmartre. For each of them, this early period of exchange provided a lasting stimulus and a knowledge of the fundamental unity of the arts. In the critical years just before the war, Apollinaire's accom-plishments as critic-impresario helped detach the new century from the old and create a frame of reference in which the word "modern" has come to mean "since sym-bolism and impressionism." His poetry cannot be fully appreciated without a knowledge of his long cohabitation with painters and painting.

Not until recent years have the circumstances of Apolli-naire's birth been brought to light. The first discoveries were made by his indefatigable biographer, Marcel Adéma. Guillaume Albert Wladimir Alexandre Apollinaire de Kos-trowitzky was born the twenty-sixth of August in the Trastevere quarter of Rome, the illegitimate son of An-gélique Alexandrine Kostrowitzky. The twenty-two-year-old, dark-haired beauty registered his birth under a false name, baptized him with his real name, and later legally recognized his birth. Her family, which belonged to lesser Polish nobility, had taken political refuge at the papal court. Convent education, however, had done little to restrain her headstrong nature. More than twenty years older than Angélique and with a brilliant military career behind him, Francesco Flugi d'Aspermont swept the girl into the romantic transports she had dreamed of. His wealthy Catholic family, originally from the province of

Grisons in Switzerland, was outraged by his affair with the extravagant "Russian." After two children had been born and sentiments had cooled on both sides, so discreet an end to the liaison was arranged that the identity of Apollinaire's father remained a mystery for nearly seventy years. Apollinaire himself took pleasure in letting it be understood that he had been sired by a high church dignitary in the Vatican—at least a cardinal. But several veiled allusions in his writings make it clear that he carried with him all his life the image of his father as a handsome, violent officer with a reputation as a philanderer. For a time, the father's brother, a prominent member of the Benedictine order, kept an eye on the struggling family and helped in the education of the children.

In 1885 Madame de Kostrowitzky settled on the Riviera to bring up her two boys, and made her own way in its cosmopolitan *demi-monde*. From the age of eight, Kostro, as Guillaume was called, attended Catholic schools in Monaco, Nice, and Cannes. A good but not brilliant student, the sallow dark-eyed boy impressed his schoolmates with his unbridled imagination, moody ambitions, and an acute ear for strange words and accents. With his earliest friend, René Dalize, he went through an intensely religious period, and in his poem "Zone" he recalls how they slipped unseen out of the dormitory and prayed all night in the school chapel. At seventeen he took a precocious interest in literature, especially in poets like Verlaine and Mallarmé, and the militant novelists Barrès and Zola. With another friend, Toussaint-Luca, he issued a handwritten anarcho-symbolist "newspaper" composed of their own poems and articles.

Fourteen years on the Côte d'Azur instilled in Apollinaire the candor, volubility, and sensuous religious awareness of the Latin temperament. He had already by that time decided on a literary career in French, a tongue that, after his earliest childhood years in Italy, always retained a faintly exotic ring for him.

The family was then under the protection of Jules Weil, a young banker and speculator, with whom Madame de Kostrowitzky lived most of her remaining years. In 1899 she and Weil visited Spa in Belgium, while Kostro and his brother boarded nearby at Stavelot, an ancient town in the Ardennes. With happy exuberance Kostro roamed the wild landscape of *"les Fagnes,"* a sort of druidic heath and traditional subject of mystery and legend. He charmed the inhabitants, including a pretty barmaid named Marie Dubois, and wrote masses of what he called *brouillons,* drafts of stories and poems. Having suffered gambling reverses at Spa, Madame de Kostrowitzky and Weil returned to Paris and instructed the boys to "skip" the pension without paying the six-hundred-franc bill. Carrying everything they could fit into a trunk and a valise, they tiptoed out in the middle of a cold October night and trudged for an hour cross country to another railroad line in order to throw off pursuers. They reached Paris frightened but safe after Kostro had been taken off the train because his name resembled that of an anarchist wanted by the police. *"Filer à la cloche de bois"* read the headline of the local Stavelot newspaper, and the article concluded that "our two de Kostrowitzkys (deep bow) were only two low swindlers." The town, however, could not hold a grudge and has in recent years erected a monument and a museum in honor of the truant French poet.

In 1900, while he was making a living by doing lowly secretarial jobs in Paris, Apollinaire saw his first work in print. But to do so he had to submit to the humiliation of becoming a ghost writer. *Que faire?*, a novel by several hands, to which Apollinaire contributed the bulk of the chapters and the central figure of Dr. Peter of Prague, appeared in installments in the newspaper *Le Matin.* It was signed by Esnard, an unreliable hack journalist, who never paid Apollinaire his fee. The extravagant, amusing, mystico-scientific adventures of the hero echo the work of Verne, Wells, Poe, and Jarry.* Apollinaire's characteristic blend of prophecy and humor is crudely handled in this sprawling text. Even greater crudity brought him a few needed francs in 1901 for his first pornographic work, *Mirely, ou le petit trou pas cher.* After the dedicated literary efforts at Stavelot, he had to submit to writing the lowest kind of potboilers. Such were his debuts.

Both in compensation for this disappointment of his literary ambitions and by natural inclination, he engaged in

---

* Dr. Peter bears a distinct similarity to Jarry's Dr. Faustroll, who had first appeared two years earlier in the *Mercure,* Faustroll's monosyllabic monkey, Bosse-de-Nage, appears to have inspired Dr. Peter's gorilla, Goliath.

a series of promiscuous and unimportant amorous adventures, of which little record remains. The one strong emotional attachment of the period provoked his first group of romantic lyrics, *Les dicts d'amour à Linda,* written to a dark-haired sixteen-year-old girl of Spanish blood.

> *Lorsque vous partirez, je ne vous dirai rien,*
> *Mais après tout l'été, quand reviendra l'automne,*
> *Si vous n'êtes pas là, zézayante, ô Madone,*
> *J'irai gémir à votre porte comme un chien.*
> *Lorsque vous partirez, je ne vous dirai rien.*

> When you leave, I shall not say a word,
> But come the fall, after summer's long day,
> If you, lisping madonna, stay away,
> I'll become a dog to whimper at your door.
> When you leave, I shall not say a word.

She thwarted him, flirted with him, and then sympathized with him as if he were a big brother; his letters to her overflow with sentimental remonstrance. For the rest of his life Apollinaire yielded at intervals to the temptation to prove himself through sexual exploits, but his best work always resulted from disappointed love.

When Linda went off for the summer, Apollinaire soon found more than mere distraction. An attractive job was offered him, that of tutor to the daughter of a wealthy German family visiting Paris. When the Viscountess of Milhau set out for Germany by automobile in August, 1901, the young French tutor was part of her entourage. He was far from indifferent to the presence of a pretty, reticent, English governess, Annie Playden, who shared his duties. During the long winter spent in the Rhineland at Honnef and in a villa called Neu-Glück at Bennerscheid, Apollinaire played the part of ardent lover—but without success. He had grown to be a striking, Roman-featured young man, who conversed brilliantly and showed an unflagging enthusiasm for every aspect of life. The shy blonde English girl both admired and feared the intensity of the young poet whose verses and stories at last began to appear in Paris reviews; she did not yield to his attack. Yet in his letters Apollinaire boasted of conquest. "I loved her carnally," he wrote his fiancée, Madeleine Pagès, fourteen years later, "but our temperaments were a long way apart."

In the spring of 1902, the viscountess released Apollinaire for a few months to travel. Free for the first time in his life and with a little money in his pocket, he went eastward: Cologne, Munich, Berlin, Vienna, finally Prague. He felt himself becoming a citizen of Europe and saw himself in the role of the Wandering Jew. Stirred by the spectacle of an entire continent bursting into bloom, his desire for Annie unabated, he composed a number of melancholy lyrics, the most characteristic of which are included in the group *Rhénanes.*

> *Le mai le joli mai en barque sur le Rhin*
> *Des dames regardaient du haut de la montagne*
> *Vous êtes si jolies mais la barque s'éloigne*
> *Qui donc a fait pleurer les saules riverains*

> May lovely May floats idle on the Rhine
> High on the slopes the women come to see
> You are so lovely but the boat moves on
> Who made the willows weep along the shore

Back in Paris in the fall of 1902, Apollinaire lived with his mother, took a job in a bank, and sought entry into literary and artistic circles. The bank soon failed, and he barely kept his head above water doing odd journalistic chores. Twice he crossed the Channel to London to see Annie and ask her to marry him; her family refused permission, and she ultimately accepted a job as governess in the United States. In despair, Apollinaire wrote the most famous and sustained of his poems, *"La chanson du mal-aimé."*

> *Regrets sur quoi l'enfer se fonde*
> *Qu'un ciel d'oubli s'ouvre à mes vœux*
> *Pour son baiser les rois du monde*
> *Serait morts les pauvres fameux*
> *Pour elle eussent vendu leur ombre*

> Regrets compose a lonely hell
> May the sky swallow my desires
> For her kiss all worldly kings
> Would die a glad and glorious death
> They'd sell their shadows for her look

Years later he was able to write of how poets "put their sufferings to good use by turning them into song."

The sunny logical spirit of Italy and the Riviera was never dislodged in Apollinaire's temperament, but the months in Stavelot and his travels across Europe instilled in him the inward vision of the North. This blend of northern and southern strains helped produce a personality that was both extroverted and reticent, and a corpus of poetry filled with contrasting images of darkness and light. That same spring of 1902, in signing his first published story, he adopted the name Guillaume Apollinaire, which appears to give primacy to the Mediterranean and Apollonian side of his temperament. This brighter side did not completely assimilate the shades and depths of his nature which turned instinctively to Germanic and Celtic folklore. But even a partial fusion allowed him to feel his strength. It is at this juncture, in his twenty-third year, that the youthful irresolute Kostro begins to disappear behind the manifold literary figure of Guillaume Apollinaire. With "La chanson du mal-aimé" his career had begun in earnest.

Around 1903 an unexpected lull came over the Paris literary scene. After the triumphs of symbolism and naturalism, after the enormous activity of the époque 1900, with its Universal Exposition and seething Dreyfus case, writers suddenly became uncertain of which way to turn next. The important Revue Blanche ceased publication, and literary supplements dwindled to the vanishing point. Reviewing the results of a large-scale survey of the contemporary literary scene, Remy de Gourmont concluded, "Thus, in every field, profound stagnation."

It was during this calm that Apollinaire encountered and became associated with three different groups of artists and writers whose friendship deeply influenced the direction his career would take. He was at the time a habitué of the weekly poetry gatherings sponsored by the review La Plume. Invited one evening to read some of his own work, Apollinaire leaned on the piano, puffed his tiny clay pipe, displayed his "centurion's head," and recited two of his poems to a not very responsive audience. On that same evening in 1903 another unfledged poet equally dissatisfied with the stillness of the literary scene recited a poem called "Le banquet." He was André Salmon, an athletic-looking young man with a certain wildness in his manner. Inevitably the two became friends. A short time later they met a celebrated writer, the better part of whose career was already behind him: Alfred Jarry. Apollinaire and Salmon together founded a little review, *Festin d'Esope*, which ran to nine lively but not revolutionary issues. Jarry, barely seven years their senior, was godfather and adviser. During lengthy conversations over absinthe in the *bistros* of the Rue de Seine, he taught them the boldness they lacked and encouraged their high spirits. Two other men joined the little group: Mecislas Golberg, an emigrant Pole with violent ideas and the appearance of a prophet and fakir, whose influence supplemented Jarry's in convincing Apollinaire of the significance of a special form of humor and distortion in art; and the "Baron" Mollet, a silent witness and literary factotum who later became Apollinaire's secretary. Apollinaire never wrote at length of this exploratory period when he was trying his hand at all sorts of writing, editing his own magazine, making numerous friends, and surveying the field. He was not, all in all, a bad literary strategist, yet he was content to say of the epoch, "We learned to laugh."

During the same winter of 1903–1904, Mollet walked Apollinaire across Paris to meet a painter in a busy café in the Rue d'Amsterdam opposite the Gare Saint-Lazare. The Criterion already had a literary history, for it is in this "tavern" that, in Huysmans' novel *A rebours,* Des Esseintes ends an aborted trip to England. The place had meanwhile become a hangout of touts and jockeys; and Alphonse Allais died in one of its booths the following year. Mollet's friend found Apollinaire conversing easily at a table full of strangers and hangers-on; the friend was a Spaniard named Pablo Picasso, aged twenty-three, on his fourth trip to Paris—this one to last thirty years. The two unknown young men became friends that day.* To the next meeting Picasso brought along the mystico-humorous poet Max Jacob, whom he had met in 1901 at the time of his first Paris show at Vollard's gallery. Jacob's impressions of Apollinaire at this first meeting were vivid.

* For this meeting the participants themselves have supplied dates ranging from 1903 to 1906. Frequently the similar Austin-Fox bar, a few doors up the street, is given as the scene. André Billy insists that it happened in 1903 in a café on the Boulevard Saint-Germain.

He was an imposing young man with a deep chest and heavy limbs. . . . He changed in an instant from childlike laughter to pale gravity. The three of us left together and Guillaume carried us off for a stroll which never came to an end. . . . Here began the best days of my life.

Before long, Salmon moved in next door to Picasso in the *bateau lavoir* up the street from Jacob, and Apollinaire spent more and more of his time in their company. From these beginnings can be traced one of the most significant literary artistic collaborations of the century.

At about this same moment, Apollinaire encountered another group of young painters in Chatou near the "villa" his mother and Weil rented in the suburb of Le Vésinet. Maurice de Vlaminck and André Derain were both enthusiastic athletes (Vlaminck had been a bicycle racer) turned artists and had met one day while painting the same suburban landscape. They took Apollinaire along with them into the most disreputable places in the locality —bargemen's cafés, hashish dens, and *maisons de passe*. They played cards and drank and launched into conversations on aesthetics and the aspirations of painting, discussions as impassioned as those between Picasso and Salmon and Apollinaire. Vlaminck describes Apollinaire at this time as keenly intelligent, naïve, and at the same time skeptical. "With all the authority he was beginning to assume," Vlaminck adds, "and with the ribald bluster of Père Ubu, he encouraged people's worst pretensions." The comment reflects principally on Apollinaire's growing preoccupation with novelty and innovation. He was beginning to come into his own.

In these three groups of new friends he found all the stimulation he needed; the Montmartre groups soon became a nucleus of artistic activity. All of them worked constantly and according to a particular method: Picasso painted all night; Apollinaire composed poetry while walking and humming to himself; Jacob had visions and told fortunes in fashionable *salons*. Together they frequented the Lapin Agile and the Cirque Médrano, and once a week they tramped all the way across the city to the Closerie des Lilas where Paul Fort's new review, *Vers et Prose*, held its wild soirees. (Salmon as editorial secretary of the review helped organize these gatherings.) While a new generation of poets and painters sparred with the old guard of symbolism, Apollinaire passed as an authority on the stock market because of his position as editor of a half-fraudulent financial magazine. The American-born poet Stuart Merrill and many others asked his advice on investments, and only Salmon and a few close friends perceived how totally ignorant he was of every aspect of the Bourse. But Apollinaire's talents were at ease in any field of fabrication. One evening after missing the last train home to Le Vésinet, he pronounced solemnly to Jacob: "Our civilization will leave to future ages only its roundhouses and its railroad tracks. Scholars will perish trying to decipher the inscriptions." He invented his world as he went along.

After the *Festin d'Esope* failed, Apollinaire and Salmon raised money among the shady Criterion and Austin-Fox crowds for another review and borrowed office space in the clinic of a doctor friend, brother of the painter F. X. Roussel. The publication was launched under the title (possibly borrowed from Gide's recently published novel) of *La Revue Immoraliste*. However, the building that housed the clinic was, as Salmon expressed it, "blessed"— that is, it belonged to the Catholic Church and housed certain religious orders. The name of the magazine did not entirely suit the surroundings, nor did its activities. Every day exceedingly eccentric and unseemly characters, *de trop pittoresques messieurs-dames*, banged at the front door and asked the nuns for the offices of *La Revue Immoraliste*. One poet, Ernest Reynaud, who always looked uncomfortable in his suits, was mistaken for a plain-clothes investigator from the vice squad. The concierge summed up the touchy situation in blunt terms: *"Dans une maison catholique, ça la fout mal"* ("In a Catholic building it louses things up"). The upshot was that Apollinaire discreetly changed the name from *La Revue Immoraliste* to—as if it would make all the difference—*La Revue Moderne*. The venture soon failed, for Apollinaire had neither the resources to support it nor truly original ideas for which to demand a hearing. He was still partially under the spell of symbolism,* and his efforts at magazine publication

* In 1904 Apollinaire contrived a certain humorous objectivity on the demise of symbolism in speaking of the epidemic of

demonstrate more than anything else his resolve to find an independent position and make his mark.

In these unbridled surroundings Apollinaire's ambitions as an art critic rapidly took shape. Jarry's bravado, Picasso's prolific talent, exalted conversations with Vlaminck and Derain, and the swirling night life of Paris fired him with a new desire to impose his tastes and whims on the amorphous artistic scene. His first writings on art, two lyric, yet observant, articles on Picasso, appeared in 1905.

> He came from far away, from the rich composition
> and brutal decoration of 17th-century Spaniards.
> . . . He has since become more Latin morally and
> more Arab in his rhythms. (*La Plume.*)

Meanwhile, his expansive, oddly informed, unpredictable personality, both merry and mystifying, commanded more attention in the literary world than is indicated by his trickle of publications in magazines. He began one season flamboyantly by making furious preparations to fight a duel. Max Daireaux, a peppery journalist, had written an account of how Apollinaire, in his cups at one of Charles Morice's literary "Dinners of the 14," ordered Apollinaris water shouting, *"C'est mon eau . . ."* ("It's my water"). The unfought affair dwindled into a petty dispute between Apollinaire and his second, Max Jacob, over café expenses incurred during negotiations for settlement. Apollinaire had already attracted his legend: obscure foreign birth, wide travel and knowledge, formidable appetites, and a capacity to converse lengthily with anyone as an equal. He grew a mustache, began putting on weight, and succeeded in sustaining multiple careers as market expert, poet, editor, journalist, Bohemian, and exotic personality. Fernande Olivier, Picasso's mistress during these years, completes the picture.

> A mixture of nobility and vulgarity due to his open
> childlike laugh. A prelate's hands with unctuous
> gestures. . . . And all this enveloped, it seemed, and
> attenuated by his friendly manner, calm and mild,
> grave and tender, which made you listen to him
> when he started talking—and he talked a lot.

memoirs being written by its veterans. "These symbolists talk like the syphilitic who, after being cured, acted as if the disease did not exist because he was thereafter immune to infection."

In 1907 Apollinaire moved into a small bourgeois apartment in the Rue Henner near his companions in the *bateau lavoir*. Wednesday evenings he entertained them simply; they all took poverty for granted. He saw a good deal of Jules Romains (five years his junior), and became loosely associated with the social and poetic experiments of the unanimists.

A new domicile and new friends, however, did not separate Apollinaire from his mother, who had arranged and furnished his apartment. She was a determined, demanding woman, who never treated her son as grown up, made little attempt to understand his literary work, yet had a say in many of his decisions. He constantly tried to prove himself in her eyes, told her everything he did, and later kept up a regular correspondence with her on every aspect of his life. In a sense, he went his own way, but he wished always to share that way with his mother, despite her inflexibility. Apollinaire visited her every Sunday in Le Vésinet, consumed the hearty meal she cooked for him, left a bundle of laundry, and occasionally took along a friend—if Madame de Kostrowitzky approved. She represented the most permanent and exacting force in his life, and he responded with unfailing devotion.

It was not only his friends and his career that brought Apollinaire to Paris to live. When one day Picasso had jokingly told him of a young woman who would make a perfect "fiancée" for him, Apollinaire did not forget. In Père Sagot's gallery he soon met her, a wide-eyed, mischievous, slender girl, still a student at the Académie Julian. Not beautiful, boasting a drop of Creole blood in her veins, she had a subtly alluring manner between childishness and sophistication that the French call *gamine*. This was Marie Laurencin. He immediately felt the challenge she seemed to embody, and approached her with all the force of his mixed temperament. It was not an understanding they reached, but a kind of intermittent truce. The question of marriage soon arose, and Apollinaire moved to Paris both to be near her and in hopes of establishing their independent ménage. His mother, however, opposed the marriage on the grounds of Marie's insufficient dowry, and he accepted the decision. Because Marie took care of her mother, they could never live together regularly. Apollinaire was a demanding, sometimes cruel, lover, and she a capricious mistress; yet their liaison lasted until the fall of 1912. Marie thrived in the carefree and intense world of poets and painters into which Apollinaire took her, painted industriously with a certain naïveté, and alternately loved and resisted him. They went everywhere together, and the affair passed through contrasting moods of devotion and exasperation. Because she both yielded to him and escaped him, he found embodied in her the unstilled rhythm of love and disappointment which stimulated him most profoundly. For six years Marie was truly his "muse," as Rousseau had the simplicity to say, and the poems she inspired have the truest ring of all his love lyrics. *"Le Pont Mirabeau"* became his favorite, one of the two he recorded in 1914 in his sinuous chanting voice.

> *L'amour s'en va comme cette eau courante*
> *L'amour s'en va*
> *Comme la vie est lente*
> *Et comme l'Espérance est violente*

> Love leaves us like this flowing stream
> Love flows away
> How slow life is and mild
> And oh how Hope can suddenly run wild

Apollinaire had the good fortune to understand that if he was now to make any deep impression on the literary scene, he would do well to launch his attack not from within but from some extraliterary stronghold. Charles Maurras, a rabid royalist, and Charles Péguy, a revolutionary Catholic, had been able to make themselves heard from adjoining positions. Apollinaire found his vantage point in the youthful energies of painting, and he mastered its secrets insofar as his temperament and sensibility allowed. He was not alone in exploiting the upsurge of artistic innovation during the years following 1900. His friends Max Jacob, an artist in his own right, and Salmon preceded him and were endowed with a more naturally perceptive eye than his. But no one set about more deliberately and zestfully than he to discover, explain, and promote the newest movements in the arts.

From 1907 to 1909 in the pages of the reviews open to him, Apollinaire campaigned for the fauves, for Matisse, and for the devastating experiments of Picasso and Braque. He also began to take a serious though somewhat condescending interest in Rousseau's work. Asked to give an important public lecture at the Salon des Indépendants in 1908 on the youngest generation of poets, he chatted about his friends in a polite and pedestrian talk to a large crowd. Then, as if the subject made all the difference, he changed his tone and wrote a trenchant perceptive account of the painting in the same Salon, praising the revolutionary work of Derain, Braque, and Vlaminck—all of them still in their twenties. This boldness did not desert him when he wrote the catalogue prefaces for Braque's first exhibition at Kahnweiler's gallery and then for an important group show of new work in Le Havre. His remarks on Braque ("he is not preoccupied with anything alien to his art") began a long contest with Vauxcelles, a bitter critic of the new school, who derisively furnished its name in an allusion to "little cubes." As spokesman for the artists concerned, Apollinaire was the first to accept the name, "cubism," and overhaul its connotations. His first important critical venture started before either his ideas or his vocabulary had taken shape. Yet he decided to leap to the defense of cubism (this fact has been unjustly questioned) as soon as it began to emerge as a movement distinct from fauvism and without waiting for time to mollify public protest.

The ebullient demonstrations of the Rousseau banquet climaxed this first period of strenuous participation in the arts. It showed Apollinaire fully established as principal representative of the group of artists soon to be known as the cubists. He made his own contribution to the movement at the end of the busy year 1908. Kahnweiler, the art dealer most sympathetic to the group, published Apollinaire's semidramatic, semilegendary *L'enchanteur pourrissant,* with handsome woodcuts by Derain. Appollinaire's blurb stresses the artistic quality of the book as well as its literary merits. "Few books show better than *L'enchanteur pourrissant* a perfect accord between the talents of author and artist." The volume included a long prose poem, *"Onirocritique,"* the most advanced piece of writing he had done to date.

The sky was full of feces and onions. I cursed the unworthy stars whose light flowed out over the earth. . . . Ships of gold, unmanned, crossed the horizon. Gigantic shadows passed across the distant sails. Several centuries separated me from these shadows. I despaired. But I was conscious of the different eternities of men and women. Shadows of different kinds darkened with their love the scarlet of the sails, while my eyes multiplied in rivers, in cities, and on mountain snows.

Rimbaud? Lautréamont? Jarry? Their impress is unmistakable. Five years later, when the chronology of such matters was already blurred, Apollinaire was to insist on the "importance of 'Onirocritique' in respect to the road taken by the modern movement, particularly futurism."

Apollinaire's rise to prominence as interpreter of new movements in the arts and his increasingly frequent publication in literary reviews by no means earned him a living. The few journalistic chores that came his way added only a pittance, and he was obliged by sheer material need to find some means of earning his keep. Since he could no longer pretend to be a banker or a financial authority, the only commercial commodity he had to offer was his sketchy but wide-ranging knowledge in many semiliterary fields, information he had picked up during years of vagabond reading. He had a great fondness for libraries and bookstalls, and an inexhaustible curiosity about rare volumes, strange cults and customs, and the vast half-acknowledged limbo of literature; forgeries, hoaxes, pornography, pirated texts, suppressed confessions, and the like. In 1907, finding himself in desperate straits, he had turned out two pieces of pornography: *Les mémoires d'un jeune Don Juan* and *Les onze mille verges*. He was not the first poet to tap the resources of the trade, and these two volumes, the one farcical, the other partially serious, are not without qualities of style and psychological perceptiveness.

It is far from surprising, then, considering his need and his familiarity with the field, that Apollinaire accepted a contract with an enterprising young publisher named Briffault to edit a series of texts, both old and new, generally classed as pornography. It was better than having to write

his own. Called *Les maîtres de l'amour,* the series began
in 1909 with selections from the Marquis de Sade and the
Divine Aretino and concluded eight years later with Baudelaire's *Les fleurs du mal.* Counting also a similar series
issued by the same publisher, Apollinaire introduced, translated in part, annotated, and supplied bibliographies for
twenty-seven licentious texts, including Crébillon *fils* and
John Cleland's standard *Memoirs of Fanny Hill.* The assertive style he was developing on the subject of painting became even more pronounced in the erudite introductions
he produced for these erotic and obscene writings. The
Sade volume set the tone: ". . . this man, who appeared
to be of no importance through the whole of the nineteenth
century, may well dominate the twentieth." Such a statement helped produce the very effect it predicted.

These marginal literary activities must be seen in their
proper light, for they have frequently been misrepresented
as either pure drudgery entirely divorced from Apollinaire's
literary talents, or as the secret, the very core of his genius.
The truth lies between. He undertook so vast a project in
order to assure himself a regular income, and in this respect the arrangement had a reasonable success. Yet at the
same time, certain parts of the series elicited from him a
labor of love. They are not the work of a mere hack, nor
of a depraved purveyor of smut. The scholar, the liberator
of human behavior, and the commercial writer in him
combined forces to produce works in the recognized and
reputable tradition of *œuvres libres.*

After these years of struggle, Apollinaire emerged at
last onto the first plateau of his career. Between 1909 and
1911 he did not rest, but for the first time he could survey
the distance he had come. Just turning thirty, he published
his first important book, found himself accepted as a *chef
d'école,* and had enough work to keep him busy. To a young
poet this was prosperity.

Early in 1909, while the futurists were preparing their
frenzied manifesto for *Le Figaro* and Diaghilev was re-
upholstering the Châtelet theater for the first visit of the
Ballets Russes, Apollinaire added to his reputation as a
wag by taking over a regular column on women authors
(*"la littérature féminine"*) in the lively review *Les Marges.*
Under the name of Louise Lalanne he supplied coy articles

on lady poets, wrote "feminine" poems of his own, and threw in a few by Marie Laurencin. To halt the hoax a year later, the review announced that Mademoiselle La-lanne had been abducted by an army officer, and finally revealed her true identity. Under his own name Apollinaire then contributed a series of articles on literary figures, "*Les contemporains pittoresques.*" In an anecdotal style that treated man and work as a single phenomenon, he discussed Ernest La Jeunesse, Remy de Gourmont, and Jean Moréas, and, with special attention, Jarry. It was the first major article to be published on Jarry, and the impassioned tone tells a good deal about its author. In Jarry, Apollinaire admired the unsparing humor, the erotic motifs, and the sacrifice of personality to a literary creation. "His smallest actions, his pranks, everything was literature." Writing on Gourmont, Apollinaire singled out his vast erudition, the scientific approach to all subjects, and the scrupulous attention to style. With time and a means of doing so, Apollinaire would probably have set about establishing a new canon of literary classics to include, along with Jarry and Gourmont, Rimbaud, Gogol, Verne, Goethe, Nerval, Whitman, and Poe; to exclude Stendhal, most nineteenth-century novelists, Hugo, and Claudel's spiritual flatulence. Painting, however, claimed the greater part of his critical energies.

In May, 1909, after what appears to have been a delay of several years because the manuscript had been misplaced, the *Mercure* published the fifty-nine stanzas of "*La chanson du mal-aimé.*" The poem made a deep impression on Paul Léautaud, Vallette, and Gourmont, of the *Mercure* staff, and on many readers. Some time later, when Apollinaire proposed that he write a regular *chronique* for the *Mercure,* to be called "*La vie anecdotique,*" the editors accepted with alacrity. The opportunity to write as he chose in one of the most important literary reviews in Paris came as a godsend. His first installment in 1911 begins with a humorous and tactful story about Jules Romains and then turns to what was uppermost in Appollinaire's mind at the time: painting. In a few charming paragraphs he mentioned the names of all the painters he was championing. After this beginning he treated any subject that struck his fancy—singular personalities, speech habits, literary gossip, aesthetic theory. In his pungent style they all fuse into the single spacious realm of anecdote, where he was entirely at home.

Exceptionally, the lengthy second installment is devoted entirely to the life of the Douanier Rousseau, who had just died and for whom a retrospective exhibit had been organized in the Salon des Indépendants. Amid so much exploration of new territory in the arts, there probably lingered in Apollinaire's sensibility a yearning for simplicity and even conventionality. Rousseau was the one modern artist who could satisfy the yearning without betraying the hard-won principles of new painting; for Rousseau is blessed by a paradox. He can be regarded as an awkward yet totally genuine representative of traditional academic painting. He can also be regarded as an intuitive modern whose techniques suggested solutions far different from his intentions. Thus Rousseau served doubly as a minor aesthetic weakness indulged by the modern school (admiring a caricature of what it rejected) and as a major proponent of the new vision. Apollinaire started by patronizing Rousseau and came slowly around to being the foremost exponent of his cult. Must we cry hoax?

Rousseau's role as envisaged by Apollinaire and the cubists is perfectly legitimate. Whatever their original motives may have been in taking him up, they established the reputation of a great painter. In order to become Rousseau's impresario, Apollinaire had to go back and unearth a career already lost in the past. The article on Rousseau which took shape out of these pages in the *Mercure* is the longest he wrote on any artist and gives an idea of the kind of thorough treatment of personality and work that Apollinaire might have produced on many other painters. Had he lived another thirty years, Apollinaire could have written a new Vasari's *Lives* for the school of Paris.

One reason why Apollinaire now enjoyed sufficient prominence to have a regular *chronique* in the *Mercure* was the publication in 1910 of his collected stories, *L'hérésiarque et cie*. Warmly received by many critics, the volume consisted mostly of stories written five to ten years earlier. Apollinaire was disappointed when he did not receive the Prix Goncourt (his book led the first ballot), yet even without the prize he gained wide recognition through these stories.

Meanwhile, he had to work steadily at the jobs that kept

him alive. He spent entire days in the Bibliothèque Nationale examining licentious texts. In 1910, helped by his friend
Fernand Fleuret, he delivered to Briffault a total of fourteen completed volumes. Then, since they clearly had
greater familiarity with the material than the staff, the
two authors started assembling a critical bibliography of
the *Enfer* (forbidden books) of the Bibliothèque Nationale.
The *Mercure* published the book two years later, and it
remains a definitive reference work.

Apollinaire was also trying to extend his activities as a
journalist, for the lull of a few years earlier was coming
to a close. A perfect opportunity came his way in the spring
of 1910 when Salmon, who had for two years been the
regular art critic for *L'Intransigeant*, was offered a better
position on another paper. He asked Apollinaire to replace
him. Delighted at the prospect of reaching an audience
even larger than that of *Mercure*, Apollinaire began by
contributing a series of four articles on the Salon des
Indépendants. The headlines are unmistakably his: *Attention! Wet paint.* . . . *The Salon of Independent Artists.* . . .
The rout of Impressionism. . . . *Young artists return to
composition.*

Until 1914 Apollinaire performed his journalistic task
faithfully, submitting copy about three times a week, from
short notices of one paragraph to lengthy and detailed
articles running several days on the big official Salons. As
time went on he made increasingly explicit his convictions
about the new schools of painting, especially cubism. By
the spring of 1911 his position was so clear that he was
asked to organize an exhibit of cubist painting for the
Cercle d'Art in Brussels and to contribute a preface to the
catalogue.

These activities would have kept most people more
than occupied; Apollinaire was able to add endlessly to
the dimensions of his life until it appeared to be truly a
form of enchantment. In Paris he was everywhere, and
nowhere for long. As Salmon had already done and Picasso
was soon to do, he left Montmartre in 1909. The flood
waters of the Seine in 1910 inundated his new apartment
in Auteuil, three second-story rooms over a saddle maker's
shop, chosen for their closeness to where Marie Laurencin
lived with her mother. He moved a few streets away, and
it fell to Marie to attempt to keep house amid a growing

collection of rare and odd books, Negro sculpture, curios
of all descriptions, from department-store inkwells to old
Polish icons, early cubist paintings, and, dominating everything else, a large canvas by Marie vying with the double
portrait of Apollinaire and Marie by Rousseau.* Apollinaire
invited friends to dinner Thursday nights for the ritual
bœuf en daube, ruled his household with a mixture of
bourgeois frugality and hospitable negligence, and worked
no one knew when. He returned almost daily to Montmartre to see the artists who lingered there despite the
rising tide of tourists and professional Bohemians. He
never missed the weekly wassail at the Closerie des Lilas,
and, until it was no longer possible, he loved to take groups
of friends to Rousseau's studio in the Plaisance quarter
for the *soirées artistiques et familiales.* Most regularly he
frequented two quarters whose subsequent reputation as
artistic centers is due in great part to Apollinaire's mag-
netic presence. First of all, he found in the large cafés,
small *bistros,* cheap restaurants, and art academies of
Montparnasse a substitute for the steeper slopes of Montmartre. Faithfully he reported to his *Mercure* readers the
migration of artistic Paris across the river to a new home.
But he was even more attached to Saint-Germain-des-
Prés, with its old church and abbey, narrow streets, busy
markets, and convenient location. Every Tuesday it became his headquarters. He spent a few hours in Briffault's
office (in the lovely little Square de Furstenberg) correct-
ing proofs of the *Maîtres de l'amour* series, lunched gen-
erously in the Rue de Seine, occupied his customary table
in the Café de Flore, and attended the weekly afternoon
reception of the *Mercure* in the Rue de Condé. In any
free moments, Apollinaire was an indefatigable walker
and explorer. He roamed across Paris, usually accompanied
by an acquaintance and interrupting their conversation to
remark on historical landmarks, little-known curiosities,

---

* The spring of 1909 this portrait, *Le poète et sa muse,* hung
in the Salon des Indépendants, and several critics gleefully
recognized its subjects. Apollinaire, who had laughed at first
at Rousseau's methods, became angry when he discovered the
nature of what Rousseau considered a likeness. He seemed
surprised that anyone could recognize the portrait. However,
his esteem for Rousseau's qualities had been growing since
1908.

exotic restaurants (where the proprietor invariably knew him), and the quirks of metropolitan architecture. His connoisseurship reached into many realms—especially the art of cooking, which he enjoyed with prodigious appetite and an epicurean palate. During peregrinations in a remote quarter, he might at any moment abruptly bid good-by to his companion and disappear for several days from all his haunts. Murmurs drifted back to his friends of "distant orgies" with admirers from social circles usually closed to Bohemian poets; in the triumphant days following publication of *L'hérésiarque et cie.*, he tried his hand at opium smoking and other excesses. But Apollinaire's temperament did not require artificial stimulation. His expansive, volatile nature flowed inexhaustibly on and left behind it poems and lyric texts which seemed to flower effortlessly out of his enthusiasms. His manner became increasingly eccentric, for he often adopted Jarry's bombastic *parler Ubu,* filled his conversation with erudite and vulgar allusions, and forgot nothing he saw or heard. His mental appetite equalled his gastronomic voraciousness, and many people saw in him simply a talented purveyor of secondhand knowledge and mannerisms. The border line in his mind between originality and imitation is truly difficult to ascertain; yet all his acts and remarks were peculiarly his. He could borrow with impunity, for his borrowings became his own by a process of complete assimilation and rediscovery. Established by 1911 as an art critic, a witty *chroniqueur* in the *Mercure,* a successful story writer, a poet, and a man of conversational brilliance and mysteriously attractive personality, Apollinaire could still look ahead to his most productive years as a writer.

In August of 1911, however, disaster struck Apollinaire's flourishing career. Today it seems inevitable that his picturesque character should have attracted attention, as indeed he intended; but international notoriety was more than he bargained for. One of Apollinaire's acquaintances from poorer days, who had worked briefly as his secretary, an itinerant Belgian named Géry Pieret,* had twice stolen small statuettes from the Louvre out of pure bravado. He sold the first lot to Picasso and left some with Apollinaire.

* Apollinaire had written about Pieret's extravagant career in one of the stories in *L'hérésiarque et cie.* called *"L'Amphion faux messie."*

Shortly after Pieret's second escapade, the theft of the
Mona Lisa, on August 21, made sensational headlines all
over the world. Pieret proceeded to sell one of the stolen
statuettes to the *Paris-Journal*, which used it for publicity
purposes to taunt Louvre officials about the laxness of pre-
cautions against theft. Apollinaire and Picasso, both of
them suddenly terrified of arrest and deportation as unde-
sirable foreigners, packed Pieret out of Paris, debated
throwing the remaining statuettes into the Seine, and finally turned all the goods over to the *Paris-Journal* for
anonymous restitution. In reality, Pieret was innocent of
the Mona Lisa theft. Nevertheless, the Sûreté uncovered
Apollinaire's name, searched his apartment, cluttered with
all kinds of statues and paintings, and arrested him on
September 7. Stoutly defended by most of his friends, but
deserted by others, he spent six miserable days in prison.

> From the moment the heavy gate of La Santé
> prison closed behind me, I had a sensation of death.
> However the walls of the court where I stood in the
> clear night were covered with climbing vines. But
> beyond the second door I knew that the zone of
> vegetation was passed, and it seemed to me after
> that that I occupied a place situated outside of our
> world and that I was going to my destruction.
> (*"Mes Prisons."*)

The police were convinced they had the culprit, and Apollinaire was stripped, searched, and put in solitary. He was
taken out only for long interrogations and, finally, hearings
before a judge at the Palais de Justice. In prison he wrote a
series of short poems entitled *A la Santé*, which are more
plaintive than bitter.

> *Avant d'entrer dans ma cellule*
> *Il a fallu me mettre nu*
> *Et quelle voix sinistre ulule*
> *Guillaume qu'es-tu devenu*
>
> Before I could enter my cell
> I had to strip to the skin
> A dire voice whimpered its spell
> Guillaume what have you done

But imprisonment was by no means the worst blow. During
the hearings Apollinaire listened in astonishment while Pi-

casso, under questioning, denied having any part in the affair and finally even denied knowing his friend. Picasso's name was not officially mentioned in the records, and they remained friends. No conclusive evidence was produced, and the prisoner was given a provisional release. Apollinaire's dossier almost caused deportation proceedings to be initiated against him, however.

The humiliation crushed his spirits. The article *"Mes Prisons,"* which he wrote the day after his release for the *Paris-Journal,* still expresses more sadness than wrath, and he avoided indignation until several years later in a letter:

> That then is the unique, incredible, tragic, and amusing story of how I was the only person arrested in France in connection with the theft of the Mona Lisa. And on top of all that, the police did everything they could to justify their action; they cross-examined my concierge, the neighbors, asked if I brought in young girls, or little boys, and I don't know what else. (*Tendre comme le souvenir.*)

Despite his acquittal, newspapers continued to attack him for several months, victimizing his position in the avant-garde and citing his foreign birth and his work as editor of licentious texts. He stoutly went on writing about cubism and the new aesthetic in his *chroniques,* but Apollinaire had been brought low. The winter of 1911–1912 began with discouragement and new financial need.

Aware of his poor spirits, a few of Apollinaire's friends performed the simple miracle that began his recovery. André Billy, the novelist and critic he had seen intermittently since 1903, founded a review of which Apollinaire was asked to be associate editor, with Salmon and Dalize as contributing editors. In February, 1912, the *Soirées de Paris* appeared in a dignified chocolate-brown cover and led off with a near manifesto by Apollinaire justifying the abandonment of "resemblance" and "subject matter" in modern painting. The article made even his fellow editors shudder, but Apollinaire was resolved to recapture the position of prominence from which the Louvre scandal had dislodged him. His resilience astonished everyone, and subsequent issues carried equally assertive articles. He even began traveling out of town to give lectures, one of which, delivered to a large audience in the Grand Skating Rink of Rouen, treated the subject of "Sublimity in Modern Art." There is no record of how it was received.

The summer of 1912 Apollinaire vacationed in the Jura Mountains with Picabia, the Spanish painter, and his wife. During the stay he read to them a nearly finished version of the nostalgic modernist poem *"Zone,"** an example of how he could weave together the past and the future.

> *C'est Dieu qui meurt le vendredi et ressuscite*
> *le dimanche*
> *C'est le Christ qui monte au ciel mieux*
> *que les aviateurs*
> *Il détient le record du monde pour la hauteur*
> *Pupille de Christ de l'œil*
> *Vingtième pupille des siècles il sait y faire*
> *Et change en oiseau ce siècle comme Jésus*
> *monte dans l'air*

> It's God who dies Friday and rises again on Sunday
> It's Christ who climbs into the sky better than
> any aviator
> He holds the world's altitude record
> Pupil Christ of the eye
> Twentieth pupil of the centuries he knows what
> he's about
> And the century become a bird climbs skyward
> like Jesus

The summer turned into another period of excited speculation about the destiny of the arts, and when the Picabias offered Apollinaire financial support and encouragement for it, he decided to assemble a book on modern painting which would include many texts he had already published in reviews and newspapers. Back in Paris, he lent his support to a new cell of cubists who had founded a gallery called La Section d'Or, and he began praising in his articles two totally unknown painters recently arrived in Paris and whom he had just met: the Russian Chagall

---

* The significance of this title has been much debated. According to Gabrielle Picabia, it was originally inspired by the name of the frontier region in the Jura Mountains where they were staying. It also refers to a band of squalid workers' suburbs surrounding Paris. The poem invokes cities in the principal zones of the terrestrial globe. Apollinaire later wrote in a poem: "And I smoke ZONE tobacco." The original title was *"Cri."*

and the Italian Chirico. Of his own work he was saying
(to Billy, as recorded in the October *Soirées*):

> For some time I have been trying new themes far
> different from those around which you have seen
> me entwine my verses up to now. I believe that I
> have found a source of inspiration in prospectuses
> . . . catalogues, posters, advertisements of all sorts.
> Believe me, they contain the poetry of our epoch.
> I shall make it spring forth.

In these sentiments he was not entirely alone, for a new
freedom and urgency was making itself felt in French
poetry. The unanimists had returned to a simple and
sincere lyricism with distinct populist leanings.The adventuresome figure of Blaise Cendrars, sailor and tramp, arrived in Paris after wide international travel; *"Pâques à
New-York,"* his first poem of cosmopolitan incantation,
appeared in 1912. There can be no doubt of the impact of
Cendrars' work on Apollinaire (especially in *"Zone"*) and
vice versa.[*] Their work formed the core of a sturdy poetic
renaissance which embraced Salmon and Jacob, Romains
and Jouve, Valery Larbaud, and the short-lived "drama-
ticism" of Henri-Martin Barzun.

During the closing months of 1912, Apollinaire found
himself entangled in two uncomfortable situations. His
long affair with Marie Laurencin was drawing to a close,
and he was receiving violent and conflicting advice from
all sides about how to write his book on the new painters.
Fleeing his troubles, he lived during November and December in the studio of Robert and Sonia Delaunay, a
couple he had met earlier in the year. Immediately he was
dazzled by Delaunay's experiments with spectrum-like
arrangements of pure color. The painter called them "windows by simultaneous contrast." (The last two words are
taken from Chevreul's treatise on the optics of color.) Late
in 1912 Delaunay pushed these color compositions across
the frontier of completely nonfigurative painting with his
"formes colorées." This departure in Delaunay's career
matched the achievements of Kandinsky in Germany in

---

[*] "Apollinaire /1900–1911/ for 12 years the only poet in
France," wrote Cendrars in 1914, implying, perhaps, that now
there were two. Apollinaire published Cendrars' poetry regularly in the *Soirées*.

1910, of Mondrian in Holland, and of the Czech Kupka in Paris. The significance of the event was not lost on Apollinaire.

Working at a breathless pace, he chose for Delaunay's art the ancient term "orphism," connoting mystery and poetry, published the manifesto-like *"Zone"* in the December *Soirées*, and composed *"Les Fenêtres,"* a poem closely related to Delaunay's nonfigurative compositions.

> *Du rouge au vert tout le jaune se meurt*
>
> . . .
>
> *Tu soulèveras le rideau*
> *Et maintenant voilà que s'ouvre la fenêtre*
> *Araignées quand les mains tissaient la lumière*
> *Beauté pâleur insondables violets*

> The yellow fades from red to green
>
> . . .
>
> You will lift the curtain
> And now look at the window opening
> Spiders when hands wove the light
> Beauty paleness unfathomable violet tints

At this same moment he was renaming, recasting, repunctuating, and revising the proofs of a major collection of his poetry for the *Mercure*. Writing as lyrically as he had seven years before on Picasso, Apollinaire produced a series of brilliant texts on Delaunay's work and in January, 1913, went with him to deliver a lecture at his exhibition in Berlin. Out of orphism there soon grew the more general term "simultanism."

Apollinaire was carried into 1913 on this flood tide of activity; his associations with painters were now propelling him through a more rapid evolution in artistic convictions than at any other moment of his career. In the middle of it all he changed lodgings for the last time—principally in order to detach himself from memories of Marie Laurencin, from whom he was finally separated. His new quarters were hidden away on the sixth floor of an apartment building on the Boulevard Saint-Germain near Saint-Germain-des-Prés; henceforward he resided at the very center of the universe he had created for himself on the left bank. This *pigeonnier* was composed of half a dozen little rooms like connecting corridors, overlooking neighboring roofs and soon filled to overflowing with books, knick-knacks, paintings, sculpture, and ill-assorted furniture. The two most significant locations were the tiny desk at a window, where Apollinaire worked, and the equally small kitchen, where he supervised or performed most of the cooking. With its steep entrance stairs, terrace, sloping walls, mysterious upper room, and frequent visitors, the apartment embodies the bizarre comfort and intimacy that characterized its occupant. Like Jarry's *Chasublerie,* this lodging was (and still is) Apollinaire's most appropriate monument.*

The climax of Apollinaire's career coincided with the paroxysm of activity on the artistic scene in Paris and elsewhere in 1913† The *avant-guerre* was about to fulfill its wild promise. For him April was the month of richest harvest: his two most significant volumes appeared in appropriate order—simultaneously. *Alcools, "poèmes* 1898–1913,"* with a portrait of Apollinaire by Picasso as frontispiece, coincided with *Méditations esthétiques; les peintres cubistes,* which included reproductions of forty cubist paintings. The former volume, published by the *Mercure de France,* contained the recently composed free verse *"Zone"* but not the distinctly experimental *"Les Fenêtres."* The collection was generally reviewed with severe reservations about its cavalier treatment of literary tradition, its mixture of styles, and its shocking lack of punctuation. In a bold gesture (possibly inspired by some poems he had just read by the painter Rouault as well as by his new simultanist ideas), he had deleted all punctuation from the page proofs and defended his action before the assembled editors of the *Mercure.* They acquiesced. Then Georges Duhamel, reviewing the collection for the June *Mercure,* where Apollinaire hoped for favorable treatment, took him harshly to task.

Nothing could be more reminiscent of a junk shop than this collection of verse published by M. Guil-

---

* His widow has carefully preserved the apartment, and in recent years Paris municipal authorities have considered acquiring it as a museum. But it could never hold more than a handful of visitors.

† See pp. 27–28.

laume Apollinaire . . . a mass of heterogeneous objects with a few valuable things among them but no one of which is the product of the dealer's own talents.

Apollinaire was with difficulty restrained from sending his seconds to Duhamel. For all their motley, however, *Alcools* left a clear imprint on modern poetry.

Les peintres cubistes might well have borne the date 1905–1913. Over half the text is lifted from Apollinaire's earlier writings, some of it revised, some of it reproduced intact. It omits the material on Delaunay, a fact explained either by his intention to reserve it for a subsequent volume (*"Méditations esthétiques"* was chosen to designate Apollinaire's contributions to a general series under his direction, *Tous les arts,* which never materialized), or by his hesitation to include in the book his most recent and untried opinions.

The text stands as the monument to Apollinaire's championing of cubism and immediately reveals the unsystematic but penetrating nature of his criticism. Beyond a doubt he succeeds in picking the major cubists: Picasso, Braque, Metzinger, Gleizes, Marie Laurencin, Gris, Léger, Picabia, Marcel Duchamp, and Duchamp-Villon. One could take exception only to Marie Laurencin, whose talents are agreeable but severely limited and scarcely cubist, and perhaps Picabia, who did not fully live up to the promise he showed in 1913.[*] Two books on cubism had appeared the previous year, Gleizes' and Metzinger's highly theoretical *Du cubisme* and Salmon's general survey of the scene in *La jeune peinture française.* Neither carried the impact of *Les peintres cubistes,* the essential parts of which had been written before the other two volumes.

The famous fourfold classification of cubism inserted in the proofs of his book was in reality Apollinaire's attempt to reconcile his wide-ranging aesthetic enthusiasms. It was not a success. Scientific, physical, orphic, and instinctive cubism did not denote four distinct strands in the development of the new movement. The first two have become

[*] The other young painters Apollinaire steadily supported but did not discuss in this volume are Matisse, Derain, Delaunay, Chagall, and Chirico. For Braque, Derain, Delaunay, and Chagall he wrote prefaces for the catalogues of their first public exhibits.

"analytic" and "synthetic" cubism (though no nomenclature is universal); orphism falls outside the movement; "instinctive" was the dubious catchall heading for Marie Laurencin and others—even Rousseau, one supposes, if Apollinaire had dared. Nevertheless, the attempted classification shows considerable boldness for the year 1913.

Frequently, the accusation is made—and has been from the very beginning—that cubism is an enormous hoax dreamed up by the hashish-smoking, pistol-carrying, half-starved inhabitants of Montmartre who had been impregnated with Jarry's 'Pataphysics and the pseudo mathematics of the fourth dimension. (An imaginative and articulate mathematician, Princet, was originally a member of the *bateau lavoir* group.) Without doubt, much of the inspiration for the speculations that produced cubist theory came from these sources. Yet two further points temper this estimate. First, the sources are perfectly valid, are, in fact, integral parts of all modern inspiration. Jarry and Satie, as well as Henri Monnier and Alphonse Allais, were predecessors in this line of perpetrators of hoaxes who took their own antics seriously. The Chat Noir and the Lapin Agile were truly the *salons* of the new art. What started as a humorous indulgence of the imagination in confronting eternal artistic problems became a serious endeavor.

The second point is that these buffooneries helped produce cubist theory, but not its works. To spend several days or weeks painting a difficult and elaborate cubist composition (or to spend year after year writing about these paintings) required total dedication. There is a headily improvised side of cubism that can be called "dreamed up," but the genuineness of the whole movement cannot be challenged. Too many monumental figures lived it. Part of the greatness of cubism consisted in its willingness to entertain speculations which other minds would have dismissed as foolishness or mere bluff. In Apollinaire's declamations we feel some of the precariousness of cubism's early researches into the shifting appearances of things, yet his confidence helped establish the movement. Such confidence came partly from his facility with words, his ability to construct a provisionally habitable edifice out of untested materials. Thus, while the cubists produced a magnificent collection of paintings defying the entire tradition of post-Renaissance art, Apollinaire was the first to transform their ideas from incoherence into persuasive intelligibility. Others, like Salmon, Gleizes, and Metzinger helped, but his was the honor.

The high spirits that produced cubism acted as a safeguard in a manner lost sight of today because of the unrelieved seriousness with which cubism is treated. The enjoyment of a good hoax—insofar as it was a hoax—prevented most painters from capitulating totally to the theoretical side of the school. Gleizes' and Metzinger's book lacks this perspective of self-irony, and its intense earnestness slightly removes it from the central current of cubist thought. Beneath their sweeping metaphors, Salmon and Apollinaire do far better in conveying the probationary nature of cubist theory. It was not a rigid doctrine, and the idea that it was continues to cause misunderstanding. In the spring of 1953 every art critic in Paris worth his salt wrote at length of the large retrospective show of cubism; the results were revealing. Forty years after the fact, the only flimsy point they could find to agree on was that *Les demoiselles d'Avignon* was the first cubist composition. Art history has not yet fixed any better than Apollinaire did the chameleon color of this school, which understood that a good hoax can be as salutary as it is entertaining. "The modern school of painting," he wrote, "appears to me to be the most audacious that has ever existed. It has posed the question of what is beautiful in itself."

Apollinaire finished the spring with two extravagant gestures. First, he devised an epic account of Whitman's funeral in Philadelphia, describing it as an all-day orgiastic barbecue complete with watermelons, speeches, and Whitman's former lovers of both sexes in attendance.

> At sundown a huge cortege formed with a ragtime
> band in the lead. Whitman's coffin followed, carried
> by six drunken pallbearers, and after it the crowd.

Because of a low door, the pallbearers carried the coffin into the tomb on all fours. Through the preceding fifteen years a group of admiring European critics had distorted Whitman's exotic figure beyond recognition. With this one facetious chronicle Apollinaire exploded the legend. The international polemic he provoked over Whitman's respectability and sexual mores spiced the pages of the *Mercure* for a year to come and tended to replace one misapprehension with another. Apollinaire cooly extricated himself from the free-for-all once it was well under way.

The second and final gesture of the spring was to compose, in his apartment situated "65 meters above the Boulevard Saint-Germain," a belated futurist manifesto, *L'antitradition futuriste*. In a poster-like arrangement of typography, it proclaimed "suppression of poetic grief . . . syntax, punctuation, lines and verses, houses, boredom." Set innocently to music, *mer . . . de* was bestowed upon critics, museums, and various authors from Montaigne to Baudelaire. *Rose*, signifying approval, without benefit of music, was awarded to a long list of contemporary artists from Delaunay to Apollinaire. Significantly, the manifesto was for publication not in Paris, where he tended to be more circumspect in his pronouncements, but in Milan.

By now Apollinaire was sustaining a headlong pace of artistic enterprise and production. A talented Russian painter, Serge Jastrebzoff, and his sister, the "Baroness" Œttingen, financed Apollinaire in acquiring full ownership of the *Soirées* from Billy in November, 1913. Under Apollinaire's enthusiastic editorship, every number now included a special section of articles and reproductions on a young artist. His choice was unerring: Picasso, Rousseau, Derain, Matisse, Braque, Vlaminck, Gleizes, Archipenko. The review also declared itself boldly in favor of the literary work of Jarry (his correspondence ran for three numbers), Max Jacob, and the *Fantômas* detective series. These miraculously successful adventure tales of unbridled fantasy and melodrama were raised—and seriously—to the status of "classics." In the late afternoon, the editorial offices of the review on the Boulevard Raspail overflowed with such habitués as Jacob, Picasso, Fernand Léger, Chirico and his musician brother Alberto Savinio,* Chagall, Zadkine, Modigliani, and Cendrars. Apollinaire, congenial and inexhaustible, presided over them as master of ceremonies and principal attraction. Amid these new preoccupations he could begin to forget his grievous separation from Marie.

In March, 1914, having involved himself in two duels,

---

* Savinio's violent piano technique particularly impressed Apollinaire. He usually ended a performance only after he had covered the keyboard with blood and broken the instrument.

Apollinaire began taking fencing lessons. Trivial in themselves, these ultimately bloodless disputes reveal the prominent and vulnerable position he had reached. One was with the boxer-Bohemian Arthur Cravan, who, in a ribald article in *Maintenant*, called Apollinaire a Jew and insulted Marie Laurencin. The other concerned Ottman, a painter who violently protested Apollinaire's well-meant remark that Ottman had been influenced by Delaunay. Partly as a result of the latter incident, Apollinaire was dropped from his position on *L'Intransigeant*. Within two months he was hired to write the art reviews for the *Paris-Journal*. This paper published daily a full page entitled "The Literary and Artistic Movement," and during three months from May, 1914, to the outbreak of war, Apollinaire's name was missing only three days from that page. He discussed Russian ballet, the textile museum at Lyon, Jarry as a woodcut artist, and almost every art exhibit in the city, in addition to carrying on a vast and violent polemic with Barzun over the paternity of simultanism. This was the moment at which the plastic ideas that Apollinaire had been championing for so long erupted in the typographical derangement of his own work. The June *Soirées* carried an article on simultanism in poetry illustrated with *"Lettre-Océan,"* the first "calligram." In a kind of visualized mental geography, he collected verbal oddments on the page in a pattern considerably more orderly than the collages in which Braque and Picasso had been delighting since 1912. The article speaks of "conversation poems, where the poet at the center of life records its ambient lyricism," and relates them to the discoveries of simultanist painting.

It was natural and logical that Apollinaire's enthusiasm should carry him beyond cubism. Cubism severely restricted the role of the subject in painting without ever abolishing it. The example of Delaunay's work in 1912 plus that of Kandinsky and Mondrian, whose painting he saw in Berlin and Paris, led Apollinaire to contemplate a realm of painting beyond the French school. Having named it orphism, he went on to survey the more general category of simultanism in all the arts. In 1913 orphism did not stop the presses on *Les peintres cubistes*, already near completion, except for one highly charged paragraph. Yet what he wrote there foretells the trajectory of his thinking for the next two years.

The works of the orphic artists must simultaneously present pure aesthetic pleasure, a self-evident construction, and a sublime significance, that is, a subject. This is pure art.

His strongest pronouncements on the doctrine were made at first to non-Parisian audiences under circumstances which appear to have liberated his Italo-Slav imagination from the demands of French logic. In his article on Delaunay in the Berlin review *Der Sturm* (December, 1912), Apollinaire quotes several superb pages of the artist's notes to the effect that proportion and vision can themselves be the "subject" of painting. Apollinaire adds only a few lines. It is through this extreme strand of his thinking that plastic ideas most readily found their way into Apollinaire's poetic practice. Cubism afforded only difficult literary application until it had been generalized into simultanism in the winter of 1912–1913. The following spring he suppressed all punctuation in his work. Then after a year of meditation he came back refreshed in 1914 to the idea of simultanism as the basis for his calligrammatic poems. He considered them his most important innovation, and they are a clearer instance of the influence of pictorial theories on his work than the tenuously "cubist" poems of earlier years.

The doctrine and practice of simultanism in Apollinaire's work as the natural outgrowth of cubism has not received the attention it deserves, for the critical texts have never been assembled from the newspapers and reviews where they were originally published. They make it perfectly clear, however, that during the most active years of his career, 1912–1914, the simultanist manner of thought and vision formed the armature of his modernism in poetry and the basis of his sympathy with the plastic arts. This was his ultimate innovation. The war caught him at the peak of his powers and arrested his literary career for over a year. Undismayed, he plunged into the new life with gusto and a sense of active participation in history.

Despite his Italian birth, Apollinaire decided to apply for French citizenship and volunteer. When his first enlistment was refused, he left Paris for the Mediterranean haunts of his youth, and in the frenzied atmosphere of

Nice he met Louise de Coligny-Chatillon, a beauty of aristocratic birth and fiery, unstable temperament. On the verge of volunteering again, Apollinaire abandoned himself to a voluptuous interlude of opium smoking, unbridled passions, and all the pleasures of the Riviera. He took himself in hand when Lou seemed to draw back, signed up abruptly, and left for Nîmes with the artillery. As he hoped, Lou followed him, and his first days in the army coincided with a sustained erotic adventure that haunted his memory long after she left him. It could not last; Lou went back to Nice, and for several months they continued a correspondence of incredible richness, much of his in verse and addressed to *l'ombre de mon amour*—"the shadow of my love." Many of these letters were later reworked into the best poems in *Calligrammes,* published after the war.

> *Je vois briller cette étoile mystique*
> *Dont la couleur*
> *Est de tes yeux la couleur ambiguë*
> *J'ai ton regard*
> *Et j'en ressens une blessure aiguë*
> *Adieu c'est tard*

> I watch the glitter of that mystic star
> Whose shifting tint
> Matches the misty color of your eyes
> I keep your look
> To wound me where my darkest feeling hides
> Good-by it's late

After the loss of Marie, he was reluctant to relinquish Lou even when he knew their time was up. Nothing, however, could prevent the army from agreeing with him.

To Paul Léautaud, December, 1914:

> I'm not getting any thinner here in spite of the violent training; they even call my constitution *very good.* . . . All day long, polishing till your knuckles bleed, theory up to your ears, drill, saber, rifle, revolver, horsemanship, riding, jumping, theoretical and practical study in detail of the 75 which is a beautiful piece, as beautiful, as strong, as tender as one of my poems.

To Serge Férat, January 4, 1915:

> I'm fine and it seems that a soldier's life is the
> right life for me. I like that. My friend [Lou] keeps
> saying that I act all the time as if I were at the opera
> and it's true.

In the lowly rank of *"deuxième canonnier-conducteur,"*
Apollinaire left for the front on Easter Day, 1915. The
abundance of his correspondence became staggering, almost compulsive now that he was separated from Lou
and all his attachments. It showered not only old friends
and loves, but on a new acquaintance, Madeleine Pagès.
He had met her briefly in the train between Nice and
Marseille, a pretty, quiet girl from Oran in North Africa,
where she taught school. In order to fill the vacancy Lou
had left in his life, Apollinaire reached out toward the
remembered image of Madeleine in long, increasingly
sensual letters. With a mixture of earnestness and pure
pretense he pursued and virtually seduced her by letter,
asked her to marry him, and wrote a formal request for
her hand to the mother. This truncated and absentee court-
ship ended in their engagement the last days of August,
when he was still writing intimately to Lou.

Meanwhile, life on the front had dazzled Apollinaire
and set him to combining his images with new freedom.

To Lou, April 10, 1915:

> *Les obus miaulaient un amour à mourir.*
> *Les amours qui s'en vont sont plus doux que les autres*
> *Il pleut, Bergère, il pleut et le sang va tarir*
> *Les obus miaulaient entends chanter les nôtres.*
> *Pourpre Amour salué par ceux qui vont périr!*

> The shells were bellowing a love-till-death
> The loves which leave us are sweeter than the rest
> Rain, rain, go away and blood will staunch its flow
> The shells were bellowing listen to ours sing
> Purple love saluted by those about to die!

A new liaison assignment and hopes of promotion filled
him with exultation.

To Lou, April 11, 1915:

> I was inexpressibly happy. The rain had stopped.
> It was five o'clock. I was mighty proud. Four

months of service and already making yourself
useful, even in subaltern position (but dangerous
and secret)—that can give you a good idea of yourself. Even to a poet whose work is a good deal like
a whore's, for like them we prostitute our feelings
to the public.

To André Billy, April 26, 1915:

Je te le dis André Billy que cette guerre
        C'est Obus-Roi
Beaucoup plus tragique qu'Ubu mais qui n'est guère
        Billy crois moi
Moins burlesque ô mon vieux crois moi c'est très comique.

I'm telling you André Billy that this here war
        Is King Shell
A long sight more tragic than Ubu but for sure
        Believe me Billy
No less burlesque in fact old boy it's rich

To Lou, May 11,1915:

>   *Un seul bouleau crépusculaire*
>   *Sur le mont bleu de ma Raison . . .*
>   *Je prends la mesure angulaire*
>   *Du cœur à l'âme et l'horizon*

>   A solitary twilit beech
>   On the blue rise of my Reason's field . . .
>   I plot the angle in degrees
>   From heart to soul to horizon's tree

To Lou, June 1, 1915:

>   My sensibility has become as tender as that of a
>   crab when it sheds its shell.

In June, Apollinaire printed from gelatine plates in multicolored inks twenty-five copies of *Case d'armons,* a collection of his army verse. Its lively drawings, the arrangement
of its handwritten text on the page, and the clever montage
inclusion of an armed forces correspondence card express
the high spirits with which he undertook the task. He not
only wrote, but published, his poetry under fire in the front
lines.

Having volunteered for service in the trenches, Apollinaire was commissioned a second lieutenant on November 20 and transferred to an infantry company in the bitter Champagne offensive. From then on it was the letters to Madeleine in North Africa that overshadowed the rest.

To Madeleine, November 30, 1915:

> It's fantastic how much you can put up with. There is hardly any coal, but they have to furnish the regular officers' ration. So I have brought my two sergeants in to sleep with me, and the men who are cold can warm themselves four at a time. My fire heats our soup as well. They are very happy, the poor fellows.

To ————, December, 1915:

> To my way of thinking it is an ascetic and theatrical life, and, strange to say, the legend and music of Parsifal come close to giving that impression of sublime abandon and watchfulness which never slacks off, of infinite chastity, of white metallic monotony.

Apollinaire spent his Christmas furlough in Oran, where, instead of conquering lover, he had to play the part of official fiancé for Madeleine's large bourgeois family. And her tenderness demanded of him behavior far different from that with which he had met Lou's willful transports. He was unaccustomed to such discipline of his appetites, yet the visit apparently pleased them both. On the return trip he stopped in Paris only long enough to tell his mother of the engagement, then rejoined his unit for maneuvers. In March the regiment returned to the front near Berry-au-Bac; his spirits were high.

At four o'clock on the afternoon of March 17th, a fairly quiet day in the sector, he was sitting in a trench reading the latest *Mercure de France,* to which he had again begun sending his regular *chronique,* "*La Vie anecdotique.*" A shell came fairly close, and after ducking for the burst, he turned back to his reading. He did not realize what had happened until blood started dripping onto the page; shrapnel had pierced his helmet over the right temple. Two days later he could write Madeleine, "I'm admirably well cared for and it appears to be not too serious." The blood-encrusted *Mercure* and the ripped helmet became his most precious souvenirs.

But it was serious. The shell fragments were removed at two in the morning along the evacuation route to Château-Thierry, and a week later he was moved to Paris. His brief letters to Madeleine speak only of persistent fatigue, a little paralysis and vertigo, and general depression. But something very mysterious and almost sinister had happened to him. Because of his uncertain condition, he was trepanned on May 11. Medically the operation was counted a success. However, it is as if the surgeon removed without leaving a trace that part of Apollinaire's brain which had been the seat of his feelings for Madeleine. His daily outpourings to her by mail ceased abruptly. He wrote only twice more to her after the operation, brief letters separated by months instead of hours, and both of them simply to ask for the return of manuscripts and books he had sent her for safekeeping. Without explanation or apology he turned from the young fiancée who had been preparing to come to Paris to take care of him and meet his mother. Something had altered his emotional nature, which had been capable of unfaithfulness but not of indifference. Yet in other ways he appeared to be recovering.

While his strength was returning under good care and the personal attentions of the wife of the Italian ambassador, Apollinaire, who had been admitted to the Italian hospital, assembled various stories and prose works written since *L'hérésiarque*. He entitled the motley volume *Le poète assassiné*. His behavior and the opinions he voiced in interviews with the press became unexpectedly guarded, for he had heard a rumor that he might be eligible for nomination of the Légion d'honneur. His irascibility did not disappear, however, and he underwent a disturbing physical change which modified the shape of his head, thickened his body, and gave a withdrawn, calculating expression to his features. He was not the same person when he left his bed at the end of 1916, wearing a horizon-blue officer's uniform and an imposing head bandage, like a set of earphones. After an affair with an anonymous Mademoiselle B., who had come daily to pick him up at the hospital in her carriage, he met Jacqueline Kolb, handsome and red-haired, whom he had met once before, in 1914. Back in the *pigeonnier* on the Boulevard Saint-Germain, he found with "Ruby" a peace and domesticity he had never previously known. Distressed by the war and the death of his oldest friend, René Dalize, he was nevertheless full of new plans and appeared to be finding his stride once again.

Always attentive to literary protocol and remembering what Apollinaire had been through, his remaining friends in Paris concluded there was only one way to celebrate the publication of *Le poète assassiné* and to welcome the poet resuscitated back to literary circles. A banquet had to be held. Organized by Juan Gris, Picasso, Paul Dermée, Max Jacob, Reverdy, and Blaise Cendrars, the feast, on December 31, 1916, overflowed the dining room of the Palais d'Orléans, Avenue du Maine, where an uproarious banquet for Verlaine had been held a quarter-century before. While the African troops billeted in the building stared in amazement, ninety guests* sat down to a meal whose menu announced a dozen courses, such as *"Hors d'œuvres cubistes, orphistes, futuristes,* etc.," *"Méditations esthétiques en salade," "Café des Soirées de Paris,"* and, inevitably, *"Alcools."* Toward the end of the meal the lady who was to begin the speeches was shouted down, and in the competition for the floor a brawl developed among rival factions of cubists. Blaise Cendrars took it upon himself to knock down a journalist. Apollinaire, magnificently attired in a new uniform, finally calmed the gathering with a recitation and toast. A few days later he wrote to Maurice Raynal: "My dinner was a sort of magnesium flash, exactly what it should have been, explosive and dangerous, brief, but carried to the verge of paroxysm." Apollinaire was thirty-six, a war hero, a recognized poet, and a spokesman for the avant-garde in literature and the arts. The banquet was a genuine tribute but not, like Rousseau's ten years earlier, an apotheosis; nor did it temper his mood. Irritability and an increasingly petty desire for official recognition warped his temperament so severely that his friends wondered if there had been damage to his brain. The source of his purest spontaneity seemed to have dried up.

No longer eligible for active service, he found a job censoring magazines and newspapers. The year 1917 opened with a series of events that re-established his prom-

* Including Jacques Copeau, Jules Romains, André Gide, Jean Cocteau, André Salmon, Alfred Vallette, Blaise Cendrars, Henri de Régnier, Paul Fort, Braque, Matisse, and Vlaminck.

inence on the Paris scene. The same group that had staged the banquet for him founded the review *Nord-Sud* in March, 1917, with this opening statement.

> What could be less astonishing than that we judge the moment has come to group ourselves around Guillaume Apollinaire. More than anyone today he has broken new ground, opened new horizons. He has the right to all our fervor and admiration.

With Tristan Tzara and André Breton in its pages, the review found the open road which led to Dada and surrealism. A show of Negro sculpture at the Paul Guillaume gallery gave Apollinaire the opportunity to write a preface that emphasized the "audacity in taste which accepted these objects as works of art." After attending rehearsals with Diaghilev, Picasso, Satie, and Cocteau, he wrote a text for the program of *Parade* which describes "a sort of sur-realism in which I see the point of departure for a series of manifestations of that New Spirit which . . . promises to modify the arts and the conduct of life [*mœurs*] from top to bottom in a universal joyousness." *Parade,* in May, 1917, one of the most important artistic events of the war, far outshone his own play, *Les Mamelles de Tirésias,* for which he also used the word "surrealism" when it was performed a month later before a suitably excited audience. He completed two more works in verse for the stage, but his ambitions as a dramatist were never to be fulfilled. After *Parade,* Apollinaire corresponded with Satie about possible collaboration on a ballet or an opera, but they came to no agreement. Auric relates the disappointment Satie felt on hearing Apollinaire read parts of *Les mamelles.*

The *Maîtres de l'amour* edition of Baudelaire's poems (recently come into public domain) appeared in 1917. Apollinaire's preface contains his first clear critical retreat. Acknowledging Baudelaire as one of the greatest modern poets, "who can still teach us that an elegant manner is not incompatible with great freedom of expression," he took him severely to task for "the moral side of his work . . . a certain pessimistic dilettantism by which we are no longer duped." Apollinaire's new concern with physical and moral health could not approve of Baudelaire's spleen, and he censured a state of mind that he had previously admired in Rimbaud, Poe, and Baudelaire himself. This attempt to separate poet from moralist was not without its dangers and provoked strong protest.

At the end of the year Apollinaire's cautious mood found complete expression in the lecture *L'esprit nouveau et les poètes,* delivered with poetry readings at Jacques Copeau's Vieux Colombier theatre. Even as he revised it for publication in the *Mercure,* it is far from his best piece of critical writing. The style, halfway between a harangue and a manifesto, is not sustained by any clear development. His obvious desire to be comprehensive tempts one to believe that Apollinaire had a premonition that this text would become his literary last will and testament.

The text begins with patriotic insistence (the war was in its fourth year) that the great new aesthetic, *l'esprit nouveau,** was "a particular lyric expression of the French nation, just as the classic spirit is a sublime expression par excellence of the same nation." And he stoutly asserts the importance of discipline in the arts and of a strong literary tradition. Against this background he considers the possibility of experiment and innovation. Calling poets the "alchemists" of today, he proclaims that we are surrounded by fresh possibilities for poetry: new technical means of recording by film, phonography, and typography, all leading toward an exciting synthesis of the arts; new domains of knowledge in technology and science, which challenge the imagination and even the language of the poet; and a whole new source of effects, *surprise.*

> We can hope, then, in regard to what constitutes the material and manner of art, for a freedom of unimaginable opulence. Today poets are serving their apprenticeship to this encyclopedic liberty. In the realm of inspiration their freedom cannot be less than that of a daily newspaper which, on a single sheet, treats the most diverse matters and ranges over distant countries.

* The term had two significant precedents. In 1890 Havelock Ellis published a book entitled *The New Spirit* which approaches the modern sensibility as a reconciliation of religion and science. The following year François Paulhan applied almost identical analysis to *l'esprit nouveau* in a work aptly called *Le nouveau mysticisme.*

Forty years later, the text reads like an enormous cliché of modernism shot through with conciliatory statements about traditional values. It is true that in his final years Apollinaire launched two terms that have achieved historical importance: *surréalisme* and *l'esprit nouveau*. But they do not belong to the most original part of his criticism, written before the war. After the long apprenticeship which led to the first expression of his artistic convictions in *Les peintres cubistes*, and after his rapid gathering of cubism into the more extensive aesthetic of simultanism, this last pronouncement of Apollinaire's comes as an awkward recasting of ideas. The attempt to please all parties did not become him. Thus publication in March, 1918, of *Calligrammes* (again with a frontispiece portrait by Picasso) appears almost as an attempt to recoup his position. Along with poems in traditional forms it contains his most frankly experimental works composed in the simultanist vein. But out of the whole volume only two poems had been written since his wound.

In the beginning of 1918 Apollinaire's health began to waver again, and he relied increasingly on the care and affection of Ruby. She had inspired the only important poem of the last two years, *"La jolie rousse."* On May 2, they were quietly married in the Eglise Saint-Thomas-d'Aquin around the corner; Picasso and Ambroise Vollard were witnesses. The war moved on into its final agony, and Apollinaire kept himself unflaggingly at work despite headaches, fatigue, and vertigo. At this juncture the Légion d'honneur passed him over, partially because of the unforgotten Mona Lisa incident; he became unwarrantedly depressed.

In November a flu epidemic swept through Paris, and Apollinaire succumbed. He fought the germ five days, desperately wanting to recover, but his resistance had fallen lower than anyone realized. He died quietly late in the afternoon of November 9, and was laid out in his lieutenant's uniform with a crucifix clasped in his hands. For the next few days the apartment was filled with his friends, some of whom turned up after many years' absence. His mother, now a stiff remote figure, appeared briefly and carried off his officer's cap without a word or a tear. When the Armistice was proclaimed on November 11, the city demonstrated wildly—the kind of wake Apollinaire would have wished. *"A bas* Guillaume," they cried outside his window. Funeral services were held in the same church where he had been married only six months before, and a long cortege followed the casket through the festive streets of Paris, again at peace.

Barely four months later, his mother died. For over ten years Picasso delayed his design for a tombstone, and Madame Apollinaire finally had Serge Férat choose a simple granite column on which were inscribed two stanzas from *"Les Collines"* which conclude, "I can die smiling." In 1951, on the anniversary of his death, the municipality of Paris renamed in his honor a short street that runs between the Rue Bonaparte and the Rue Saint-Benoît. In the prewar years of enthusiasm and productivity, the poet-enchanter of Paris would have scoffed mightily at the Légion d'honneur and would have been deeply moved by the thought that one day a street in the very heart of Saint-Germain-des-Prés would bear the name, Rue Guillaume-Apollinaire. It is monument enough.

{ 10 }

PAINTER-POET

Brilliant in conversation and endowed with a capacious memory for piquant detail, Apollinaire early discovered a great facility in every field of writing—stories, poetry, anecdotal description, articles, informal reflections, and letters. His spontaneous prosody made it easy for him to correspond in verse. His prose style usually flows with unlabored grace. In a confident moment he affirmed that "one must publish everything," but he knew the dangers of facility and worked uncompromisingly during his best years to revise his works for final publication in book form.

The price he paid for such literary ease, however, came earlier than the stage of revision. "My facility finds its compensation in the great trouble I have in settling down to work," he wrote to Madeleine. In 1912, after frittering away several weeks (he named himself *"le flâneur des deux rives"*), he appealed to André Billy for assistance in disciplining himself to work regularly every morning. They arranged two desks facing one another in Apollinaire's apartment. After shirking for several mornings while Billy kept his part of the bargain, Apollinaire suddenly wrote down in one sitting the first draft of *"Un fantôme des nuées,"* one of his most successful poems. When it came, so powerful an inspiration gave a limpid rhythm to his work, an unobstructed lyric flow. As time went on, however, he felt the need deliberately to jumble and rearrange his work in complex and equivocal patterns, particularly his poetry.

Apollinaire's stylistic adroitness and the alluring presence
of his personality in everything he wrote give his work its
most immediate quality. It is all one letter to the world,
never detached from a date line and salutation at the top
and a signature at the bottom. More than half his poems
carry dedications or were sent as letters to friends. Without exception they are occasional and draw on the events
of his life. His stories relate in thin disguise things that happened to him and his acquaintances, mixed freely with
fantastic incidents of his own devising. Because of the
versatility of his talent, one genre fuses easily into another.
He not only practiced the "letter-poem" (reminiscent of
Rousseau's "portrait-landscape") but on two occasions successfully carved up the text of a story into free verse* His
imagination knew no confinement, and his writing became
a vast radiation of himself in all directions—enough letters,
as was said of his mail in the army, "to kill the postman."

His power as a correspondent is best revealed in the volume *Tendre comme le souvenir*, the spacious rambling edifice of letters written to Madeleine within a period of
thirteen months in 1915 and 1916. It contains not only a
wealth of poems on war and love, but also lengthy passages
on the themes that preoccupied him then: his role as a poet
in time of war, patriotism and duty, tenderness and passion,
idolatry of the body, the conflict of his origins and his culture. The collection offers a useful introduction to the man
and his work, for the influence of amorous feelings makes
it both revealing and eloquent. What he writes to Madeleine about his epistolary style applies to all his writing.

> Perhaps also my letters shock you because you find
> in them only talk and no style. It is because in the
> end I disdain what has for a long time been called
> style in all arts and limit it to the expression of what
> is necessary and personal. Discipline and personality
> —those are the limits of style as I understand it;
> beyond that, there is only imitation not of nature,

* A story called *"L'obituaire"* was cut up into the long poem,
"La maison des morts" in *Alcools*. *"Un fantôme de nuées"* in
Calligrammes at first took the form, in the incident just related,
of a prose narrative.

but of an earlier work of art. Canons seem to me to be useful only in the artillery; in art they are above all hobbles on style. . . .

This freewheeling and sometimes explosive tendency shows up clearly in his critical writings, which must be recalled now as the channel through which certain outside influences reached his sensibility. His articles on painting and literature display two qualities that made him less a critic of the arts than their herald. As a devoted believer in the modern sensibility, he always wrote affirmatively; as a poet, even in his prose, he always wrote metaphorically. The strength and weakness of all his criticism lies here. He rarely attacked, for he did not feel the need to destroy the monuments of the past. His writing rings with proclamation, an inspired exposition of ideas which he absorbed from everywhere and everyone.* The authority he achieved arose not so much out of an innate sensitivity to the arts

---

* There were few critics of any importance to young artists in the period before 1914. One of them, the painter Maurice Denis, wrote in 1890 the celebrated definition of painting which marked the first advance since Baudelaire and inaugurated modern criticism. "Remember that a painting—before being a horse in battle or a naked woman or an anecdote of any kind— is essentially a plane surface covered with colors assembled in a certain order." Denis later attacked both fauves and cubists, even though he made use of the term "subjective deformation" to describe what he esteemed the true direction of modern painting. Félix Fénéon had stopped writing his discerning comments on painters around the turn of the century.

One of the rare direct influences on Apollinaire's critical writing is contained in the forgotten work *La morale des lignes* (1908) by his friend Mecislas Golberg. "Truth is visionary; reality in the strict sense is the result of a marvelous filtering: part thought, part understanding, plus emotion and mystery. . . . Deformation—what is commonly called deformation—is the very principle of human creation, our *animus Dei.*" Adopting a similar tone and phrasing, Apollinaire had only to replace Rouveyre's superb caricatures in *La morale des lignes* with paintings by Braque, Picasso, and Léger in order to produce the most excitingly contemporary art criticism of the prewar decade.

He may also have read the German text of Kandinsky's *On the Spiritual in Art* (1912) and the excellent texts by Marc, Kandinsky, and others in *Der Blaue Reiter*. Yet they do not appear to have had any important effect on his development as a critic.

as out of personal knowledge of the integrity of certain artists and familiarity with their aspirations. His poetic talents could transform random conversations into eloquence. Though his prose rarely remained sober for long, it became simpler when he began to contribute regularly to newspapers.

It is inevitable that some confusion and inconsistency should have arisen during almost fifteen years of steady critical writing. Color and light, fourth dimension and subtlety, composition and inspiration—he treated some words as more or less interchangeable. Yet blurred as it is by Apollinaire's shifting poetic terminology, a position emerges which centers around the words "plasticity" and "music." By "plasticity" he meant a totally free manipulation of appearances of things, a freedom that marks all phases of cubism and simultanism. It subsumes both composition, the method of putting together parts to form an artistic whole, and inspiration, the subjective state of the artist who composes. Plasticity, or freedom from conventional patterns, liberates both. "Music" was Apollinaire's metaphor for a state of painting not burdened by any fidelity to external appearances, the way musical sounds are not burdened by any semantic function of language. Arising principally out of his collaborations with Delaunay and Picabia, the concept of musicality in painting affected his own work very little even in his most extreme and short-lived innovations in poetic technique. Plasticity, on the other hand, is the mode of activity most central to his imagination and literary composition, and it enlightens his whole career as a writer.

The plasticity which Apollinaire absorbed from painting combined readily with his own stylistic flexibility, leading him to ignore established literary forms. In the field of fiction it meant that he wrote no true novels or stories. From the early gothic narratives of *L'hérésiarque et cie.* to the meandering anecdotal descriptions of contemporary events he contributed to the *Mercure,* his fiction consists entirely of "tales." Their rich documentation reveals him as a shrewd chronicler of human behavior in all its variety— language, social custom, abnormality, religious practice, bawdiness, boredom. Suffering and humiliation, tragedy and comedy in the classic sense are not the themes of his prose works. Apollinaire was preoccupied with what the

French call *mœurs,* and explicitly admired a similar preoccupation in the Italian authors of the Renaissance. " . . .
reviving high Occidental literature, dead since the fall of
Antiquity, the storytellers following Poggio and Boccaccio
studied the *mœurs,* customs, and characters in all classes
of Italian society and did so with total liberty in regard to
religion and morals." Apollinaire had also read Zola and
Anatole France. But the extravagant events that constitute
the action of his tales represent an effort to carry contemporary life into the realm of myth. The past offered its
most haunting legends: the Wandering Jew, esoteric her-
esies, fraudulent miracles, and all the pagan folklore of
Europe. The future offered the infinite promise of scientific
discovery as imagined by Poe, Verne, Wells, Jarry, Allais,
detective fiction, and the authors of *Fantômas.* The campaign in 1914 in the *Soirées* to present the *Fantômas* volumes and Nick Carter as classics testifies to Apollinaire's
attitude toward narrative line and psychological conventions. These works have more than documentary interest:
"From the point of view of imaginativeness *Fantômas* is
one of the richest works in existence." He means that it
attempts through informality to describe miraculous incidents as if they were ordinary happenings. Apollinaire's
advance from preoccupation with the social emancipation
embodied in licentious texts to preoccupation with emanci-
pated literary form in popular fiction corresponds to the
advance in his art criticism from cubism to orphism-
simultanism. In fiction Apollinaire strove increasingly to
make all experiences immediately meaningful: the adventure of being alive is to understand that we must ourselves
re-enact the great exploits of past and future. A distinctly
"mythomaniac" strain in his sensibility searched for what is
legendary in the most trivial manifestations of modern life
as well as in the most miraculous. Unsolved crimes, papal
infallibility, and the new art of the moving picture inspired
him equally. The subtitle of *La femme assise* concisely defines the scope of his tales: *"Mœurs et merveilles du temps."*

His best fiction is in *L'hérésiarque et cie.,* where the
stories have a strong, if somewhat gnarled, line and a
texture that seldom wears thin. The selections in *Le poète
assassiné* are either slim sketches or a diluted Rabelaisian
hodgepodge, and *La femme assise* amounts to a scissors-
and-paste assemblage of inferior fragments without even

the semblance of continuity. In the first two volumes especially, the style works steadily in his favor, flexible and
highly colored.

> *Elle était brune, encore belle et bien faite; elle*
> *souriait, l'air faux, en minaudant et sa peau sèche*
> *et mate comme la paille de maïs attestait seule*
> *l'approche de la cinquantaine. Sur le cou et sur la*
> *face couraient les ombres de ses années. Et sur ses*
> *yeux encore humides comme le velours d'une loutre*
> *nageant à la surface de l'eau les durs frissons du*
> *regret et d'une fin d'espoir mettaient parfois les mi-*
> *roitements bleus et froids de l'acier.* ("La favorite")

She was a brunette, still beautiful, and shapely;
she smiled with enticing guile, and her dry flesh,
lusterless as a corn husk, alone revealed that she was
approaching fifty. On her neck and face moved the
shadows of her years. And in her eyes, humid like
the velvet skin of an otter swimming on the surface
of the water, keen shivers of regret and hopeless-
ness stirred up cold blue glints of steel.

In every sentence poetic metaphor spars with raillery, and
the resulting ironic tone permits him to write with equal
ease of external appearances and intensely emotional states,
of erotic escapades and devout asceticism. This mobility of
style, this plasticity, is in itself the most sustained expression
of his attitude toward the world.

His theme was always freedom—freedom to be an individual before being a member of society.* The total
visual freedom of cubism was called depravity by the world

---

* Apollinaire saw clearly that, after loss of life, the supreme
evil of war is its effect on individual freedom. "By destroying
liberty, this war which the Germans made inevitable arouses
our curiosity about people in earlier ages who could live as
they liked. The conditions which such an existence requires
have never been met as in the 18th century. We can well fear
that, after the peace, these conditions may never return, and
that regimented men sealed off inside their nationalities, races,
professional and political groups, men organized in docile herds,
may never again dream that there was a time when one could
do what one wanted." (*Anecdotiques*.)

of 1910; the moral freedom signified by the under-the-
counter texts over which he labored many years bore the
same name. Apollinaire contested both judgments.

> Baffo, the famous syphilitic, called the "obscene,"
> whom one can esteem the greatest Priapean poet
> who ever lived [was] at the same time one of the
> most lyric poets of the eighteenth century. . . .

The Marquis de Sade, he maintained, "created, a hundred
years before Krafft-Ebing, sexual psychopathology." Apollinaire's published opinions and his persistence in developing them finally left their mark. The most challenging
sentence of all occurs in the story, *"L'hérésiarque"*: "Mysticism verges very closely on eroticism." Total liberation, then,
would finally obliterate any frontier between the spiritual
and the physical. He did not shrink from the hazardous
ground to which these roads lead. Following the decadents,
paralleling Gide, and anticipating the surrealists and existentialists, Apollinaire finally had to confront the gratuitous
act, *"l'acte gratuit,"* as the extreme instance of human
freedom. Since, in the Christian world of the West, charity
has become closely associated with reward in a life here-
after, its spontaneity and selflessness have tended to become tainted. One can maintain that the only domain of
purely disinterested action that remains in the inversion
of charity: *unmotivated evil.* It satisfies nothing deeper than
whim. This view explains how Apollinaire, having undertaken them for other reasons, became absorbed in writing
pornographic novels. The best of them, *Onze mille verges*,
presents its hero as obsessed by the liberating power of
wickedness, yet he remains untroubled by soul-searchings
such as those that affect Dostoevski's criminal-saints. It is a
story of prolonged orgiastic adventure whose narrative
shifts easily into deadpan humor. After describing a frightful debauch, Apollinaire begins the next paragraph: "For
a considerable time Mony led this monotonous life in
Bucharest." A hundred pages later, at the end of the book,
Mony, sentenced to death by the Japanese, violently de-
flowers a twelve-year-old Romanian girl who was chosen
to yield her virginity to a condemned man. The true climax
follows.

> Then Mony stood up and, since he had nothing
> more to hope for from human justice, he strangled

the little girl after having gouged out her eyes,
while all the time she uttered hideous cries.

The "purity" of this imaginary act lies not in its utter
cruelty but in the gratuitousness of its evil. Only a man
already facing death is free to act unswayed by any human
motives of right and wrong, gain and loss, pleasure and
pain. The detached, scientific tone of Apollinaire's prose
here, especially after it has been sustained through a hundred and fifty pages, concentrates the horror of deliberate
moral depravity; the act becomes both inhuman and superhuman. Yet, as in the most outrageous pages of Sade, we
can hear in these passages the cool accent of Montaigne.
Apollinaire was no true fiction writer, but an author intent
on narrating with as great flexibility as possible the myths
and manners of his time. The casual ordering and unrestricted subject matter of his tales support the major accomplishments of Proust, Gide, and Joyce in overthrowing
the conventions of the nineteenth-century novel. For him
no holds were barred.

Apollinaire's true importance as a writer, however, lies
in his poetry. This segment of his work attains an almost
total plasticity because it arises out of a condition of fruitful
conflict which does not equally affect his fiction or his
criticism. The ways in which he mastered the conflict
provide the clearest demonstration of his genius.

In his last poem, *"La jolie rousse,"* Apollinaire himself
speaks of "that long quarrel between Order and Adventure." The more one becomes familiar with his work, the
clearer it becomes that this conflict sustained his writing
not just in his mature years, but from the very biginning.
Because of his hybrid origins, he had to forge for himself
the sense of continuity with the past that most men inherit
effortlessly during childhood and schooling. The opening
sentences of *Le flâneur des deux rives* show that he could
fall into sentimentality about anything he had found in his
untrammeled life. "Men leave nothing behind without regret; and those same places, things, and people which
caused them the most unhappiness, they abandon with the
greatest grief." At the same time, this free agent, having
had no dominant loyalties and standards thrust upon him,
could look ahead into his own century without overthrowing a cultural heritage, without revolting against deeply in-

grained values. He did not himself describe his double orientation as a "quarrel" until late in life, after deliberately espousing the cause of modernism in his critical work. In his first major collection of verse, *Alcools,* the order of poems carefully precludes separation into different styles or discovery of chronological development. Apollinaire sought to take up a position that commanded all fields of poetic practice, traditional and experimental, and it is the intermingling of the two currents, not their distinctness, that represents his accomplishment.

It was from the first proofs of *Alcools* that he struck all punctuation. Some say a fit of petulance with a sloppy printer drove him to this high-handed gesture, but it is an unlikely explanation. He had already published several unpunctuated poems in 1912, and his own inclinations were undoubtedly reinforced by the publicity Marinetti was receiving for works appearing in the *Mercure* at the same moment. Apollinaire gives his own version in a letter to Henri Martineau written in July 1913 just as the reviews were appearing.

> As for the punctuation, I got rid of it only because it seemed useless to me, and really it is. The rhythm itself and the way the lines are divided—that's the only true punctuation and there's no need for any other. Most of my poems were first printed from a rough copy. I usually compose while I'm walking and singing one of two or three tunes that stay in my head. One of my friends has taken them down. Our ordinary punctuation would never lend itself to such tunes.

At least one of these tunes has in fact been found and published by Marie-Jeanne Durry. Yet even though the reasons for suppressing the punctuation were in great part melodic and conventionally rhythmic, the effect moves sharply in another direction. The naked presentation of the text that resulted retrieved even his most traditional poems from their association with symbolism and French lyric practice, and gave them the guise of modernism. Lack of punctuation alone modifies their line, for it removes the conventional signs of logical development and opens each poem to new sequences and interpretations. The subsequent spreading of his poems across the page in the "calligrams" serves the same purpose.* On the other hand, several of Apollinaire's most rash combinations wear the composed features of the alexandrine, regular octosyllabic stanzas, and a variety of verse forms. His poems inhabit their formal shapes as unpredictably as the poet sustained his imposing figure as the pope of the avant-garde. When his blending of tradition and innovation produces an anomaly, the work sometimes retains a quality of discreet irony, mocking its own mongrel composition. His best poems rise above the squirmings of divided loyalty and literary fashion and reach the realm where irreconcilable opposites can lie down together. Jarry called this realm "ethernity"; in Apollinaire it becomes the timelessness of lyric and elegiac poetry.

Much of Apollinaire's early work, still punctuated and not free of fussy conjunctions, has the feel of meticulous exposition which mysteriously rhymes and scans like some of John Donne's poetic syllogisms. But Apollinaire was already reaching out toward a style without subordination, stanzas composed of interchangeable lines lacking strict causal sequence. Unconnected and also unseparated by punctuation, they appear to be on a single level of discourse.† Such a discontinuous, mosaic style appears to have come naturally to him very early. One of his early compositions, written in Germany in 1902, carries the old madrigal title, "*Mille Regrets.*"

> *Un soir rhénan transparent pour ma nostalgie*
> *Dans l'auberge survint deux par deux une noce*
> *Nostalgie cigares pipes courbées en crosses*
> *Ci-gît m'amour mal culotté ô tabagie*
>
> *Du dicke Du L'amour revient en boumerang*
> *L'amour revient à en vomir le revenant*
> *Ils ont demandé tant de ces bouteilles longues*
> *Comme les longs cyprès d'un grand jardin rhénan*

---

* "*L'œillet,*" shaped in the form of a flower, turns out to be composed of six alexandrines with only one irregularity, and "*Le jet d'eau*" arranges in lines of falling water a perfect octosyllabic sonnet.

† Gertrude Stein wrote: "A comma by helping you along holding your coat for you and putting on your shoes keeps you from living your life as actively as you should lead it."

A Rhenish evening transparent for my gloom
A wedding party fills the inn by twos
Gloom cigars pipes twisted into crooks
Here lies my unkempt love o dim saloon

Du dicke Du love like a boomerang
Comes hurtling back till I could spew the ghost
All night they ordered bottles from the host
Tall bottles tall as cypress on a Rhenish farm

The scene is set before us with terse vividness, and afterward the emotion of the fourth line explodes the more violently for being unprepared. In his despair the poet invokes no muse or fate but the public smoking room of the tavern where he is sitting and the graceful shape of Rhine wine bottles. *Comme* is the only connective he supplies during the long sweep of feeling.

That same year, Apollinaire wrote a poem called "*Les femmes*" which sets down with the minimum of explanation the random conversation of several women sitting around a stove. No attempt is made at discursive unity. The central stanza spins itself out like conversation in a play, full of long pauses, expressing banality, jest, and earnest conviction in the same even tone.

—Encore un peu de café Lenchen s'il te plaît
—Lotte es-tu triste O petit coeur—Je crois qu'elle aime
—Dieu garde—Pour ma part je n'aime que moi-même
—Chut A présent grand-mère dit son chapelet

"A little more coffee please Lenchen"
"Are you sad Lotte dear heart" "I think she's in love"
"God help her" "As for me I love only myself"
"SSShhh Grandmother's telling her beads"

Ten years later he revived this technique, omitting punctuation and any explanation whatever of the circumstances that produced the disconnected sentences, and calling the results "conversation poems." There is ample evidence that Apollinaire deliberately recast his work with the purpose of unhinging it from normal logical sequence. The long poem "*Les fiançailles*," dedicated to Picasso, changed from a fairly clear narrative of a dream into a series of short flashes of uncertain relation. It is probable that Apollinaire left another poem in the utterly incoherent form given it

by a typesetter who misread the manuscript. He achieved
the final dismemberment of poetry as exposition in the
"calligrammatic" style, often undeniably effective, sometimes merely cute. The visual aptness of these poems is
seldom matched by appropriate qualities of sound, which
Apollinaire could easily have produced. His ideogrammic
ideas did not find such disciplined application as we find
later in e. e. cummings, Ezra Pound, and Charles Olson.

The fundamental theory of this ultimate development
was set down by Apollinaire, writing under a pseudonym
in his own *Soirées*.

> *Psychologically* it is of no importance that this
> visible image be composed of fragments of spoken
> language, for the bond between these fragments is
> no longer the logic of grammar but an ideographic
> logic culminating in an order of spatial disposition
> totally opposed to discursive juxtaposition.
>
>   . . . It is the opposite of narration, narration is of
> all literary forms the one which most requires dis-
> cursive logic.

The "opposite of narration" defines the very quality
Apollinaire finally grasped in following cubism into the
experimental work of Delaunay, the quality he named
simultanism. It represents an effort to retain a moment of
experience without sacrificing its logically unrelated variety. In poetry it also means an effort to neutralize the
passage of time involved in the act of reading. The fragments of a poem are deliberately kept in a random order
to be reassembled in a single instant of consciousness. An
unusual typographical image on the page can help suggest
this instantaneous experience and dissipate the temporal
aspect of reading. Simultanism means a telescoping of
time, a poetic technique that achieves the opposite effect
from the regulated flow of music. The ambitious and inspiring doctrine led Apollinaire to practice *"découpage
poétique"* and accounts for the apparent obscurity of some
of his simplest poems and for their blatant avant-gardism.
Surprise, the category Apollinaire unfortunately employed
in the *espirit nouveau* lecture to express all the artistic
innovation he had advocated, describes only the surface
aspect of his poems. Surprise must remain a secondary
characteristic of the two general principles toward which

Apollinaire's thinking deviously evolves: *total freedom of invention* or plasticity, leading to gratuitous or arbitrary constructions in no way imitating nature; and the unifying principle of *simultanism,* in which all parts interpenetrate and interreact through contrast and humorous conflict rather than by discursive logic or conventional perspective. These two characteristics as he found them in painting nudged his own work toward a demonstrative departure from tradition.

While the structure of Apollinaire's poems was evolving toward aggravated modernism and simultanism, his prosody, in subtle compensation, moved toward ancient measures. Beneath his innovations in rhyme,* it is the pure musical rhythms of Villon and Verlaine, Heine and Nerval that sustain his best verse. He claimed, not without justification, to have "given new life to the eight-syllable line." Traditional verse forms were no encumbrance for Apollinaire, for they lent incisiveness to his boldest imaginative leaps.

> *Soirs de Paris ivres du gin*
> *Flambant de l'électricité*
> *Les tramways feux verts sur l'échine*
> *Musiquent au long des portées*
> *De rails leur folie de machines*
> > (*"La chanson du mal-aimé"*)

> Drunk on gin the Paris nights
> Blaze with electricity
> The trolleys flashing greenish lights
> Warble along their staves of tracks
> The madness of machinery

It is the prosody here that transforms the shoddiness of modern life into something both moving and comic. He can also compress into a single line (as in the fourth, below) the association of abstract concept and physical sensation. Baudelaire would have taken an entire stanza and Proust five pages to reconnoiter the territory.

* Louis Aragon has pointed out that Apollinaire virtually redefined masculine and feminine rhymes for French poetry. He treated words whose terminal sound for the ear is a vowel as masculine, words whose terminal sound is a consonant as feminine. *Avril, heureuse, fer*—all feminine; *jolie, gens, connue*—all masculine.

J'ai cueilli ce brin de bruyère
L'automne est morte souviens-t'en
Nous ne nous verrons plus sur terre
Odeur de temps brin de bruyère
Et souviens-toi que je t'attends
                    ("L'adieu")

I picked this fragile sprig of heather
Autumn has died long since remember
Never again shall we see one another
Odor of time sprig of heather
Rmember I await our life together

The abridged syntax and unpunctuated abruptness of
each of these two examples tends to merge the moment
into a single image, into what the French aptly call an
instantané. The prosody, however, prolongs the moment
into several measures of transparent music. The gentle
conflict between qualities of arrest and flow is not a quarrel
or a crippling inconsistency. Here lies the very spell of
Apollinaire's best verse: he *sings* quietly to us of feelings
that cannot be *told* because they have no time.

It is not enough, finally, to distinguish two stylistic tendencies in Apollinaire's poetry and examine them in terms
of contrast and reconcilement. These tendencies, planted
in his versatile talents and great facility, blossomed into
several poetic styles, all of which mix ancient and modern
strains. First, there are poems in traditional metrics whose
internal coherence came to be set by poetic logic alone.
The theme that haunted him most constantly, the erosion
of time which forever threatens both our feelings of love
and our consciousness of individual identity,* usually crys-
tallizes into classic stanzas. Death, the final running out of
time, does not preoccupy him, but he suffers intensely subjective states of loss and nostalgia which seem to be his
meaning for the word *destin*. Secondly, machines, war, the
complexity and adventure of modern life—these kindred
excitements erupted in a consciously modernist tendency
applied to the surface of his verse and concentrating finally

---

* "Nothing causes more melancholy in me than the passing
of time. It is in such formal disagreement with my feelings,
with my sense of identity, that it is the very source of my
poetry." *(Lettres à sa marraine.)*

on typographical manipulation. It produced essentially simple poems, dealing with the immediate circumstances of daily life and dream. Their apparent obscurity lies in the directness of their transcription—five senses and an unfettered imagination setting down all impulses without differentiation.

In more ambitious moods, when he sought a role for himself as prophet, patriot, poet, and love of men, Apollinaire developed a third manner; an expansive, increasingly confident free verse. If time is the dimension that aligns his classic meters, a sense of space dominates the free verse poems in which *I* expands its geographical location toward limitlessness.

Mais je connus dès lors quelle saveur a l'univers

Je suis ivre d'avoir bu tout l'univers
Sur le quai d'où je voyais l'onde couler et dormir
*   les bélandres*

Ecoutez-moi je suis le gosier de Paris
Et je boirai encore s'il me plaît l'univers

Ecoutez mes chants d'universelle ivrognerie
*   ("Vendémiaire")*

But ever since then I've known the flavor
    of the universe

I'm drunk from having swallowed the entire universe
On the quay from which I saw the darkness flow and
    the barges sleep

Listen to me I am the throat of all Paris
And I shall drink the universe again if I want

Listen to my songs of universal drunkenness

The voices of Whitman, Verhaeran, and, more faintly, Rimbaud reverberate through such lines.

The fourth style Apollinaire perfected is a popular-humorous vein, in which he wrote with magnificent ease. Echoing Tristan Corbière, Jarry, and popular ditties he heard in cafés and places of less repute, he turned out irresistible drolleries.

Il a vécu	He spread his smut
En Amérique	In America
Ce petit cul	This little or-
Or	nithological butt
nithologique	
	But
Or	Enough of this
J'en ai assez	I'll take a piss
Je vais pisser	
("Chapeau-Tombeau")	

The verses in *Cortège priapique* use the direct realism of his pornographic prose. Two of Apollinaire's most uneven works, the late burlesque plays *Les mamelles de Tirésias* and *Casanova,* exploit but do not sustain these comic inclinations. However, no such thinness detracts from the blend of mocking humor, easy versification, and folk wisdom that characterize Apollinaire's early volume, *Le Bestiaire* (with handsome woodcuts by Dufy).

> *Le Paon* (The Peacock)
> *En faisant la roue, cet oiseau*
> *Dont le pennage traîne à terre*
> *Apparaît encore plus beau,*
> *Mais se découvre le derrière.*

> By spreading his tail this bird so fair,
> Whose plumage drags the forest floor,
> Appears more lovely than before,
> But thus unveils his *derrière.*

Little wonder, when he can write such gently comic, unaffected, popular verse, that a score of composers have set Apollinaire to music.

The imagery of Apollinaire's poetry, remarkable for its variety and unconventionality, does not provide the consistent link among these four styles. For poetry in which the texture of the imagery creates the principal effect, one must examine poets like Saint-Pol-Roux or Hart Crane. The great polarity of Apollinaire's images is between light and dark, values that do not correspond to good and evil, but, rather, to consciousness (lucidity) and the subconscious (shadows). He was loyal to both realms, and within this vast area take shape the other metaphorical patterns of flowing (time), eating (ingesting the universe), the city street (modern life), and war (all-encompassing adventure). In effect, his variegated imagery serves to extend the range of his poetry. Since his versification likewise modulates too freely to weld together so heterogeneous a body of work, what is its unity, if any, its most general and most profound characteristic?

Most obvious of all is the high ambition of his literary purpose. He desired to affirm both tradition and innovation as his true loyalties; he sought a means of presenting a poem not only as a succession of lines, but as a simultaneous experience; and he was inclined by temperament to mix together earthy humor, tenderness, uncensored dreams, erudition, and sophisticated modernism. In order to achieve these ends he had to develop a poetic method essentially opposed to elimination and construction of meaning. Mosaic style, truncated syntax, cancellation of punctuation—all these devices increase the inclusiveness of his poetry by keeping it open to all combinations and interpretations. The primary quality of his work, then, its unmoving pivot, is *ambiguity,* not so much of individual words and phrases as of the entire structure of a poem. The symmetrical, yet apparently gratuitous, ordering of *"La chanson du mal-aimé"* succeeds in blending an antique and a contemporary flavor. His most explosive "calligrams" can be reduced to simple messages like lyric telegrams. Ambiguity in Apollinaire's poetry corresponds to what acquaintances referred to in his personality as mystification, the capacity to confound any attempt to pin him down, to discover his secret. Because they exist in several dimensions of time and meaning, his poems suggest an infinity of human experience and represent the freedom which Apollinaire treasured as the most precious fulfillment of our nature. And it is ambiguity that permitted him to assimilate the childlike vision of Rousseau, Satie's and Allais' delicately violent humor, and Jarry's hallucinated universe. Out of the experiments of cubism and simultanism, out of plasticity, he distilled this poetic method.

But "ambiguity" falls short of the final mark. Apollinaire's "lack of identity," which sought a new self through a simultanist identification with all the universe, takes on its true aspect as a *reversal of consciousness.* This huge ambition was to him the most natural thing in the world. Through the sequence of important long poems (*"La chan-*

son du mal-aimé," "Les fiançailles," "Cortège," "Vendé-
miaire," "Zone," "Collines," and *"Merveilles de la guerre"*)
he increasingly sought himself *outside* himself. It is as if
his *I* were the exterior world from which, once he had
radiated himself into it, he could look back wistfully and
indulgently upon his old self as a pathetic object. The
relevant texts are among his best known.

Painter-Poet

> *Un jour*
> *Un jour je m'attendais moi-même*
> *Je me disais Guillaume il est temps que tu viennes*
> *Pour que je sache enfin celui-là que je suis . . .*
> *Tous ceux qui survenaient et n'étaient pas moi-même*
> *Amenaient un à un les morceaux de moi-même*
> ("Cortège")

> One day
> One day I waited for myself
> I said to myself Guillaume it's time you turned up
> So I could know just who I am . . .
> All those who turned up and were not myself
> Brought one by one the pieces of myself

✦   ✦   ✦

> *Je m'arrête pour regarder*
> *Sur la pelouse incandescente*
> *Un serpent erre c'est moi-même*
> *Qui suis la flûte dont je joue*
> *Et le fouet qui châtie les autres*
> ("Les Collines")

> I stop in wonderment to see
> Upon the incandescent lawn
> A serpent glide it is myself
> Who am the flute I play upon
> A whip to punish other men

In *"Cortège"* it is the restricted world of his friends and
past which constitute his self; in 1914, at the peak of his
confidence, *"Collines"* asserts all of creation as the locus of
his being. *Not-I is I,* he says, and reverses subject and object, the poles of consciousness itself. As he writes, his first
person passes through a series of extensions and collapses,
conquests and routs. The reason why Apollinaire's poetry

conveys so singular and intriguing a personality is this very transformation of our innermost faculty: our awareness of being ourselves. He says what appalls and wins us—you are I, I am you and everyone. For him it is not religion, but poetry as a way of living.

Such a persistent effort to encompass the whole world and discover himself in it is both foolish and admirable. Without it, untautened by the stress of conflicting meanings and poetic *selves* in equilibrium, the entire edifice of Apollinaire's work would become vacant and flimsy. Ambiguity permitted him to endow his poetry with both a clarity of the immediate world vividly experienced and a mystery of meanings which reach to infinity.

> *Rien n'est mort que ce qui n'existe pas encore*
> *Près du passé luisant demain est incolore*
> *Il est informe aussi près de ce qui parfait*
> *Présente tout ensemble et l'effort et l'effet*
> (*"Cortège"*)

> Nothing is dead but what does not yet exist
> Tomorrow is wan beside the deep-tinted past
> And formless as well next to what proffers us
> In perfect singleness both effort and effect

Though they may appear to be tranquil evocation of the past, these strict alexandrines completely reverse our usual attitude toward time. Time brings not death (which belongs, rather, to the future), but life and meaning by allowing us to behold the accomplished sequence of history. The present becomes a ressurection out of a lifeless future into the life of an available past. The stanza that makes this triumphant affirmation, however, and that approaches Proust's vision, comes at the close of a long poem whose tone verges on nostalgic melancholy. The significant ambiguity here lies less in individual words like *"rien,"* *"parfait,"* and *"présente,"* than in the equivocal mood of the entire poem. Through its shifting prosody and imagery filters a profound feeling of victory in defeat, of defeat in victory. Yet this attitude toward our mortal condition is never explicitly expressed. Our combat with the great adversary, time, can best be described by a kind of perpetual riddle, as in Rousseau's painting. It is the natural virtue of Apollinaire's poetry that it succeeds in capturing the ambiguous experience of life; the joyful and heartrending flux of immediate sensation, the unformed promise of the future, and the "perfect singleness" of recollections out of a "deep-tinted past."

Having come into prominence at the opening of the new century, it is not surprising that Apollinaire soon won a wide reputation for modernism even though he wrote few thoroughly modern poems. The outward aspect of his work deceives many. Essentially, his work lies in the savage-sentimental line of French poetry—a line that avoids the great crossroads of classicism, romanticism, and symbolism, and connects Villon, Scève, La Fontaine, Nerval, Baudelaire, and Laforgue to the twentieth century. Apollinaire had their passion and their measure. No one in this century has rhymed so sweetly.

As has been pointed out by Professor LeRoy Breunig, the dominant mood of Apollinaire's poetic inspiration alternates in a clear binary rhythm between traditional lyricism and brash modernism. The chronology of his poems establishes two relatively traditional periods, 1902–1905 and 1908–1912, which correspond to his highly emotional interludes with Annie Playden and Marie Laurencin. The intervening periods of emotional calm, 1905–1908 and 1912–1914, contain the greatest intensity of experiment and innovation. These latter periods, however, are not just free of emotional stress. They coincide exactly with Apollinaire's most important collaborations with painters; first, friendship with Vlaminck and Derain, followed by boisterous discussions in the *bateau lavoir* with Picasso, Jacob, and the rest; second, a renewed interest in painting in 1912, the founding of the *Soirées* the same year, experiment with Delaunay in orphism and simultanism, and the decision to publish *Les peintres cubistes*. During these two periods his poetry responded to the "plasticity" he discovered in the new painting by modifying its own appearance and structure. Poems like *"Crépuscule," "Saltimbanques,"* and *"Salomé"* transpose the delicate poses of Picasso's circus and pink periods (1905) more successfully than did Rilke, Max Jacob, and Cocteau. Around 1908, a montage style, which might be called cubist, emerges in the poems *"Palais"* (dedicated to Max Jacob), *"Les fiançailles"* (dedicated to Picasso), and *"Le brasier."* Then in 1913 and 1914, after a four-year interval of restrained poetic output, come the simulantist

poems: *"Liens," "Les fenêtres," "Lundi Rue Christine,"*
"Un fantôme de nuées," and sections of *"Les collines."* The
rhythm of experiment increases sharply in 1914 and takes
on a frankly plastic aspect. The "calligrams" conclude the
cycle.

Obviously, the aural side of Apollinaire's poetry—especially his important contributions to rhyme—did not develop under the direct influence of painting. Most of these
techniques, in fact, entered his verse and gave it its
particular breath well before 1905. *"La chanson du mal-
aimé,"* which contains his most thorough renovation of
versification, was composed in 1902 and 1903. After 1907,
however, his poetry, apart from an increased ease in free
verse, moves less toward a new prosody than toward a new
grasp of structure, toward freedom in assembling a poem
out of disparate parts. It seems reasonable to attribute this
evolution in great part to the enormous amount of thinking
Apollinaire did about painting.* Because of his double
career as critic and writer, Apollinaire belongs, finally, to
the rare species of *poète fondé en peinture*—a poet rooted
in painting. Baudelaire provides the only apt comparison.
Their poetic imaginations enabled them to write art criticism of discernment and sensitivity. The quality of their
poetry cannot be fully understood without a knowledge of
the painting they admired. Baudelaire did not, like his
contemporaries, merely borrow scenes and subjects from
romantic artists. Writing from the age of twenty-four about
the total sensuous experience of a work of art, he yielded
very early to what was virtually the direct dictation of
Delacroix' ideas. In the end, he evolved a combined ethics
and aesthetics of individualism and an accompanying poetic principle of correspondence between the senses, the
arts, and the entire universe. Apollinaire came to be less

---

* Mademoiselle Janine Moulin, in her careful study of Apollinaire's development as a poet, attributes his stylistic evolution primarily to the influence of Rimbaud. Unquestionably
Rimbaud's example corroborated the principles Apollinaire
gleaned from other sources. But there is not enough evidence
—unless Apollinaire deliberately covered his tracks—to make
Rimbaud the central factor in Apollinaire's progress toward a
style of modernism. Hallucination was not his genre, and the
increasingly prophetic tone of his works probably derived as
much from Verhaeren and Jules Romains as from Rimbaud.

preoccupied in his poetry with the aesthetics of evil than
with the need to pierce time itself in order to transfix the
experience of a moment. In different ways, both Apollinaire and Baudelaire learned from painting a new logic, a
new mode of unity. Baudelaire saw in the controlled violence of Delacroix' compositions (and also in Guys' *dandy-
isme*) the means to make his poetry both passionate and
elegant. The high velocity and multiple reference of Apollinaire's verse are similarly visible in the work of cubists
and simultanists.

One wonders if Baudelaire's example can have swayed
Apollinaire in his role of defender of the arts. Certain
passages may well have lodged in Apollinaire's mind.

> I sincerely believe that the best criticism is that
> which is amusing and poetic; not that cold and alge-
> braic kind which, under the pretext of explaining
> everything, displays neither hate nor love. . . . Thus
> the best account of a painting can well be a sonnet
> or an elegy.
>
> (*Salon de* 1846.)

Elsewhere, Baudelaire employed the piquant prophetic
style in which Apollinaire excelled.

> Delacroix was passionately in love with passion and
> coldly determined to search for means to express
> passion in the most visible terms.
>
> (*L'art et la vie d'Eugène Delacroix.*)

> What is pure art according to the modern concep-
> tion? It is to create a suggestive magic which con-
> tains both subject and object, the external world
> and the artist himself.
>
> (*L'art philosophique.*)

Both men reached a three-year peak of critical activity at
approximately the same stage of maturity: Baudelaire between thirty-eight and forty (1859–1861), Apollinaire
between thirty-two and thirty-four (1912–1914). The
similarities, however, must not be exaggerated. Apollinaire
had a dangerous penchant for paradox and prophetic gen-
erality; Baudelaire wrote in constant splenetic awareness
of his bourgeois public and of his own chosen pose of
aloofness. It is as *poètes fondés en peinture* that they can

be associated, for each participated directly and fruitfully in the radical vision of great painting.

Following 1900, during the three-year calm before the century truly began to turn, the arts in France cried out for a champion who would know when to be reasonable and when to be reckless. This state of affairs irresistibly attracted Apollinaire to meet the challenge of the epoch. Seen across the interval of half a century, the figure he cuts is that of a surfboard rider who balances in easy triumph on the crest of a wave. He moves by a force he neither generates nor controls, though he appears to do both. His skilled travel astonishes us, yet he would sink in a flat sea. The artistic movements of the prewar era lifted Apollinaire to a position from which he seemed to lead them into the twentieth century; in reality they carried him along in graceful but precarious stance. His comments provide an excellent description of how the wave reached the shore, but he cannot finally tell us why. His enterprise and flexible sensibility elected the role of impresario as a way of making his mark in a world where he was never entirely secure, never truly at home. Probably his death in 1918 brought a timely end to his career. His creative powers were declining and he began to entertain vain hopes of official honors. It is doubtful that he could have maintained his position of authority in the postwar crush of organized demonstration.

By then, however, he had accomplished as much as his ancestor Du Bellay, in a career of exactly equal length. The principal classics from which Apollinaire learned his lesson were contemporary painting and under-the-counter literature. Like Du Bellay, honoring the classics in *Défense et illustration de la langue française*, he scrupulously repaid in polemical and critical writing what he appropriated from these two fields into his poetry. The eclectic in him borrowed unconcernedly from every culture, from all history; his mind found room for everything. The eccentric in him ensured that his culture was different from that of people around him and that every work he published, every gesture he made, bore some trace of originality. This counterthrust of eccentric and eclectic yielded his greatest poems. Constantly he was trying to lug into the future with him the curious exotic treasure he found in the past. Yet he wrote in the opening pages of *Les peintres cubistes*: "One cannot be forever carrying one's father's corpse. It must be abandoned with the other dead." He made it a virtue to be equivocal.

The excitement of his work is due in great part to the swiftness with which he could transform personal and intimate avowals into poems that encompass the entire universe.

> *Je ne suis pas sentimental à l'excès comme le sont ces*
> *gens sans mesure que leurs actions dépassent sans*
> *qu'ils sachent s'amuser*
> *Notre civilisation a plus de finesse que les choses qu'ils*
> *employent*
> *Elle est au delà de la vie confortable*
>
> ("A l'Italie")

I am not overly sentimental like those extravagant
    people who are overwhelmed by their own ac-
    tions without knowing how to enjoy themselves
Our civilization is more subtle and exact than the ob-
    jects they make use of
There's more to it than the easy life

In critical writing, as in poetry, Apollinaire's faculties are capable of this rare equilibrium, moments of total clairvoyance in which he had mounted the crest of the wave. He could, at least, see clearly. He beheld, in an instant, the enchantment of his own zealous and supple figure and the future glistening ahead like a lost continent about to be rediscovered.

PART THREE

The Century Turned

Some years ago I myself made some observations on this aspect of nitrous oxide intoxication, and reported them in print. One conclusion was forced upon my mind at that time, and my impression of its truth has ever since remained unshaken. It is that our normal waking consciousness, rational consciousness as we call it, is but one special type of consciousness, whilst all about it, parted from it by the filmiest of screens, there lie potential forms of consciousness entirely different. We may go through life without suspecting their existence; but apply the requisite stimulus, and at a touch they are there in all their completeness, definite types of mentality which probably somewhere have their field of application and adaptation. No account of the universe in its totality can be final which leaves these other forms of consciousness quite disregarded.—William James, *The Varieties of Religious Experience*

{ **11** }

THE ART OF STILLNESS

The "great" war, which was to have made the world safe for democracy, succeeded far better in making the world safe for the artistic avant-garde. In the document signed in the railroad car near Compiègne, there was nothing about the New Spirit or the right of experiment in the arts. Yet the battles of World War I indirectly advanced the cause of modernism in the promise that a new order was at hand. After 1918 the avant-garde could never again be driven back into the sea and could devote its energies for the next twenty years to extending the foothold it had won in Paris. The intermingled careers of Rousseau, Satie, Jarry, and Apollinaire represent stages of the original campaign completed before the war. In order to start from scratch, the avant-garde had had to discover the fresh childlike vision of a man like Rousseau, a vision which Satie preserved and exploited for all it contained of humor and the absurd. Jarry, in whom innocence and eccentricity, genius and idiocy sprang from one intense wrenching of reality, hurled himself deliberately over the precipice of hallucination. A passionate and clever impresario, Apollinaire learned that through the openness of ambiguity he could use, and keep, the secrets of the other three. Rousseau's candor of simplicity became Apollinaire's candor of unabashed complexity. By heterodoxy or naïveté or mystification each of the four strove to live up to his art, to live a work of art.

However, despite the revelations they may make about the intimate mood of the Banquet Years, these traits still grievously beg the most elusive of all questions in modern art: the survival of form. After this lengthy consideration of the work of four modern artists, the question cannot be neglected. The two respects in which the arts since 1885 have most clearly moved away from the nineteenth century with its ultimate version of Renaissance style both concern form.

The first point must be treated in reference to the "spiritual revival" mentioned in the second chapter, man's search for divinity and spiritual values within the material world, above all within himself. The form of a work of art can imply this inward direction and stand for the fact that the work itself becomes the means, the locus of the search. Twentieth-century art has tended to *search itself* rather than exterior reality for beauty of meaning or truth, a condition that entails a new relationship between the work of art, the world, the spectator, and the artist.

Two complementary tendencies characterize the relationship of art to the external world. The first is to withdraw entirely and create a self-sufficient universe; the second is to seek ties with the real world either through naturalism (art imitates life) or artificiality (life imitates art). The former tendency, withdrawal, usually evolves in the direction of semi-mystical detachment from the material world; the latter moves toward adventure, reform of the world, and a desire to change life itself. Between 1885 and 1918 in France, both tendencies assumed an aspect peculiar to the turning century. Two difficult and crucial texts will help to show that what is at stake here is a theory of knowledge, a theory of consciousness itself.

> If then I know myself only through myself, it is contradictory to require any other predicate of self, but that of self-consciousness. Only in the self-consciousness of a spirit is there the required identity of object and of representation; for herein consists the essence of a spirit, that it is self-representative.
>
> (Coleridge, *Biographia Literaria*.)

It follows that an absolute can be reached only by an *intuition*, whereas the rest [of our knowledge] arises out of analysis. We here call intuition the *sympathy* by which one transports oneself to the interior of an object in order to coincide with its unique and therefore ineffable quality.

(Bergson, *Introduction to Metaphysics.*)

Coleridge's remarks, anticipating Bergson's conviction that all knowledge is subjective (identity of knower with known), suggest that art may embody its own reality and its own infinity. A self-representative expression needs no exterior world. Eighty years after Coleridge, Jarry wrote an even more obscure text in the same vein called *"Etre et vivre."* "Being, once rid of Berkeley's burden, consists . . . not in perceiving or being perceived, but in that the iridescent mental kaleidoscope *think itself and of itself* [SE *pense*]." (Mallarmé was even more cryptic: *"Ma pensée se pense."*) By the end of the article Jarry has confounded us with the serious double talk of 'Pataphysics. But why are these authors so concerned with metaphysical preliminaries to the artistic process? The answer reaches far beyond the question. When literature and painting cease to be representations or imitations of external reality in order to become self-sufficient creations rivaling reality, then the artistic function itself demands intense scrutiny. By what right can art claim to have surpassed the dogma of imitation? In answering this challenge, art has become *self-reflexive*—narcissistic. It endlessly studies its own behaviors and considers them suitable subject matter. Self-representation in art has replaced verisimilitude. Certain French artists endowed with the double genius of lyric sensibility (or *sympathy*) and ruthless analysis have given this self-reflexive tendency its most sustained and extreme expression.

Mallarmé and his poetic offspring, Paul Valéry, could never take their eyes off themselves. Valéry's lyrical-mathematical mind, very similar to Jarry's, stalked the workings of his consciousness into the reaches of solitude and solipsism. Straightforwardly or obliquely, everything he wrote concerns the nature and meaning of the creative act. It is not art for art's sake, but *art about art*. In writing of Leonardo he reaches the point of stating: "Perhaps one

can really conceive only of what one has created." Valéry
was intent upon a truly autonomous art.

In painting, the question of fundamentals has arisen as
dramatically as in literature. Redon was misunderstood
until the turn of the century because he painted objects
and figures that existed not in the world but in his subjective vision only. His works have no model but themselves.
The whole trend of cubist researches led artists to paint
paintings about painting. That explains why their works
often look like exercises or definitions. In the last analysis
it makes no difference whether one calls a radically cubist
canvas abstract or concrete: *it strives to be its own subject.*
This is the meaning of "self-reflexive." There is a passage
by Stendhal, writing about his own writing, in which he
grasps this slippery question in one sentence.

> I ceaselessly ruminate upon what interests me; by
> dint of regarding it in *different positions of mind*
> [*âme*] I end up by seeing something new in it, and
> I make it change its aspect.
>
> (*Vie de Henry Brulard.*)

As early as Stendhal, the subject of a work is beginning
to dwindle in importance before the carefully watched
positions d'âme which transform it into art. The process
of transformation (for Stendhal, crystallization followed
by disenchantment; for cubism, a methodical dissolution
of material objects, a dissociation of visual ideas) carries
all before it. The subject of a painting is not what it
started with but what it ends up with.

Of all the cubists, Juan Gris was the most exclusively
concerned with this aesthetic, and he wrote convincingly
about his methods.

> To paint is to foresee, to foresee what is going on in
> the whole composition of the painting when a cer-
> tain form or color is introduced, and to foresee what
> it suggests as reality to someone seeing it. Therefore
> it is in the role of spectator of my own work that I
> discern the subject of a painting.

Gris painted by watching himself paint, and his immaculate
compositions of tables and chessboards convey the impression of intense observation directed inward rather
than outward. In Rousseau there was little of this breath-

less self-consciousness before the creative act; for him crafts-manship and magic were one. But this much can be said about Rousseau's work: the meticulousness of his style, his scorn of the sketch as anything more than preparation, and the sure freedom with which he recomposed his scenes —these factors produced a body of work that does not so much represent reality as rival it. His world, too, was autonomous.

The relation of music to these aesthetic trends is ex-tremely complex and extremely pertinent. Music has al-ways, more than the other arts, taken itself as its subject. Every sonata is essentially "about" the sonata form. The capacity of music to be "pure," to be utterly self-reflexive, explains in part why music was welcomed back into the central tradition of the arts in France at the end of the nineteenth century after having been long considered a means of expression best suited to the Germanic romantic sensibility. The symbolists, somewhat misguidedly, admired the sensuous suggestiveness of Wagner. For Apollinaire, however, music was distinguished by its capacity to be autonomous. Music came to represent to the Banquet Years the state of complete self-reflexiveness and self-sufficiency to which all arts aspire. Sensing this, and simultaneously attracted to literature, Satie could not help toying as much with the pseudo-descriptive qualities of music as with its separateness. His work is a commentary on the auton-omous nature of music, not a denial of it.

Through self-reflexiveness, through concentration upon its own mobility or immobility, the artistic consciousness can shrink from the world into its own mirrored realm. This aesthetic retreat toward the formal position described by Coleridge and Bergson lasted well into the twentieth century during the ascendancy of decadence and symbol-ism. After 1900, as is apparent in Jarry's, Satie's, and Apol-linaire's developments, the external world was again em-braced in a gradual change of mood. But neither "realism" nor "artificiality" suffices to describe the shift. The antics it entailed were distinctive of the new century and re-sulted not in a subjection of one realm to the other but in a deliberate *cross* of art and life. It is as if, in Edmund Wilson's terms, Axel and Rimbaud could inhabit a single human being who retreats from reality by seizing it in a sustained effort of transformation. This principle, already demonstrated biographically, also resides in the formal revision which affected the arts.

The frame of a painting, the format and "style" of a work of literature, the conventions of performance for musical compositions—these factors clearly separate art from reality. The boundaries of art have long been made explicit in order to avoid confusion and to call attention to its exceptional mode of existence. No one knew quite how to react, therefore, when Jarry himself became Ubu, his own magnificently outrageous creation, and when Blaise Cendrars wrote and half painted a poem six feet long ("format attaining the height of the Eiffel Tower") which read more like a travelogue than poetry. The frame had been overrun, and art set itself up as continuous with life. The two universes engaged in mutual interference: Satie incorporated imperious comments to the audience into his scores and gave instructions that no one listen to his music. Picasso hammered nails through the back of his cubist paintings so that the points protruded through the finished surface. Their motives were not strictly aesthetic, but also destructive and playful.

It was, appropriately, Apollinaire who conceived of the "internal frame." If there is no longer a frame to segregate art from reality by establishing an external boundary, can we find its counterpart inside the composition? Apollinaire discovered it in cubist painting.

> The equivalent of Picabia's written title, of Picasso's and Braque's real objects, letters, and molded numbers is to be found in Mlle. Laurencin's paintings in the form of pictorial arabesques in depth; in Gleizes' paintings in the form of right angles which catch the light; in Fernand Léger in the form of bubble-shaped forms; in Metzinger in the form of vertical lines parallel to the sides of the frame and cut by occasional transversals. The equivalent will be found in all great painters.
>
> (*Les peintres cubistes.*)

For Apollinaire, who never developed the idea, the internal frame remained something akin to an internal signature, an emblem like Rousseau's hands and street lamps. But does not the internal frame serve the opposite purpose from an external frame? A sample of the real world erupts in the middle of a work of art and violates its separateness. The internal frame, being a gap or an intrusion, does not de-limit one realm from the other but fuses art with reality. The newspaper clippings in cubist collages serve to link them to the surrounding world of events, and real frag-ments fill the poems of Max Jacob, Cendrars, and Reverdy.

Gide employed a similar technique in his labyrinthine novel *Les faux-monnayeurs*, which interweaves fiction with the nonfiction of the author's journal. The contrived anti-literary effect of the book arises out of a short-circuiting of the creative act. Undigested gobs of journal show the artistic process which has refused to complete its trans-formation; by calculation the novel is left full of holes. Similarly, the very typography or notation of Apollinaire's, e. e. cummings', and Ezra Pound's poetry leaves gaps which let us read through the surface of their verse back into the intermittent texture of experience. Jokes about the holes in Henry Moore's sculpture come close to doing justice to its most significant aspect: the tendency of mate-rial in his hands, even at the cost of contortion or ugliness, to embrace and bring to life its own opposite, *vacancy*.

This is no longer mere self-reflexiveness, art about art, but, rather, a disconcerting and amusing subversion of artistic immunity. We see through the internal frame (a fragment of reality) to ourselves seeing the work which now contains us. When the distinctions of art and reality have broken down, we are ourselves incorporated into the structure of a work of art. Its very *form* importunes us to enter an expanded community of creation which now includes artist and spectator, art and reality.

The second departure of twentieth-century art from nineteenth-century conventions can best be approached through the classical concept of unity. The unities of the Greek theater amounted to a single value of *proximity* within the dimensions of place, time, and characterization. "Action" meant a reasoned arrangement of events in series. With its profoundly dramatic vision, the Renaissance im-posed these restrictions on painting, on much of literature, and, in a tenuous way (through the tonal-harmonic system and new musical forms), on music. Romanticism enlarged every dimension and treated unity as a breath-taking ex-pansion of the same categories. The romantic abandon to the desire to be somewhere else, in another time, and in another person swelled the unities beyond recognition, and only the privileged personality of the artist could hope for fulfillment of these yearnings. The modern sensibility, however, began to proceed not so much by untrammeled expansion of the unities as by a violent dislocation of them in order to test the possibility of a new coherence. The fundamentally discursive unities could not serve. Just as a phenomenon in nature could no longer be understood as existing *there* in the simple location of classic physics, so a work of art—play or painting—no longer had a simple *here and now,* but a very complex unity. Be it a Gris still life, a poem by Apollinaire, a passage from Proust, or even a polytonal composition, a work of art began to co-ordinate as equally present a variety of times and places and states of consciousness. The process, because it seeks to hold these elements in a meaningful relationship, relinquishes both classic unity and also the quality of self-forgetfulness which characterizes romanticism. Not self-forgetful, the artist of the twentieth century seeks the means to become totally *self-remembering,* self-reflexive, without conventions of location and of logical consistency. This is the still-emergent unity of his work.

In shying away from the word "unity," however, criticism in all the arts has unwittingly settled on another term to convey the idea of how the parts of a modern work of art are put together. Scarcely a page of analysis can be written today without it. The word has been arbitrarily excluded from the preceding chapters; used without definition, it glides too smoothly over basic questions of unity and form as if they had been long since resolved. Yet its general acceptance is significant. This factotum word is *juxtaposition:* setting one thing beside the other without connective. The twentieth century has addressed itself to arts of juxtaposition as opposed to earlier arts of *transition.*

Transition refers to those works that rely upon clear articulation of the relations between parts at the places they join: connection at the edges (though other, inner connections may exist as well). It means one event, one sensation, one thing at a time, and is the effective result of the great Renaissance disciplines. In literature, both grammar and rhetoric tended to put a conjunction between all phrases. The copulative function of language used classically made every transition smooth and clear. In painting, linear perspective related every object to every other object along imaginary lines representing space. In music, the connections of harmonic progression permitted melodic intervals, and voice leading wove a single thread of consecutiveness from one moment to the next. The whole "classic" idea of style in art arose from the undisputed supremacy of transition. It ruled that in any artistic experience each part must follow from the last; witness the logical sequence of a tragedy or the massive symmetry of classic architecture. In great part its reward lies in the steadiness with which it carries the spectator along from beginning to end.

The arts of juxtaposition offer difficult, disconcerting, fragmented works whose disjunct sequence has neither beginning nor end. They happen without transition and scorn symmetry.

> *Trois becs de gaz allumés*
> *La patronne est poitrinaire*
> *Quand tu auras fini nous jouerons une partie*
> *   de jacquet*
> *Un chef d'orchestre qui a mal à la gorge*
> *Quand tu viendras à Tunis je te ferai fumer du kief*
> *Ça a l'air de rimer*
>
> *("Lundi Rue Christine.")*

> Three lit gas jets
> The proprietor has lung trouble
> When you've finished we'll have a game of
>   backgammon
> A conductor who has a sore throat
> When you come to Tunis I'll have you smoke
>   some kiff
> It seems to rhyme

An utterly random sequence of experiences while sitting in a café could set Apollinaire's sensibilities in motion. Instead of imposing logical order, he retains the raw lump of thought halfway between daydream and casual conversation. Edouard Dujardin's gropings in the direction of interior monologue (in the novel *Les lauriers sont coupés*, 1887) are contrived and unconvincing in comparison. A forceful modern style of juxtaposition broke out like a rash around 1910 in the writings of unanimists and futurists, and of simultanists like Apollinaire, Cendrars, and Reverdy. They recorded the world in the still-scrambled order of sensation, and the style soon affected the work of Ezra Pound, Wyndham Lewis, Virginia Woolf, James Joyce, and Valery Larbaud. All of them knew prewar Paris intimately and drew in part from that source a form of fictional or poetic montage. Hemingway, when he put the little "chapters" between the short stories of *In Our Time*, was not inserting transitions but creating intervals. The stories had to have space to swing free and seek their separate postures. However, to construe the style of juxtaposition as something more than a collapse of man's capacity to create lasting forms will require closer examination of each of the arts.

Juxtaposition in literature has few clear precedents in the three centuries preceding 1885.* Yet one of them is of particular relevance in the present context. The English "nonsense" writers of the eighteenth century, Christopher Smart and Laurence Sterne, exploited a humorous and apparently rambling style which relied to a great extent on juxtaposition of incongruities. Their only true progeny, Edward Lear and Lewis Carroll, long remained on the sidelines of literature. Today, after the second looks of several critics culminating in the work of Elizabeth Sewell, we know better where to place them. In *The Field of Nonsense* Dr. Sewell distinguishes between the universe of poetry and dream, which experiences so vast a pattern of relations between objects that we run the risk of losing all sense of order, and the universe of nonsense, which systematically defends order by seeking absolute control over its objects through use of number and of words in isolation, without the interpenetration of kindred meaning. Nonsense consists in a game played with rigidly distinct counters *against* the

* No history of literature begins to examine the question with the perceptiveness of Sergei Eisenstein in his writings on film. He discusses Leonardo da Vinci, Milton, El Greco, the Chinese ideogram, Japanese Kabuki theater, Dickens, and jazz with an insight derived in part from the nature of the medium he worked in. Having no subordinate conjunctions and no punctuation except the retarded timing of the fade and the mix, film *is* organically juxtaposition, and Eisenstein set out boldly in search of its heritage and its true identity.

forces of dream, association, and disorder. "The Non-sense universe must be the sum of its parts and nothing more. There must be no fusion and synthesis, no calling in of the dream faculty to lend to the whole so formed new significance beyond the grasp of logic." The distinction is important, for artists like Jarry or Klee produced works which cross and recross the fine line between highly suggestive dream sequence and utterly cool, playful nonsense. Why this alternation, which is often imperceptible and tantalizing? Because it represents a desire both to respond to the voice from within—subconscious, memory, race consciousness, et cetera—and to dominate our mental products, to assert supreme control *as creators* over the small part of the world which falls within our reach. It is the ambition of much modern art to be active *and* passive. The former tendency at its extreme point may reach the purely logical, confined, and comically fussy arrangements of non-sense; the latter opens itself to the vivid, all-encompassing, and eloquent associations of dream. As spectators of painting or readers of poetry we become lost principally when we no longer know what universe surrounds us—that of atomistic order or that of the unity of all things.

Any provisional line in literature dividing the new style of juxtaposition (which may deliberately produce both these effects) from the old style of transition must be drawn after Mallarmé (d. 1898), who has too often been mislabeled a "cubist" poet. He remains symbolist through his avoidance of direct statement, and classic through the structure of his writings. *Un coup de dés* is the ultimate instance of classic style. One enormously complex and comprehensive sentence, syntactically correct and explicit in its conjunctions, accumulates meaning to the verge of dissolution. Yet it perilously sustains its discursive unity, even though obscure and distended. The poem's typographical arrangement depicts levels of meaning and reference, and demonstrates its reasonableness and coherence. The impression of Mallarmé as a cubist author—as creating a new disjointed reality of juxtaposed elements—results from incomplete comprehension. When we cannot succeed in assembling the parts, we accept striking bits of disconnected discourse as the true poem. Misread, Mallarmé seems a "modernist" who gathered impressions in random sequence on the page. It is highly possible that the cubists and even Apollinaire deliberately misread him in this fashion, for his obcurity then became suggestive of their methods. But Mallarmé, like Yeats, never lost touch with discursive thought, with the unity of a sentence. His importance to art is that his works attenuate their subject through meticulous analysis to a point where the medium almost obliterates the subject. Almost. Mallarmé's work comes close to violating our normal powers of thinking; it does not, however, advance beyond the last frontier of reason. Juxtaposition in modern literature began where Mallarmé stopped. He reached a point from which any advance must abandon the possibility of *meaning* in the classical sense.

There is no one in music to fill a comparable role. The long transitional passages which fill compositions of the previous three centuries rapidly disappear after Satie and Debussy and *les Six*. (The audacities of Beethoven's last quartets dispensed with transition, but it was sixty years before they received proper recognition.) Atonal music removes the very conventions by which our ears have been trained to hear harmonic transition, and composers work increasingly with small, mosaic-like pieces which keep their distinctness. Like films, modern music often links two passages not so that one leads easily into the other, but so that we feel their conflict.

When Renaissance painting developed its miraculous representation of space, the objects portrayed tended to become segments of space more than individual entities. Their outlines were forever foreshortened and shadowed and modeled so as to lead the eye away to other volumes in space. In contrast, what characterizes modern painting more than heavy outline? It insists on the detachment of an object from its surroundings. Rousseau and Léger and Rouault are not concerned about what is in front and what behind. The spectator can interpolate his own orientation. The important thing is that each object—even each facet and feature of the object—should occupy its separate space. The carefully etched planes of Mondrian after 1910, with their suggestion of visual puzzles, and the multiple images of futurism—these, too, employ methods of juxtaposition. The great overcrowded shows of the Indépendants from 1885 to 1914 introduced a total change in the vision and structure of painting.

Though it is difficult to follow the course of the formal revolution that took place early in this century, the technique of juxtaposition soon showed two distinct tendencies. It is possible that this distinction may become more meaningful for the twentieth century than the categories of classic and romantic. One can, in the first place, juxtapose heterogeneous elements and produce an explosive, exciting texture in which connectives are actively missed. We are surrounded with conflict and contrast and cannot expect to reach a point of rest or understanding in the conventional sense. In 1913 Cendrars wrote a poem appropriately entitled "Contrast."

> *Il pleut les globes électriques*
> *Montrouge Gare de l'Est Métro Nord-Sud*
>   *bateauxmouche monde*
> *Tout est halo*
> *Profondeur*
> *Rue de Buci on crie* l'Intransigeant *et* Paris-Sports
> *L'aérodrome du ciel est maintenant embrasé,*
>   *un tableau de Cimabue*

>   (*Dix-neuf poèmes élastiques.*)

> It's raining electric light bulbs
> Montrouge Gare de l'Est subway North-South
>   river boats world
> Everything is halo
> Profundity
> In the Rue de Buci they're hawking *l'Intransigeant*
>   and *Paris-Sports*
> The airdrome of the sky is on fire, a painting
>   by Cimabue

Heterogeneous elements juxtaposed produce an art that replaces the romantic tradition. It arouses the emotions, asserts the personality of the artist, and tends to demonstrate its feelings in unconventional typography, instrumentation, and surface texture.

The classical strain of juxtaposition combines homogeneous elements to produce a far different effect.

> However, the life of an honest man must be an apostasy and a perpetual desertion, an honest man must be a perpetual deserter, the life of an honest man must be perpetual unfaithfulness. For the man

who wishes to remain faithful to truth must make himself constantly unfaithful to all constant, successive, indefatigable, renascent errors. And the man who wishes to remain faithful to justice must make himself constantly unfaithful to inexhaustibly triumphant injustice.

(*Cahiers de la quinzaine*, VIII, 3.)

Péguy's exhortation assumes the rhythm of a litany. Here the stress is not on the opposition of parts, but upon their near identity. Yet the illusion of smoothness and rhetorical progression rapidly disintegrates. By their very repetitiveness the parts establish their independence like the blows of a hammer on an anvil. Style here becomes circularity, a distortion of linear development and direction in the traditional sense: *an absence of style*. This kind of juxtaposition developed later than the first, most prominently in the "a rose is a rose is a rose" manner of Gertrude Stein. Some years later, in one of his most brilliant pieces of criticism, Sartre analyzed this modern form of classicism in commenting on the "white" style of Camus' first novel, *L'étranger*. Sartre perceives that it represents a conception of reality.

But what is the postulate implied by this kind of narrative? It amounts to this, that out of what used to be melodic organization has been made a simple addition of invariable elements; the succession of mere *movements* is asserted as rigorously identical with the act in its totality. Are we not dealing here with an analytical postulate which maintains that every reality is reducible to a sum of elements? But, if analysis is an instrument of science, it is also the instrument of humor. . . . Mr. Camus' narrative is analytic and tends toward the humorous. He lies like every good artist—because he wishes to record experience in the raw, because he slyly filters out all significant connectives, which also belong to experience. (*Situations I.*)

Sartre goes on to discover this absurd sense of life-without-links in "the discontinuousness of his chopped-up sentences." What he states about the latent humor of Camus' style is something often recognized in Kafka and Gertrude

Stein, perhaps, but long overlooked in Hemingway and in the terse style of detective fiction.

The *absurd*, expressed by a lack of connectives in experiencing the world, clearly intersects *nonsense*, expressed by a very few precise relationships (numbers, for instance, or chess moves, or gravitation) grafted onto totally disparate objects. Alice has just told Humpty Dumpty her age:

> "Seven years and six months!" Humpty Dumpty repeated thoughtfully. "An uncomfortable sort of age. Now if you'd asked *my* advice, I'd have said, 'Leave off at seven'—but it's too late now."
>
> . . . she said, "One can't help growing older."
>
> "One can't perhaps," said Humpty Dumpty, "but *two* can. With proper assistance, you might have left off at seven."

Or the end of *The Twelve Days of Christmas:*

> Five gold rings,
> Four colley birds,
> Three French hens,
> Two turtle doves, and
> A partridge in a pear tree.

The formal techniques of juxtaposition, with the components of play, nonsense, and the absurd, provide the most apt vehicle for the mood and content of the arts in the Banquet Years. The child-man who travels in a world of incipient humor, dreams, and multiple meanings, must so dispose the elements of his mind that they represent both his reason and his unreason.

Inevitably the two categories of juxtaposition entail a set of characteristics often criticized in modern art—obscurity, illogicality, inept style, abruptness. "Abruptness," in fact, means, precisely, lack of transition. Apollinaire dubbed it *surprise* and singled it out as one of the fundamental traits of our era. The idea of art which was erected by classic theater and classic architecture included no central role for suddenness, for abruptness. In the old tradition the spectator knows in essence what must happen, and while the action unfolds we experience not surprise but verification of certain general truths. The peripety is fated from the start. Thus, any important event occurs, in effect, twice —and this analysis can be applied to Greek tragedy, to the early French novel, and to baroque architecture. The classic art of anticipation and verification is by no means expiring, but beside it has grown up a different scheme of things. In developing a new form, art lost its calm, something that has happened to an entire way of life. Every symphony became a surprise symphony. We can no longer expect to find in the arts only verification of knowledge or values deeply rooted within us. We will, instead, be surprised or dismayed.

Abruptness, the rawness of art, seen from a slightly different standpoint, reveals the extent to which we accept as finished, works that by former standards are blatantly unfinished. The modern school since Cézanne does not hesitate to leave bare patches of canvas in a completed signed painting. Satie and Auric cut short their amusing compositions without coda or cadence. The dominant trait of the prewar poems of Reverdy and Salmon and Apollinaire has been described as "negligence." To "finish" in the sense of removing all traces of sketch and struggle and uncertainty became the surest way of destroying the authenticity of their work. Malraux wrote discerningly of the fragmentary nature of all old art: ". . . always amputated, and, first of all, from its time." Modern art, possibly because it has become profoundly aware of the nature of our artistic heritage, has anticipated the action of time. In refusing to finish and polish their work, artists have produced fragments at the start. For completion they demand the spectator's active collaboration in pursuing developments and associations that have been barely suggested. The artist's process of creation stops at the stage of the sketch.

The freshness of the sketch, however, has a deeper significance than that of requiring someone else's participation to complete a work. The good artist is not lazy, but he understands that by luring the spectator into his work he has discovered a new attribute in the very structure of his art. He exploits an *intimacy of form*—one is attracted and not kept at a distance by the formal qualities of a poem or painting. In the theater, for example, the modern tendency has been to break down the separation not only between audience and actors, but also between on stage and backstage. The entire production partakes of the excitement, the undressed candidness of backstage. Things have reached the point where we watch all art not from "out front"—where proscenium and sets allow us to see only what we are meant to see—but from the wings, where we can keep our eyes on everything. We miss, it is true, the final dramatic effect of the tableau as it appears only to the spectator seated in the auditorium. Instead, we enjoy an intimate look into the alluring world where art and reality mingle among painted props, sweaty costumes, and muffed lines.*

Satie's *musique de placard* is the extreme form of musical intimacy. The casualness of structure in all postsymbolist poetry of unanimists, cubists, futurists, and the like amounts to free admission to a literary backstage. The oblique vision of Jacob or Prévert is explained by the fact that they never present the world to us in a composed fullface portrait. Their lack of formal arrangement is the basis of their candidness.

At last an answer begins to emerge to the question of why the seemingly rough and arbitrary technique of juxtaposition has shaped so many modern works, why it is art at all. The intimacy of the voyeur relationship to art, watching it from the wings, represents a yearning to be in touch with the subconscious world which produced it. This candidness is turned inward. Interest in the inaccessible resources of the human mind induced the arts to model themselves less and less on the rational polite disciplines of the past. They sought what Sergei Eisenstein called "inner speech." Subconscious thought processes—dream and memory and wit—function by sudden leaps the way a spark jumps a gap. The arts have sought to duplicate these inner creative processes, to portray them without putting them through rigorous realignments of dramatic development, linear perspective, or tonality. Self-reflexiveness aims a work of art at itself, at its own development, as both subject and form. Juxtaposition, with its surprises and intimacy of form, brings the spectator closer than ever before to the abruptness of creative process. The film, for example, an art of pure juxtaposition, conveys the restlessness of the

---

* The ultimate demonstration of the backstage tradition is not so much the dramatic efforts which connect Pirandello with Thornton Wilder, but the weekly matinee performance at the Folies-Bergère, which is staged from beginning to end with the curtain up.

mind in action. Bergson felt this dynamic so deeply that he sounds as if he were writing about film, or cubism.

> Now the image has at least this advantage, that it keeps us in the concrete. No image can replace the intuition of duration, but many diverse images, borrowed from very different orders of things, may, by the convergence of their action, direct the consciousness to the precise point where there is a certain intuition to be seized. By choosing images as dissimilar as possible, we shall prevent any one of them from usurping the place of the intuition it is intended to call up. . . . (*Introduction to Metaphysics.*)

A great diversity employed to suggest and delimit a point in another dimension aptly describes juxtaposition.

In the end it comes to this. Till the end of the nineteenth century it was the transitions in a work of art to which the artist confided his running commentary on the materials he assembled. His *buts* and *becauses* and *althoughs* contained the evaluation made by his subjective sensibility regarding and arranging objective content. Think of Madame de Lafayette or Henry James,* of Handel or Poussin or David. With transition dropped altogether, postromantic works at first manifested a certain remoteness, and imperviousness, as if the artist's sensibility had disintegrated. The *I* that could guide us through these strange passages seems missing until one perceives that the discontinuous fragments are *all I* —purely subjective. Is it true, then, that Jarry and Chirico and their ilk are indulging in pure narcissistic nonsense? In the jacket copy of the play *Him,* e. e. cummings answers for them all.

---

* Witness these two sentences in which Henry James is present and at work in every measured connective and adverb. "He thought of those fellows from whom he was so to differ, in English; he used, mentally, the English term to describe his difference, for, familiar with the tongue from his earliest years, so that no note of strangeness remained with him either for lip or ear, he found it convenient, in life, for the greatest number of relations. He found it convenient, oddly, even for his relations with himself—though not unmindful that there might still, as time went on, be others, including a more intimate degree of *that* one, that would seek, possibly with violence, the larger or finer issue—which was it?—of the vernacular." (*The Golden Bowl.*)

Public: So far as I'm concerned, my very dear sir, nonsense isn't everything in life.

Author: And so far as you're concerned "life" is a verb of two voices—active, to do, and passive, to dream. Others believe doing to be only a kind of dreaming. Still others have discovered (in a mirror surrounded with mirrors), something harder than silence but softer than falling; the third voice of "life," which believes itself and cannot mean because it is.

Public: Bravo, but are such persons good for anything in particular?

Author: They are good for nothing but walking upright in the cordial revelation of the fatal reflexive.

The subjective-objective distinction breaks down into a single category of self-reflexiveness, the consciousness reporting objectively upon itself. Works uttered by this active-passive third voice of life are not representations, but in Coleridge's words, "self-representative," not romantically self-forgetful but self-remembering. In deceptively objective terms they describe a purely subjective world.

The final result of the arts of juxtaposition has already been suggested. Juxtaposition, through its fusion of subject and object, achieves not so much a new style, as an absence of style in the old sense of expressed transitions. One of its most successful manifestations has been "functional" architecture, which allows all parts to show in a building almost as if they constituted its subconscious. Any form of decoration, transition, or arbitrarily imposed symmetry would begin to hide those parts or functions. In other arts the discontinuous jumpy nature of the mind's functioning has been similarly exposed. The logically biased intelligence was prevented from tampering with it to impose a style.

If, instead of perpetuating a stylistic tradition, certain artists began after 1885 to "unmake" their art as they went along in order to investigate their own consciousness, then we have finally come full circle. The obscurity and surprise, the disjunct, importunate nature of their art, which appear at first to indicate a high degree of sophistication, in reality establish its primitiveness. What, in the end, did they find in their return to fundamentals, to the "natural" behaviors of consciousness? They found what has been known in every age but never well enough, and what the romantics had been the last to rediscover: that man is forever vacillating between passive inactivity (the extinction of consciousness in habit) and insatiable restlessness (dissatisfaction with all his accomplishments; spiritual, moral, and intellectual yearnings exceeding his capacities). Few men ever attain the equilibrium necessary to live fully with what they have. The romantics, while exploiting it, were still wary of this profound unsteadiness in us, and even as they preached liberation of the natural man they covertly acknowledge that something dangerous lurks within. The Banquet Years moved away from the "decadent" preoccupation with vice and unnaturalness which haunted the close of the nineteenth century from Baudelaire to Remy de Gourmont to D'Annunzio. Only Henri Rousseau, that sophisticate, had the capacity to be satisfied with his lot. Satie and Apollinaire and Jarry affirmed that wisdom and virtue lie in man's apprehension of his own "primitive" characteristics—his capacity for boredom and his overweening aspirations to achieve new being, new status. Man is, by nature, an unnatural animal, and it requires a suitably primitive art not to distort this nature, but to reveal it.

Whatever the virtues and vices, whatever the value may be of dream logic and abruptness and humor, a significant segment of the modern arts has been constructed by juxtaposition of mutually reacting units. They do not observe smooth transition through unified development. Conflict, as opposed to connection, produced a different strain of expression. The most lasting monuments of man, the pyramids, were raised as demonstrations of absolute unbroken mass. The Egyptians were the first men to dress stone so clean it fitted together without crack or fault. The past hundred years have attained a contrasting and less imposing goal—an art composed in the rough on the principle of interval and tension between parts. Painters, writers, and musicians learned how to arrange fragments of experience, how to "cut" in montage style, how to vivisect consciousness in order to reconstruct our "inner speech." Made not for our gods nor even for posterity, our works do not achieve the simple stablity of monuments. We have created for ourselves a complex art, perishable perhaps, of self-awareness.

The term juxtaposition, which has served till now, finally breaks down. The "nextness" which it connotes reveals itself as an inaccurate description of the structure of the arts. Juxtaposition implies succession, even if it is at random or provoked by conflict. Exactly here one can go astray. Had the montage form of art been concerned with a real succession of events, transitions would have been included rather than suppressed, for transitions supply the guided tour, an order of events. But since instead of transition we have contrast and conflict, the successive nature of these compositions cannot sustain itself. Ultimately it becomes apparent that the mutually conflicting elements of montage—be it movie or poem or painting—are to be conceived not successively but *simultaneously*, to converge in our minds as contemporaneous events. The conflict between them prevents us from fitting them smoothly end to end; what appeared an arbitrary juxtaposition of parts can now take its true shape of enforced *superposition*. The diversity of Apollinaire's "calligrams," the associations of *Le rêve* by Rousseau, and the assortments of Satie's ballets should reach us as *co-incidence*. The aspiration of simultanism is to grasp the moment in its total significance or, more ambitiously, to manufacture a moment which surpasses our usual perception of time and space.

The history of the attitude that produced simultanism reaches as far back as human consciousness. Most religious experience expresses it. Yet having been twice pushed out of the central tradition of Western art, first by the Greeks and then by the Renaissance, it has been given recognition only under the restricted heading of unitive knowledge. The sensibilities of mystics, visionaries, occultists, and poetic dreamers have often achieved a vision of the universe which remained ineffable in terms of traditional composition—a play, a formal portrait, a fugue. In protest, the eighteenth and nineteenth centuries began, first gingerly, then more boldly, to test the limits of art. After the turn of the twentieth century, the futurists were among the first to lay claim to simultanism as a technique available to all. They confined its application to objects in motion— trains, cyclists, runners, et cetera. A natural succession of events was telescoped into an overlay. A larger application of simultanism, as it was envisioned by Apollinaire, Barzun, Cendrars, Romains, Delaunay, and the cubist painters, did not restrict itself in subject, place, or time. Any event that impinged on their consciousness was artistically valid. Simultanism soon reached the point of assuming a significant relation between all coincidental happenings, objective and subjective, even when the relation was not immediately clear. Such is the premise of James Joyce's stream of consciousness style in *Ulysses*.

Simultanism, the general heading under which we can place a large segment of modern art, establishes other sources of meaning than causal sequence. It reaches a position comparable to that of Chinese *I Ching*. This Oriental discipline interprets the present through the fall of yarrow sticks, a hazard that reveals the essential state of the universe at any single moment. Stars, cards, tea leaves —such readings are based on a similar "chance," which implicates all things. The American edition of *I Ching* contains a preface by Jung in which he touches on several crucial ideas.

> . . . the hexagram [formed by a throw of the yarrow sticks] was understood to be an indication of the essential situation prevailing at its moment of origin.
>
> This assumption involves a certain curious principle that I have termed synchronicity, a concept that formulates a point of view diametrically opposed to that of causality. Since the latter is merely a statistical truth and not absolute, it is a sort of working hypothesis of how events in space and time evolve out of one another, whereas synchronicity takes the coincidence of events in space and time as meaning something more than mere chance, namely a peculiar interdependence of objective events among themselves as with the subjective (psychic) states of the observer or observers.

Simultanism in the arts, like Jung's synchronicity, seizes upon what is, for our culture, a new kind of coherence, a

new unity of experience.* The Aristotelian dicta on beginning, middle, and end, on singleness of place and time and
character, cannot apply to works that seek neither the
balance of classic architecture nor the schematic psychology of classic theater. Like the portraitist who can begin
his sketch with the necktie and end with the pupil of the
eye, or vice versa, artists have claimed a freedom to begin
anywhere and end anywhere. Without causal progression,
everything is middle. All things in that universal middle
exist in the rudimentary order (apparent disorder) of conflict, an order we conceive only when we experience its
parts as simultaneous. Unity becomes not progression but
intensification by standing still, a continuous present in
which everything is taken together and always. Memory
and attention, the two prime faculties of human consciousness, can be trained to conceive unitively in simultaneous
occurrence as well as historically in chronological unfold-
ing. Only certain natural happenings in the world sustain
our thinking in historical terms. Henri Focillon observes:

> The historian of a world that was perpetually flooded
> with steady light, a world without day or night,
> month or season, would be able to describe only
> a more or less complete present.
> (*La vie des formes dans l'art*.)

It is out of this world that Rousseau created "the time of
abstract art," that Satie heard the almost motionless pulse
of *Socrate*, and that Jarry wrote *Les jours et les nuits*. In
that novel, which first appears to stress the succession of
events, we gradually become aware of the simultaneous
incidence in the hero of sleeping and waking—the source
of the visionary tone of the book.

Another version of the continuous present occurs in some
of the works of Gertrude Stein, works that absorbed much
of the feeling of the Banquet Years through her residence
in Paris after 1904. An infinitely long series of details constantly turns back upon itself, an illusion of movement in
stillness. Her works have neither beginning nor end, only

* Two significant texts will help elucidate the nature and
history of this state of mind in the arts: Paul Valéry's forgotten
article inspired by Wells and Jarry, "*Méthodes*," *Mercure, mai*
1899; and Joseph Frank's "Spatial Form in Modern Literature,"
The Sewanee Review, Spring, Summer, and Autumn, 1945.

duration of feeling and incident. Her poems and narratives do not progress from one point to another, but establish themselves deeper and deeper in a perpetual mode of existence.° In his book on Gertrude Stein, Donald Sutherland distinguishes between what he calls the prolonged and the continuous present.

> The difference between a prolonged and a continuous present may be defined as this, that a prolonged present assumes a situation or a theme and dwells on it and develops it or keeps it recurring, as in much opera, and Bach for example. The continuous present would take each successive moment or passage as a completely new thing essentially, as with Mozart or Scarlatti, or, later, Satie.

The passage closely parallels Sartre's description of Camus' style. Yet in the case of both Stein and Satie the "completely new thing" is only an appearance; both artists practice a juxtaposition of homogeneous, nearly identical parts. This is the structure that produces the effect of monotony and reiteration in their works, movement without advance. Unity of action, considered in the light of the continuous present, changes its aspect from a progress in time to a fixed posture of deepening awareness and "spiritual exercise."

The juxtaposition of heterogeneous elements, the art of violent dislocation, affects us slightly differently. We are thrown back upon a desperate effort of assimilation—the basic feat of simultanism. In the confined art of Stein and Satie we must hold in our minds a number of parts so nearly identical as to escape our attention by being indistinguishable. In the carefully detonated art of Apollinaire and of cubist collages, we must bring together parts so divergent from one another as to exceed the span of our attention. In both cases a technique of juxtaposition—or, more accurately, superposition—forces us to experience the world as simultaneous and continually present. Since the

---

° The suppressed conjunctions, haunting use of the imperfect, and deliberately flat style of Flaubert sets the clearest precedent here. Flaubert was also fully aware of the dramatic-ironic effects of juxtaposing conflicting elements. All the crucial scenes of *Madame Bovary* are constructed as a montage of two contrasting actions.

end of the last century, the arts have dared approach the pace of life in no longer relying on the classic *modus vivendi* of one-thing-at-a-time (except as it culminates in the tidily atomized realm of nonsense). Simultanism and all the related isms of the Banquet Years carried the arts into the realm of all-at-once.

The logic of simultanism, however, if it has a logic, does not discreetly tend toward a Hegelian resolution of opposites. It requires that our minds entertain concurrently and without synthesis two or more contradictory propositions. (In this system more than two are possible.) Jarry's 'Pataphysics rests on the truth of contradictions and exceptions. In the paintings of Delaunay's *Les fenêtres* series we are simultaneously indoors and out of doors, inside an object and on all sides of it. Satie is simultaneously spoofing and in earnest. There is no compromise: truth, *logical* truth in the works of art that have been considered here, consists in the conjunct occurrence of contradictions— namely, absurdity. In the way it confounds conventional thought processes, has not this "logic" steered a parallel course to relativistic physical science which has had to describe the universe in such poetic metaphors as "light-years," "bent" space, absolute negative temperatures, and "audible" radio stars?

Simultanism evolved as both a logic (or an a-logic) and an artistic technique. It found a childlike directness of expression free of any conventional order. It reproduced the compression and condensation of mental processes. It maintained an immediacy of relationship between conscious and subconscious thought. It encompassed surprise, humor, ambiguity, and the unfettered associations of dream. Cohering without transition, it gave the illusion of great speed though always standing still. Speed represented its potential inclusiveness, its freedom from taboos of logic and polite style. Stillness represented its unity, its continuous present, its sole permanence.

Simultanism did not mean, however, an utterly literal recording of every impression that reaches the consciousness. That came later, in the surrealist practice of automatic writing and painting. The style of Apollinaire and Cendrars differs from that of Breton and Desnos precisely in that it remained controlled and could be revised and tightened, thus avoiding the intermittent quality of automatic writing.

Whereas automatic writing strove to divulge the subconscious mind by grasping everything that approaches its surface, simultanism strove to reveal the entire universe in its potential unity at a moment of time. In the latter case the pristine subjective order was not kept as an inviolable absolute. Simultanism registered as great a portion of the universe as possible by extending consciousness itself. Baudelaire, entranced by a seascape, wrote: "What a delight to drown one's gaze in the immensity of the sky and sea . . . all those things think through me, or I think through them (for in the vastness of revery, the I quickly loses itself) . . . ." It is one of Baudelaire's most lucid moments, a purely self-reflexive perception. Henri Michaux, a poet writing eighty years later, disciplines himself to abdicate his personality and attains the same reversal of consciousness, the same simultaneous attunement: "One no longer dreams. One is dreamed." Between these two statements lie the works of art that embody the deepest yearnings of the early years of this century.

There is a final word to be said about the art that has been depicted in this chapter as one not of progression, but of position, of fixity. Before our era, have come the great styles of progression. The linear, purposeful nature of Egyptian art expressed the inexorable march toward death of a people obsessed by the idea of life after death. The movement of classic Greek tragedy related the fulfillment of a human destiny, of a fate as inexorable as Egyptian death. The aspirations of Gothic architecture rose in irrepressible arches and spires toward heaven. Renaissance style in architecture and painting grew to magnificence in response to the swelling temporal power of individual and state.

In contrast to these ambitious arts of progress and development, the paintings, poems, and compositions of the Banquet Years turn back upon themselves and lie quiet. They imply that by being sufficiently still, by becoming for an instant exactly identical with ourselves, nothing more nor less, we can allow the universe to move around us. This is the meaning in art of relativity. An object in motion has difficulty taking into account other motions. Only by achieving rest, *arrest*, can we perceive what is happening outside ourselves. Simultanism, the third voice of life, signifies an approach to immobility and thus an extremely sensitive attunement to the infinite universe. Baudelaire, Bergson, and cummings are all describing this state. Arrest is achieved not by absence of power to move, but by an equilibrium of forces, whence the dynamic nature of works we call modern. The paradox is that even arrest has no final peace, for it continues to be relative motion; nothing can attain absolute stillness in our physical and spiritual system. Yet this remains the goal of the dynamic upheaval in the arts during the Banquet Years.

In 1899, with his customary blend of absurdity and conviction, Jarry composed his *Commentaire* telling how to construct a time machine in your cellar. The principle he puts forward is that in order to obtain freedom of travel in time, one must establish absolute immobility in space.

> We move with Time and at the same speed, being ourselves part of the present. If we could remain immobile in absolute space, through the course of time, that is if we could suddenly enclose ourselves in a Machine which isolates us from time . . . all future and past moments . . . would be successively explored, the way the sedentary spectator of a moving panorama has the illusion of a rapid voyage through successive landscapes.

In order to construct such a totally rigid machine, Jarry proposes a frame equipped with three mighty gyroscopes, which would isolate the occupant from (or in) normal space and therefore from the normal advance of time. He describes the gyroscopic device with specific details and mathematical formulas.* He was thinking, obviously, of the bicycle on which he traveled every day.

Since Jarry many minds have understood the aptness of the gyroscope to represent the elusive *form* of art in the twentieth century. Like a gyroscope, it sustains itself by a concentration of forces in self-reflexiveness, art turning upon itself. This inwardness reveals itself in a posture of total arrest—the juxtaposition of parts around a moment of profound awareness. Through all the whirl of contradiction

---

* "Lobatchewski" *(sic)*, W. Thomson (the future Lord Kelvin in an abstruse and significant article on the composition of the ether), Aristotle, and Dr. Faustroll are the authorities cited. All this dazzling hypothesis precedes the special theory of relativity by nearly a decade.

and dream and nonsense we can reach the still center, and from there we can behold the world at once and for all time as revolving around us and as indistinguishable from us. One of the most awesome statements of this heightened condition of mind came from an artist whose categorical and embittered condemnation of modern art could not prevent him from belonging to our era. Ten months before his death, ailing and distraught by domestic conflicts, Leo Tolstoi wrote thus in his journal, as if his eyes had just opened to perceive reality.

> I have keenly experienced consciousness of myself today, at 81 years, exactly as I was conscious of myself at 5 or 6 years. Consciousness is motionless. And it is only because of its motionlessness that we are able to see the motion of that which we call time. If time passes, it is necessary that there should be something which remains static. And it is consciousness of self which is static.
>
> (January 15, 1910)

The art and the science of the twentieth century have not yet shown any signs of being able to surpass the state of human consciousness here expressed. Contrary to all expectation, this century may one day be known as the age of stillness, of arrest.

THE LAST BANQUET

When the *avant-guerre* ended in 1914 with the first hostilities in Europe for almost half a century, the cultural
capital of that prosperous world seemed a different place
from what it had been in 1885. It was not merely that
Paris was being equipped with electric lights, telephones,
motorbuses, taxis, and elevators. It was not merely that the
American bar, the English tearoom, and the international
music hall had established themselves for good. Fashionable society, seeming to sense that things would never be
the same again, galloped through these last years in a
paroxysm of activity. It is best represented by the dazzling
figure of Boni de Castellane, an indigent marquis who married the American heiress Anna Gould. Their Pink Palace
on the Avenue du Bois, their sumptuous parties in the Bois
itself, and his injection of taste and refinement into the
most extreme luxury made him the hero of an expiring
way of life. His memoirs chronicle the close of an era.

At the opposite end of the disintegrating social order one
comes upon a new domain, not of elegance but of the
sporty proletarian truculence spawned by the avant-garde.
The aristocratic prestige of the arts, embodied in Robert de
Montesquiou's dandified behavior in the nineties, could
no longer resist the onslaught of a figure like Arthur
Cravan. This robust, trilingual nephew of Oscar Wilde was
a professional boxer, traveling to title bouts all over
Europe until he switched to literature in 1911 at the age of
thirty and made his mark in Paris. He published a one-

man magazine called *Maintenant,* which he peddled from
a wheelbarrow around sports arenas and subway en-
trances. Handsome, unpredictable, photographed more
often in tights than fully clothed, Cravan had an ebullience
that carried him into belligerent defiance of convention.
In its systematic provocation, his writing resembles a
literary transposition of boxing techniques. He baited Apollinaire into challenging him to a duel, insultingly interviewed Gide, overturned every idol in his path, and fled
conscription during the war to Madrid where, reeling
drunk, he faced former world champion Jack Johnson in
the ring. After the knockout (to satisfy the contract, Johnson waited three rounds, whereupon Cravan virtually lay
down all by himself), he came to America on a so-called
lecture tour. At his most legendary performance, he began
wildly undressing during a talk in the Grand Central Galleries, until the police handcuffed him. He stayed on, first
in the United States, then in Mexico, in the classic roles of
physical instructor, chauffeur, private secretary, and permanent house guest. Like Hart Crane a decade later, he
probably drowned in the Gulf of Mexico.

The Banquet Years had achieved this casual absurdity;
Paris could no longer keep her offspring at home. Yet it
was Paris that bred them, and part of the spell that lies
over the whole period arises out of the character of the
city itself. *La belle époque,* the long entertainment the
city staged for itself in its own streets at a time when the
structure of society was gradually capsizing, remains one
of the supreme expressions of that city's sense of time.
Every city lives differently with its past and its future and
inflicts its mood on residents and visitors alike. Paris treats
its history lightly. One of the oldest cities in Western
Europe, it is never deeply concerned with its past. Citizens
take scant notice of their monuments and are not, like
Venetians or Londoners, eager to enlighten a tourist. They
know the streets are old and the buildings steeped in
momentous events. But streets and buildings are also still
used and find their character as they stand today. Neglect-
ful of its past, the city nevertheless resists change. The
skyline is sacred, and any new construction on a large
scale enrages an entire quarter. There will be no second
Haussmann; catastrophe will come first. New store fronts

and improved traffic routing are only sops to an endlessly pricked sense of progress. But if you lift your eyes above street level, Paris remains the same. The city has not been seduced by the future.*

It is the present Paris inhabits. Halfway between the old world and the new, it lives happily unto itself and seeks neither to advance nor to retreat. The city sustains itself in the moment, not a fleeting, but an everlasting moment, and when its pulse one day flags, the city will come to rest where it stands in time. *Le vieux Paris* is in essence not a place but a point of view shared by antique dealers, photographers, and tourists. Parisians simply live there. The "school of Paris," a fine-sounding phrase for a legion of artists since the middle of the eighteenth century, is meaningless except in this sense of self-sufficiency in time, aliveness to the present, which is the secret charm of Paris. The worker clad in blue denim who sweeps the streets with Seine water and a faggot broom is neither a stage prop for Americans nor a disgruntled municipal employee agitating for shorter hours and mechanized equipment. In every quarter he belongs. All Paris lives in a time it sets for itself.

This sense of the present is peculiar to no single epoch of the city's history. The Banquet Years, however, lived it to the utmost. It is the medium that supported the theatricality of *la belle époque* and the scandals of the avant-garde. Having been so complete an expression of the spirit of Paris, the era rapidly became one of the most attractive embodiments of its past. Fashion, the expression far more of a sense of the past than of a departure into the future, will never cease making excursions back to the turn of the century. A few American expatriates after World War I sensed that they had just missed the real thing. In his introduction to one of the oldest books the twenties produced, *This Must Be the Place* by Jimmie the Barman (of Le Dingo bar), Ernest Hemingway sounds rueful. "Like everyone else in the Montparnasse the most interesting

---

* Ten years later, these statements are open to serious challenge. New building has begun to modify the skyline; the automobile has occupied the city like an invading army. However, I cannot bring myself to rewrite the words which belong to the original text and to the original inspiration of this book.

part of his [Jimmie's] life was before he crossed to the left bank of the Seine, but, like most everyone else there, he did not realize that."

At bottom the only general change after the crossing of the Seine and after the war was that people slowly began to sense that something had happened in the past thirty years. The new review *Littérature* conducted a well-remembered symposium in 1919 on the subject: *Why do you write?*° The question caught every writer, without exception, trying to be wittily destructive of his profession.

RACHILDE: Because I like silence.

JACOB: In order to write better.

GIDE: You will be able to classify writers occording to whether their answers begin with "in order to," "out of," or "because."

There will be those for whom literature is above all an end, and those for whom it is principally a means.

In my case I write because I have an excellent pen and in order to be read by you. . . . But I never contribute to symposia.

VALERY: Out of weakness.

PAULHAN: I am touched that you should want my reasons, but after all I write very little. Your reproach scarcely touches me.

JAMMES : I write because, when I write, I don't do anything else.

COPEAU: I have very little time to write. That's why I take pains to write only in order to say something.

VANDERPYL: I don't write, I *yell* [*gueule*].

KNUT HAMSUN: I write to pass the time of day.

Imagine the symbolist generation answering the same question in the nineties, and measure the change in tone. Not so much the war, as the entire *avant-guerre* had pulled the rug out from under artists, and new they danced wildly to keep their balance.

° Edited by Aragon, Breton, and Soupault and soon becoming openly Dada after a conservative beginning, early numbers of *Littérature* found reason to publish texts by, or speak at length about, Jarry (No. 1), Apollinaire (Nos. 2, 8, 9), Satie (No. 2), and Rousseau (No. 5)—alongside texts by Mallarmé, Gide, and Valéry.

Dada and surrealism accomplished the feat of acting as if this were exactly the way they wanted things to be, and so it continued for fifteen years. The difference was basically one of organization. The postwar schools announced themselves from the housetops and found strength in numbers and solidarity. During the Banquet Years the motive force in the arts came from individuals, reacting to one another and occasionally discovering a common end, yet never surrendering their integrity. Except for the casual grouping of talents among the Hydropaths in the eighties, no important movement established itself by deliberating a program, choosing a name, and declaring its principles. Like the impressionists before them, symbolists, fauves, and cubists were all first ridiculed from outside under those names which, in defiance, they finally accepted as designating some form of common purpose. Jarry was a symbolist, Braque a fauve, and Delaunay a cubist only by chronological accident, not by self-proclamation or lasting affinity. The artists of these years remained individuals, whom only critics and enemies lumped together, in order to have a bigger target. And it was as individuals that they achieved the greatest of all essentials to creative endeavor: courage. One does not live; one dares to live. Forty years after the Banquet Years, in an era of social adjustment, mass communication, and normal response, the resolve to be oneself and live one's life in the face of misunderstanding and disapproval has come increasingly to be branded nonconformity—and even schizophrenia. But conformity, in life and in art, in love and in work, must be to one's inner being and not to the world. The most notable artistic figures of the Banquet Years practiced external nonconformity in order to attain a conformity within the individual. Outstanding among them, Rousseau, Satie, Jarry, and Apollinaire did not seek courage in numbers; they found it in themselves. We see them variously as children and determined humorists, as dreamers and mystifiers, and they played all these roles. But their ultimate virtue lies deeper, lodged beneath all their vices. They had the wisdom, already rare, to know themselves, and the courage, which is far rarer, to be themselves.

Galvanized by this determined individuality, the arts in France at the turn of the century attract or repel with vehemence. They tolerate no indifference. Rousseau's tranquil career is as difficult to judge objectively as Jarry's self-inflicted inquisition. When the arts are not radical they are at least importunate, disturbing. Their accomplishments demand response more than appraisal. The four figures considered here were among the principal importunates of the era, who refused ever to let well enough alone. With their pranks and outrages they ask not for toleration or indulgent laughter, and least of all for clinical classification. They ask to be taken to heart.

A reader who has progressed this far may feel that he has been offered a goodly sum of picturesque counterfeit currency without value outside the closed game of the arts in the Banquet Years. But a little perseverance may bring him to the point where he suddenly finds the currency declared valid and legal tender. The old coin of the realm has become worthless; the reversal of values, the *conversion* has taken place. By an evolution that only today begins to become clear, the Banquet Years yielded the arts of the twentieth century.

The period has survived in the history of the arts despite a set of backhanded adjectives to describe its contributions. Postimpressionism, postsymbolism, post-Wagner—the terms pass harsh judgment on the period by suggesting that it had no character of its own. Were these years merely an aftermath, as is often supposed, a lull during which a few isolated figures like Cézanne and Proust, Gide and Ravel worked steadily on, awaiting the publicity of the postwar years? The very opposite is true. The first war whoop of Dada in 1916 was the beginning of the end for one of the most fertile eras for the arts in France. By then the great themes had been chosen. The modernist movement of the twenties acted out with energetic devotion a drama conceived and dedicated before the war.

Today, during the second half of the twentieth century, we have in no respect left behind the issues broached fifty years ago. Looking backward to the turn of the century, we discover not a defunct segment of history, but a still-vigorous ancestry, whose contribution to our present state of health we have been too inclined to forget. Time and syntax swiftly harden around our experience and our inheritance, and we must constantly shuck off the shell of pat phrase and accepted opinion in order to touch the quick of ourselves. The past tense, which inhabits our lives, as it fills the pages of history, can claim significance and urgency only if it insinuates a concurrent present. Given the courage, we live by moments of interference between past and present, moments in which time comes back into phase with itself. It is the only meaning of history. We search the past not for other creatures but for our own lost selves.

The celebrations of the *avant-guerre* bear witness that the era had found itself. Essentially it embraced the attitude of "morbid-mindedness," which William James defined as ranging over "a wider scale of experience" than healthy-mindedness. In other words, the era acknowledged the vitality of certain areas conventionally called evil and lunatic. But the presence within us of these forces does not oblige us to be forever dispirited, condemning man's iniquity and depravity. On the contrary, these forces can be transformed into the source of new strength. Thus Apollinaire pursued eroticism into mysticism, and Satie boredom into inspiration. These morbid artists, from Rousseau to Picasso, from Jarry to Proust, found reason to take courage in aspects of human consciousness that would dismay weaker minds. They celebrated the discovery not that man is superficially good and happy, but that his richest potentialities are lodged deepest within him. To this truth they lifted their glasses.

The glow lasted for nearly a half-century. The last banquet, old style, took place in 1925, a month before Satie's death. Starting in serious homage to a poet, it developed into a gala insurrection so widely publicized that it became a civic issue. In June, 1925, the review *Les Nouvelles Littéraires* published a special issue to honor the aging writer Saint-Pol-Roux, the neglected "Rabelais of poetry" during the symbolist period. His violent vivid imagery lent itself to exploitation by the recently organized surrealists. Inevitably, the tribute culminated in a vast banquet in honor of the poet at the Closerie des Lilas, which had been the scene of the *Vers et Prose* evenings twenty years earlier. Along with all the young bloods of surrealism, such venerable figures as Lugné-Poe and Rachilde were present. These former collaborators of Jarry's were now considered reactionary. When, in the middle of the meal, Rachilde stoutly affirmed the patriotic sentiment that "a Frenchwoman must never marry a German," sufficient provocation had been provided for the start of hostilities. André Breton rose to defend the insulted nationality of Max Ernst, the German surrealist painter, present at the banquet. It is said Breton went so far as to fling his napkin in Madame Rachhilde's face and call her a *fille à soldats*. While shouts of *Vive l'Allemagne* resounded through the building, the tumult centered around the figure of Philippe Soupault, who was swinging from the chandelier capsizing glasses and dishes with his feet. The traditional pieces of overripe fruit found their mark among dignitaries of the banquet. An irate crowd formed outside, ready to attack the *sales artistes* who were now yelling out the window "Down with France." There was considerable damage inside the restaurant, and the police could barely prevent a lynching as the banqueters emerged. The affair ended violently with several arrests and injuries.

The following day the press broke into shrill protest and agreed to "quarantine" the surrealists for their scandalous behavior by refusing to mention their stunts. In *L'Action Française:*

> It remains to be seen if the courts will give their due to these creatures who are not only poor Frenchmen and boors, but several of whom are armed as well and conducted themselves like common criminals. . . . We shall take measures to silence them.

The exuberant spirits of the *Mercure* banquets in the eighties and nineties, the serious-farcical hoax of the Rousseau banquet in 1908, and the fisticuffs of Apollinaire's war-hero dinner, could now be elevated in retrospect to the recognized status of crime. There was no further evolution; following this last banquet everything was, for a time, postscript. The celebrations of the Banquet Years had fallen into public domain.

WORKS OF ROUSSEAU
MENTIONED IN TEXT

The works are oil on canvas unless specified to the contrary. Dates and dimensions (in inches) are in many cases approximate. Figures in brackets give page references. Italic numbers indicate pictures reproduced in this book. The most valuable recent list of paintings is in Dora Vallier's book (148a).

1. *Petit moulin avec attelage* (*Mill and Peasant Cart*, 1st version), 1879 (dated), 12" x 16". Konstmuseum, Göteborg. [90]
2. *Petit moulin avec attelage* (2nd version), 1880 (dated). [90]
3. [*Lac de Genève*, 1880–1885?, on wood, 12" x 16". Museum of Fine Arts, Boston. Doubtfully attributed to Rousseau.]
4. *La falaise* (*Sea Cliffs*), 1880–1885?, 8½" x 14". Private collection, Paris. [90]
5. *Portrait de Monsieur Stevenc*, 1884 (dated), 8" x 6". [83, 85]
6. *Portrait de Madame Stevenc*, 1884 (dated), 8" x 6". [83, 85]
7. *Un soir de carnaval*, 1886 (dated), 45" x 34¼". Louis E. Stern Collection, Philadelphia Museum of Art. [19, 55, 56, 82, 83, 91, 92, 97]
8. *Autoportrait à la lampe*, 1890, 10" x 8". Collection Picasso. [83, 85, 86]
9. *La femme de l'artiste à la lampe*, 1890, 10" x 8". Collection Picasso. [85]
10. *Moi-même, portrait-paysage*, 1890 (dated), 57½" x 45". National Gallery, Prague. [55, 63, 86, 87, 98]
11. *Portrait de Pierre Loti*, c. 1890, 22½" x 20". Kunsthaus, Zurich. [87, 99]
12. [*Portrait d'homme*, 1890?, c. 48" x 36", Formerly Neumann Gallery, New York City.] [81n]

362]

13. *Bouquet de poète,* 1890–1895?, 15″ x 18″. Collection William S. Paley, New York City. [94]
14. *Promenade dans la forêt,* 1890–1900, 28″ x 24″. Kunsthaus, Zurich. [91, 92]
15. *Paysage exotique: l'orage,* 1891 (dated), 50½″ x 63½″. Collection Mr. and Mrs. Henry Clifford. [87n, 95n]
16. *Un centenaire de l'indépendance,* 1892 (dated), 44¾″ x 62½″. Formerly Düsseldorf; whereabouts unknown. ("The people dance around the two republics, that of 1792 and that of 1892, joining hands to the tune 'Auprès de ma blonde, qu'il fait bon, fait bon dormir.'") [55, 94, 95, 104, 107, 110]
17. *Bonne fête,* 1892 (dated). Collection Charles Laughton, London. [94, 99]
17a. *Le paradis,* c. 1893. Former collection Serge Jastrebzoff (Férat). [95n, 104]
18. *La guerre,* 1894, 44½″ x 76″. Musée du Louvre, Paris. ("She spreads terror where she passes, leaving behind her despair, weeping and ruin.") [55, 91, 93, 95n, 196]
19. *La première femme de l'artiste,* c. 1895, 80″ x 46″. Collection Baron Gourgaud, Paris. [87]
20. *Le parc Montsouris,* 1895, 17½″ x 15½″. Collection Picasso. [97]
21. *La passerelle de Passy* (*The Passy Footbridge*), 1895, 17¼″ x 20″. Collection Morton R. Goldsmith. [97]
21a. *Les artilleurs,* c. 1895, 36″ x 45″. Solomon R. Guggenheim Museum, New York City. [104]
22. *Les bords de l'Oise* (1st version), c. 1895. [103]
23. *Les bords de l'Oise* (2nd version), c. 1895, 12″ x 20″. Wertheim Collection, Fogg Museum of Art, Cambridge, Mass. [103]
24. *L'enfant aux rochers,* 1895–1897?, 21½″ x 18″. Chester Dale Collection, Philadelphia Museum of Art. [88, 99]
25. *Fleurs,* 1895–1900?, 12″ x 9″. Collection Louis Stern, New York City. [94]
26. *Tour Eiffel et Trocadéro,* 1895–1900?, 20″ x 26″. [98]
27. *La fabrique de chaises* (*The Chair Factory*), 1897, 12″ x 17″. Private collection, Paris. [102]
28. *La bohémienne endormie* (*The Sleeping Gypsy*), 1897 (dated), 51″ x 70″. Museum of Modern Art, New York City. [60, 82, 86, 91, 92]
28a. *Portrait de Mlle M.,* 1897, 59″ x 39½″. Collection Picasso. [66]
29. *L'octroi* (*The Toll Gate*), c. 1900, 14¾″ x 12¾″. S. Courtauld Collection, London. [97, 102]
30. *Pêcheur à la ligne avec aéroplane,* c. 1900, 18″ x 22″. Private collection, Paris. [104]

31. *Vue d'un coin du château de Bellevue, c.* 1900. Collection Mrs. Henry D. Sharpe, Providence. [84]
32. *Petit paysage, c.* 1900, 8½" x 11". Collection Hansloser, Winterthur. [97]
32a. *Paysage, c.* 1900. [90]
33. *Bois de Vincennes,* 1901, 17¾" x 21¾". Whereabouts unknown. [90, 104]
34. *Mauvaise surprise,* 1901. Barnes Foundation, Merion, Pa. [91]
35. *Bouquet des fleurs,* 1903, 24" x 20". Tate Gallery, London. [94]
36. *Pour fêter le bébé; l'enfant au polichinelle,* 1903, 40" x 37". Kunsthaus, Winterthur. [88]
37. *Portrait d'enfant,* 1905, 30" x 23". Private collection, Paris. [88]
38. *Une noce à la campagne (Country Wedding),* 1905, 63¾" x 44¾", Musée du Louvre, Paris. [88, 97, 99]
39. *Le lion ayant faim (The Hungry Lion),* 1905, 80" x 120". Private collection, Zurich. ("The hungry lion throws himself on the antelope and devours it; the panther anxiously awaits the moment when it also will have a share. Carnivorous birds have pecked out a piece of flesh from the side of the animal, which weeps a bitter tear. Sunset.") [61, 82n, 91, 107]
40. *La liberté invitant les artistes,* 1906, 69½" x 47½". Sidney Janis Gallery, New York City. ("Liberty invites the artists to take part in the 22nd Exhibition of Independent Artists.") [94, 95, 97]
41. *L'été, le pâturage (Landscape with Milkmaid)* (1st version), 1906 (dated). McNay Art Institute, San Antonio, Texas. [103]
42. *L'été, le pâturage* (2nd version), 1907 (dated), 16" x 21". Musée du Louvre, Paris. [103]
43. *Les représentants des puissances étrangères viennent saluer la république,* 1907. Collection Picasso, Paris. [94]
44. *Pensée philosophique, présent et passé, c.* 1907. Barnes Foundation, Merion, Pa.

> *Etant séparés l'un de l'autre*
> *De ceux qu'ils avaient aimé [sic]*
> *Tous deux s'unissent de nouveau*
> *Restant fidèles à leur pensée.*

45. *Les joueurs de football (The Football Players),* 1908 (dated), 40" x 22". Solomon R. Guggenheim Museum, New York City. [75, 94, 98, 103n, 107, 110]
46. *La charmeuse des serpents,* 1907 (dated), 75" x 84½". Musée du Louvre, Paris. [61, 91]

47. *La carriole du père Juniet,* 1908, 38¼" x 50¾". Collection
     Mme. Paul Guillaume, Paris. [96, 97, 100, 104]
48. *Vue de Malakoff,* 1908 (dated). Collection A. Villard,
     Paris. [97]
49. *Nègre attaqué par un léopard, c.* 1908, 42½" x 67½". Kunst-
     museum, Basel. [91, 92]
50. *Portrait de Joseph Brummer,* 1909 (dated), 45¼" x 35".
     Collection Dr. Franz Meyer, Zurich. [83, 88, 96, 99]
51. *Le poète et sa muse* (1st version), 1909 (dated). Museum
     of Modern Western Art, Moscow. [74, 88, 254–55,
     274]
52. *Le poète et sa muse* (2nd version), 1909 (dated), 41" x
     27½". Kunstmuseum, Basel. [74, 88, 254–55, 274]
53. *Le rêve,* 1910 (dated), 80" x 118½". Museum of Modern
     Art, New York City. [63n, 75, 82, 92, 105, 111]

> *Yadwigha dans un beau rêve*
> *S'étant endormie doucement*
> *Entendait les sons d'une musette*
> *Dont jouait un charmeur bien pensant.*
> *Pendant que la lune reflète*
> *Sur les fleuves, les arbres verdoyants,*
> *Les fauves serpents prêtent l'oreille*
> *Aux airs gais de l'instrument.*

SKETCHES AND DRAWINGS

54. *Tour Eiffel et Trocadéro,* 1895–1900?, oil. [98, 101]
55. *Portrait de l'artiste,* 1895, pen and ink. Collection Antonio
     Santamarina, Buenos Aires. [86]
56. *Vue de Malakoff,* 1906 (dated; probably painted *c.* 1900),
     oil, 7½" x 11¼". Collection Max Weber. [84]
57. *Paysage avec pêcheur, c.* 1900, oil, 8" x 12". Collection
     Rees Jeffreys, London. [101]

BIBLIOGRAPHY

The following lists are highly selective. Designed to provide the most basic titles relating to the period and the four figures studied, they supplement or complement existing bibliographies. Place of publication of books is Paris unless otherwise stated.

The following scheme has been followed:

An * indicates a work that has been published in English translation. In three sections, numbers in brackets give page references. Principal cross references are in italics.

I

The most useful bibliogaphy (over 100 items) on the literary background of the period is in Billy (12). Except for titles particularly relevant to this study, the following list does not duplicate Billy. For other bibliographies see 3, 4, 5, 6, 7, 35, 57, 58, 75, 82, 99, 122.

1. Aegerter, E., et Labracherie, P., *Au temps de Guillaume Apollinaire*, 1945

2. Antoine, André, *Mes souvenirs sur le Théâtre Libre*, 1921
3. Balakian, Anna, *The Literary Origins of Surrealism*, New York, King's Crown Press, 1947
3a. ———, *Surrealism*, New York, Noonday Press, 1959
4. Barr, Alfred H., Jr., *Cubism and Abstract Art*, New York, Museum of Modern Art, 1936
5. ———, ed., *Fantastic Art, Dada, Surrealism*, New York, Museum of Modern Art, 1936
6. ———, *Matisse, His Art and His Public*, New York, Museum of Modern Art, 1949
7. ———, *Picasso, Fifty Years of His Art*, New York, Museum of Modern Art, 1946
8. Bell, Clive, *Since Cézanne*, London, 1928
9. Bercy, A. de, *et* Ziwès, A., *A Montmartre . . . le soir*, 1951
10. Bertaud, Jules, *Paris 1870–1935*, London, 1936
11. Billy, André, *L'époque contemporaine*, 1956
12. ———, *L'époque 1900*, 1951
13. Bloy, Léon, *Belluaires et porchers*, 1905
14. Boisson, Marius, *Les attentats anarchistes*, 1931
15. Breton, André, *Les pas perdus*, 1924
16. Burnand, Robert, *Paris 1900*, 1951
17. Carco, Francis, *La belle époque au temps de Bruant*, 1954
18. ———, *De Montmartre au quartier latin*, 1927
19. ———, *Nostalgie de Paris*, 1952
20. ———, Depaquit, Jacob, Apollinaire, *et al.*, *Les veillées du Lapin Agile*, 1919
21. Cœuroy, André, *La musique française moderne*, 1922
22. ———, *Panorama de la musique contemporaine*, 1928
23. Colette, *Mes apprentissages*, 1936
24. Cooper, Martin, *French Music* (*1869–1924*), London, 1951
25. Coquiot, Gustave, *Les indépendants*, 1920
26. *Debussy, Claude, *Monsieur Croche, l'antidilettante*, 1921
26a. Décaudin, Michel, *La crise des valeurs symboliste*, 1960
27. Denis, Maurice, *Théories 1890–1910*, 1913
28. Donnay, M., Bonnaud, D., *et* Hyspa, V., *L'esprit montmartois*, 1938
29. Dorgelès, Roland, *Le bouquet de bohème*, 1948
30. Dorival, Bernard, *Les étapes de la peinture française contemporaine*, 3 vols., 1943, 1944, 1946
31. Dumesnil, René, *La musique contemporaine en France*, 1930
32. ———, *La musique en France entre deux guerres*, 1948
33. ———, *Portraits de musiciens français*, 1938

34. Durand, Jacques, *Quelques souvenirs d'un éditeur de musique,* 2 vols., 1924, 1925
35. *Duthuit, Georges, *Les fauves, Genève,* 1949
36. Fargue, Léon-Paul, *Portraits de famille,* 1947
37. Fels, Florent, *Propos d'artistes,* 1925
38. Fénéon, Félix, *L'art moderne,* 2 vols., 1919
39. Fort, Paul, *Mes mémoires,* 1944
40. Fosca, François, *Histoire des cafés de Paris,* 1934
41. Fouquier, Marcel, *Les jours heureux d'autrefois,* 2 vols., 1941, 1944
42. Friedrich, Hugo, *Die Struktur der modernen Lyrik von Baudelaire bis zur Gegenwart,* Hamburg, 1956
43. Gauguin, Paul, *Avant et après,* 1923
44. Gaunt, William, *The March of the Moderns,* London, 1949
45. Georges-Michel, Michel, *Peintres . . . que j'ai connus,* 1942
46. *Gleizes, A., *et* Metzinger, J., *Du cubisme,* 1912
47. Goldwater, Robert J., *Primitivism in Modern Painting,* New York, Harper, 1938; rev. ed. *Primitivism in Modern Art,* New York, Vintage Books, 1967
48. Goudeau, Emile, *Dix ans de bohème,* 1888
49. Gourmont, Remy de, *Dans la tourmente,* 1916
50. *———, *Le Livre des masques,* 2 vols., 1896, 1898
51. ———, *Promenades littéraires,* 1904–1927
52. *Guitry, Sacha, *Souvenirs I,* 1934
53. Haas, Dr. Albert, "Souvenirs," *Soirées de Paris, mai* 1914
54. Hill, Edward Burlingame, *Modern French Music,* Boston, Houghton Mifflin, 1924
55. Hope, Henry R., *Georges Braque,* New York, Museum of Modern Art, 1949
56. Hull, Eaglefield, *Music: Classic, Romantic and Modern,* London, 1927
57. *Huyghe, René, *Les contemporains,* 1939
58. ———, ed., *Histoire de l'art contemporain,* 1934 (articles by Huyghe, Cogniat, Rey, Salmon, Uhde Lhote, Bazin, *et al.*)
59. Jacob, Max, *Correspondance I,* 1953
60. Jean-Aubry, G., *La musique française d'aujourd'hui,* 1916
61. Jeanne, R., *et* Ford, C., *Histoire encyclopédique du cinéma I,* 1947
62. Jimmie the Barman (James Charters), *This Must Be the Place,* introd. Ernest Hemingway, New York, Lee Furman, 1937
63. Jourdain, Francis, *Nés en 76,* 1951
64. *Kahnweiler, Daniel-Henry, *Juan Gris,* 1946
65. Kœchlin, Charles, *Debussy,* 1927
66. *———, *Gabriel Fauré,* 1927

67. ———, *"Les tendances de la musique moderne française,"* in *Encyclopédie de la musique du Conservatoire de Paris,* 1925

67a. Kramer, Katz, *et al., The Turn of the Century, Arts Yearbook I,* 1957

68. Kyrou, Ado, *Le surréalisme au cinéma,* 1953

69. Laloy, Louis, *Debussy,* 1944

70. ———, *La musique retrouvée,* 1928

71. Léautaud, Paul, *Entretiens avec Robert Mallet,* 1951

71a. ———, *Journal littéraire,* I–III, 1954–56

72. Lemaître, Georges, *From Cubism to Surrealism in French Literature,* Cambridge, Harvard, 1941

73. Lugné-Poe, Aurélien, *Acrobaties 1894–1903,* 1931

74. MacOrlan, Pierre, *Le mémorial du petit jour; mémoires,* 1955

75. Michaud, Guy, *Message poétique du symbolisme,* 3 vols., 1947

76. Milhaud, Darius, *Etudes,* 1927

77. *———, *Notes sans musique,* 1949

77a. Mollet, le Baron, *Mémoires,* 1963

77b. Monnier, Adrienne, *Rue de l'Odéon,* 1960

78. Montfort, Eugène, ed., *Vingt-cinq ans de littérature française,* 2 vols., 1922

79. *Morand, Paul, *1900,* 1931

80. Moreno, Marguerite, *La statue de sel,* 1926

81. Morice, Charles, *Paul Gauguin,* 1919

82. Motherwell, Robert, ed., *The Dada Painters and Poets,* New York, Wittenborn, Schultz, 1951

83. *Nadeau, Maurice, *Histoire du surréalisme,* 1947

84. *Olivier, Fernande, *Picasso et ses amis,* 1933

85. Ozenfant, Amedée, *The Foundations of Modern Art,* New York, Brewer, Warren and Putnam, 1931

86. ———, *et* Jeanneret, A., *La peinture moderne,* 1925

87. Paulhan, François, *Le nouveau mysticisme,* 1891

88. Paulhan, Jean, *Félix Fénéon ou la critique,* 1945

89. Polignac, La Princesse de, *"Memoirs," Horizon,* August 1945

90. *Portraits du prochain siècle–poètes et prosateurs,* 1894

91. Praz, Mario, *The Romantic Agony,* London, 1933

92. Puy, Michel, *Le dernier étape de la peinture,* 1910

93. *Raymond, Marcel, *De Baudelaire au surréalisme,* 1933

94. Raynal, Maurice, *Modern French Painters,* New York, Brentano's, 1928

95. *———, *Histoire de la peinture moderne,* 3 vols., Genève, 1949

96. Régnier, Henri de, *De mon temps,* 1933

97. Rémond, Georges, *"Souvenirs," Mercure de France,* mars–avril 1955

98. Renard, Jules, *Journal*, 1887–1910, 1927

99. Rewald, John, *Post-Impressionism*, New York, Museum of Modern Art, 1956

99a. Richter, Hans, *Dada: Art and Anti-Art*, New York, McGraw-Hill, 1965

100. Robsjohn-Gibbings, T. H., *Mona Lisa's Moustache*, New York, Knopf, 1947

101. Rohozinski, L., ed., *Cinquante ans de musique française*, 1925

102. *Roland-Manuel, *Maurice Ravel*, 1914

103. Sadoul, Georges, *L'histoire générale du cinéma*, 1946

104. Salmon, André, *La jeune peinture française*, 1912

105. ———, *Souvenirs sans fin*, 2 vols., 1955–1956

106. *———, *La négresse du Sacré-Coeur*, 1920

107. Sert, Misia, *Misia*, 1952

108. Soby, James Thrall, *Giorgio de Chirico*, New York, Museum of Modern Art, 1955

108a. Soupault, Philippe, *Profils perdus*, 1963

109. Stein, Gertrude, *The Autobiography of Alice B. Toklas*, New York, Harcourt, Brace, 1933

110. ———, *Dix portraits*, 1930

111. Stein, Leo, *Appreciations*, New York, Crown, 1947

112. *Stravinsky, Igor, *Chroniques de ma vie*, 2 vols., 1935

113. Tailhade, Laurent, *Quelques fantômes de jadis*, 1919

114. Thétard, Henry, *La merveilleuse histoire du cirque*, 2 vols., 1947

114a. Torre, Guillermo de, *Historia de las literaturas de vanguardia*, Madrid, 1965

115. Tourette, F. Gilles de la, *Robert Delaunay*, 1950

116. *Vallas, L., *Claude Debussy et son temps*, 1932

117. Vlaminck, Maurice, *Portraits avant décès*, 1943

118. ———, *Tournant dangereux*, 1924

119. *Vollard, Ambroise, *Souvenirs d'un marchand de tableaux*, 1948

120. Warnod, André, *Les berceaux de la jeune peinture*, 1925

121. ———, *Ceux de la Butte*, 1947

122. Wilenski, R. H., *Modern French Painters*, New York, Harcourt, Brace, 1949; Vintage Books, 2 vols., 1960

123. Wilson, Edmund, *Axel's Castle*, New York, Scribner, 1931

Reviews of the period: *L'Art Littéraire, Bulletin de la S.I.M., Le Canard Sauvage, Le Chat Noir, Le Coeur, L'Esprit Nouveau, Essais d'Art Libre, Le Festin d'Esope, La Gazette des Arts, Littérature, Les Marges, Le Mercure de France Montjoie!, Nord-Sud, La Nouvelle Revue Française, La Phalange, La Plume, La Révolution Surréaliste, La Revue Blanche, La Revue Indépendante, La Revue Musicale, Les Soirées de Paris, Vers et Prose, La Vogue.*

Newspapers: *Comoedia, Le Figaro, Le Gaulois, Gil-Blas,*

L'Humanité, L'Intransigeant, Le Matin, Paris-Journal, Paris-Midi, Le Temps.

II. HENRI ROUSSEAU

The only extensive bibliography on Rousseau is in Rich (131), and it is brought up to date in section C. below.

A. Selected sources (see also 25, 30, 37, 45, 47, 57, 58, 84, 86, 94, 95, 100, 104, 105, 109, 111, 115, 117, 118, 119, 122, 292 and titles in section B, below)

124. Cann, Louise Gebhard, "An Artist of the People," *International Studio*, July 1925
124a. Certigny, Henri, *La vérité sur le douanier Rousseau*, 1961
125. Chassé, Charles, *D'Ubu Roi au Douanier Rousseau*, 1947
126. Cooper, Douglas, *Rousseau*, 1951
127. Delaunay, Robert, "Mon ami, Henri Rousseau," *Les Lettres Françaises* (*Tous-les-arts*), 14, 21, 28 août, 4 sept. 1952
128. Eichmann, Ingeborg, "Five Sketches by Henri Rousseau," *Burlington Magazine*, June 1938
129. Gauthier, Maximilien, *Henri Rousseau*, 1949
130. Melville, Robert, "Rousseau and Chirico," *Scottish Art and Letters*, no. 1, 1944
131. Rich, Daniel Catton, *Henri Rousseau*, New York, Museum of Modern Art, 1946
132. Roh, Franz, "*Henri Rousseaus Bildform und Bedeutung für die Gegenwart,*" *Die Kunst*, Jan. 1927
133. *Soirées de Paris, jan. 1913* [*sic* for 1914] (Special number on Rousseau: letters, articles by Apollinaire and Raynal)
134. Sweeney, James Johnson, *Plastic Redirections in Twentieth Century Painting*, Chicago, University of Chicago, 1934
135. Tzara, Tristan, "*Préface,*" in 151
136. Uhde, Wilhelm, *Five Primitive Masters*, tr. Ralph Thompson, New York, Triangle Books, 1949
137. ———, *Henri Rousseau*, 1911
138. Weber, Max, "Rousseau As I Knew Him," *Art News*, Feb. 15, 1942

B. Principal volumes of reproductions (see also 95, 126, 128, 129, 131, 137, 162)

139. Basler, Adolphe, *Henri Rousseau*, 1927
140. ————, *Henri Rousseau le Douanier*, 1930
141. Courthion, Pierre, *Henri Rousseau le Douanier*, Genève, 1944
142. Duca, Lo, *Henri Rousseau dit le Douanier*, 1951 (contains forgeries)
143. Grey, Roch, *Henri Rousseau*, 1943 (contains forgeries)
144. Payró, Julio E., *El Aduanero Rousseau*, Buenos Aires, 1944
145. Raynal, Maurice, *Rousseau*, Geneva and New York, Skira, n. d.
146. Salmon, André, *Henri Rousseau dit le Douanier*, 1927
147. Soupault, Philippe, *Henri Rousseau, le Douanier*, 1927
148. ————, *Henri Rousseau le Douanier*, 1949
148a. Vallier, Dora, *Henri Rousseau*, 1961
149. Zervos, Christian, *Rousseau*, 1927

C. Supplement to bibliography in Rich (131) (see also 30, 95, 100, 105, 111, 115, 117, 118, 125, 126, 127, 129, 135, 136, 142, 145, 148)

150. Rousseau, Henri le Douanier, *La vengeance d'une orpheline russe*, Genève, 1947
151. ————, *Une visite à l'exposition de 1889*, Genève, 1947
152. ————, *"Carnets," Labyrinthes, juillet* 1946
153. Bernard (née Rousseau), Jeanne, *"La petite fille d'Henri Rousseau raconte la vie de son grand-père," Beaux-Arts,* 17 oct. 1947
154. Carrà, Carlo, *"Rousseau le Douanier and the Italian Tradition," Magazine of Art,* Nov. 1951
155. Cocteau, Jean, *"Introduction"* to *Collection John Quinn, tableaux modernes (vente),* 28 oct. 1926
156. Diberdier, Yves le, *"Rousseau copiste," Beaux-Arts,* 26 dec. 1947
157. Garçon, Maurice, *Le Douanier Rousseau, accusé naïf,* 1953
158. Goodrich, Lloyd, *Max Weber*, New York, Macmillan, 1949
159. Kandinski, Wassily, *"Über die Formfrage," Der Blaue Reiter,* München, 1912
160. Read, Herbert, *A Coat of Many Colors*, London, 1947
161. Shattuck, Roger, *"The Rousseau Banquet," Arts,* Oct. 1955
162. Tzara, Tristan, *"Le Douanier Rousseau,"* in *Henri Rousseau* (catalogue), Sidney Janis Gallery, 1951

III. ERIK SATIE

No systematic bibliography of works on Satie exists. Templier (229) and Myers (216) contain the greatest concentration of material, and the latter includes a complete list of Satie's published compositions. Page references in italics indicate musical illustrations in the text.

A. Principal works (for piano solo unless otherwise specified)

163. *3 Sarabandes*, 1887 [118, 125, 142, 146]
164. *3 Gymnopédies*, 1888 [117–120, 137, 141, 142, 143, 146]
165. *3 Gnossiennes*, 1890 [118, 140, 141, 143]
166. *3 Préludes pour Le fils des étoiles*, 1891
167. *Prélude pour La porte héroïque du ciel*, 1895 [146]
168. *Messe des pauvres*, 1895, [125, 127, 138]
169. *Pièces froides*, 1897 [127–130, 138, 146]
170. *Geneviève de Brabant*, 1899 [170, 183]
171. *Jack-in-the-box*, 1899 [170, 183]
172. *3 Morceaux en forme de poire*, 1903 (piano, four hands) [136–142, 143, 146, 176n]
173. *Aperçus désagréables* (*Disagreeable Remarks*), 1908 (piano, four hands) [114]
174. *Véritables préludes flasques* (*pour un chien*) (*True Flabby Preludes* [*for a Dog*]), 1912 [114, 146]
175. *Choses vues à droit et à gauche* (*sans lunettes*) (*Things Seen from Right and Left* [*without Glasses*]), 1912 (violin and piano)
176. *Descriptions automatiques*, 1913 [114]
177. *Embryons desséchés* (*Dried Embryos*), 1913 [178]
178. *Croquis et agaceries d'un gros bonhomme en bois* (*Sketches and Twitchings of a Big Wooden Fellow*), 1913 [146]
179. *Chapitres tournés en tous sens* (*Chapters Turned Every Whichway*), 1913 [146]
180. *Enfantines*, 1913 [170, 176]
181. *Vieux sequins et vieilles cuirasses* (*Old Sequins and Breastplates*), 1914
182. *3 Poèmes d'amour*, 1914 (songs for solo voice and piano) [176]
183. *Heures séculaires et instantanées*, 1914 [147n]
184. *3 Valses du précieux dégoûté*, 1914
185. *5 Grimaces*, 1914
186. *Sports et divertissements*, 1914 [147–150, 176; see translation of Satie's notes by Ronald Johnson, Dunsyre, Wild Hawthorn Press, 1965]

187. *3 Mélodies,* 1916 (songs for solo voice and piano)
188. *Avant-dernières pensées,* 1915
189. *Parade (ballet réaliste),* 1917 (orchestra) [152–158, 183, 294]
190. *Sonatine bureaucratique,* 1917
191. *5 Nocturnes,* 1919 [176n]
192. *Socrate (drame symphonique),* 1919 (voices and orchestra) [159–168, 183]
193. *3 Petites pièces montées,* 1919 (orchestra) [170]
194. *4 Petites mélodies,* 1920 (songs for solo voice and piano)
195. *Ludions (Bottle-Imps),* 1923 (songs for solo voice and piano, words by Léon-Paul Fargue)
196. *Mercure (poses plastiques)* 1924 (orchestra) [173, 183]
197. *Relâche (ballet instantanéiste)* (piano reduction of film score published as Cinéma), 1924 (orchestra) [170–174]

Orchestral arrangements have been made of the following works: nos. 164 (Claude Debussy), 165 (Francis Poulenc), 167 (Roland-Manuel), 168 (David Diamond), 170 (Roger Désormière), 171 (Darius Milhaud).

Too large a portion of Satie's music has been recorded to list conveniently here. Many recordings are still available and are described in current catalogues and publishers' listings.

With the exception of *Le Piège de Méduse* (1921), Satie's writings have never been collected in a volume. Principal periodical publications:
Action, août 1921; *Bulletin de la S.I.M., avril* 1912, *fév.* 1913, *jan.* 1914; *Le Cartulaire, passim,* 1895; *Le Coeur à Barbe avril* 1922; *Le Coq, passim,* 1920; *Esprit Nouveau, avril* 1921; *Feuilles Libres, fév., juin, oct.* 1922; *mars, sept.* 1923; *jan.* 1924; *L'Oeil de Veau, fév.* 1912; *La Revue de Musicologie, juillet-déc.* 1962, *391, juin, juillet* 1924

B. Selected sources (see also 21, 22, 24, 31, 32, 33, 34, 54, 56, 59, 60, 63, 65, 67, 69, 70, 76, 77, 84, 85, 101, 102, 107, 109, 110, 112, 116, 122)

198. Auric, Georges, "Chronique sur Parade," *La Nouvelle Revue Française, fév.* 1921
199. ————, "Parade et Socrate," *Littérature, mars* 1919
199a. Cage, John, *Silence,* Middletown, Wesleyan University Press, 1961
200. Chennevière, Rydhyar D., "Erik Satie and the Music of Irony," *Musical Quarterly,* Oct. 1919
201. *Cocteau, Jean, *Rappel à l'ordre,* 1926

202. Cœuroy, André, "Erik Leslie Satie," in *Larousse mensuelle, nov.* 1925

203. Collet, Henri, *"Un livre de Rimsky et un livre de Cocteau —les cinq Russes, les six Français et Erik Satie," Comœdia,* 16 & 23 *jan.,* 1920

203a. Contamine de Latour, J.-P., *"Erik Satie intime,"* Comœdia, 5 août 1925

204. Cortot, Alfred, *"Le Cas Satie," La Revue Musicale, avril–mai* 1938

205. ———, *La musique française de piano,* vol. III, 1944

206. Guichard, Léon, *"Erik Satie et la musique grégorienne," La Revue Musicale, nov.* 1936

207. Jeanneret, Albert, *"Erik Satie," L'Esprit Nouveau,* no. 2, 1920

208. ———, *"Socrate," L'Esprit Nouveau,* no. 9, 1921

209. Lambert, Constant, *Music Ho!,* London, 1934

209a. Leiris, Michel, *"L'Humour d'Eric Satie," Air du Mois,* jan., 1938

210. Lieberman, William, *"Parade* and the New Spirit," *Dance Index,* Nov.–Dec. 1946 (see also *Dance Magazine,* Sept. 1957)

211. *Maritain, Jacques, *Frontières de la poésie,* 1935

212. Marnold, Jean, *"Chroniques de musique," Mercure de France, sept.* 1917, *sept.* 1919, *avril* 1920, *oct.* 1924

213. Mellers, Wilfred, *Studies in Contemporary Music,* London, 1947

214. Milhaud, Darius, *"Note sur Erik Satie,"* in *Œuvres Nouvelles,* New York, Maison Française, 1946

215. ———, *"Les derniers jours d'Erik Satie," Le Figaro Littéraire,* 23 *avril* 1949

216. Myers, Rollo, *Erik Satie,* London, 1948

217. Newman, Ernest, *A Musical Motley,* New York, Knopf, 1925

218. Renshaw, Rosette, *"Erik Satie," La Nouvelle Revue Canadienne, avril–mai* 1951

219. *La Revue Musicale, mars* 1924 (important articles by Charles Kœchlin, Georges Auriol, and Jean Cocteau)

220. ———, *"Hommage à Erik Satie," août* 1925 (articles by Georges Auric and Jean Cocteau)

221. ———, *"Erik Satie, son temps et ses amis,"* ed. Rollo Myers, *juin* 1952 (texts by Roland-Manuel, Virgil Thomson, Jean Cocteau, Stanislas Fumet, Francis Poulenc, Pierre Bertin, Roger Shattuck, Fernand Léger, Valentine Hugo)

222. Roberts, W. Wright, "The Problem of Satie," *Music and Letters,* Oct. 1923

223. Roland-Manuel, *Erik Satie* (*"Causerie faite à la Société Lyre et Palette"*), 1916

224. Rosenfeld, Paul, *Musical Chronicle,* New York, Harcourt, Brace, 1923
225. Roussel, Albert, *"A propos d'un récent festival,"* Le Gaulois, 12 juin 1926
226. Schlœzer, Boris de, *"Le cas Satie,"* La Revue Musicale, août 1924
227. Schmitt, Florent, "Erik Satie," *Montjoie!,* 14 mars 1913
228. Shattuck, Roger, "Erik Satie, Composer to the School of Paris," *Art News* Annual XXXVII, 1957
229. Templier, P.-D., *Erik Satie,* 1932
230. Thomson, Virgil, *Music Left and Right,* New York, Holt, 1951
231. ———, *The Musical Scene,* New York, Knopf, 1945
232. van Vechten, Carl, *Interpreters and Interpretations,* New York, Knopf, 1917
233. ———, *Excavations,* New York, Knopf, 1926
233a. Wiener, Jean, *Arts,* 13 & 20 juillet, 1945

IV. ALFRED JARRY

The richest bibliographical material on Jarry is contained in the *Cahiers du Collège de 'Pataphysique,* no. 10, catalogue of the "Expojarrysition" (257). Items 254, 268, 270, and 271a also contain bibliographies.

A. Principal works

234. *Les minutes de sable mémorial (Minutes of Memorial Sand),* 1894 [194–95, 226, 240–41, 243–46, 247]
235. *César-Antéchrist,* 1895 [194, 226, 245]
236. *°Ubu Roi,* 1896 (re-ed. 1921, 1950; tr. Barbara Wright, New York, New Directions, 1951; tr. Beverly Keith and G. Legman, New York, Boar's Head, 1953; tr. Michael Benedikt and George Wellworth, in *Modern French Theatre,* New York, Dutton, 1964; tr. Wallace Fowlie, in *Four Modern French Comedies,* New York, Putnam, 1960) [32, 34, 108, 191, 203–11, 224, 229, 245]
237. *Les jours et les nuits,* 1897 (re-ed. 1948, 1964) [35, 200–201, 218, 231–32, 241–43]
238. *L'amour en visites,* 1898 [197, 218, 231, 246]
239. *Almanach du Père Ubu,* 1899 (*Almanach illustré,* 1901) [62. 212n, 218]
240. *L'amour absolu,* 1899 (re-ed. 1952, 1962, 1964) [200n, 218, 232, 234, 236, 249]

241. *Ubu enchaîné*, 1900 [227–28]
242. *Messaline*, 1901 (tr. Louis Coleman, introd. Matthew Josephson, *The Garden of Priapus*, New York, Black Hawk Press, 1932) [217, 233]
243. *Le surmâle* (*The Supermale*), 1902 (tr. Ralph Gladstone and Barbara Wright in *New Directions* 18, 1964) [218, 220, 233, 239]
244. *Par la taille*, 1906
245. *Pantagruel*, 1911, [218]
246. *Gestes et opinions du docteur Faustroll 'pataphysicien*, 1911 (re-ed. 1923, 1955) [218, 229n, 241n–42, 244, 247, 248–50, 258n]
247. *Gestes*, 1921 [218, 244]
248. *La Dragonne*, 1943 [40, 219, 221, 235, 245]
249. *Ubu cocu*, 1944 (tr. by Keith and Legman; see 236)
250. *Oeuvres poétiques complètes*, 1945
251. *Oeuvres complètes*, Monte Carlo and Lausanne, 1948 [244]
252. *La revanche de la nuit* (*The Revenge of Night*), 1949
253. *Commentaire pour servir à la construction pratique de la machine à explorer le temps*, 1951 [351]
254. *Alfred Jarry* (*Poètes d'aujourd'hui*, no. 24), 1951
255. *L'objet aimé*, 1953 [234]
255a. *Tout Ubu*, ed. Maurice Saillet, 1962
255b. *Selected Works of Alfred Jarry*, ed. Roger Shattuck and Simon Watson Taylor, New York, Grove Press, 1965

B. Selected sources (see also 3, 11, 12, 15, 36, 39, 52, 53, 59, 63, 71, 72, 73, 77a, 78, 85, 93, 97, 98, 113, 119, 122, 125, 148a, 195, 292)

255c. Arnaud, Noel, "*La vie nouvelle d'Alfred Jarry*," *Critique*, déc. 1959
256. Artaud, A., et Vitrac, R., *Le Théâtre d'Alfred Jarry et l'hostilité publique*, n.d., 1930
256a. *———, Le théâtre et son double*, 1938
257. *Cahiers du Collège de 'Pataphysique*, 1949– (see especially nos. 1, 3–4, 5–6, 8–9, 10, 15, 20, 22–23, 26–27; see also *Dossiers* and *Subsidia* du Collège de 'Pataphysique)
258. Chauveau, Paul, *Alfred Jarry*, 1932
258a. Daumal, René, *Chaque fois que l'aube paraît*, 1953
259. Fitzgerald, P. M., "The Strange Case of Père Ubu," *World Review*, Jan. 1951
260. Gens-d'Armes, Gandillon, "*Alfred Jarry au lycée Henri IV*," *Les Marges*, jan. 1922

261. Géroy, "Mon ami Alfred Jarry," Mercure de France, juillet 1947
262. Gide, André, Les faux-monnayeurs (Chap. VIII), 1925
263. ———, "Le groupement littéraire qu'abritait le Mercure de France," déc. 1946
264. ———, et Gourmont, Rémy de, "Minutes de sable mémorial," Mercure de France, oct. 1894
265. Grubbs, H. A., "Alfred Jarry's Theories of Dramatic Technique," Romanic Review, Oct. 1936
266. Hertz, Henri, "Jarry collégien et la naissance d'Ubu Roi," Ecrits Nouveaux, nov. 1921
267. Jean, M., et Mezei, A., Genèse de la pensée moderne, 1950
268. Lebois, André, Jarry l'irremplaçable, 1950
269. Levesque, Jacques-Henri, "Alfred Jarry," in 254
270. Lot, Fernand, Alfred Jarry, 1934
271. Lormel, Louis, "Alfred Jarry," La Phalange, déc. 1907
271a. Perche, Louis, Alfred Jarry, 1965.
271b. Pronco, Leonard, Avant-garde: the Experimental Theater in France, Los Angeles, Calif., 1962
272. Quillard, Pierre, "De l'imagination et de l'expression chez Jarry," La Revue Blanche, jan. 1902
273. Rachilde, Alfred Jarry ou le surmâle des lettres, 1928
273a. Robichez, Jacques, Le symbolisme au théâtre: Lugné-Poe et les débuts de l'Oeuvre, 1957
274. Saillet, Maurice, "L'oeuvre de Jarry," Critique, fév. 1949
275. ———, Sur la route de Narcisse, 1958
276. Salmon, André, "Alfred Jarry ou le Père Ubu en liberté," Ami du Lettré, 1924
277. Shattuck, Roger, "Le tic et le type," in 255
277a. Shattuck, Watson, Taylor, et al., "What is 'Pataphysics?" Evergreen Review, 13, 1960
277b. Soupault, Philippe, "Confrontations: Alfred Jarry," Cahiers de la Compagnie Renaud-Barrault, mai 1958
278. Vallette, Alfred, "La mort d'Alfred Jarry," Mercure de France, nov. 1907

V. GUILLAUME APOLLINAIRE

The most complete bibliographies of Apollinaire's work may be found in Adéma (304) and in Oeuvres poétiques (303). See also 328b and 333. The second section below gives a number of important items in English neglected by Adéma and others.

A. Principal works

279. *Les onze mille verges*, 1907 [269, 305]
280. *L'enchanteur pourrissant* (*The Decomposing Enchanter*), 1909 [268]
281. *Les maîtres de l'amour* (series of titles), 1909–1917 [270, 274, 294]
282. °*L'hérésiarque et cie.* (*The Heretic and Co.*), 1910 (re-ed. 1922, 1945, 1954) [272, 275, 292, 302, 303, 305]
283. *Le bestiaire ou le cortège d'Orphée*, 1911 (red-ed. 1914) [314]
284. °*Les peintres cubistes: méditations esthétiques*, 1913 (re-ed. 1922, 1950, 1965; tr. by Lionel Abel, New York, Wittenborn, Schultz, 1949) [281–83, 286, 293, 318, 321–22]
285. °*Alcools, poèmes 1898–1913*, 1913 (re-ed. 1920, 1934, 1950; tr. William Meredith, New York, Doubleday, 1964; tr. Anne Hyde Greet, University of California Press, 1965) [281, 300n, 307, 308–10, 314–16, 317]
286. *Le poète assassiné*, 1916 (re-ed. 1927, 1945) [292, 293, 303–04]
287. *Vitam impendere amori*, 1917
288. *Les mamelles de Tirésias* (*The Teats of Tiresias*), 1918 (re-ed. 1948) [294, 314]
289. *Calligrammes, poèmes de la paix et de la guerre, 1913–1916*, 1918 (re-ed. 1925, 1930) [288–90, 296, 300n, 307, 309–11, 315–17, 319]
290. *Le flâneur des deux rives* (*Idler on Both Banks*), 1918 (re-ed. 1928, 1945) [299–306]
291. *La femme assise*, 1920 (re-ed. 148) [303]
292. *Il y a*, 1925 (re-ed. 1947, 1949) [34, 214]
293. *Anecdotiques*, 1926 (re-ed. 1955) [271–72, 304n]
294. *Ombre de mon amour*, Genève, 1947 [288–91]
295. *Poètes d'aujourd'hui: Guillaume Apollinaire* (ed. A. Billy), 1947
296. *Lettres à sa marraine*, 1948 [312]
297. *Que faire*, 1950 [254, 258]
298. °*Selected Writings* (tr. and ed. Roger Shattuck), New York, New Directions, 1950
299. *Tendre comme le souvenir*, 1952 [277, 360]
300. *Le guetteur mélancolique* (*The Melancholy Watchman*), 1952
301. *Casanova*, 1952 [314]
302. *Textes inédits* (ed. J. Moulin), Genève, 1952
303. *Oeuvres poétiques* (ed. M. Adéma *et* M. Décaudin; préface d'André Billy), 1956
303a. *Chroniques d'art* (ed. L. C. Breunig and J.–Cl. Chevalier), 1960

303b. *Oeuvres complètes* (ed. Michel Décaudin), 4 vols. &
    4 vols. facsimile, 1965–1966

B. Selected sources (see also 1, 3, 3a, 11, 12, 15, 18, 19, 29,
    39, 58, 59, 64, 71, 72, 77a, 78, 84, 85, 93, 95, 100, 105, 106,
    108, 108a, 109, 110, 111, 115, 117, 118, 120, 121, 122, 125,
    148a, 161, 221)

304. *Adéma, Marcel, *Guillaume Apollinaire le mal-aimé*, 1952
305. Aegerter, E., *et* Labracherie, P., *Guillaume Apollinaire*,
    1943
306. Balakian, Anna, "Apollinaire and the Modern Mind," *Yale
    French Studies*, IV, 2
307. Bates, Scott, *Guillaume Apollinaire*, New York, Twayne
    Publ. 1967
308. Billy, André, *Apollinaire vivant*, 1923
309. Bowra, C. M., "Introduction" to Apollinaire, *Choix de
    poésies*, London, 1945
310. ———, *The Creative Experiment*, London, 1949
311. Breunig, LeRoy, "Apollinaire," *The Kenyon Review*,
    Spring 1951
312. ———, "Apollinaire since 1950," *The Romanic Review*
    Feb. 1955
312a. ———, "Apollinaire's 'Les Fiançailles,'" *Essays in
    French Literature*, Nov. 1966
313. ———, "The Chronology of Apollinaire's *Alcools*,"
    PMLA, Dec. 1952
313a. Butor, Michel, "*Monument de rien pour Apollinaire*,"
    Nouvelle Revue Française, mars 1965
314. Cadou, René-Guy, *Testament d'Apollinaire*, 1945
315. ———, *Guillaume Apollinaire ou l'artilleur de Metz*, 1948
316. Cameron, J. W., "The Manuscript of Apollinaire's 'Sang-
    lots,'" *Modern Language Notes*, June 1953
317. Carmody, Francis J., *The Evolution of Apollinaire's Po-
    etics*, Berkeley, 1963
317a. Cendrars, Blaise, *Selected Writings* (ed. Walter Albert),
    New York, New Directions, 1966
318. Champigny, Robert, "*Le temps chez Apollinaire*," *PMLA*,
    March 1952
318a. ———, "*Analyse du Pont Mirabeau*," *PMLA*, Sept. 1963
319. *Cocteau, Jean, *La difficulté d'être*, 1947
319a. Cranston, Mechthild, "Apprendre '*Le Larron*' de Guil-
    laume Apollinaire," *PMLA*, Oct. 1967
320. Davies, Margaret, *Apollinaire*, New York, St. Martin's
    Press, 1964
320a. Décaudin, Michel, *Le Dossier d' "Alcools*," 1960
320b. ———, "*Obscurité et Composition chez Apollinaire*,"

    Cahiers de l'Association Internationale des Etudes Françaises, mars 1963

321. Durry, Marie-Jeanne, *Guillaume Apollinaire: Alcools,* 3 vols., 1956–1965

322. *L'Esprit Nouveau,* n.d., 1924 (special number on Apollinaire, with important articles by Roch Grey, André Salmon, Paul Dermée, etc.)

322a. *Europe,* Nov.–Dec. 1966 (special number on Apollinaire)

323. Fabureau, Hubert, *Guillaume Apollinaire, son oeuvre,* 1932

324. Fabre-Favier, Louise, *Souvenirs sur Guillaume Apollinaire,* 1945

325. Fettweis, Christian, *Apollinaire en Ardenne,* Bruxelles, 1934

326. *Le Flâneur des Deux Rives,* 1954–1955 (Review devoted to Apollinaire studies)

326a. Fonteyne, André, *Apollinaire prosateur,* 1964

326b. Francastel, Pierre, *Du cubisme à l'art abstrait: les cahiers inédits de Robert Delaunay,* 1957

327. Giedion-Welcker, Carola, *Die neue realität bei Guillaume Apollinaire,* Bern, 1945

327a. Golding, John, "Guillaume Apollinaire and the Art of the Twentieth Century," *The Baltimore Museum of Art News,* summer–autumn 1963

327b. Ghothot-Mersch, Claudine, "Apollinaire et le symbole: 'Le Larron,' " *Revue de l'Histoire Littéraire de la France, juillet-sept.* 1967

328. Gray, Christopher, *Cubist Aesthetic Theories,* Baltimore, Johns Hopkins University, 1953

328a. Greet, Anne Hyde, "Puns in Apollinaire's Alcools," *Wisconsin Studies in Contemporary Literature,* autumn 1965

328b. "Guillaume Apollinaire," annual numbers of *La Revue des Lettres Modernes,* 1962 ff.

328c. Hackett, C. A., "Rimbaud and Apollinaire," *French Studies,* July 1965

329. Klingopulos, G. D., "Guillaume Apollinaire," *Scrutiny,* Dec. 1946

330. Lawler, James R., "Music in Apollinaire," *French Studies,* Oct. 1956

331. Mackworth, Cecily, "Je suis Guillaume Apollinaire," *Horizon,* Feb. 1945

332. Moulin, Janine, "*Introduction*" in 302

332a. Orecchioni, Pierre, *Le thème du Rhin dans l'inspiration de Guillaume Apollinaire,* 1956

333. Pia, Pascal, *Apollinaire par lui-même,* 1954

334. Picabia, Gabrielle, "Apollinaire," *Transition,* 6, 1950

334a. *Revue des Sciences Humaines,* special number, *ed.* Michel Décaudin, *oct.–dec.* 1956

335. Rhodes, S. A., "Guillaume Apollinaire," *French Review,* Jan., Feb. 1938

336. Rosenfeld, Paul, *Men Seen,* New York, Dial Press, 1925

337. Rouveyre, André, *Apollinaire,* 1945

338. ———, *Souvenirs de mon commerce,* 1921

339. Salmon, André, "*Vie de Guillaume Apollinaire,*" *La Nouvelle Revue Française, nov.* 1920

340. Shattuck, Roger, "Apollinaire at the Opéra Comique," *Theatre Arts,* Jan. 1948

341. ———, "Apollinaire and the Automatic Life," *Poetry New York,* 2, 1950

341a. ———, "Apollinaire's Great Whitman Happening," *City Lights Journal,* 3 (1966)

342. ———, "Introduction" in 298

343. Soby, James Thrall, "The Wedding of the Arts: Guillaume Apollinaire," *Saturday Review of Literature,* Oct. 7, 1950

343a. Steegmuller, Francis, *Apollinaire: Poet Among the Painters,* New York, Farrar, Straus, 1963

344. *La Table Ronde, sept.* 1952 (special number on Apollinaire with articles by Adéma, Breunig, *et al.*)

345. *Times Literary Supplement,* Sept. 22, 1950; Sept. 29, 1950; Dec. 26, 1952

346. Toussaint-Luca, A., *Guillaume Apollinaire,* 1920, 1954

347. Wolf, E. M., *Guillaume Apollinaire und das Rheinland,* Dortmund, 1937

INDEX

ABOUT THE AUTHOR

Roger Shattuck was born in 1923. He took his B.A. at Yale and was appointed to the Society of Fellows at Harvard. He has been a recipient of both a Fulbright and a Guggenheim grant and is at present Professor of Romance Languages at the University of Texas. He has published criticism and verse in *Harper's, Accent, The Hudson Review, Poetry, The Saturday Review,* and other magazines, and has also published translations from the French. He is the author of *Proust's Binoculars* and a volume of verse, *Half Tame*. Mr. Shattuck is also on the Advisory Board of the National Translation Center and holds the title of Provéditeur Général du Collège de 'Palaphysique.

VINTAGE CRITICISM: LITERATURE, MUSIC, AND ART

VINTAGE BELLES—LETTRES